500 VEGAN RECIPES

500 VEGAN RECIPES

An Amazing Variety of Delicious Recipes, From Chilis and Casseroles to Crumbles, Crisps, and Cookies

Celine Steen and Joni Marie Newman

First published in the USA in 2009 by
Fair Winds Press, a member of
Quayside Publishing Group
100 Cummings Center
Suite 406-L
Beverly, MA 01915-6101
www.fairwindspress.com

13 12 11 10 2 3 4 5

ISBN-13: 978-1-59233-403-2
ISBN-10: 1-59233-403-2

Library of Congress Cataloging-in-Publication Data

Steen, Celine.
500 vegan recipes : an amazing variety of delicious recipes : from chilis and casseroles to crumbles, crisps, and cookies / Celine Steen and Joni-Marie Newman.
p. cm.
Includes index.
ISBN-13: 978-1-59233-403-2
ISBN-10: 1-59233-403-2
1. Vegan cookery. I. Newman, Joni-Marie. II. Title. III. Title: Five hundred vegan recipes.
TX837.S735 2009
641.5'636--dc22

2009026711

Printed and bound in Canada

This book is dedicated to the furry and the feathered, the scaly and the prickly. To the friends that share our home, and the friends we enjoy from afar. This book is for all the animals that give us joy and share our planet in peace.

Contents

What Is a Vegan Diet?

If you are holding this book in your hands, you definitely have some interest in learning more about the vegan diet and lifestyle (or you're a vegan already!). Maybe you just want to reduce your meat consumption, or you find yourself considering making the switch to a completely animal-free lifestyle. In this introduction, we hope to answer many of the questions you may have.

Of course, you could also already know 99.99 percent of what there is to know about veganism and simply be on the lookout for new recipes to play with, in which case we hope a whopping five-hundred of them will be enough to keep you busy in the kitchen—and well fed—for a long, long time.

Merriam-Webster's Dictionary defines *vegan* as: A strict vegetarian who consumes no animal food or dairy products; also: one who abstains from using animal products (as leather).

Vegan not only describes the food someone eats, but often also refers to a lifestyle that vegans follow. Most vegans refrain not only from eating any animal products but also from using beauty products that contain animal derivatives; wearing animal products such as leather, wool, or fur; and generally using any type of animal product in their lives.

People who decide to follow a vegan diet do so for many reasons, some of which may include animal compassion, better health, environmental as well as economic issues, and religion. Maybe a friend or family member has decided to become a vegan, and you want to show support.

From the standpoint of those who decide to follow a vegan lifestyle for compassionate reasons, most feel that all living creatures have the same right to live a life without fear of being killed or tortured for a meal. Most vegans who follow the lifestyle for this reason are often also involved in animal rights groups and tend to volunteer at animal shelters.

A VEGAN DIET IS HEALTHY FOR YOU

There is no doubt that leading a vegan lifestyle is better for your health. By its nature, the diet has zero cholesterol, very little saturated fat, and typically an astronomical amount of vitamins, nutrients, and minerals from a wide variety of plant-based sources. Those who choose to go vegan for better health need to understand that simply giving up meat and dairy in favor of french fries and pasta is not going to make them healthier. When making the decision to eliminate animal foods from your diet, it is imperative to understand how to successfully achieve optimum health through plant-based sources.

The question that is asked most often is how to get enough protein. There seems to be a lot of misinformation out there that claims the human body needs more protein than it actually does. There are many plant-based sources of protein that can easily provide the body with more than enough. Beans, nuts, lentils, soy products such as tempeh and tofu, and gluten-based foods such as seitan and grain meats are all excellent sources of heart-healthy proteins.

It is also important to ensure that vitamin and mineral needs are met through diet. Iron can be obtained through legumes, nuts, and seeds, as well as through enriched grains. Leafy greens such as kale and collards, broccoli, soymilk and other fortified nondairy milks, almonds, tofu, and figs can be excellent sources of calcium. Sea vegetables such as algae, kelp, and seaweed can be great sources of essential fatty acids and iodine.

Two of the most difficult vitamins to obtain through a vegan diet are vitamin D and vitamin B_{12}. To increase the body's absorption of vitamin D, make sure you get plenty of sun exposure during the warm months. Nutritional and dietary supplements such as nutritional yeast can easily be added to the diet to substantiate the vitamin B_{12} intake.

A VEGAN DIET IS HEALTHY FOR THE ENVIRONMENT

From an environmental standpoint, the vegan diet is undoubtedly a sustainable way to eat. Each year the United States imports about 200 million pounds (90 million kg) of beef from Central America. Fuel costs and pollution aside, where does this beef come from? The grazing land needed to raise these cattle is often found by clear-cutting dense forests and rainforest land. Studies estimate that the necessity for more grazing land means that for every minute of every day, a land area equivalent to seven football fields is destroyed in the Amazon basin. For each hamburger that originated from animals raised on rainforest land, approximately 55 square feet (16.8 m) of forest have been destroyed. It's not just the rainforest. In the United States, more than 260 million acres of forest have been clear-cut for animal agriculture. With increased per capita meat consumption, and an ever-growing population, we can only expect to see more deforestation in the future.

In addition to needing land for raising meat, animal agriculture also requires water. In the United States, the amount of water needed for animal consumption is almost equivalent to all other uses of water combined. To grow 1 pound (0.45 kg) of beef requires about 2,500 gallons (9,463 L) of water. Compare that to 1 pound (0.45 kg) of soy, which only requires 250 gallons (946 L), or a pound (0.45 kg) of wheat, which requires only 25 gallons (94.6 L). In addition, it is an inefficient use of resources because it takes years to grow that single pound of beef. Think about it: the amount of water needed to produce just one hamburger is enough to take a nice long, hot shower every day for two and a half weeks. With numbers like these, eating vegan is surely the green way to go.

Beyond the waste is the pollution: agricultural pesticides and manure seep into the groundwater, eventually finding their way to the rivers and oceans. In addition to water pollution, the effect of animal agriculture on fossil fuels is tremendous. Each animal grown and slaughtered for food must be fed. The feed ranges from grain to soy products. The production of this feed requires energy to grow and transport. Imagine the amount of people that could be fed if we focused our agriculture on wheat and grain grown for human consumption rather than growing food for livestock.

A report in the *New Scientist* estimated that driving a hybrid car rather than an average vehicle would conserve a little over one ton of carbon dioxide per year. A vegan diet, however, consumes one and a half tons fewer than the average American diet. Adopting a vegan diet actually does more to reduce emissions than driving a hybrid car!

A VEGAN DIET IS HEALTHY FOR YOUR POCKETBOOK

From an economic standpoint, it can be much cheaper to maintain a plant-based diet. Purchasing bulk pantry staples, such as dried beans, rice, and other grains, and supplementing them with fresh fruits and vegetables can save hundreds, possibly thousands, of dollars on your yearly grocery bill.

Many cultures and religions also have strict dietary guidelines. Following a plant-based diet can easily be adjusted to meet the guidelines of most cultures and religions.

Making the decision to eliminate animal-sourced ingredients, however, can be tricky, regardless of the reason. Ingredients you've probably never even heard of before will now become a part of your everyday language, and label reading will also become part of your shopping routine. In the beginning, this can add a little time to your trip to the market, but rest assured that in no time, it will become second nature.

There are countless websites and resources that have lists of ingredients (check the resource section at the end of this book, page 500) that are animal-derived. Following is a concise list of the major offenders.

Animal-Derived Ingredients

* denotes that product can be animal- or plant-derived

albumin
calcium stearate
carmine
cochineal
capric acid
casein
clarifying agent (also known as fining agent)
disodium inosinate
emulsifiers (also known as surfactants)
flavor enhancers (such as disodium guanylate)
folic acid*
glycerols or glycerine*
isinglass (except Japanese isinglass, which is made from agar)
lactic acid*
lactose
lanolin
lard
lecithin*
magnesium stearate*
mono-, di-, or triglycerides*
MSG*
myristic acid or tetradecanoic acid*
natural flavorings*
oleic or oleinic acid

palmitic acid*
pancreatin
pepsin
propolis
rennet
royal jelly
shortening*
sodium stearoyl lactylate*
stearic acid or octadecanoic acid
suet
surface-acting agents*
tallow (found in many waxed papers, but not Reynold's)
vitamin A*
vitamin A_2*
vitamin D*
wetting agents
whey

When in doubt, seek out information from the manufacturer. Call the number on the label or send an email requesting the information. You'll be surprised how helpful most manufacturers will be.

No matter the reason behind your decision to give the vegan diet a try, we hope that this book, filled with more than 500 delicious meat- and dairy-free options, will help you make a seamless and pleasurable transition.

A NOTE ABOUT FOOD ALLERGIES

A food allergy is a response from the immune system when it mistakenly believes that a food is harmful. Because of how the immune system works, the human body will produce antibodies that can become reactive every time a certain type of food is eaten. Allergic reactions can range from mild irritation to anaphylactic shock, which can lead to death.

There are many types of food allergies. Some of the most common ones include milk, eggs, peanuts, tree nuts, fish, shellfish, soy, and wheat. By following a vegan diet you can eliminate the worry of at least half of these.

Throughout this book, we have done our best to mark recipes that are free of soy-based products and wheat ingredients. However, in today's global market, it is important to be vigilant when it comes to the ingredients that can sneak into your foods.

Celiacs, and others who must maintain a strict gluten-free diet, should use extreme caution, even when preparing recipes that are marked as being gluten free, because some ingredients not normally associated with wheat, such as soy sauce, vinegar, vanilla and other extracts, and oats, can sometimes contain small or trace amounts of gluten.

We are not nutritionists or dieticians, but a couple of gals with a passion for good, nutritious, vegan food. If you have particular food allergies, we recommend that you consult your physician before trying new foods that may contain certain allergens.

Chapter 1

How to Use This Book

In an attempt to make your cooking life just a little easier, you will find the following notations next to the recipes that follow these four specifications:

Under 30 Minutes Recipes that can be prepared quickly, based on the idea that you have intermediate skills in the kitchen.

Keep in mind that it may take you a little longer than that if preparing your own meals from scratch is an entirely new endeavor for you, but hang in there: it's all a question of practice, and you'll do it all in five seconds flat, with your eyes closed, in no time. (Okay, maybe not, but we can dream, can't we?)

Low Fat Recipes that contain 3 grams or less of fat per serving, if part of the reason why you are switching or have switched diets is to shed those few "hard to reach" extra pounds.

Gluten Free Recipes that do not contain gluten, in case of food allergies. As noted in the introduction, be sure to double-check all ingredients on food labels before using.

Soy Free Recipes that do not contain soy, in case of food allergies. Remember to double-check labels, for your own safety. Thankfully, almost all recipes that call for soymilk can be replaced with other nondairy milks (such as rice, almond, or hemp), although we have found that recipes calling for "sour" or "curdled" milk work best with soymilk.

NEW-TO-YOU INGREDIENTS

You might find yourself wondering what on earth some of the ingredients used in this book could possibly be, if veganism or healthier eating isn't something you are too familiar with quite yet. Fear not!

Soy sauce, tamari, and Bragg's Liquid Aminos are all interchangeable, in a ratio of 1:1. Bragg's only contains a small amount of natural sodium, without added table salt, and is also free of gluten. Its flavor differs from soy sauce and tamari, and is more of an acquired taste. It is also more expensive.

Nondairy butter has gotten quite the bad rap in recent headlines. When choosing a nondairy butter, look for products that don't contain any hydrogenated fats. One of our favorites is Earth Balance, though there are many on the market. Also, note that all margarines are not necessarily nondairy. Check labels for sneaky ingredients such as whey or casein, which are dairy derivatives.

Vegetable broth or bouillon is a very important staple in the vegan kitchen. Although it is best to use homemade broth so you can control ingredients and sodium content, it can be hard to find the time to prepare it from scratch. Experiment with different broths, powders, and cubes until you find one that suits your needs. There are many types, ranging from straight vegetable to chicken-flavored and even beef-flavored vegetable broths. Be sure to check the labels and do your best to avoid those containing hydrogenated oils and fats.

Agar flakes and powder are derived from seaweed. Agar-agar, also known as kanten, is commonly used as a thickener for soups, desserts, and jellies in Japan but has recently become readily available in health food stores and international markets, and even online. It works wonders as a vegetarian alternative to gelatin. Normally sold in flakes or powder, it can also sometimes be found in huge rods. If you are lucky enough to find it this way, which is much cheaper, you will need to break it down into flake form in a food processor. As with gelatin, agar requires heat to be activated.

If you need agar for a recipe that calls for flakes when you only have powder, or vice versa, it is important to know that 1 teaspoon of the powder is roughly equivalent to 1 tablespoon of the flaked version.

TVP, otherwise known as textured vegetable protein, is a versatile meat substitute that, in its smaller granulated form, has the appearance of Grape-Nuts. For the purposes of this book, only the smaller granules are used. When reconstituted with vegetable broth or water, it can be used to mimic the texture of ground meats. It has very little flavor on its own and, much like tofu or seitan, takes on the flavor of whatever it is prepared with. Very low in fat and high in protein and fiber, it is produced from defatted soy flour, then cooked under pressure and dried.

Gluten is the protein portion of wheat. It can be purchased as flour. (Note that *vital wheat gluten flour* is not the same as *high-gluten flour*.) Vital wheat gluten flour has a variety of uses in the vegan kitchen. It can be added to breads for softness and stretch, or used for making seitan, a gluten-based wheat meat.

Nutritional yeast is a simple yellow flake usually grown on molasses. It yields a nutty, rich, almost cheesy flavor and is a favorite for vegans and vegetarians looking for a homemade alternative to cheese. Be sure to seek out "vegetarian-support" yeast flakes. They can normally be found in the vitamin aisle of your local health food store. An excellent source of fiber, B_{12}, and a multitude of other vitamins and minerals, nutritional yeast is sure to become a must-have staple in your pantry.

Egg replacers, which come in many forms, play the role of binder in baked goods. We will always mention which egg replacer we use in each recipe, but feel free to play around if the one we chose isn't to your liking. Here is a succinct list of them:

To replace one single egg, you can choose between:

- ½ banana, mashed

- ¼ cup (60 g) soy yogurt or blended silken tofu

- 1½ teaspoons Ener-G egg replacer powder, a commercially made powder that needs to be whisked with 2 tablespoons (30 ml) water

- 2½ tablespoons (18 g) ground flaxseed whisked with 3 tablespoons (45 ml) water

- ¼ cup (61 g) applesauce, preferably unsweetened

Nut butters come in a wide array of varieties; if you are allergic to a specific nut, you may find there are many other nut butters you can eat and enjoy.

We mostly use the natural type that only contains the nut in question, and eventually some salt, but no added oil or sweetener, which is a fact that is particularly welcome when using nut butters in savory dishes. Choosing creamy or crunchy nut butters will usually depend on the recipe, but also on personal preference.

Making your own nut butter is even better for guaranteed freshness, provided you own a fairly efficient food processor, or even a coffee grinder.

Although the latter can make for a bit of a messy cleanup, we have found that the nuts are made into butter even more quickly than with a food processor.

Keep in mind that the consistency of nut butters varies tremendously, so the results of baked goods could also vary in turn. If what you have access to is really dry, adding a little more liquid (nondairy milk or oil, for example) might be necessary.

Tofu, which is also known as soybean curd, is a protein-packed food that has a rather bland taste on its own, which allows for endless ways for its preparation and uses. With such a generous variety of tofu firmness and quality, it would be easy getting a bit lost. Here are the main categories:

- *Silken tofu* is usually used for sauces, smoothies, and desserts. It comes in soft, firm, and extra-firm qualities. It can be found in aseptic packages and is often shelf-stable.

- *Regular tofu* comes in soft, firm, extra-firm, and even super-firm qualities. Extra-firm and super-firm are the best to use for panfrying, because they keep their shape more easily than any of the other firmness levels do.

This type of tofu can be found in the refrigerated section of the supermarket, usually packed in water, and requires draining and pressing, depending on the recipe, for best results. If you can find fresh tofu from a local health food or international market, you will be greatly rewarded with substantially better taste and texture.

Please note that when nothing is specified in our recipes, we are talking of the regular kind of tofu. We will make note of when the silken kind is needed.

Tofu usually comes packed in water. To remove the excess moisture from the tofu, we recommend first draining it, and then pressing it. An easy way to press tofu is to fold a kitchen towel, place the tofu on it, place another folded towel on top of it, and then weight it down with a heavy pan or book. Let it sit for about 30 minutes, and then proceed with the recipe directions.

Seitan, or wheat meat, is made from gluten and spices. Seitan is a popular meat substitute because it is very simple to manipulate the flavor and texture to mimic many different types of meat. The way in which it is prepared, be it boiled or baked, will have a definite effect on the texture of the final product. Most recipes calling for seitan will be specific as to which type to use.

Tempeh is made from fermented soybeans that are bound together into a cake form. Like tofu, it is high in protein, but because it is a whole bean product, it has an even higher protein, fiber, and vitamin profile than that of tofu. The flavor is a bit stronger and the texture quite firmer than tofu.

Agave nectar, which comes from the agave cactus, is the vegan alternative to honey. It can be used in a ratio of 1:1, and it has a tendency to brown quickly when baked: the oven temperature needs to be at a lower setting, and baked goods will benefit from being loosely covered with foil when they aren't quite done but take on the appearance of being ready. The nectar is not only delicious, although rather neutral in flavor, but it also has a low glycemic index, making it a suitable replacement for most diabetics. We use what is called "light agave" in our recipes, unless otherwise mentioned.

Molasses comes in several varieties; blackstrap molasses happens to be the only one that retains its minerals, as opposed to regular molasses. It also has a rather strong flavor that not all people seem to enjoy. We often use blackstrap in our recipes to benefit from its richness in iron and calcium, but substitute regular for it if you prefer a mel-lower flavor.

Sweeteners come in a wide variety, and many aren't quite as bad for you as good old granulated or brown sugar can be. As is the case with almost every food, moderation is key. Everyone is "blessed" with a different degree of a sweet tooth, so be sure to adjust our recipes, depending on your liking.

With choices such as Sucanat, the nonrefined cane sugar that contains calcium, iron, and vitamin B_6, it is possible to make being the proud owner of a sweet tooth just a touch less sinful after all.

If Sucanat is not available, it can be easily replaced with light or dark brown sugar in a 1:1 ratio. When we use brown sugar, we usually "pack" it, but a note will be made in each recipe that uses this ingredient.

Another healthier sweetener is turbinado sugar, often sold as "raw sugar" or "sugar in the raw." We do not recommend substituting turbinado for Sucanat, or vice versa, in muffins, brownies, or cookies, because we have found the coarser texture of the former to change the outcome of several baked goods. Feel free to use them interchangeably in yeast breads, granolas, crisps, and pies, though.

We prefer using unrefined evaporated cane juice as a substitute for granulated sugar. It is substituted in a 1:1 ratio with granulated. It is slightly darker in color, because it is not bleached. The bleaching and refining process of traditional cane sugar requires the use of bone char, and therefore is not vegan.

As for liquid sweeteners, an obvious albeit expensive choice is pure maple syrup. What would waffles and pancakes do without their daily dose of syrup? Do not try to substitute what is known as "pancake syrup" for it, because the latter is composed of high-fructose corn syrup, which cannot even compete with pure maple syrup when it comes to flavor or health benefits.

Other liquid sweeteners include brown rice syrup, barley malt, and the agave nectar that we previously mentioned in this chapter.

Nondairy versions of traditionally dairy items are hot products these days. With the popularity of veganism and vegetarianism on the rise, as well as with the ever-increasing population of lactose-intolerant people, many companies have come up with products that are strikingly similar to their dairy counterparts.

One of the many benefits of these products is their long shelf life. Most major supermarket chains now carry items such as nondairy yogurt, sour cream, cream cheese, and even mayonnaise. We have tried to include recipes for as many nondairy replacements as possible, but sometimes the convenience of picking up a ready-made package can't be beat. Be sure to choose varieties without hydrogenated fats. Brands such as Tofutti and Follow Your Heart are excellent sources. If you can't find these items on your market shelf, don't be afraid to ask! Most markets are more than happy to place special orders for their customers.

Nondairy milks come in a wealth of choices. So many milks, so little time! If local stores are conscientiously stocked, you should be able to choose among soymilk, rice milk, almond milk, hemp milk, oat milk, and even hazelnut milk. All of these delicious milks come in different flavors, including chocolate and vanilla, but can also be found in plain and unsweetened versions. Needless to say, the last two are especially useful when preparing savory foods.

We like to get all the nutrients we can from the foods we eat, which is why it's important to choose milks that are fortified with calcium.

Not all milks are created equal when it comes to flavor, creaminess, and thickness; your personal preference might make it important to test several milks before finding your perfect match.

If you find yourself consuming a lot of milk, and would rather save on packaging and cost, while at the same time having complete control over the ingredients, purchasing a soymilk maker may be a good investment. There are several good-quality brands out there, so consider doing some research to find the one that would best meet your needs.

Salt and pepper, while certainly not "new", are often followed by the notation "to taste" in our recipes. It is obvious that this is most definitely a matter of personal taste, and while we will give guidelines to the approximate amount that works well in each recipe, you are strongly encouraged to adjust them according to your own needs.

Both salt and pepper come in many different varieties and types: when it comes to salt, we favor fine and sometimes coarse sea salt, because not only are they affordable options, but sea salt also naturally retains trace minerals. If you'd rather stick to the more common table or even kosher salt, the difference in the outcome would be next to nil.

As for pepper, we prefer to have a pepper mill at hand to grind the black or white versions of it fresh each time we need it, because the flavor will be kept more intense and intact, but any sort of pepper will do just fine.

INGREDIENT SUBSTITUTIONS

Most of the ingredients that are used in this book are getting increasingly easier to find in common supermarkets. International food markets and online stores are also great options for getting your hands on harder-to-find items. It might take a bit more work, but by doing some research and shopping around, it is usually possible to find affordable options. If none of these options is feasible where you live, here is a list of substitutions for the ingredients we use the most:

• **Arrowroot powder** can be replaced with equal amounts of cornstarch, which is more readily available at grocery stores. Although arrowroot produces clearer results than cornstarch does in sauces, it is also more expensive. Both thickening agents yield great results.

• We generally use **mild-flavored oils** in our baked goods, but if you are opposed to using canola oil due to the GMO controversy, you can choose vegetable or any other mild-flavored oil instead.

• **Whole-grain flours** contain a lot of vitamins, nutrients, and fiber that all-purpose flour is lacking, but if you find the flavor of whole wheat, white whole wheat, or whole wheat pastry flours to be too strong and heavy for your liking, you can use half all-purpose and half any of these flours, or even choose to use all-purpose completely on its own instead.

All the aforementioned flours are pretty much interchangeable, but expect denser results if using whole wheat or white whole wheat flours in cookies or muffins: therefore, we recommend using whole wheat pastry flour instead, or as mentioned above, a combination of unbleached all-purpose and white whole wheat flours.

The fact that whole wheat and bread flours contain more gluten actually makes these flours especially well suited for yeast breads.

Also note: In this book, flours are measured by lightly spooning them with a separate measure or spoon, and leveling them with the flat side of a knife. Keep in mind that scooping packs the flour and makes a noticeable difference in the outcome, especially in baked goods.

• **Light spelt flour** can replace wheat flour, and vice versa, but you will usually need up to ¼ cup (30 g) more of it than you would wheat flour. You will have to experiment judging on texture, but our recommendation is that unless a recipe is already using 100 percent spelt flour, you only substitute half of it along with any wheat flour, instead of using it alone.

• **Oat flour** makes a wonderful addition to bread, cookies, and other baked goods. We like to make our own because it is often cheaper than purchasing ready-made at the store. Simply finely grind a large amount of quick or old-fashioned oats in a food processor, and keep it handy for future use.

• The most common types of **dry yeast** you will see used in this book are bread machine yeast and active dry yeast. We have used them interchangeably without any issue, but we will still specify which one is used in each recipe.

Bear in mind that while bread machine yeast does not need to (and shouldn't) be dissolved prior to being used, active dry yeast does. Proofing active dry yeast is necessary to make sure the yeast is indeed active, and it only takes 10 minutes of extra preparation time. We will describe the process in every recipe that calls for active dry yeast.

When in doubt, follow the instructions that can be found on the package itself.

• Choosing **foods that are fresh, local, and organic** is always best, but sometimes it just isn't practical depending on where you live or the size of your pocketbook. When it comes to subbing veggies and fruits for something other than fresh, try to pick frozen over canned, because frozen veggies retain more of their vitamins and nutrients than canned vegetables do. If you can only get canned vegetables, try to go for the "no salt added" options, or rinse thoroughly before using, whenever possible.

• If you do not have access to **fresh herbs**, the dried versions make a fine substitution: simply use 1 teaspoon of dried herb (e.g., basil, thyme, parsley) for 1 tablespoon of the fresh version.

TIPS FOR ULTIMATE COOKING SUCCESS

• Some of the baked good recipes yield amounts for a cake, or jumbo muffins, but if you want to change the size of the baked good, be sure to adjust the baking time accordingly; standard-size muffins or cupcakes need a shorter baking time than larger versions. Check for doneness by inserting a wooden toothpick, or the tip of a knife, into the center of the baked good; it should come out dry (or with a few crumbs) and without wet batter stuck to it.

• Using an oven thermometer is important to making sure your oven is well calibrated, so that you can get the best possible results.

• It is preferable for ingredients to be at room temperature when baking in general, but this is especially important when making yeast bread, because the yeast reacts to differences in temperature and could fail to rise properly if the ingredients that accompany it are either too cold or too hot.

We hope these tips will help you on your way to becoming an expert at cooking and baking delicious vegan feasts. Be sure to have a look at the end of this book for links to websites that are packed with even more useful information to make your transition to veganism even easier.

Chapter 2

Breakfast

There's nothing better than waking up late on a Sunday morning and fixing a big, elaborate breakfast in your fuzzy slippers. This chapter offers plenty of inspiration for those mornings, with mouthwatering recipes for pancakes, waffles, and tofu scrambles, while covering the rest of the week with quick, healthy breakfast recipes, such as granola, energy bars, and on-the-go options that will fuel you through hectic days.

Macadamia Yogurt Granola

Very lightly sweetened, this granola is an ideal snack to munch on when you're on the go. If macadamia nuts aren't your cup of tea, rest assured that any other nut is equally lovely in this recipe.

¼ cup (29 g) wheat germ
2 cups (160 g) old-fashioned rolled oats
2 tablespoons (16 g) arrowroot powder
¼ teaspoon fine sea salt
¼ cup (34 g) macadamia nuts, coarsely chopped
2 tablespoons (30 ml) melted coconut oil
2 tablespoons (30 ml) pure maple syrup
¼ cup (60 g) vanilla soy or other nondairy yogurt

Preheat the oven to 350°F (180°C, or gas mark 4). Have a large-size rimmed baking sheet handy.

Combine the wheat germ, oats, arrowroot, salt, and nuts in a medium-size bowl.

Whisk together the oil, syrup, and yogurt in a small-size bowl.

Combine the wet ingredients with the dry, and stir until well coated. Spread the mixture evenly on the baking sheet.

Bake for 8 minutes. Stir well.

Bake for another 8 minutes, or until golden brown.

Let cool on the baking sheet before transferring to a tightly closed container. Store in the fridge once completely cooled.

Yield: About 3 cups (366 g)

White Chocolate Raspberry Granola

Eating chocolate for breakfast probably should not be an every morning event, but a sweet tooth sometimes has to be tended to, no matter what the time of day.

1 cup (80 g) old-fashioned rolled oats
¼ cup (40 g) brown rice flour
¼ cup (23 g) shredded coconut
8 Brazil nuts or other nuts of similar size, coarsely chopped
¼ cup (27 g) chopped pecans
1 tablespoon (8 g) sesame seeds
¼ teaspoon fine sea salt
2 tablespoons (30 ml) canola oil
¼ cup plus 1 tablespoon (105 g) agave nectar
½ teaspoon pure vanilla extract
¼ cup (30 g) dried raspberries
¼ cup (50 g) nondairy white chocolate chips

Preheat the oven to 350°F (180°C, or gas mark 4). Have a large-size rimmed baking sheet handy.

Combine the oats, flour, coconut, Brazil nuts, pecans, sesame seeds, and salt in a medium-size bowl.

Whisk together the oil, agave, and vanilla in a small-size bowl.

Combine the wet ingredients with the dry, stirring until well coated. Spread the mixture evenly on the baking sheet.

Bake for 8 minutes. Stir well.

Bake for another 10 minutes, or until golden brown. Be sure to keep a close eye on the granola as it bakes, because agave nectar browns quickly.

Remove from the oven, and stir in the raspberries and white chocolate chips while the granola is still hot so that the chips melt and coat the granola.

Let cool on the baking sheet before transferring to a tightly closed container. Store in the fridge once completely cooled.

Yield: About 3 cups (366 g)

VARIATION

If you cannot find vegan white chocolate chips or dried raspberries where you live, substitute the same amount of nondairy semisweet chocolate chips and dried cherries, or any other dried fruit you prefer.

Peanut Butter and Chips Granola

Not quite as harsh on sensitive gums the way other super crispy granolas can be, thanks to the addition of flax meal, this granola invites any sort of vegan chip to join the party: carob, white, or semisweet. It will be a treat no matter which you choose. As a bonus, and a way to make up for the addition of chocolate, flax also contains a lot of fiber, as well as omega-3s, which have been shown to help lower "bad" cholesterol and high blood pressure.

1 cup (80 g) old-fashioned rolled oats
¼ cup (40 g) brown rice flour
¼ cup (28 g) flax meal
¼ teaspoon fine sea salt
2 tablespoons (32 g) natural peanut butter
1 tablespoon (15 ml) canola oil
2 tablespoons (42 g) agave nectar or (30 ml) pure maple syrup
⅓ cup (58 g) nondairy semisweet or (66 g) white chocolate or (40 g) carob chips

Preheat the oven to 350°F (180°C, or gas mark 4). Have a large-size rimmed baking sheet handy.

In a large-size bowl, combine the oats, flour, flax meal, and salt.

In a small-size bowl, whisk together the peanut butter, oil, and agave until emulsified.

Combine the wet ingredients with the dry, stirring until well coated. Spread the mixture evenly on the baking sheet.

Bake for 8 minutes. Stir well.

Bake for another 8 minutes, or until golden brown.

Remove from the oven, and stir in the chocolate chips while the granola is still hot so that the chips melt and coat the granola.

Let cool on the baking sheet before transferring to a tightly closed container. Store in the fridge once completely cooled.

Yield: About 3 cups (366 g)

Crunchy Carob Almond Granola

Carob is often expected to taste like chocolate, but it has a wonderful flavor of its own and is free of caffeine, too. If you aren't sold on it—it can be a bit of an acquired taste—go ahead and use nondairy chocolate chips instead.

⅓ cup plus 2 tablespoons (154 g) brown rice syrup
¼ cup (60 ml) canola oil
1 teaspoon pure vanilla extract
½ teaspoon blackstrap or regular molasses
2½ cups (200 g) old-fashioned rolled oats
½ cup (58 g) wheat germ
¼ teaspoon fine sea salt
½ teaspoon ground cinnamon
½ cup (47 g) shredded coconut
⅓ cup (40 g) nondairy carob chips
⅓ cup (36 g) slivered almonds
¼ cup (27 g) chopped pecans
¼ cup (40 g) raisins (optional)

Preheat the oven to 300°F (150°C, or gas mark 2). Line a large-size rimmed baking sheet with parchment paper or a silicone baking mat, such as Silpat.

In a medium-size bowl, whisk together the rice syrup, oil, vanilla, and molasses.

In a large-size bowl, combine the oats, wheat germ, salt, cinnamon, coconut, carob chips, almonds, pecans, and raisins, if using.

Combine the wet ingredients with the dry, stirring until well coated. Spread the mixture evenly on the baking sheet.

Bake for 15 minutes. Stir well.

Bake for another 15 minutes, or until golden brown.

Let cool on the baking sheet before transferring to a tightly closed container. Store in the fridge once completely cooled.

Yield: About 8 cups (732 g)

Peanut Butter and Jam Granola

A twist on a childhood favorite, this granola is easy and quick to prepare. It tastes just like a thumbprint cookie, if you've ever had one, but is just a touch more appropriate than cookies for breakfast.

¼ cup (64 g) creamy peanut butter
2 tablespoons (24 g) raw sugar
¼ cup (60 ml) water
¼ cup (40 g) brown rice or other flour, divided
½ teaspoon ground cinnamon
¼ teaspoon fine sea salt
1½ cups (120 g) old-fashioned rolled oats
¼ cup (80 g) jam of choice

Preheat the oven to 350°F (180°C, or gas mark 4). Have a large-size rimmed baking sheet handy.

In a microwave-safe bowl, combine the peanut butter, sugar, and water. Heat in the microwave for 30 to 60 seconds so that the peanut butter is more manageable.

Stir in 2 tablespoons (20 g) of the brown rice flour, and the cinnamon, salt, and oats. The mixture will be thick and rather unmanageable at this point, so place it on the baking sheet, and combine using your fingers. Sprinkle the remaining 2 tablespoons (20 g) of brown rice flour on top, and work it in gently until it dissolves. Try not to break the granola chunks too much while doing this.

Add the jam in little pieces; you don't want it to coat the granola, but rather to form bits of it throughout.

Spread the mixture evenly on the baking sheet.

Bake for 8 minutes. Stir well.

Bake for another 10 minutes, or until golden brown.

Let cool on the baking sheet before transferring to a tightly closed container. Store in the fridge once completely cooled.

Yield: About 4 cups (488 g)

Cookie Crumble Granola

This granola is perfectly suited for special occasions and opens the door to endless possibilities, giving your favorite cookie recipes a chance to shine in a whole new way.

For the Chocolate Almond Cookie Dough:

1 cup (140 g) whole roasted almonds
1 cup (78 g) quick-cooking oats
½ cup (96 g) raw sugar
Pinch fine sea salt
1 tablespoon (8 g) arrowroot powder
½ teaspoon baking powder
3 ounces (85 g) nondairy semisweet chocolate, coarsely chopped, melted, and cooled
¼ cup (60 ml) soy or other nondairy milk

For the Oatmeal Raisin Cookie Dough:

½ cup (60 g) whole wheat pastry flour
½ cup (39 g) quick-cooking oats
½ teaspoon ground cinnamon
¼ teaspoon baking soda
¼ teaspoon fine sea salt
2 tablespoons (32 g) creamy peanut butter
2 tablespoons (30 ml) peanut oil
2 tablespoons (30 ml) soy or other nondairy milk
⅓ cup (64 g) Sucanat
1 teaspoon pure vanilla extract
¼ cup (40 g) raisins

Preheat the oven to 350°F (180°C, or gas mark 4). Have a large-size rimmed baking sheet handy.

To make the Chocolate Almond Cookie Dough: Place the almonds, oats, sugar, salt, arrowroot, and baking powder in your food processor. Process until finely ground.

Add the chocolate and milk. Process until thoroughly mixed.

To make the Oatmeal Raisin Cookie Dough: In a medium-size bowl, whisk together the flour, oats, cinnamon, baking soda, and salt.

In a small-size bowl, whisk together the peanut butter, oil, and milk until emulsified. Add the Sucanat and vanilla.

Stir the wet ingredients into the dry. Stir in the raisins.

Crumble both preparations evenly onto the baking sheet.

Bake for 12 minutes, stirring once halfway through.

Let cool on the baking sheet before transferring to a tightly closed container. Store in the fridge once completely cooled.

Yield: About 6 cups (732 g)

Under 30 Minutes

Noggy Bulgur

This is the type of breakfast that's guaranteed to stick to your ribs! The bulgur will thicken up the longer it sits, so be prepared to add a little more soy nog or nondairy milk, if needed. If you can't find soy nog, use your favorite nondairy milk and add a pinch nutmeg and ½ teaspoon of ground cinnamon to it. It won't be quite the same, but it will be good, too!

2 cups (470 ml) soy nog or other nondairy milk
¼ cup (48 g) raw sugar
¼ cup (40 g) raisins
1 tablespoon (15 ml) rum (optional)
⅛ teaspoon ground cinnamon
Pinch fine sea salt
1 tablespoon (8 g) arrowroot powder
1 cup (140 g) uncooked bulgur
Handful chopped pecans (optional)

In a medium-size saucepan, whisk together the nog, sugar, raisins, rum, cinnamon, salt, and arrowroot.

Bring to a low boil, then turn off the heat; remove from the stove while pouring the bulgur in.

Place the pan back on the still-hot stove, cover with a lid, and let stand for 15 minutes.

Stir well and remove from the stove; let stand, covered with a lid, for another 10 minutes.

Enjoy warm, at room temperature, or even cold. Sprinkle with the chopped pecans, if desired, upon serving.

Yield: 4 small-size servings

Whole Wheat Couscous Bowl of Comfort

Cold cereal flakes can look anything but appetizing in the middle of winter, so why not turn to this healthy and belly-warming breakfast instead? You also control the amount of sweetener added to it, if using any, which is another plus over store-bought cereal, where sugar can be high on the ingredients list.

1½ cups (260 g) uncooked whole wheat couscous
3 cups (705 ml) soy or other nondairy milk
2 teaspoons pure vanilla extract
½ teaspoon ground cinnamon
1 cup (109 g) chopped pecans
¾ cup (120 g) raisins

Combine all the ingredients in a medium-size saucepan. Cover with a tight-fitting lid, bring to a boil, lower the heat, and let simmer for 5 to 10 minutes, or until all the liquid is absorbed. Fluff with a fork.

Divide into 6 portions. Serve immediately, or let cool and freeze for later use.

If frozen, simply thaw out individual portions the night before, add a little nondairy milk, pop into the microwave for a minute or so, and throw in your favorite sweetener or other add-ins.

Yield: 6 servings

NOTE

Drizzle with maple syrup, agave nectar, or more nondairy milk, or add fresh fruit upon serving.

Cinna-vanilla Rice

This hot "cereal" is a hearty breakfast and a great way to use up last night's leftovers!

1½ cups (355 ml) soy or other nondairy milk (use rice milk and this dish is soy free, too!)
1 teaspoon ground cinnamon
3 cups (522 g) cooked rice (we like Jasmine, but any will do)
1 teaspoon pure vanilla extract
¼ cup (60 ml) pure maple syrup
Pinch salt

In a pot, bring the milk and cinnamon to a boil. Add the rice and stir to thicken. Remove from the heat. Stir in the vanilla, maple syrup, and salt. Serve warm, topped with a little extra maple syrup, if desired.

Yield: 4 servings

Under 30 Minutes

Banana Oat Morning Fuel

This is perfect for those days when you need as much energy as you can get, but can't be bothered whipping up a batch of pancakes, or when even toasting a slice of bread sounds like too much work. Note that if you use a frozen banana, the beverage will be even thicker and, of course, more smoothie-like.

1 small ripe banana, fresh or frozen, sliced
¼ cup (20 g) quick-cooking oats
1 tablespoon (16 g) creamy natural peanut butter
1 cup (235 ml) soy or other nondairy milk
½ teaspoon pure vanilla extract
1 tablespoon (5 g) unsweetened cocoa powder
1 to 2 tablespoon(s) (21 to 42 g) agave nectar or (15 to 30 ml) pure maple syrup, to taste

Using an immersion or countertop blender, blend all ingredients until perfectly smooth.

Serve immediately.

Yield: 1 serving

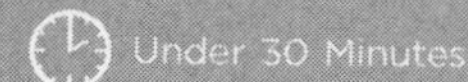
Under 30 Minutes

Pumpkin Spice Coffee

If you are like millions of people who need their coffee to start the day on the right foot, but would rather avoid forking out an entire paycheck for a single cup, you're in luck: this coffee tastes like the kind you'd get at your favorite coffee shop, which will put a smile on your face—until you realize you still have to go to work/school.

1 cup (235 ml) almond milk or other nondairy milk
3 tablespoons (45 g) pumpkin purée
1 tablespoon (15 ml) pure maple syrup
½ teaspoon pure vanilla extract
1 teaspoon instant espresso powder
¼ teaspoon ground cinnamon
⅛ teaspoon ground ginger

Whisk all ingredients in a small-size saucepan, heat on medium-low, and let simmer for about 8 minutes. Pour into your favorite mug, and enjoy.

Yield: 1 serving

NOTE

If you want to have a perfectly smooth drink, strain the liquid through a fine-meshed sieve upon serving. You can also prepare the drink in advance, let it sit in the fridge until ready to use, strain it (if desired), and heat it up in the microwave until it is warm enough for you, but not boiling.

Mexican Hot Mocha

Bring some heat into your mornings by whipping up a perfect cup of coffee enhanced with flavorful spices and made even more luscious with the addition of chocolate chips.

1 cup (235 ml) plain soy or other nondairy milk
1 tablespoon (3 g) instant espresso powder
2 tablespoons (10 g) unsweetened cocoa powder
1½ tablespoons (18 g) Sucanat
¼ teaspoon ground cinnamon
⅛ teaspoon mild to medium chili powder, to taste
1 tablespoon (11 g) nondairy semisweet chocolate chips

Combine the milk, espresso powder, cocoa powder, Sucanat, cinnamon, and chile powder in a small-size saucepan. Let chill in the fridge for 1 hour, to let the flavors develop.

Bring the mixture to a low boil, reduce the heat, and simmer for 4 minutes, whisking occasionally. Stir in the chocolate chips until melted, and serve.

Yield: 1 serving

Under 30 Minutes

Pumpkin Yogurt Smoothie

If your smoothie looks a little too thick, as it can depend upon the quality of the nondairy yogurt and pumpkin purée, simply add a little more nondairy milk until it reaches a thinner consistency. This makes an excellent and nutritious quick breakfast for mornings when you aren't feeling too ravenous, or when you're simply in too much of a hurry to take the time to sit down.

2 cups (470 ml) vanilla soy or other nondairy milk
1¼ cups (290 g) vanilla soy or other nondairy yogurt
½ cup (122 g) pumpkin purée
2 tablespoons to ¼ cup (42 to 84 g) agave nectar, to taste
½ teaspoon rum extract or 1 tablespoon (15 ml) spiced rum
½ teaspoon ground cinnamon
¼ teaspoon ground ginger

Combine all the ingredients in a large-size bowl, whisking vigorously until blended.

Enjoy chilled.

Yield: 3 servings

Soy Free

Banana Peanut Oat Breakfast Biscuits

These crispy-outside, soft-inside little breads are absolutely scrumptious on their own, or covered with some jam for breakfast. Bet you can't eat just one!

- 1 large-size ripe banana, mashed, placed in a large-size measuring cup, and topped with enough water to equal 1 cup
- 2 tablespoons (30 ml) peanut oil
- 2 tablespoons (42 g) agave nectar
- 1 teaspoon fine sea salt
- ½ cup (39 g) quick-cooking oats
- 1½ cups (180 g) white whole wheat or whole wheat pastry flour, plus about an extra ⅓ cup (40 g) for kneading
- ½ cup (76 g) grouned or very finely chopped dry-roasted peanuts
- 1½ teaspoons bread machine yeast
- 1 tablespoon (14 g) nondairy butter, melted, to brush on top

With an immersion blender or in a countertop blender, purée the banana with water, oil, agave, salt, and oats.

In the bowl of your stand mixer, with the dough hook, or by hand, whisk together the flour, peanuts, and yeast.

Pour the wet ingredients into the dry, and start stirring, adding more flour as needed until a dough starts forming.

You can either knead by hand or let the stand mixer do the work: the kneading will have to last between 6 and 8 minutes. The resulting dough will be rather stiff.

Preheat the oven to 375°F (190°C, or gas mark 5). Line a large-size rimless baking sheet with parchment paper or a silicone baking mat, such as Silpat.

Roll out the dough to about ½-inch (1.3-cm) thickness. Using an approximately 3½-inch (9-cm) round cookie cutter, and rerolling the dough as needed, cut out 6 pieces of dough in all.

Place on the baking sheet.

Brush the pieces of dough with the melted nondairy butter, cover with plastic wrap, and let rest while the oven is preheating, for about 25 minutes.

Remove the plastic wrap, and bake for 22 to 24 minutes, until golden on the bottom.

Let cool on a wire rack.

Yield: 6 biscuits

Butternut Drop Biscuits

Not crumbly or dry the way some biscuits can be, these turn out a beautiful yellow-orange color and are the perfect healthy accompaniment to both sweet and savory meals.

2 cups (240 g) light spelt flour
½ cup (39 g) quick-cooking oats
1 tablespoon (12 g) baking powder
1 teaspoon fine sea salt
¾ cup (180 g) butternut squash purée
¾ cup plus 2 tablespoons (210 ml) almond or other nondairy milk
¼ cup (60 ml) canola oil
2 tablespoons (42 g) agave nectar
½ cup (32 g) fresh cranberries (optional)
Zest of ½ orange (optional)

Preheat the oven to 375°F (190°C, or gas mark 5). Line a baking sheet with parchment paper or a silicone baking mat, such as Silpat. You could also coat 8 individual cups in a standard muffin tin with nonstick cooking spray.

In a large-size bowl, whisk together the flour, oats, baking powder, and salt.

In a measuring cup using an immersion blender or in a regular blender, blend together the squash, milk, oil, and agave until perfectly smooth.

Fold the wet ingredients into the dry, being careful not to overmix.

Fold in the cranberries and zest, if desired.

Drop 8 equal portions of the batter (about ⅓ cup [100 g]) onto the prepared sheet or into the muffin cups.

Bake for 18 to 20 minutes, or until golden brown. Transfer to a wire rack to cool.

Yield: 8 biscuits

Chocolate Breakfast Cake

The sugar content was kept rather low in this cake, to make it a bit more suitable for breakfast. Enjoy a slice of it lathered with your favorite all-fruit spread, or with Ginger Cranberry Sauce with Cinnamon Cream Cheese Spread (page 78). You can even add a handful of chocolate chips or your favorite nuts to the batter, if you feel like indulging a bit more.

Nonstick cooking spray
1¾ cups (210 g) whole wheat pastry flour
2 teaspoons baking powder
¼ teaspoon fine sea salt
1 cup (235 ml) almond or other nondairy milk
¼ cup (60 ml) canola oil
1 ripe banana
⅓ cup (64 g) Sucanat
½ cup (40 g) unsweetened cocoa powder
1 teaspoon pure vanilla extract

Preheat the oven to 350°F (180°C, or gas mark 4). Lightly coat an 8-inch (20-cm) square baking pan with nonstick cooking spray.

In a large-size bowl, sift together the flour, baking powder, and salt.

With an immersion blender, or in a countertop blender, purée the milk, oil, banana, Sucanat, cocoa powder, and vanilla until smooth.

Fold the wet ingredients into the dry, being careful not to overmix.

Pour the batter into the prepared pan and bake for 30 minutes, or until a toothpick inserted into the center comes out clean.

Leave the cake in the pan, on a cooling rack, for about 30 minutes. Remove from the pan, and let cool completely before slicing.

Yield: 6 to 8 servings

Pull-Apart Cinnamon Sticky Buns

These sticky buns are reminiscent of the ones you can buy from the Amish folk in Intercourse, Pennsylvania. These buns are best served hot out of the oven. They're sweet on their own, but if you need that extra sugar boost, you can top them with the simple icing that follows the recipe.

For the dough:

2 envelopes (¼ ounce, or 7 g each) active dry yeast
1 cup (235 ml) warm water
½ cup plus 1 tablespoon (113 g) evaporated cane juice or granulated sugar, divided
3 cups (375 g) all-purpose flour
¼ teaspoon ground cinnamon
2 tablespoons (28 g) nondairy butter, melted
1 teaspoon pure vanilla extract
¼ teaspoon canola oil

For the cinnamon filling:

2 cups (440 g) firmly packed brown sugar
1 teaspoon ground cinnamon
1 stick (4 ounces, or 112 g) nondairy butter, softened

To make the dough: Dissolve the yeast in the warm water and 1 tablespoon (13 g) of the cane juice. Let sit until bubbly and foamy, about 5 minutes.

Meanwhile, mix together the flour and cinnamon. In a separate bowl, mix together the remaining ½ cup (100 g) of cane juice, and the melted butter, vanilla, and yeast mixture.

Add the wet ingredients to the dry and begin to knead until a nice elastic dough forms, adding a touch more flour if it is too sticky or a touch more water if it is too dry. Turn out onto a well-floured surface and knead for about 5 minutes.

Form into a ball, lightly coat with a thin layer of the oil, place on the center of a plate, and lightly cover with plastic wrap. Let rise for 1 hour.

To make the filling: Mash together the brown sugar and cinnamon with the softened butter until uniform. Set aside.

Have ready a 9 × 12-inch (23 × 30.5-cm) glass baking dish.

Punch down the dough. On a flat floured surface, press out the dough into a rectangle about 9 x 12 inches (23 × 30.5 cm) using your hands.

Spread the cinnamon filling evenly all over, leaving about ½-inch (1.3-cm) border on both of the short edges.

Starting at the short edge, roll up. When you get to the end, crimp the dough to seal.

Using a serrated or very sharp knife, cut the rolled-up dough into 12 equal pieces.

Place the dough, cut side up, equally spaced in the baking dish. Let sit for an additional 45 minutes to 1 hour for the second rise. They will be touching in the baking dish.

Preheat the oven to 400°F (200°C, or gas mark 6).

Bake for 15 to 20 minutes, or until golden brown. Let rest (and soak up the juices) for about 5 minutes before serving.

Serve upside down so that all of the juices are on top and ooze down the sides. Top with icing, if desired (recipe follows).

Yield: 12 rolls

Simple Icing:

¼ cup (60 ml) soy or other nondairy milk, vanilla or plain
2 cups (240 g) powdered sugar

Stir the milk into the sugar until all the sugar has been dissolved and a thick, smooth icing is formed. Drizzle over the hot cinnamon buns.

As-You-Like It Energy Bars

These versatile bars are packed with simple, energy-boosting, and healthy ingredients. Substitute your favorite nuts and dried fruits for the ones listed here, and you'll be hard-pressed to concoct a version that isn't a success.

Nonstick cooking spray
4 teaspoons (9 g) flax meal
1½ tablespoons (23 ml) warm water
2 tablespoons (42 g) agave nectar
½ teaspoon pure vanilla extract
2 tablespoons (20 g) brown rice flour
⅛ teaspoon baking powder
⅛ teaspoon baking soda
⅛ teaspoon fine sea salt
1 cup (121 g) equal amounts dried cranberries and dried raspberries, coarsely chopped
1 cup (99 g) pecan halves, coarsely chopped

Preheat the oven to 350°F (180°C, or gas mark 4). Lightly coat an 8 × 4-inch (20 × 10-cm) loaf pan with nonstick cooking spray.

In a small-size bowl, whisk together the flax meal and water until combined. Whisk in the agave and vanilla.

In a medium-size bowl, combine the flour, baking powder, baking soda, salt, and chopped fruits and nuts.

Fold the wet ingredients into the dry.

Press down firmly with the back of a spoon into the prepared pan, and bake for 30 minutes, or until golden brown and set. If it browns up too quickly because of the addition of agave, loosely cover the pan with a piece of foil.

Let cool on a wire rack, still in the pan, for about 15 minutes. Remove from the pan and let cool completely before cutting.

Yield: 4 bars

 Soy Free

No-Bake Pecan Brittle Bars

If you are looking for breakfast or snack bars that are a little bit crunchy, a little bit chewy, just a touch crumbly, and most of all, very easy to grab from the fridge when you're in a rush to get out in the morning, this recipe is a perfect match.

4 cups (320 g) old-fashioned rolled oats
1 cup (109 g) chopped pecans
¼ teaspoon fine sea salt
3 tablespoons (45 ml) coconut oil
⅓ cup (64 g) raw sugar
½ teaspoon ground cinnamon
3 tablespoons (63 g) agave nectar or brown rice syrup
1 tablespoon (22 g) blackstrap or regular molasses

Line an 8 × 4-inch (20 × 10-cm) loaf pan with parchment paper.

Toast the oats, pecans, and salt in a large-size saucepan over medium heat, stirring constantly, until lightly browned and fragrant. Place in a large-size bowl.

In the same saucepan, combine the oil, sugar, cinnamon, agave, and molasses. Cook over medium heat until it bubbles and the sugar is melted, about 2 minutes.

Fold the wet ingredients into the dry until coated.

Place the mixture in the prepared pan, pressing down firmly with an extra piece of parchment to avoid a sticky mess.

Chill in the fridge while still in pan for an easier time slicing into bars.

Yield: 4 bars

Pumpkin Molasses Power Bars

Instead of spending astronomical amounts of your hard-earned cash on store-bought energy bars, why not make your own, wrap them in waxed paper that you can save and use again later, and take them to go? You will find that they are not only cheaper but also fresher and far tastier.

Nonstick cooking spray
1 cup (244 g) pumpkin purée
⅓ cup (117 g) blackstrap or regular molasses
¼ cup (48 g) Sucanat
2 tablespoons (30 ml) canola oil
2 teaspoons pure vanilla extract
1½ cups (117 g) quick-cooking oats
1 cup (120 g) light spelt flour
1 teaspoon ground cinnamon
½ teaspoon ground ginger
¼ teaspoon fine sea salt
⅓ cup (41 g) dried cranberries or other dried fruit or nut

Preheat the oven to 350°F (180°C, or gas mark 4). Lightly coat an 8-inch (20-cm) square baking pan with nonstick cooking spray.

In a large-size saucepan, heat the pumpkin, molasses, Sucanat, and oil until smooth and combined, about 2 minutes. Stir in the vanilla.

Fold in the oats, flour, cinnamon, ginger, salt, and cranberries.

Press the mixture into the prepared pan, and bake for 25 minutes. Let cool on a wire rack. Chill in the fridge while still in the pan for an easier time slicing into bars.

Yield: 8 bars

VARIATION

If you want to drizzle the bars with icing: Sift ⅓ cup (40 g) powdered sugar into a bowl. Add nondairy milk, about ½ teaspoon at a time, stirring vigorously to obtain a smooth mixture. It should be thick enough to stick to the back of a spoon, but thin enough to spread with ease. Drizzle on top of the bars.

Pumpkin Chocolate Barley Bars

The perfect union of chocolate and pumpkin will have you reach for more of these crunchy, mellow-flavored bars.

Nonstick cooking spray
3 ounces (85 g) nondairy semisweet chocolate, coarsely chopped
3 tablespoons (42 g) nondairy butter
1 cup (244 g) pumpkin purée
1 teaspoon pure vanilla extract
⅓ cup (64 g) raw sugar
1 cup (116 g) wheat and barley cereal, such as Grape-Nuts
1 cup (78 g) quick-cooking oats
½ teaspoon baking powder
¼ teaspoon fine sea salt
¼ cup (27 g) chopped pecans (optional)

Preheat the oven to 350°F (180°C, or gas mark 4). Lightly coat an 8-inch (20-cm) square baking pan with nonstick cooking spray.

Combine the chocolate and butter in a microwave-safe bowl and heat in the microwave, in 30-second increments, until melted. Check often to avoid burning and stir well to accelerate melting. Stir in the pumpkin and vanilla.

In a large-size bowl, combine the sugar, cereal, oats, baking powder, and salt.

Stir the wet ingredients into the dry, being careful not to overmix. Stir in the nuts, if desired.

Pour the batter into the prepared pan. Bake for 25 minutes. Let cool on a wire rack. Chill in the fridge while still in the pan for an easier time slicing into bars.

Yield: 6 bars

Banana Barley Bars

Here is a satisfying recipe for a portable and highly addictive version of the fiber-rich, healthy, and nutty cereal.

Nonstick cooking spray
1 ripe banana, mashed
¼ cup (84 g) agave nectar
¼ cup (64 g) creamy natural peanut butter
1 teaspoon pure vanilla extract
2 cups (232 g) wheat and barley cereal, such as Grape-Nuts
1 teaspoon ground cinnamon
¼ teaspoon fine sea salt
¼ cup (30 g) nondairy carob or (44 g) semisweet chocolate chips

Preheat the oven to 325°F (170°C, or gas mark 3). Lightly coat an 8-inch (20-cm) square baking pan with nonstick cooking spray.

In a medium-size bowl, combine the banana, agave, peanut butter, and vanilla.

In a large-size bowl, combine the cereal, cinnamon, and salt.

Fold the wet ingredients into the dry. Stir in the carob chips.

Pour the batter into the prepared pan. Bake for 25 minutes. Let cool on a wire rack.

Chill in the fridge while still in the pan for an easier time slicing into bars.

Yield: 6 bars

Peanut Butter Oat Bars

These dense, nutty bars are packed with fiber thanks to the use of whole grains, are rich in protein from the addition of nut butter, and are kept deliciously moist with applesauce.

Nonstick cooking spray
1 cup (235 ml) organic corn syrup
¼ cup (61 g) unsweetened applesauce
½ cup (128 g) crunchy natural peanut butter
1½ cups (117 g) quick-cooking oats
1 cup (116 g) wheat germ
⅓ cup (53 g) raisins
¾ teaspoon ground cinnamon

Preheat the oven to 350°F (180°C, or gas mark 4). Lightly coat an 8-inch (20-cm) square baking pan with nonstick cooking spray.

Combine the corn syrup, applesauce, and peanut butter in a small-size saucepan, and warm over low heat until melted and emulsified.

Combine the oats, wheat germ, raisins, and cinnamon in a large-size bowl.

Fold the wet ingredients into the dry, and combine until coated.

Press the mixture into the prepared pan, and bake for 20 minutes.

Let cool on a wire rack.

Chill in the fridge while still in the pan for an easier time slicing into bars.

Yield: 8 bars

VARIATION

Use maple syrup, agave nectar, brown rice syrup, or a combination of any liquid sweetener you prefer, instead of the organic corn syrup. And if you don't like peanuts or are allergic to them, using any other nut butter will yield scrumptious results as well. The raisins can also be replaced by another favorite dried fruit or nut.

Banana Fritters

With no added sugar, these little fritters have just enough sweetness to make for a tasty, potassium-rich breakfast. Not sweet enough for you? Try sprinkling with powdered sugar and topping with warm maple syrup.

4 ripe bananas (about 2 cups, or 310 g), mashed
¼ teaspoon ground cinnamon
1 cup (80 g) panko-style bread crumbs
3 tablespoons (42 g) coconut oil

In a mixing bowl, mash the bananas together with the cinnamon. Mix in the bread crumbs until well combined.

Roll about 2 tablespoons of the mixture into a ball, then flatten, and repeat with the rest of the mixture to make 12 fritters.

Preheat the coconut oil in a frying pan. Panfry for 3 to 5 minutes per side, or until golden brown and crispy.

Yield: 12 silver dollar–size fritters

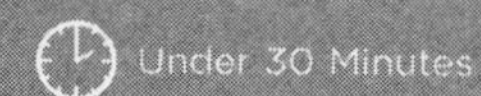

No-Fail Buttermilk Pancakes

This recipe is very simple. It is an adapted version of the Buttermilk Pancake recipe in the good old red and white Better Homes and Gardens Cookbook.

1 tablespoon (15 ml) lemon juice
1 scant cup (220 ml) vanilla soymilk (use soy here, or your milk might not curdle)
1 cup (125 g) all-purpose flour
1 tablespoon (13 g) granulated sugar
1 teaspoon baking powder
¼ teaspoon baking soda
¼ teaspoon salt
2 tablespoons (30 ml) vegetable oil
Equivalent of 1 beaten egg (see note below)
Nonstick cooking spray (optional)
Nondairy butter, for serving
Pure maple syrup, for serving

Combine the lemon juice and soymilk in a medium-size bowl; it will curdle and become like buttermilk.

In a mixing bowl, mix together the flour, cane juice, baking powder, baking soda, and salt.

Add the oil and egg replacer to the buttermilk mixture and whisk together until smooth.

Create a well in the center of the flour mixture and pour in the wet ingredients. Stir until there are very few lumps.

Heat a skillet or frying pan over high heat. You can use nonstick spray if you don't have a really good nonstick pan.

Drop about ⅓ cup (50 g) of batter onto the hot skillet and cook until the edges begin to lift and the uncooked side is nice and bubbly. Flip and cook for an additional minute.

Serve warm with a huge dollop of nondairy butter and a very generous puddle of dark amber pure maple syrup.

Yield: 6 medium-size pancakes

NOTE

Bob's Red Mill brand egg replacer works well in this recipe, but a flax egg will work here as well. A mashed banana will also work, but would add a banana-y flavor.

Chocolate Chocolate Chip Pancakes

Want to surprise your family with a special breakfast? Topped with soy whipped topping or strawberry jam, these are sure to please even the pickiest of eaters (spouses and kids included)!

2 cups (250 g) all-purpose flour
⅓ cup (27 g) unsweetened cocoa powder
1 teaspoon baking powder
1 teaspoon baking soda
¼ teaspoon salt
1½ to 2 cups (355 ml to 470 ml) soy or other nondairy milk
½ cup (120 ml) canola oil
½ cup (100 g) evaporated cane juice or granulated sugar
½ cup (88 g) nondairy chocolate chips
Nonstick cooking spray (optional)

In a mixing bowl, mix together the flour, cocoa powder, baking powder, baking soda, and salt.

In a separate bowl, mix together 1½ cups (355 ml) of the milk, oil, and sugar.

Add the wet ingredients to the dry and stir until there are virtually no lumps, adding more milk if your mixture is too thick. Fold in the chocolate chips.

Preheat a frying pan over high heat. You can use nonstick spray if you don't have a really good nonstick pan. Drop about ½ cup (75 g) of batter onto the hot skillet and cook until the edges begin to lift and the uncooked side is nice and bubbly. Flip and cook for an additional minute.

Yield: 6 medium-size pancakes

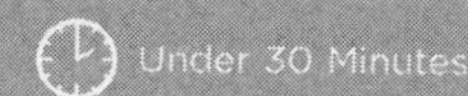

Peanut Butter Pancakes

These are great with maple syrup or their natural cohort—jelly!

2 tablespoons (30 ml) lemon juice
1 cup (235 ml) soymilk (use soy here, or your milk might not curdle)
2 cups (250 g) all-purpose flour
2 tablespoons (25 g) granulated sugar
1 teaspoon baking soda
1 teaspoon baking powder
¼ cup (60 ml) canola or other vegetable oil
1 cup (235 ml) soy creamer or additional soymilk
½ cup (128 g) creamy natural peanut butter
Nonstick cooking spray (optional)

Combine the lemon juice and soymilk in a medium-size bowl; it will curdle and become like buttermilk.

In a separate mixing bowl, combine the flour, sugar, baking soda, and baking powder.

Add the oil, soy creamer, and peanut butter to the buttermilk mixture and whisk together until smooth.

Add the wet ingredients to the dry and whisk together until there are very few lumps. If your mixture is too thick, you can add a little more soymilk.

Preheat a frying pan over high heat. You can use nonstick spray if you don't have a really good nonstick pan. Drop about ⅓ cup (50 g) of batter onto the hot skillet and cook until the edges begin to lift and the uncooked side is nice and bubbly. Flip and cook for an additional minute.

Yield: 10 medium-size pancakes

Wheat Germ Raisin Pancakes

Low in fat and full of fiber, these pancakes are sure to please! Drizzling a nice amount of pure maple syrup on top won't feel so sinful after all.

1 cup (120 g) light spelt flour
2 tablespoons (15 g) wheat germ
2 teaspoons baking powder
Pinch fine sea salt
½ teaspoon ground cinnamon
½ cup (120 ml) prune or other fruit juice
¼ cup (60 ml) soy or other nondairy milk
1 teaspoon vegetable oil
¼ cup (40 g) raisins
Nonstick cooking spray
Pure maple syrup or other accompaniment, for serving

In a large-size bowl, whisk together the flour, wheat germ, baking powder, salt, and cinnamon.

In a small-size bowl, whisk together the juice, milk, and oil.

Fold the wet ingredients into the dry, being careful not to overmix. Fold in the raisins. If the batter is too thick, add more milk.

Preheat a pan lightly coated with nonstick cooking spray. Pour a little less than ¼ cup (40 g) of batter, spreading it with the back of a spoon. Cook until bubbles appear in the center of the pancake, then flip over and cook for another 2 minutes, or until golden brown. Repeat with the rest of the batter, spraying with oil in between each pancake.

Serve with pure maple syrup or your favorite pancake topping.

Yield: 6 medium-size pancakes

Under 30 Minutes

Lemon Currant Cornmeal Waffles

Currants are a bit tarter and stronger in taste than good old raisins. It is time to give these less famous, smaller dried grapes a chance, and these hearty, lemony waffles are a great way to let their flavor shine.

2 cups (240 g) whole wheat pastry flour
1 cup (120 g) cornmeal
¼ teaspoon fine sea salt
1 teaspoon baking powder
2 cups (470 ml) soy creamer or nondairy milk
2 tablespoons (30 ml) canola oil
¼ cup (84 g) agave nectar
1 teaspoon pure lemon extract
¼ cup (36 g) dried currants

In a large-size bowl, whisk together the flour, cornmeal, salt, and baking powder.

In a separate large-size bowl, whisk together the soy creamer, oil, agave, and lemon extract until well combined.

Fold the wet ingredients into the dry, being careful not to overmix. Fold in the currants.

Prepare the waffles according to the waffle iron manufacturer's instructions.

Yield: 12 standard waffles

Under 30 Minutes

Blackberry Nut Butter Waffles

No matter which nut butter you like best, it'll fit right into these lovely waffles. Feel free to use whichever berry is in season, or the one you favor the most. Be sure to serve them with a generous drizzle of pure maple syrup!

2 cups (240 g) light spelt flour
1 cup (78 g) quick-cooking oats, finely ground
1 teaspoon baking powder
½ teaspoon fine sea salt
¼ cup (48 g) raw sugar
1 teaspoon ground cinnamon
2 teaspoons pure vanilla extract
2½ cups (590 ml) plain soy or other nondairy milk
½ cup (128 g) nut butter
1 cup (151 g) blackberries

In a medium-size bowl, whisk together the flour, ground oats, baking powder, salt, sugar, and cinnamon.

In a small-size bowl, whisk together the vanilla, soymilk, and nut butter.

Fold the wet ingredients into the dry, being careful not to overmix. If the batter is too dry, add 1 or 2 tablespoons (15 or 30 ml) of milk. Gently fold in the blackberries.

Prepare the waffles according to the waffle iron manufacturer's instructions.

Yield: 12 standard waffles

Under 30 Minutes

Carob Chip Waffles

You might already be an aficionado of the little carob chip, or it could be your first time trying it, but these waffles are a great way to enjoy the tasty caffeine-free treats without suffering from a guilty conscience.

If you prefer your waffles without added frills when it comes time to eat (i.e., plain), consider increasing the amount of maple syrup they contain before cooking them in the waffle iron.

2 cups (160 g) finely ground old-fashioned rolled oats
1 cup (120 g) chickpea or other flour
¼ teaspoon fine sea salt
1 teaspoon baking powder
2 cups (470 ml) soy creamer or nondairy milk
2 tablespoons (30 ml) canola oil
3 tablespoons (45 ml) pure maple syrup
2 teaspoons pure vanilla extract
¼ cup (30 g) nondairy carob chips

In a large-size bowl, whisk together the ground oats, flour, salt, and baking powder.

In a separate large-size bowl, whisk together the soy creamer, oil, syrup, and vanilla until well combined.

Fold the wet ingredients into the dry, being careful not to overmix. Fold in the carob chips.

Prepare the waffles according to the waffle iron manufacturer's instructions.

Yield: 12 standard waffles

Sweet Potato Ginger Waffles

The delicious crunch of the candied nuts joins forces with spicy ginger in a breakfast that will give you a great start to the day.

For the candied ginger nuts:

- ½ cup (60 g) pecan halves
- 2 tablespoons (28 g) packed light brown sugar
- 1 tablespoon (14 g) nondairy butter
- 1 tablespoon (15 ml) Triple Sec, dark rum, or water
- 2 teaspoons grated gingerroot

For the waffles:

- 1 cup (235 ml) plain soymilk (use soy here, or your milk might not curdle)
- 2 teaspoons apple cider vinegar
- 1 cup (120 g) whole wheat pastry flour
- 2 tablespoons (16 g) arrowroot powder
- 1 teaspoon ground cinnamon
- 1 teaspoon ground ginger
- 1 teaspoon baking powder
- ¼ teaspoon fine sea salt
- ⅔ cup (170 g) homemade or canned sweet potato purée
- 2 tablespoons (30 ml) pure maple syrup
- 2 tablespoons (30 ml) canola oil

To make the nuts: Place all the ingredients in a small-size saucepan. Cook over medium-high heat until the liquid is mostly gone and the nuts are golden brown, about 5 minutes. Keep an eye on the nuts and stir often so that they don't burn.

Set aside to cool.

To make the waffles: Combine the soymilk and vinegar in a medium-size bowl; it will curdle and become like buttermilk.

In a large-size bowl, whisk together the flour, arrowroot powder, cinnamon, ginger, baking powder, and salt.

Add the sweet potato, maple syrup, and oil to the buttermilk mixture, and whisk until combined.

Fold the wet ingredients into the dry, being careful not to overmix. If the batter is too thick, stir in a little extra soymilk, 1 tablespoon (15 ml) at a time, until it is more manageable.

Fold in the candied ginger nuts.

Prepare the waffles according to the waffle iron manufacturer's instructions.

Yield: 12 standard waffles

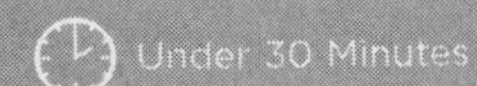

Pumpkin Tofu Scramble

Breakfast without tofu scramble? Not on our watch! This delicious version is boosted with all the fantastic color, vitamins, and fiber the wondrous squash known as pumpkin has to offer.

1 tablespoon (15 ml) peanut oil
2 cloves garlic, grated
⅓ cup (53 g) chopped onion
¼ cup (30 g) nutritional yeast
¼ teaspoon ground black pepper, to taste
½ teaspoon fine sea salt
1 teaspoon dried sage
⅛ teaspoon ground nutmeg
½ teaspoon paprika
½ teaspoon dried oregano
16 ounces (454 g) firm tofu, drained and crumbled
1½ cups (366 g) pumpkin purée

In a large-size skillet, heat the oil over medium heat. Cook the garlic and onion until tender and fragrant, about 2 minutes.

Add the yeast, pepper, salt, sage, nutmeg, paprika, and oregano. Cook for 1 minute.

Add the tofu and cook until slightly browned, about 5 minutes.

Stir in the pumpkin and cook until just heated through, about 2 minutes.

Serve immediately.

Yield: 2 to 4 servings

Buttermilk Biscuits and Gravy

A diner breakfast at home!

For the biscuits:

1 cup (235 ml) soymilk (use soy here, or your milk might not curdle)
2 tablespoons (30 ml) lemon juice
2 cups (250 g) all-purpose flour
¼ cup (36 g) vital wheat gluten flour
2 tablespoons (26 g) granulated sugar
1 teaspoon baking powder
½ teaspoon baking soda
½ teaspoon salt
2 tablespoons (28 g) nondairy butter, melted

For the gravy:

3 tablespoons (42 g) nondairy butter
¼ cup (32 g) all-purpose flour
2 cups (470 g) vegetable broth
1 teaspoon black pepper
8 ounces (227 g) crumbled seitan or your favorite meat substitute

To make the biscuits: Preheat the oven to 350°F (180°C, or gas mark 4).

Line a baking sheet with parchment or a silicone baking mat, such as Silpat.

Combine the soymilk and lemon juice in a small-size bowl; it will curdle and become like buttermilk. Set aside.

In a mixing bowl, mix together the flours, sugar, baking powder, baking soda, and salt.

Add the melted butter to the buttermilk mixture.

Add the wet ingredients to the dry and knead into a soft dough. Add a little more flour if the dough is too sticky, or a little more water if it is too dry.

Turn out onto a well-floured surface and, using your hands, flatten the dough into a disk about 1 inch (2.5 cm) thick.

Using a pint glass or a 3-inch (7.5-cm) cookie cutter, cut the dough into 6 biscuits and place on the baking sheet. Reform the dough if necessary to cut out more biscuits.

Bake for 18 to 23 minutes, or until the tops are beginning to brown.

To make the gravy: It is important to premeasure all of your ingredients and have them at hand, because this process is quick!

Preheat a pot over medium-high heat. Add the butter. When fully melted and just beginning to bubble, add the flour and whisk vigorously. A thick yellow paste will form.

Immediately and slowly pour in the broth and continue to whisk until the desired consistency is reached.

Remove from the heat and add the pepper and crumbled seitan.

Pour a generous amount of gravy over an open-faced biscuit.

Yield: 6 to 8 biscuits and enough gravy for all of them

Muffin Cup Quiche in Phyllo Crust

Here you will find two variations of quiche, a Mediterranean-influenced sun-dried tomato and spinach version, and a broccoli "cheddar" version, complete with fake bacon. The recipe for the base quiche mix is given, as well as what is added for the different variations, but seriously, you can make these any old way you want to. In fact, you don't even have to make individual cups. One recipe would fill a premade pie crust quite nicely.

Nonstick cooking spray

Basic Quiche Mix:

12 ounces (336 g) extra-firm tofu, drained and pressed
1 teaspoon onion powder
1 teaspoon garlic powder
¼ teaspoon turmeric
1 tablespoon (15 g) prepared yellow mustard
¼ cup (30 g) nutritional yeast
¼ cup (30 g) chickpea flour
¼ cup (60 ml) extra-virgin olive oil

For the crust:

1 package (1 pound, or 455 g) frozen phyllo dough, thawed according to package directions
Olive oil, for brushing

Preheat the oven to 350°F (180°C, or gas mark 4). Prepare your muffin pan by spraying the cups liberally with nonstick spray.

To make the quiche mix: In a mixing bowl, crumble the tofu, add all the remaining ingredients, and mash together using your hands. Mix until well incorporated. Set aside.

To make the crust: Following the instructions on the box, carefully unroll the package of dough, and, using a pizza cutter, cut the entire stack of dough into 8 even pieces.

Oil each layer lightly, and divide into 3 or 4 layers for each "cup." Press it into the muffin pan to form the crust.

Scoop 1⁄12 of the quiche mixture into each cup.

Bake for 15 minutes, checking them after 10 minutes. Remove from the oven when the crusts begin to brown.

Yield: 12 mini quiches

VARIATIONS

For a Mediterranean-style quiche, add 2 cups (60 g) fresh spinach leaves, tightly packed, then cut into a chiffonade, and about 6 sun-dried tomatoes packed in oil, chopped into little pieces.

For a broccoli "cheddar" quiche, add ½ of a white onion, finely diced, 1 tablespoon (18 g) of mellow white miso, about 2 cups (142 g) of broccoli florets, and ¼ cup (208 g) of Imitation Bacon Bits (page 212).

Chipotle Sweet Potato Latkes

These latkes are kosher for Passover, as long as you purchase kosher for Passover ingredients. Serve traditionally with sour cream and applesauce, or go chipotle crazy and serve with Chipotle Ranch Dressing (page 129), but be careful not to go overboard unless you like it HOT! HOT! HOT!

1 large-size sweet potato, shredded (3 cups, or 350 g)
1 cup (160 g) diced yellow or white onion
¾ cup (170 g) plain nondairy yogurt
3 chipotle peppers in adobo sauce, diced
1 tablespoon (15 ml) adobo sauce (from the can)
1 cup (120 g) matzo meal
½ cup (80 g) currants or raisins
Salt and pepper to taste
Enough canola or vegetable oil to make ¼ inch (6 mm) in your frying pan

In a mixing bowl, combine the shredded sweet potato, onion, yogurt, peppers, adobo sauce, matzo meal, currants, salt, and pepper. Using your hands, mash everything together until well incorporated.

Preheat a frying pan with ¼ inch (6 mm) of oil.

Form the mixture into patties about 4 inches (10 cm) in diameter and ½ inch thick (1.3 cm).

Panfry in hot oil for about 3 to 5 minutes per side, until golden brown and crispy.

Transfer to a paper towel–lined plate to absorb any excess oil.

Yield: 10 to 12 latkes

Zucchini Fritters

You can make four out of this recipe, if you like 'em pretty big, or you can make six smaller ones. They're great served alongside a nice tofu scramble.

2 cups (248 g) shredded zucchini (1 cup [124 g] green and 1 cup [124 g] yellow)
2 cups (250 g) all-purpose flour
¾ cup (170 g) plain nondairy yogurt
¼ cup (60 ml) canola or other vegetable oil, plus more for frying
¼ cup (60 ml) plain soy or other nondairy milk
¼ teaspoon paprika
Salt and pepper to taste

Combine the zucchini, flour, yogurt, ¼ cup (60 ml) oil, soymilk, paprika, salt, and pepper in a mixing bowl and mix together until well incorporated. Your mixture should be wet, like a very thick pancake batter.

Preheat a frying pan over medium-high heat with a good amount of oil (about ¼ inch [6 mm]). Plop down the batter into the pan and fry for about 5 to 7 minutes per side. Flip when you see the edges beginning to brown.

Yield: 4 to 8 fritters

Cast-Iron Skillet Frittata, Four Ways

Sometimes the same old tofu scrambles can just get tiresome. That's when a nice frittata comes in to save breakfast. It's a quick and easy one-pan meal that really satisfies! The possibilities are really quite endless. Here are four favorite ways to make a frittata, but you can easily add just about anything you want to make it your own.

Frittata Base:

Oil or nonstick cooking spray
12 ounces (336 g) extra-firm tofu, drained and pressed
1 cup (120 g) chickpea flour
¼ cup (30 g) nutritional yeast
1 tablespoon (8 g) garlic powder
1 tablespoon (8 g) onion powder
½ teaspoon turmeric
½ cup (120 ml) plain soy or other nondairy creamer
¼ cup (60 ml) vegetable or canola oil
Salt and pepper to taste
Add-ins of your choice; see below

Frittata Denver:

1 red bell pepper, seeded, cored, and diced
1 green bell pepper, seeded, cored, and diced
1 cup (160 g) diced red or yellow onion
1 cup (150 g) diced Ham Fauxsage (page 200)

Frittata Mediterranean:

8 sun-dried tomatoes (packed in oil), chopped
12 large-size basil leaves, tightly packed, then cut into a chiffonade
1 tablespoon (15 g) minced garlic

Frittata Lorraine Americana:

½ cup (50 g) imitation bacon bits, store-bought or homemade (page 212), or 1 recipe Seitan Bacon Crumbles (page 209)
14 ounces (392 g) frozen or canned spinach, thawed and drained
2 tomatoes, seeded and diced

To make the frittata base: Preheat the oven to 350°F (180°C, or gas mark 4).

In a food processor or blender, blend all the ingredients until smooth. Set aside.

In a separate bowl, mix together all the add-in ingredients and divide in half.

Transfer the base mixture to a mixing bowl and fold in one-half of the add-ins.*

Pour the base mixture into a well-oiled (you can use nonstick cooking spray here, too) cast-iron skillet (10 inches [25 cm] is a perfect size for this, but if you don't have a cast-iron skillet you can use a pie pan instead).

Sprinkle the remaining add-ins on top of the mixture.

Bake, uncovered, for 45 minutes. Remove from the oven and let set for 10 minutes.

Slice as you would a pie and serve.

*For the Frittata Mexicana, mix all of the add-ins to the base.

Yield: 8 servings

Frittata Mexicana:

1 cup (110 g) store-bought soy chorizo or 1 recipe Seitan Chorizo Crumbles (page 209)
½ cup (32 g) diced scallion
½ cup (48 g) fresh cilantro leaves, chopped
1 teaspoon ground cumin
1 teaspoon ground coriander
Nondairy sour cream, store-bought or homemade (page 302), and additional chopped scallion, for topping

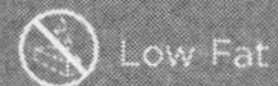 Low Fat

Maple Hickory Tofu Strips

These are a simple, nice accompaniment to tofu scrambles and hotcakes. These aren't supposed to be bacon . . . they're not! They are just a sweet and savory breakfast side, okay?

12 ounces (340 g) extra-firm tofu, drained and pressed
½ cup (120 ml) pure maple syrup
¼ cup (60 ml) orange juice
1 teaspoon ground black pepper
1 tablespoon (15 ml) hickory-flavored liquid smoke

Cut the tofu into 14 thin strips about ¼ inch (6 mm) thick.

Mix together the syrup, orange juice, black pepper, and liquid smoke to make a marinade. In a shallow dish or resealable plastic bag, place the tofu in the marinade and let rest for 20 minutes to 1 hour.

Preheat a flat, nonstick or cast-iron skillet over very high heat. Remove the tofu from the marinade and panfry until dark brown and crispy on each side, about 5 minutes per side.

Yield: 14 strips

VARIATIONS

This marinade would work the same with thin slices of tempeh or seitan. The Ham Fauxsage (page 200) recipe comes to mind.

Chapter 3

Sweet and Savory Muffins

We all know that breakfast is the most important meal of the day, but many of us don't have the time to make healthy, wholesome choices in our mad morning dash out the door. Instead, we swing through the local coffee shop and grab something (most likely) laden with hydrogenated oil, cholesterol, and calories.

This chapter comes to your rescue. In it, you will find healthy and satisfying recipes for muffins and scones that will nourish your appetite and delight your taste buds until it is time to worry about the next meal. Better yet, you can bake a batch of these guilt-free delights and keep some in the freezer for emergencies. After cooling, just pack the baked goods in freezer-safe containers, then bring them to room temperature before enjoying. And don't forget to pack an extra for snack time!

Savory Tomato Olive Muffins

Need something to go with your creamy tomato soup? Look no further! These muffins are the perfect companions to something savory, including soups, salads, or stews.

Nonstick cooking spray
2 teaspoons apple cider vinegar
1½ cups (355 ml) unsweetened soymilk (use soy here, or your milk might not curdle)
3 tablespoons (21 g) ground flaxseed
¼ cup (60 ml) water
2 cups (240 g) whole wheat pastry flour
1 cup (120 g) cornmeal
1 teaspoon fine sea salt
1 teaspoon baking soda
¼ cup (60 ml) extra-virgin olive oil
1 tablespoon (2 g) dried basil
2 teaspoons dried minced onion
½ teaspoon cracked black pepper
8 sun-dried tomatoes packed in oil, drained, finely chopped
16 black olives, finely chopped

Preheat the oven to 350°F (180°C, or gas mark 4). Lightly coat a standard muffin tin with spray.

Combine the vinegar and soymilk in a medium-size bowl; it will curdle and become like buttermilk.

Combine the ground flaxseed with water in a small-size bowl. Set aside.

In a large-size bowl, whisk together the flour, cornmeal, salt, and baking soda.

Whisk the flaxseed mixture into the buttermilk mixture, along with the oil, basil, onion, and pepper, until combined.

Fold the wet ingredients into the dry, being careful not to overmix. Fold in the chopped tomatoes and olives.

Divide the batter equally among the muffin cups.

Bake for 18 minutes, or until a toothpick inserted into the center comes out clean.

Remove the muffins from the pan, and let cool on a wire rack.

Yield: 12 standard muffins

Spicy Chick-Wheat Savory Muffins

If the tahini you use is rather thick and dry, be sure to add a few extra tablespoons of milk to it so that the muffins turn out fluffy and tender, judging on the quality of the batter. If you like your food to be even spicier, feel free to increase the amount of crushed chile peppers. On the other hand, if you prefer milder foods, reduce the amount of, or simply do not add, the peppers.

1 cup (120 g) chickpea flour
3 cups (360 g) whole wheat or whole wheat pastry flour
4 teaspoons ground cumin
4 teaspoons garam masala, store-bought or homemade (page 305)
2 teaspoons dried crushed chile peppers
2 teaspoons baking powder
1 teaspoon baking soda
2 teaspoons fine sea salt
½ cup (128 g) tahini
¼ cup (60 ml) peanut or toasted sesame oil
4 teaspoons agave nectar
2½ cups (590 ml) plain soy, almond, or other nondairy milk

Preheat the oven to 350°F (180°C, or gas mark 4). Line two standard muffin tins with about 20 paper liners.

In a large-size bowl, whisk together the flours, cumin, garam masala, chile peppers, baking powder, baking soda, and salt. Set aside.

In a medium-size bowl, whisk together the tahini, oil, agave, and milk.

Fold the wet ingredients into the dry, being careful not to overmix.

Divide the batter equally among the muffin cups.

Bake for 18 minutes, or until a toothpick inserted into the center comes out clean.

Please note that if you see them brown up too quickly, you can cover them with a piece of foil until they're done baking.

Remove from the pan and transfer to a wire rack to cool completely before storing.

Yield: 20 standard muffins

Jam-Filled Soda Rolls

A cross between Irish soda bread and a slightly sweet muffin, these rolls are ideal for breakfast. When using a savory-friendly preserve such as fig, they can also be served alongside your favorite soup or stew.

Nonstick cooking spray
1 tablespoon (15 ml) apple cider vinegar
1¼ cups (295 ml) plain soymilk (use soy here, or your milk might not curdle)
1 cup (120 g) white whole wheat or whole wheat pastry flour
1¼ cups (150 g) light spelt flour
2 tablespoons (24 g) raw sugar
2 teaspoons baking powder
½ teaspoon baking soda
¼ teaspoon fine sea salt
2 tablespoons (30 ml) canola oil
¼ cup (61 g) unsweetened applesauce
¼ cup (80 g) jam, preserves, or all-fruit spread
Melted nondairy butter, to brush tops

Preheat the oven to 400°F (200°C, or gas mark 6). Lightly coat a standard muffin tin with spray.

Combine the vinegar and soymilk in a medium-size bowl; it will curdle and become like buttermilk.

In a large-size bowl, whisk together the flours, sugar, baking powder, baking soda, and salt. Incorporate the oil with a fork.

Whisk the applesauce into the buttermilk mixture, and add to the flour mixture. Stir until just combined.

Place 1 heaping tablespoon of batter in each muffin cup, add 1 teaspoon of jam in the center, and top with 1 final heaping tablespoon of batter.

Bake for 15 minutes. As soon as the rolls are removed from the oven, brush the tops with a little nondairy butter.

Remove from the pan and place on a cooling rack, or enjoy them while they're still warm.

Yield: 12 standard muffins

VARIATION

Fold ½ cup (80 g) raisins, currants, blueberries, or nuts into the batter.

You can also skip the jam and add-ins completely and enjoy as plain rolls.

Banana Muffin Tops

These flavorful, moist, and not exceedingly sweet muffins can be prepared in a muffin top pan, if you are the proud owner of such a gadget, or in a more conventional muffin tin.

Nonstick cooking spray
1 cup (93 g) finely shredded coconut
¾ cup (59 g) quick-cooking oats
1 cup (120 g) whole wheat pastry flour
½ teaspoon baking powder
¼ teaspoon baking soda
¼ teaspoon fine sea salt
¼ cup (60 ml) canola oil
½ cup plus 2 tablespoons (120 g) raw sugar
2 tablespoons (44 g) blackstrap or regular molasses
1 ripe banana
3 tablespoons (45 ml) almond or other nondairy milk
1 teaspoon pure vanilla extract
⅓ cup (58 g) nondairy semisweet chocolate chips

Preheat the oven to 350°F (180°C, or gas mark 4). Lightly coat a muffin top pan, jumbo, or standard muffin tin with spray.

In a large-size bowl, combine the coconut, oats, flour, baking powder, baking soda, and salt.

In a medium-size bowl, using an immersion blender, purée the oil, sugar, molasses, banana, milk, and vanilla until smooth.

Fold the wet ingredients into the dry, being careful not to overmix. Fold in the chocolate chips.

Divide the batter equally among the muffin cups.

Bake for 16 to 20 minutes, until firm and golden brown, or until a toothpick inserted into the center comes out clean.

Leave in the pan for a few minutes before transferring to a wire rack to cool.

Yield: 6 muffin tops, 6 jumbo muffins, or 12 standard muffins

Lemon Poppy Seed Muffins

A nice balance between cupcake and muffin, these sophisticated treats can be enjoyed for breakfast or dessert. Or both.

¼ cup plus 2 tablespoons (54 g) poppy seeds
¼ cup (84 g) agave nectar
¼ cup (60 ml) fresh lemon juice
4 teaspoons grated lemon zest
½ cup (112 g) nondairy butter
½ cup (96 g) raw sugar
1 tablespoon (8 g) arrowroot powder
1 cup (240 g) nondairy sour cream, store-bought or homemade (page 302)
2 cups (240 g) light spelt flour
2 teaspoons baking powder
1 teaspoon baking soda
¼ teaspoon fine sea salt

Preheat the oven to 350°F (180°C, or gas mark 4). Line a standard muffin tin with 12 paper liners.

In a medium-size bowl, cream together the poppy seeds, agave, lemon juice, lemon zest, nondairy butter, sugar, arrowroot, and sour cream.

In a large-size bowl, whisk together the flour, baking powder, baking soda, and salt.

Fold the wet ingredients into the dry, being careful not to overmix.

Divide the batter equally among the muffin cups.

Bake for 20 minutes, or until a toothpick inserted into the center comes out clean. If you see the muffins are browning up too quickly, cover with foil.

Let cool on a wire rack while still in the tin for at least 15 minutes before transferring directly onto the wire rack.

Yield: 12 standard muffins

Coffee Toffee Muffins

If you wake up in dire need of something that screams "caffeine," or if you need an extra boost of energy in the middle of the afternoon to make it through your day at the office, these little muffins will have your back.

For the muffins:

- Nonstick cooking spray
- ¾ cup (90 g) whole wheat pastry flour
- 1½ cups (180 g) light spelt flour
- 2 teaspoons baking powder
- ¼ teaspoon fine sea salt
- 4 teaspoons instant espresso powder
- ¼ cup plus 2 tablespoons (30 g) unsweetened cocoa powder
- ¼ cup (60 g) blended silken tofu
- ¾ cup plus 2 tablespoons (168 g) raw sugar
- ¼ cup plus 2 tablespoons (84 g) nondairy butter
- 1 cup plus 2 tablespoons (265 ml) unsweetened soy or other nondairy milk
- 2 teaspoons pure vanilla extract

For the topping:

- 2 tablespoons (24 g) Sucanat
- 2 tablespoons (28 g) nondairy butter

To make the muffins: Preheat the oven to 350°F (180°C, or gas mark 4). Lightly coat a standard muffin tin with spray.

In a medium-size bowl, sift together the flours, baking powder, and salt.

With an immersion or countertop blender, blend the espresso powder, cocoa powder, tofu, sugar, butter, milk, and vanilla until perfectly smooth.

Fold the wet ingredients into the dry, being careful not to overmix.

Divide the batter equally among the muffin cups.

To make the topping: Sprinkle ½ teaspoon Sucanat, then place ½ teaspoon butter on each top.

Bake for 18 minutes, or until a toothpick inserted into the center comes out clean.

Leave in the tin for about 10 minutes before transferring the muffins onto a wire rack to cool.

Yield: 12 standard muffins

Apple Candy Muffins

The preparation may look involved at first glance, but these muffins couldn't be simpler (or quicker) to prepare. Their texture is breadlike, and the crunchy apples and sugar mixture are what brings the sweetness. If you'd rather have a sweeter experience, feel free to double the amount of sugar in the muffins themselves. You can also substitute any kind of nuts for the apples.

For the sugar-coated apples:

½ cup (80 g) dried apple bits, super packed
1 tablespoon (15 ml) water
1 tablespoon (14 g) nondairy butter
2 tablespoons (28 g) packed light brown sugar

For the sugar mixture:

2 tablespoons (24 g) raw sugar
2 tablespoons (24 g) Sucanat
¼ teaspoon ground cinnamon
¼ teaspoon ground ginger
¼ teaspoon ground cardamom
Pinch allspice

For the muffins:

Nonstick cooking spray
1 tablespoon (15 ml) apple cider vinegar
1 cup (235 ml) plain soymilk (use soy here, or your milk might not curdle)
1 teaspoon bread machine yeast
2 cups (240 g) whole wheat pastry flour
¼ cup (48 g) raw sugar
½ teaspoon ground cinnamon
½ teaspoon baking powder
½ teaspoon baking soda
¼ teaspoon fine sea salt
¼ cup (60 ml) canola oil

To make the sugar-coated apples: Place all the ingredients in a small-size saucepan. Heat over medium-high heat and cook, stirring constantly, until the liquid has evaporated and the apple bits are glossy and browned, about 6 minutes.

Remove from the heat and let cool in the fridge. The coating will firm up just a bit.

To make the sugar mixture: Combine all the ingredients in a small-size bowl.

To make the muffins: Preheat the oven to 375°F (190°C, or gas mark 5). Lightly coat a jumbo muffin tin or 16 standard muffin cups with spray.

Combine the vinegar and soymilk in a medium-size bowl; it will curdle and become like buttermilk.

In a large-size bowl, whisk together the yeast, flour, sugar, cinnamon, baking powder, baking soda, and salt.

Whisk the oil into the buttermilk mixture.

Fold the wet ingredients into the dry, stirring vigorously for a minute or two.

Divide half of the batter among the muffin cups, and sprinkle with the sugar mixture. Cover with the rest of the batter.

Divide the sugar-coated apples into 6 (or 16, if making standard muffins) equal portions and lightly press on top of each muffin.

Bake for 16 to 18 minutes, or until golden brown, if making standard muffins, or 25 minutes if making jumbo muffins. Immediately remove from the pan, and transfer to a wire rack.

Let cool completely before enjoying.

Yield: 6 jumbo or 16 standard muffins

Ginger Cranberry Muffins

Tender, gingery, and quite healthy to boot, these muffins are a great way to start your day off on the right foot. Blackstrap molasses is the most nutrient-rich type of molasses, but if you find the flavor to be too strong for you, use regular molasses instead.

2 cups (240 g) whole wheat pastry flour
¼ cup (20 g) unsweetened cocoa powder
1 teaspoon baking powder
½ teaspoon baking soda
¼ teaspoon fine sea salt
½ cup (96 g) raw sugar
¾ cup (180 ml) almond or other nondairy milk
½ cup (120 g) vanilla soy or other nondairy yogurt
¼ cup (60 ml) canola oil
¼ cup (88 g) blackstrap or regular molasses
4 teaspoons (8 g) grated gingerroot
⅔ cup (42 g) fresh cranberries, halved

Preheat the oven to 350°F (180°C, or gas mark 4). Line a standard muffin tin with paper liners.

In a large-size bowl, sift together the flour, cocoa, baking powder, baking soda, and salt. Whisk in the sugar. Set aside.

In a small-size bowl, whisk together the milk, yogurt, oil, molasses, and ginger.

Fold the wet ingredients into the dry, being careful not to overmix. Fold in the cranberry halves.

Divide the batter equally among the muffin cups. Bake for 20 minutes, or until a toothpick inserted into the center comes out clean. Let cool on a wire rack.

Yield: 12 standard muffins

Double Chocolate Muffins

You will find it nearly impossible to distinguish these muffins from their nonvegan counterparts. The only difference is that our muffins are free of cholesterol and rather low in fat, especially if using the nondairy milk instead of the creamer. If you're feeling extra indulgent, drizzle some Chocolate Ganache (page 74) on top, and have your chocolate sensor go into overdrive.

Nonstick cooking spray if making jumbo muffins
1 cup (120 g) white whole wheat or whole wheat pastry flour
½ cup (63 g) all-purpose flour
¼ teaspoon fine sea salt
1 cup (120 g) powdered sugar
¼ cup (20 g) unsweetened cocoa powder
1 teaspoon baking soda
¼ cup plus 1 tablespoon (76 g) unsweetened applesauce
1 tablespoon (15 ml) apple cider vinegar
1 teaspoon pure vanilla extract
1 cup (235 ml) plain soy creamer or any nondairy milk
⅓ cup (58 g) nondairy semisweet chocolate chips

Preheat the oven to 350°F (180°C, or gas mark 4). Line a standard muffin tin with paper liners, or lightly coat a jumbo muffin tin with nonstick cooking spray.

In a large-size bowl, sift together the flours, salt, sugar, cocoa, and baking soda. Set aside.

In a small-size bowl, whisk together the applesauce, vinegar, vanilla, and soy creamer.

Fold the wet ingredients into the dry, being careful not to overmix. Fold in the chocolate chips.

Divide the batter equally among the muffin cups. Bake for 16 to 20 minutes for standard muffins, 25 minutes for jumbo muffins, or until a toothpick inserted into the center comes out clean. Let cool on a wire rack.

Yield: 12 standard or 6 jumbo muffins

Pumpkin Carob Muffins

A bit more virtuous than chocolate, carob is free of caffeine and packed with calcium, magnesium, and potassium. A common mistake is to compare carob's flavor to that of chocolate; carob has a delicious taste all its own.

½ cup (168 g) agave nectar
1¼ cups (305 g) pumpkin purée
½ cup (120 ml) soy creamer or any nondairy milk
¼ cup (60 ml) canola oil
1¼ cups (150 g) whole wheat pastry flour
½ cup (60 g) carob powder
2 teaspoons baking soda
¼ teaspoon fine sea salt
1 teaspoon ground cinnamon
½ teaspoon ground ginger
¼ teaspoon ground nutmeg
⅛ teaspoon ground cloves
⅛ teaspoon ground cardamom
½ cup (60 g) nondairy carob chips

Preheat the oven to 325°F (170°C, or gas mark 3). Line a standard muffin tin with paper liners.

In a medium-size bowl, whisk together the agave, pumpkin, creamer, and oil.

In a large-size bowl, sift together the flour, carob powder, baking soda, salt, cinnamon, ginger, nutmeg, cloves, and cardamom.

Fold the wet ingredients into the dry, being careful not to overmix. Fold in the carob chips.

Divide the batter equally among the muffin cups. Bake for 20 minutes, or until a toothpick inserted into the center comes out clean.

Let cool in the tin for 15 minutes before transferring the muffins to a wire rack to cool completely.

Yield: 12 standard muffins

Matcha Almond Muffins

Although it can sometimes feel like you are searching for the Holy Grail, finding pure matcha powder is absolutely worth it. If the cost or effort is too much, though, the matcha-less version is quite tasty, too.

⅔ cup (147 g) packed light brown sugar
1 cup (226 g) unsweetened applesauce
2 teaspoons pure almond extract
2 teaspoons rose water
½ cup (120 ml) canola oil
¼ cup (60 ml) unsweetened soy or other nondairy milk
1½ cups (240 g) brown rice flour
½ cup (60 g) whole wheat pastry flour
4 teaspoons (16 g) matcha green tea powder
1 tablespoon (8 g) arrowroot powder
1 teaspoon baking powder
½ teaspoon baking soda
¼ teaspoon fine sea salt
⅔ cup (92 g) salted, dry-roasted almonds, coarsely chopped

Preheat the oven to 350°F (180°C, or gas mark 4). Line a standard muffin tin with paper liners.

In a medium-size bowl, whisk together the sugar, applesauce, almond extract, rose water, oil, and milk until smooth.

In a large-size bowl, sift together the flours, matcha, arrowroot, baking powder, baking soda, and salt.

Fold the wet ingredients into the dry, being careful not to overmix. Fold in the almonds.

Divide the batter equally among the muffin cups.

Bake for 18 minutes, or until a toothpick inserted into the center comes out clean.

Let cool completely on a cooling rack.

Yield: 12 standard muffins

Chocolate Orange Marmalade Muffins

Chocolate and orange flavors make a beautiful pair in these delicate and elegant muffins that teeter on the edge of being called cupcakes, accentuated by the fact that they barely reach the top of the liner. If you want a higher rise, simply make 10 muffins instead of 12 and increase the baking time by a few minutes.

⅔ cup (213 g) all-fruit orange marmalade
2 teaspoons pure vanilla extract
¼ cup (84 g) agave nectar
2 tablespoons (30 ml) canola oil
½ cup (120 ml) plain almond or other nondairy milk
1 cup (120 g) whole wheat pastry flour
¼ cup (20 g) unsweetened cocoa powder
1 tablespoon (8 g) cornstarch
½ teaspoon baking soda
¼ teaspoon baking powder
¼ teaspoon fine sea salt
½ cup (88 g) nondairy semisweet chocolate chips

Preheat the oven to 350°F (180°C, or gas mark 4). Line a standard muffin tin with paper liners.

In a medium-size bowl, whisk together the marmalade, vanilla, agave, oil, and milk.

In a large-size bowl, sift together the flour, cocoa, cornstarch, baking soda, baking powder, and salt.

Fold the wet ingredients into the dry, being careful not to overmix. Fold in the chocolate chips.

Divide the batter equally among the muffin cups.

Bake for 16 minutes, or until a toothpick inserted into the center comes out clean.

Let cool completely on a cooling rack.

Yield: 12 standard muffins

Peanut Butter Muffins

There's really something irresistible about peanut butter, or is it just us? We'll pretend it's the protein it contains. As always, if you cannot have peanut butter—or just want to try something different—use another nut butter in its place.

Nonstick cooking spray
1 cup (256 g) creamy or crunchy natural peanut butter
½ cup (96 g) raw sugar
¼ cup (61 g) unsweetened applesauce
1 cup (235 ml) almond or other nondairy milk
¼ teaspoon fine sea salt
2 teaspoons pure vanilla extract
1 cup (80 g) old-fashioned rolled oats, finely ground
½ cup (60 g) whole wheat pastry or whole wheat flour
1 teaspoon ground cinnamon
2 teaspoons baking powder
⅔ cup (116 g) nondairy semisweet chocolate chips

Preheat the oven to 350°F (180°C, or gas mark 4). Lightly coat a standard muffin tin with spray.

In a large-size bowl, whisk together the peanut butter, sugar, applesauce, milk, salt, and vanilla until well blended.

Add the ground oats, flour, cinnamon, and baking powder on top of the wet ingredients.

Fold the dry ingredients into the wet, being careful not to overmix. Fold in the chocolate chips.

Divide the batter equally among the muffin cups.

Bake for 25 minutes, or until a toothpick inserted into the center comes out clean.

Let cool for a few minutes before transferring to a wire rack to cool completely.

Yield: 12 standard muffins

Quinoa Raisin Muffins

The quinoa gives heartiness to these muffins, as well as a protein boost, making them an ideal meal to keep you satisfied and satiated throughout the morning.

1 cup (120 g) white whole wheat or whole wheat pastry flour
⅔ cup (128 g) raw sugar
1 tablespoon (12 g) baking powder
1 teaspoon ground cinnamon
½ teaspoon ground ginger
¼ teaspoon ground nutmeg
1 cup (256 g) creamy natural nut butter
⅔ cup plus 2 tablespoons (190 ml) soy or other nondairy milk
2 teaspoons pure vanilla extract
⅔ cup (123 g) cooked and cooled quinoa
½ cup (80 g) raisins

Preheat the oven to 350°F (180°C, or gas mark 4). Line a standard muffin tin with paper liners.

In a large-size bowl, whisk together the flour, sugar, baking powder, cinnamon, ginger, and nutmeg.

In a medium-size bowl, whisk together the nut butter, milk, and vanilla.

Fold the wet ingredients into the dry, being careful not to overmix. Fold in the quinoa and raisins.

Divide the batter equally among the muffin cups. Bake for 20 to 25 minutes, or until a toothpick inserted into the center comes out clean.

Let cool on a wire rack.

Yield: 12 standard muffins

Blueberry Orange Muffins

A hint of citrus takes one of America's favorite muffin flavors to new heights.

2 cups (240 g) whole wheat pastry flour
½ cup (96 g) Sucanat
1 tablespoon (12 g) baking powder
¼ teaspoon fine sea salt
¼ cup plus 2 tablespoons (92 g) unsweetened applesauce
¾ cup (180 ml) fresh orange juice
¼ cup plus 1 tablespoon (75 ml) canola oil
1 cup (145 g) fresh blueberries

Preheat the oven to 375°F (190°C, or gas mark 5). Line a standard muffin tin with paper liners. In a large-size bowl, whisk together the flour, Sucanat, baking powder, and salt. In a medium-size bowl, whisk together the applesauce, juice, and oil. Fold the wet ingredients into the dry, being careful not to overmix. Fold in the blueberries. Divide the batter equally among the muffin cups. Bake for 18 to 20 minutes, or until a toothpick inserted into the center comes out clean. Let cool on a wire rack.

Yield: 12 standard muffins

Cherry Pistachio Scoffins

The poor pistachio gets such a bum rap. Always stuck in fluorescent green ice cream or attacked with bright red dye and shoved in plastic bags. Why can't the poor guy be the star of the show? After all, he boasts more antioxidant power in one little ounce than in a whole cup of green tea! He's also low on the glycemic index and provides a good dose of heart-healthy fats, not to mention copper, manganese, thiamin, and vitamin B_6. Well, we let him be the star here, packing him into this cross between a scone and a muffin (hence the name) with some equally delicious dried cherries.

3 cups (360 g) whole wheat pastry flour
2 tablespoons (15 g) wheat germ
1 teaspoon baking soda
1 teaspoon baking powder
½ teaspoon ground cardamom
¼ teaspoon salt
1½ cups (355 ml) rice or other nondairy milk
¾ cup (170 g) nondairy yogurt
¼ cup (60 ml) canola or vegetable oil
¼ cup (50 g) sugar
1 teaspoon pure almond or vanilla extract
1 cup (120 g) shelled pistachios
1 cup (160 g) dried cherries (or raisins or cranberries)

Preheat the oven to 350°F (180°C, or gas mark 4). Line a standard muffin tin with 12 paper liners.

In a large-size bowl, mix together the flour, wheat germ, baking soda, baking powder, cardamom, and salt. Set aside.

In a separate bowl, whisk together the milk, yogurt, oil, sugar, and almond extract.

Fold the wet ingredients into the dry, being careful not to overmix. Fold in the pistachios and cherries.

Fill the muffin cups all the way to the top. These will rise, but they don't spread, so overflow is not going to be an issue.

Bake for 18 to 20 minutes. Let cool for 5 minutes before transferring to a wire rack to cool completely.

Yield: 12 standard scoffins

Zucchini Poppy Seed Muffins

If you are looking for a way to sneak a healthy amount of fruit, nuts, and veggies into your breakfast, this muffin will certainly fit the bill. Chock-full of heart-healthy walnuts, fiber-filled raisins, and vitamin C–packed zucchini, they're a well-balanced way to start your day.

- Nonstick cooking spray
- 1 cup (200 g) evaporated cane juice or granulated sugar
- ½ cup (73 g) brown sugar, spooned and leveled (not packed)
- ½ cup (113 g) nondairy butter
- ½ cup (128 g) unsweetened applesauce
- ½ cup (118 ml) soy or other nondairy milk
- ¾ cup (170 g) soy or other nondairy yogurt
- 1 teaspoon pure vanilla extract
- 1 teaspoon pure orange extract
- 3 cups (375 g) all-purpose flour
- 1 teaspoon baking powder
- 1 teaspoon baking soda
- 1 teaspoon salt
- 1 teaspoon ground cinnamon
- ½ teaspoon ground ginger
- 2 cups (195 g) finely grated zucchini
- 1 cup (160 g) raisins or other dried fruit
- ⅔ cup (70 g) chopped walnuts
- 1 tablespoon (10 g) poppy seeds

Preheat the oven to 350°F (180°C, or gas mark 4). Line two standard muffin tins with paper liners. Spray cooking spray into the liners to make it easier to peel the muffins off the papers.

Using an electric mixer, beat together the cane juice, brown sugar, and butter until fluffy. Add the applesauce, milk, yogurt, vanilla, and orange extract and beat until smooth.

In a separate bowl, mix together the flour, baking powder, baking soda, salt, cinnamon, and ginger.

Fold the wet ingredients into the dry, being careful not to overmix. Fold in the zucchini, raisins, walnuts, and poppy seeds.

Fill 24 muffin cups two-thirds full for standard muffins or fill 16 muffin cups all the way to the top for more dome-shaped muffins. Bake for 20 to 25 minutes, or until a toothpick inserted into the center comes out clean.

Let cool for 5 minutes before transferring to a wire rack.

Yield: 16 to 24 standard muffins

VARIATION

Substitute half of the flour for whole wheat pastry flour for an extra bit of fiber.

Speculaas Muffins with Chocolate Ganache

Spicy and buttery Danish "speculaas" cookies combine with dark chocolate just about as well as peanut butter and jam do, and work wonders together as a muffin! Just remember to check for suspicious ingredients upon purchasing the cookies, because not all brands are animal-friendly.

For the muffins:

Nonstick cooking spray
14 ounces (400 g) speculaas cookies, finely ground
1 cup (78 g) quick-cooking oats, finely ground
1 tablespoon (12 g) baking powder
1½ cups (355 ml) almond or other nondairy milk
¼ cup plus 2 tablespoons (90 g) blended silken tofu or soy yogurt
¾ cup (144 g) Sucanat

For the Chocolate Ganache:

¼ cup (60 ml) plain soy or other nondairy milk
½ cup (88 g) nondairy semisweet chocolate chips
1 tablespoon (15 ml) pure maple syrup or (21 g) agave nectar

To make the muffins: Preheat the oven to 375°F (190°C, or gas mark 5). Lightly coat a standard muffin tin with spray.

Whisk together the cookie crumbs, ground oats, and baking powder in a large-size bowl.

Blend the milk, tofu, and Sucanat in a medium-size bowl with an immersion blender (or use a countertop blender or a food processor).

Fold the wet ingredients into the dry, being careful not to overmix.

Divide the batter equally among the muffin cups.

Bake for 20 minutes, or until a toothpick inserted into the center comes out clean.

Let cool on a wire rack.

To make the ganache: Scorch the milk in a small-size saucepan over medium-high heat; remove from the heat. Add the chocolate chips and stir until melted. Stir in the maple syrup.

Drizzle on top of the cooled muffins.

Yield: 12 standard muffins

Caramel Apple Muffin Tops

This recipe yields tasty, wholesome, and tender muffins that are easy to prepare. Keep in mind that you're not aiming for applesauce when cooking the apple, so pick one that will retain its shape well, such as Granny Smith.

For the caramel apple pieces:

1 unpeeled apple (5 ounces, or 138 g), quartered, cored, and chopped into small, bite-size pieces
2 tablespoons (28 g) nondairy butter
2 tablespoons (24 g) Sucanat
½ teaspoon ground cinnamon

For the muffin tops:

½ teaspoon apple cider vinegar
¼ cup plus 2 tablespoons (90 ml) soymilk (use soy here, or your milk might not curdle)
¾ cup (59 g) quick-cooking oats, finely ground
¾ cup (90 g) white whole wheat or whole wheat pastry flour
¼ cup (48 g) raw sugar
¼ teaspoon baking soda
¼ teaspoon fine sea salt
¼ cup (60 ml) canola oil
1½ tablespoons (23 g) unsweetened applesauce

To make the caramel apple pieces: Place the apple pieces, butter, Sucanat, and cinnamon in a small-size saucepan.

Over medium-high heat, melt the butter, and bring to a low boil. Lower the heat to medium, and cook for about 6 to 8 minutes, stirring constantly, until the apple pieces are tender and the preparation turns dark, sticky, and syrupy. Remove from the heat and set aside.

To make the muffin tops: Preheat the oven to 375°F (190°C, or gas mark 5). Line a large-size rimless baking sheet with parchment paper or a silicone baking mat, such as Silpat.

Combine the vinegar and soymilk in a medium-size bowl; it will curdle and become like buttermilk.

In a large-size bowl, whisk together the ground oats, flour, sugar, baking soda, and salt. Sprinkle the oil on top; combine with your fingertips or with a fork until it resembles a coarse meal.

Whisk the applesauce into the buttermilk mixture, and add to the flour mixture, being careful not to overmix. Fold in the caramel apple pieces.

To create the "muffin tops," pour a little over ¼ cup (60 g) of the batter into six places on the baking sheet.

Bake for 20 to 22 minutes, or until golden brown and firm. Leave on the baking sheet for 2 minutes, then transfer to a wire rack to cool completely.

Yield: 6 large-size muffin tops

Chapter 4

Dips and Spreads

If you are looking for healthy ways to get your snacking on while still nourishing your body with vitamin- and nutrient-filled vegetables, try dipping veggie sticks into the following cholesterol-free, lower fat dips and spreads. They're a great way to help keep your tummy satisfyingly full without breaking the calorie bank.

Ginger Cranberry Sauce with Cinnamon Cream Cheese Spread

This is a really simple sauce and spread combination that tastes absolutely scrumptious sandwiched between cookies or slathered on top of your favorite sweet bread. Note that the cranberry sauce can be enjoyed on its own alongside both savory and sweet items.

For the cranberry sauce:

⅓ cup (112 g) agave nectar
2 teaspoons grated gingerroot
12 ounces (340 g) fresh cranberries

For the cream cheese spread:

½ cup (120 g) nondairy cream cheese
½ teaspoon ground cinnamon

To make the cranberry sauce: Place all the ingredients in a medium-size saucepan. Bring to a low boil, partially cover with a lid to avoid splatter, and lower the heat.

Let simmer for 10 minutes.

To make the cream cheese spread: Combine both ingredients together. Refrigerate until ready to use.

Yield: About 1½ cups (375 g) for the cranberry sauce, about ½ cup (115 g) for the cream cheese spread

Soy Free

Red Pepper Spread

A bit of a cross between good old hummus and muhammara, this spread is ideal for days when you don't feel like eating beans, but still fancy something other than plain nondairy butter on your bread or in your sandwiches. It also tastes amazing when stirred into soups or stews, or you can keep it simple and enjoy it with crackers, crudités, or chips.

⅓ cup (27 g) whole wheat panko or other bread crumbs
9 ounces (255 g) fire-roasted bell pepper, drained
1 clove garlic, grated
1 teaspoon grated gingerroot
1 teaspoon toasted sesame oil
1 tablespoon (15 ml) fresh lemon juice
1 teaspoon ground cumin
¼ cup (64 g) tahini
½ teaspoon coarse sea salt, to taste

Place all the ingredients in a food processor. Blend until somewhat smooth, scraping the sides with a rubber spatula several times.

Serve chilled.

Yield: About 2 cups (500 g)

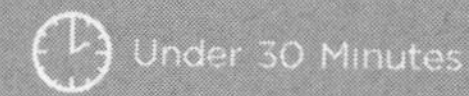

Kale Tofu Spread

This flavorful spread is perfect on bread and crackers, alongside baked potatoes, or stirred into soups or stews. We've even been known to eat it plain.

12 ounces (340 g) kale, stems and ribs removed, torn into small pieces, thoroughly cleaned, and spun dry
2 cloves garlic, grated
Juice of ½ lemon (about 1 tablespoon [15 ml])
1 teaspoon ume plum vinegar or fine sea salt
14 ounces (397 g) soft tofu, drained and simmered (Bring water to a boil in a medium-size saucepan, add tofu, and simmer for 5 minutes. Drain well.)
¼ cup (30 g) nutritional yeast
¼ cup (64 g) tahini or natural peanut butter
Zest of ½ lemon (organic, if possible; about 1 teaspoon)
2 teaspoons white miso

Place the kale, garlic, and lemon juice in a large-size saucepan. Cook over medium heat until the leaves are wilted and the liquid evaporates, about 4 minutes.

Transfer to a food processor, using tongs to avoid grabbing any potential leftover liquid.

Pulse a few times.

Add the vinegar, tofu, yeast, tahini, lemon zest, and miso and process, scraping the sides once or twice, until smooth.

Serve chilled.

Yield: About 3 cups (750 g)

Under 30 Minutes · Low Fat

Zucchini White Bean Spread

Although eating vegan foods usually means having an easier time getting enough of the daily recommended amount of fiber, you might still be looking for ways to boost your intake of raw vegetables. Adding them to your favorite bean spread makes life just a touch easier, and more delicious, too.

1 zucchini, cleaned, trimmed, and grated
2 cloves garlic, grated
1 can (15 ounces, or 425 g) cooked cannellini beans, drained and rinsed
2 tablespoons (30 ml) fresh lemon juice
1 tablespoon (4 g) nutritional yeast
1 tablespoon (21 g) white miso
1 tablespoon (16 g) tahini
Ground black pepper, to taste
Fine sea salt, to taste

Place all the ingredients in a food processor or blender and process until smooth, scraping the sides with a rubber spatula once or twice.

Serve chilled.

Yield: About 2 cups (500 g)

Under 30 Minutes · Low Fat · Gluten Free · Soy Free

Sesame Bean Spread

If you are a big fan of the flavor that sesame oil lends to dishes, you will love dipping crackers into this spread. It's equally tasty stirred into carrot, pumpkin, or butternut squash soup.

1 can (15 ounces, or 425 g) cooked garbanzo beans, drained and rinsed
1 tablespoon (15 ml) fresh lemon juice
2 cloves garlic, grated
1 tablespoon (15 ml) toasted sesame oil
Freshly ground white pepper, to taste
Pinch red pepper flakes (optional)

Place the garbanzo beans, lemon juice, garlic, oil, salt, and red pepper flakes, if using, in a food processor or blender and process until smooth, scraping the sides with a rubber spatula once or twice.

Serve chilled.

Yield: About 2 cups (440 g)

 Under 30 Minutes  Gluten Free  Soy Free

Parsley Pesto Spread

Made vibrantly green thanks to the addition of parsley, this spread goes beautifully with the Peanut and Spice Rolls (page 350) and takes the Cumin Carrot Soup (page 141) to new heights of flavor.

⅔ cup (85 g) roasted salted sunflower seeds
¼ cup (60 ml) extra-virgin olive oil
Zest and juice of 1 small-size lemon (optional)
2 cloves garlic, grated
1 cup (60 g) fresh curly parsley
1 can (15 ounces, or 425 g) cooked garbanzo beans, drained and rinsed
Salt and pepper, to taste

Place the sunflower seeds in a food processor and process until finely ground.

Add the oil, lemon zest and juice, if using, garlic, parsley, beans, salt, and pepper and process until perfectly smooth, scraping the sides several times and adjusting the seasoning to taste.

Serve chilled.

Yield: About 2 cups (500 g)

 Under 30 Minutes  Low Fat  Gluten Free  Soy Free

Salsa Fresca

Nothing scores higher on the healthy snack scale than salsa. After all, it's just fresh chopped vegetables tossed together to make a yummy dip. This makes an extra large batch, so you can share with your amigos!

2 cups (500 g) diced tomatoes
1 cup (160 g) diced red, white, or yellow onion
1 cup (64 g) chopped fresh cilantro leaves
1 cup (250 g) yellow corn kernels
¼ cup (60 ml) lime juice
3 scallions, chopped
2 jalapeño peppers, diced
2 tablespoons (30 g) minced garlic
Salt and pepper, to taste

Toss all the ingredients together in a bowl. Keep refrigerated until ready to serve. Serve with tortilla chips.

Yield: About 6 cups (1350 g)

Under 30 Minutes  Gluten Free  Soy Free

Creamy Raw Avocado Spread

This spread contains heart-healthy fats and has a spicy kick!
Serve on sandwiches or use as a dip.

Flesh of 2 avocados
1 cup (138 g) raw cashews
½ cup (80 g) diced red onion
1 jalapeño pepper, seeded
Salt and pepper, to taste

Add all the ingredients to a food processor or blender and purée until smooth.

Yield: About 1½ cups (338 g)

 Gluten Free  Soy Free

Traditional Hummus

Hummus is the quintessential vegan dip. Tasty, tangy, creamy, full of heart-healthy fats and protein, oh, and delicious! This is a traditional, plain hummus, so feel free to add a little somethin' to it to kick it up a notch. Garlic, cayenne pepper, chopped olives, even balsamic vinegar will bring it into a whole new dimension.

2 cans (15 ounces, or 420 g each) garbanzo beans, with their liquid
½ cup (256 g) tahini, roasted or raw
½ cup (120 ml) extra-virgin olive oil
2 tablespoons (30 ml) lemon juice*
Salt, to taste

***If you like a tangier hummus, use ¼ cup (60 ml) lemon juice**

In a pot, add the beans with their liquid, tahini, and olive oil. Bring to a boil and reduce to a simmer. Simmer, uncovered, for 15 minutes.

Use an immersion blender, or carefully transfer the mixture to a countertop blender, and purée until smooth. Stir in the lemon juice and add salt to taste.

Serve warm, or refrigerate in an airtight container until ready to serve.

Yield: About 4½ cups (1013 g)

Under 30 Minutes · Gluten Free · Soy Free

Curried Butternut Squash Hummus

Although this spread is absolutely spectacular served on its own with freshly baked bread or crackers, it also shines as a filling for Butternut Squash Hummus White Lasagna (page 222).

2 cups (400 g) chopped roasted butternut squash (see note)
1 can (15 ounces, or 425 g) cooked garbanzo beans, drained and rinsed
1 large-size clove garlic, grated
1 tablespoon (15 ml) extra-virgin olive oil
¼ cup (64 g) tahini
2 tablespoons (30 ml) fresh lemon juice
1 heaping tablespoon (8 g) mild to medium curry powder
1 teaspoon ground cumin
½ teaspoon coarse sea salt, to taste
¼ teaspoon ground black pepper, to taste

Place all the ingredients in a food processor or blender and process until smooth, scraping the sides with a rubber spatula once or twice.

Serve chilled, at room temperature, or even warm, with crackers, pita bread, or chips.

Yield: About 3 cups (675 g)

NOTE

To roast the squash: Cut into 8 pieces, brush the flesh with a little oil, sprinkle pepper and salt on top, and bake (flesh side down) for 45 minutes in a 400°F (200°C, or gas mark 6) preheated oven, or until tender.

Under 30 Minutes  Gluten Free  Soy Free

Broccoli Hummus

If you are looking for ways to boost your intake of green vegetables and calcium, this hummus will help you accomplish just that. The fact that it's extremely flavorful and delicious won't hurt, either. If your kids are usually reluctant to eat vegetables, they might not even be aware of their presence in this spread. We won't tell them if you don't.

1 cup (150 g) chopped steamed broccoli
1 can (15 ounces, or 425 g) cooked garbanzo beans, drained and rinsed
1 teaspoon lemon zest
1½ tablespoons (23 ml) fresh lemon juice
2 tablespoons (30 ml) extra-virgin olive oil
2 tablespoons (32 g) tahini
2 teaspoons toasted sesame oil
2 teaspoons ground cumin
1 teaspoon fine sea salt, to taste
¼ teaspoon ground black pepper, to taste

Combine all the ingredients in a food processor or blender and process until smooth, scraping the sides with a rubber spatula several times.

Serve chilled.

Yield: About 3 cups (675 g)

 Under 30 Minutes  Gluten Free  Soy Free

Avocado Cilantro Hummus

This hummus is bright green and full of flavor! As if avocados weren't tasty enough on there own, this dip takes these vitamin K- and potassium-rich fruits to a whole new level.

1 can (15 ounces, or 420 g) garbanzo beans, drained, but not rinsed
Flesh of 2 avocados
1 cup (48 g) fresh cilantro leaves
½ cup (120 ml) extra-virgin olive oil
¼ cup (60 ml) sesame oil
2 tablespoons (30 ml) lime juice
Salt and pepper, to taste

Add all the ingredients to a food processor or blender, and process until smooth, scraping the sides with a rubber spatula several times.

Serve chilled.

Yield: About 4 cups (900 g)

Baba Ghanoush

This is a Lebanese-style baba ghanoush, or mashed eggplant dish. Top this dip with a little olive oil and serve with warm pita or crackers.

1 eggplant (about 1 pound, or 455 g)
¼ cup (60 ml) lemon juice
¼ cup (64 g) tahini
3 tablespoons (12 g) fresh parsley or 1 tablespoon (4 g) dried
2 tablespoons (30 g) minced garlic
Salt and pepper, to taste
Olive oil, for garnish

Preheat the oven to 375°F (190°C, or gas mark 5).

Prick holes all over the eggplant with the tines of a fork. Place the eggplant in the oven, directly on the rack, and roast for about 45 minutes.

Remove from the oven, place in a bowl, and cover. Let sit for about 15 minutes to cool.

Peel the eggplant, reserving the flesh and discarding the skin.

Add the lemon juice, tahini, parsley, garlic, salt, and pepper and mash until smooth.

If you prefer a smoother dip, transfer to a blender and purée until smooth.

Serve with a drizzle of olive oil on top.

Yield: Just over 2 cups (about 500 g)

Fu-ttage Cheese

Sprinkle this tasty "cheese" on top of your favorite salad mix, use it as a filling in baked manicotti or lasagna, or use it in Fu-ttage Cheese Mini Baguettes (page 337).

2 tablespoons (28 g) vegan mayonnaise, store-bought or homemade (page 301 or 302)
1½ tablespoons (23 ml) apple cider vinegar
1 teaspoon dried minced onion
¼ teaspoon fine sea salt, to taste
Ground white pepper, to taste
¼ teaspoon dry mustard
12 ounces (340 g) regular firm tofu, pressed, crumbled

In a medium-size bowl, whisk together the mayonnaise, vinegar, onion, salt, pepper, and mustard.

Add the tofu, stir with a fork at first, then squeeze it with your hands or mash with a potato masher for a couple of minutes, until perfectly combined.

Serve chilled. Store in a tightly covered container in the fridge.

Yield: About 2 cups (450 g)

Under 30 Minutes  Gluten Free  Soy Free

Butter Bean Dip

Bright and fresh with a very green flavor, this dip tastes great with tortilla chips, veggie sticks, or pita bread.

1½ cups (9 ounces, or 247 g) canned butter beans, drained and rinsed
1 cup (63 g) chopped scallion (white and green parts)
1 teaspoon garlic powder
1 tablespoon (8 g) onion powder
½ teaspoon ground cumin
½ cup (120 ml) canola or other vegetable oil
Salt and pepper, to taste

Add all the ingredients to a blender or food processor and purée until smooth.

Yield: About 2 cups (450 g)

 Low Fat  Gluten Free

Tzatziki

Fresh and tangy, this recipe works well with falafel, in a pita sandwich, or as a dip for warm pita triangles or flatbread.

12 ounces (340 g) plain soy or other nondairy yogurt, strained (see note)
1½ cups (160 g) seeded and finely diced cucumber (1 cucumber)
1 tablespoon (8 g) fresh dill
1 tablespoon (15 g) minced garlic
1 tablespoon (15 ml) lemon juice
1 tablespoon (15 ml) extra-virgin olive oil
Salt and pepper, to taste

Mix all the ingredients together. Keep refrigerated in an airtight container until ready to use. This should keep for about a week.

Yield: Just over 2 cups (500 g)

NOTE

To strain the excess liquid from the yogurt, pour the yogurt into the center of several folded layers of cheesecloth, tie off the cheesecloth, and suspend it over a bowl. Tie the cheesecloth to the handle of a wooden spoon, and then rest each end of the spoon over the edge of a mixing bowl. Let sit for a few hours, then use your newly made "yogurt cheese" to make the dip.

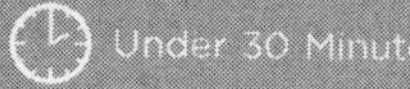
Under 30 Minutes Gluten Free

Tangy Dill and Caper Dip

Why not try dipping your veggie sticks and chips into this tangy dip instead of ranch dressing at your next get-together?

¾ cup (168 g) plain nondairy yogurt
3 tablespoons (48 g) capers
2 tablespoons (7 g) chopped fresh dill
2 tablespoons (6 g) chopped chives
2 tablespoons (30 ml) lemon juice

Mix all the ingredients together in a small-size bowl. Keep refrigerated until ready to serve.

Yield: 1 cup (225 g)

 Under 30 Minutes  Gluten Free

Mushroom Pâté

Traditional pâtés involve cooking or boiling meat with fat and then baking. Most commonly used is goose liver (aka foie gras*). This cruelty-free and healthy spin on the classic delivers a nice punch of spiciness from the black pepper and paprika.*

Nonstick cooking spray
1 tablespoon (15 ml) extra-virgin olive oil
8 ounces (227 g) button mushrooms, sliced
8 ounces (227 g) chopped onion
1 cup (2⅓ ounces, or 66 g) chopped leeks
6 ounces (170 g) extra-firm tofu, drained and pressed
3 tablespoons (12 g) chopped fresh parsley
1 tablespoon (8 g) ground black pepper
1 tablespoon (7 g) smoked paprika
1 tablespoon (8 g) cornstarch
Salt, to taste

Preheat the oven to 400°F (200°C, or gas mark 6).

Prepare a 5 × 3 × 2.5-inch (12.5 × 7.5 × 6.5-cm) loaf pan (a standard mini loaf pan) by lightly spraying with nonstick spray.

Preheat the oil in a frying pan over medium-low heat. Add the mushrooms, onion, and leeks, and sweat the vegetables until reduced in size by about half, 10 to 15 minutes.

Carefully transfer to a food processor. Add the tofu, parsley, pepper, paprika, cornstarch, and salt. Pulse until smooth.

Press the mixture into the loaf pan and bake, uncovered, for 30 minutes. Let cool in the refrigerator to set for several hours.

Invert onto a serving plate, slice, and serve with crackers.

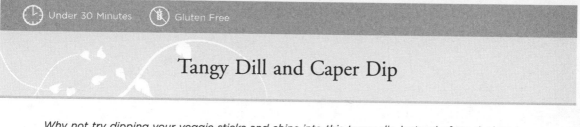

Yield: 20 slices

Nutty Cheese

Let's face it, there isn't a really good vegan cheese out there. Most of them taste all chemically and weird. Giving up cheese seems to be the most difficult for vegetarians making the transition to veganism. And with good reason: cheese tastes good. Not only that, but it also contains high levels of casein, which acts similarly to opiates (so it really is addictive!). Although it does take time, giving up dairy-based cheeses in favor of nut- and yeast-based cheeses like this one will eventually curb your cravings. And they won't clog your arteries!

Nonstick cooking spray
1 ounce (28 g) agar flakes or powder
3 cups (705 ml) water
2 cups (275 g) raw cashews, finely ground into a powder
3 tablespoons (45 ml) fresh lemon juice
2 tablespoons (30 ml) sesame oil (olive oil will work, too)
¼ cup (30 g) nutritional yeast
2 teaspoons fine sea salt
½ teaspoon onion powder
½ teaspoon garlic powder

Prepare a loaf pan (or other deep rectangular container) by lightly oiling or spraying with cooking spray.

Place the agar in the water and bring to a full boil, then boil for 5 minutes, stirring often to prevent it from boiling over.

Place the cashew powder, lemon juice, oil, yeast, salt, onion powder, and garlic powder in a food processor and blend until smooth.

Pour the mixture into the water-agar mixture and stir until creamy and smooth, then remove from the heat.

Quickly pour into the oiled loaf pan and refrigerate until set.

Yield: 1 loaf

VARIATIONS

Add fresh herbs and spices to the mix. If you want a Mediterranean-flavored cheese, add about 8 chopped sun-dried tomatoes and 5 or 6 chopped fresh basil leaves. If you want a Mexican-flavored cheese, add 1 teaspoon of cumin and 6 or 7 jarred jalapeño slices, chopped. If you want a smoky cheese, add ¼ to ½ teaspoon of liquid smoke flavoring. It's limitless!

Brazil Nut Bleu

Slightly reminiscent of blue cheese, this vegan version has a slight pungent flavor and works well crumbled onto salads, sliced on sandwiches, or cut onto crackers.

Nonstick cooking spray
8 ounces (227 g) shelled, raw Brazil nuts
2 tablespoons (9 g) chia seeds
½ teaspoon sea salt
¼ cup (30 g) nutritional yeast
¼ cup (60 ml) extra-virgin olive oil
1 tablespoon (20 g) whole-grain prepared brown mustard
1 tablespoon (10 g) onion powder
4 teaspoons (8 g) agar powder
3 cups (705 ml) water

Prepare a loaf pan (or other deep rectangular container) by lightly oiling or spraying with cooking spray.

Place the Brazil nuts in a food processor or blender and grind into a powder.

Add the chia seeds, salt, nutritional yeast, olive oil, prepared mustard, and onion powder. Blend until smooth.

Place the agar in the water and bring to a full boil, then boil for 5 minutes, stirring often to prevent it from boiling over.

Add the Brazil nut mixture. Return to a boil, stirring constantly, and boil for 1 minute.

Quickly pour into the oiled loaf pan and refrigerate until set.

Yield: 1 loaf

Smoky Black Pepper Cheese

Enjoy on crackers or on a sandwich, such as a zesty grilled cheese.

Nonstick cooking spray
2 cups (470 ml) soy or other nondairy milk
¼ cup (10 g) agar flakes
½ cup (69 g) cashews
½ cup (60 g) nutritional yeast
2 tablespoons (36 g) white or yellow miso
2 tablespoons (30 ml) soy sauce or tamari
1 tablespoon (15 ml) liquid smoke
1 tablespoon (16 g) tahini paste
1 tablespoon (6 g) onion powder
1 tablespoon (6 g) garlic powder
1 tablespoon (6 g) ground mustard seed
1 teaspoon ground black pepper

Spray a loaf pan with nonstick cooking spray.

Place the milk and agar flakes in a pot and bring to a boil.

Meanwhile, place the cashews, yeast, miso, soy sauce, liquid smoke, tahini, onion powder, garlic powder, mustard seed, and pepper in a blender and purée until smooth.

After the milk and agar have come to a full boil, add the blended mixture and stir vigorously.

Remove from the heat and immediately pour into the loaf pan. Refrigerate until set.

Yield: 1 loaf

 Under 30 Minutes

Walnut and Currant Veganzola Balls

Who says vegans can't have cheese balls? Seriously, these are very, very cheeselike. Besides spreading on crackers, this also tastes amazing crumbled over a green salad or as a sandwich spread.

10 ounces (280 g) extra-firm tofu, drained and pressed
2 tablespoons (30 ml) extra-virgin olive oil
2 tablespoons (16 g) flax meal mixed with 2 tablespoons (30 ml) warm water
1 tablespoon (18 g) white miso
2 teaspoons minced garlic
1 teaspoon liquid smoke
1 cup (120 g) walnuts, broken into small pieces
½ cup (80 g) currants
Salt and pepper, to taste

In a mixing bowl, crumble the tofu until it resembles ricotta cheese. Add the olive oil, flax mixture, miso, garlic, and liquid smoke. Mash together until uniform. Mix in the walnut pieces, currants, and salt and pepper. Form into two equal balls, form into a log, or simply place in a serving bowl.

Yield: About 2½ cups (563 g)

Under 30 Minutes  Gluten Free

Easy Garlic Spread for Bread

This is super yummy spread on French bread and put into the toaster oven or broiler until toasty. It's also a necessary ingredient for Garlic Rolls (page 348).

- ½ cup (112 g) nondairy butter, softened
- 1 tablespoon (7 g) all-purpose seasoning, such as Spike or Mrs. Dash (see note)
- 1 teaspoon garlic powder
- 1 teaspoon onion powder
- 1 teaspoon dried basil
- ¼ teaspoon paprika

Mix all the ingredients together and spread on bread.

Yield: Just over ¼ cup (about 60 g)

NOTE

If you are salt sensitive, use a salt-free all-purpose seasoning or unsalted margarine, or both!

 Under 30 Minutes  Gluten Free  Soy Free

Sun-Dried Tomato Pesto

Serve as a spread on crackers or sandwiches, over pasta or rice, or mixed with mayonnaise for a sun-dried tomato pesto aioli.

- 10 fresh basil leaves
- 1 cup (140 g) sun-dried tomato pieces, packed in oil
- 1 tablespoon (15 g) minced garlic
- ¼ cup (60 ml) extra-virgin olive oil
- ⅓ cup (46 g) cashews
- ⅓ cup (45 g) pine nuts

Add all the ingredients to a blender or food processor and purée until smooth.

Yield: Just over 1 cup (about 225 g)

Warm Chili Con Queso Dip

Maybe you've heard of it? The original is a combo of chili and a block of Velveeta processed cheese food. At football games and get-togethers, it's typically kept warm in a slow cooker and served alongside tortilla chips and Fritos next to it for dipping. This version makes enough to serve a crowd, too, but in a much healthier manner.

1 cup (225 g) tomato sauce
1½ cups (250 g) pinto beans (drained and rinsed if using canned)
1 cup (235 ml) vegetable broth or water
1 cup (160 g) finely diced onion
1 tablespoon (8 g) garlic powder
1 tablespoon (8 g) onion powder
1 tablespoon (8 g) chili powder
1 teaspoon cumin
5 to 10 slices nacho-style jalapeño peppers, diced (use less or more to taste)
1 cup (235 ml) soy creamer or other nondairy milk
1 cup (180 g) nondairy sour cream, store-bought or homemade (page 302)
¼ cup (30 g) nutritional yeast
1 tablespoon (18 g) white miso
1½ cups (150 g) TVP granules

In a pot, combine the tomato sauce, beans, vegetable broth, onion, garlic powder, onion powder, chili powder, cumin, and jalapeño peppers. Bring to a boil.

Stir in the creamer, sour cream, nutritional yeast, and miso. Return to a boil.

Stir in the TVP and remove from the heat. Let stand for 10 minutes to thicken.

Serve warm with tortilla chips or corn chips for dipping, or pour over a plate of tortilla chips for nachos.

Yield: 5 to 6 cups (1175 to 1410 g)

VARIATION

Stir in some of your favorite salsa for that extra zip!

Nacho Queso

Yet another cheesy sauce to add to your repertoire! This one is spicy and zesty and gets its girth from the cannellini beans. Add more or less jalapeños, with or without the seeds, to meet your spice needs.

2 cups (470 ml) vegetable broth
1 can (15 ounces, or 420 g) cannellini beans, drained and rinsed
2 to 3 jalapeño peppers, sliced
1 teaspoon ground cumin
1 teaspoon onion powder
¼ cup (30 g) nutritional yeast
2 tablespoons (30 g) prepared yellow mustard
2 tablespoons (16 g) all-purpose flour
½ cup (75 g) diced red bell pepper
Salt and pepper, to taste

Add the broth, beans, jalapeños, cumin, and onion powder to a pot and bring to a boil.

Reduce to a simmer and stir in the nutritional yeast, mustard, and flour. Stir until thickened. Remove from the heat.

Carefully transfer to a blender and purée until smooth.

Transfer back to the pot and stir in the diced red pepper. Season to taste with salt and pepper.

Pour over tortilla chips, or place in a serving bowl to serve as a dip.

Yield: About 3 cups (675 g)

Chapter 5

Snacks, Appetizers, and Finger Foods

When you are having friends or family over, the last thing you want to do is spend hours in the kitchen, preparing food and doing dishes. One of the best ways to make sure you will get to enjoy spending time socializing is to serve a multitude of make-ahead snacks instead of a more involved meal. Here is one of the chapters that will help you have everything you need for your party to be a healthy and satisfying success, without even having to ask for some help drying the dishes.

 Under 30 Minutes  Gluten Free Soy Free

Chili Roasted Peanuts

This is a deliciously spicy and dangerously addictive snack on its own, and is an indispensable addition to the Multigrain Pilaf (page 251). If you prefer hotter foods, adjust the amount of cayenne and other spices to your own personal taste.

12 ounces (336 g) raw Spanish peanuts
1 tablespoon (15 ml) peanut or canola oil
½ teaspoon Sucanat or light brown sugar
½ teaspoon fine sea salt
1½ teaspoons mild to medium chili powder
1 teaspoon ground cumin
¾ teaspoon unsweetened cocoa powder
Heaping ⅛ teaspoon ground cinnamon
Heaping ⅛ teaspoon cayenne pepper, to taste

Preheat the oven to 350°F (180°C, or gas mark 4). Have a large-size rimmed baking sheet ready.

In a medium-size bowl, combine the peanuts, oil, sugar, and salt. Spread the peanuts evenly on the baking sheet, and bake in 7-minute increments, stirring the nuts to keep them from burning.

Bake for a total of 18 to 20 minutes, until the nuts have darkened without burning and are fragrant.

In the meantime, combine the spices together in a bowl. Stir them into the peanuts once they are removed from the oven. Let cool before storing.

Yield: About 2¼ cups (325 g)

VARIATION

Use 2 to 3 tablespoons (15 to 22 g) of the Garam Masala Mix (page 305) for an alternate version; keep the peanuts, oil, and salt the same way they appear in this recipe, but replace the spices with the garam masala.

Cheezy Quackers

These crackers were dubbed "quackers" because of the small duck-shaped cookie cutter we always use to prepare them. You'll soon find out it is utterly impossible to resist munching on these salty treats, no matter what cookie cutter shape you decide on. Celine's recipe can also be found in Alisa Fleming's Go Dairy Free *book.*

1 cup (125 g) all-purpose flour
⅓ cup (40 g) nutritional yeast
½ teaspoon black pepper
1 teaspoon fine sea salt
4 tablespoons (56 g) nondairy butter
¼ cup (60 ml) water or any nondairy milk

Combine the flour, yeast, pepper, and salt. Cut the butter on top and combine with a mixer, a fork, or your fingers, until it has the appearance of a coarse meal. Add the water, 1 tablespoon (15 ml) at a time, and combine until a dough forms.

You can choose to wrap the dough in plastic and place it in the fridge for later use, or roll it out immediately.

Preheat the oven to 350°F (180°C, or gas mark 4). Line two baking sheets with parchment paper or silicone baking mats, such as Silpat.

Roll out the dough between two pieces of parchment or Silpats, a little less than ¼ inch (6 mm) thick. Cut out shapes using very small cookie cutters, about 1 to 2 inches (2.5 to 5 cm) in diameter. Repeat until you run out of dough, rolling it out again between batches.

Place the crackers on the prepared sheets. Bake for 15 to 18 minutes, depending on the thickness, until the crackers are light golden brown on the bottom.

Place on a rack to cool. These crackers freeze well, if you manage to keep them around long enough for that.

Yield: About 60 small crackers, depending on the size of the cookie cutter

VARIATION

Add cayenne pepper, red pepper flakes, or dried herbs of choice, to taste. Choose different flours, such as a combination of spelt, chickpea, brown rice, or whole wheat, to get different textures and flavors.

Peanut Butter Crackers

You will either think of us fondly while nibbling on these crispy, buttery crackers or shake your fists at us because you are doomed to eat the entire batch in one second flat. We're sorry?

- 1½ teaspoons tamari or soy sauce
- 1 teaspoon hot chili oil (or another teaspoon canola oil)
- 1 teaspoon canola oil (or another teaspoon hot chili oil)
- 3 tablespoons (48 g) peanut butter of choice
- ¼ cup (40 g) brown rice flour
- ⅓ cup (40 g) white whole wheat flour
- 3 tablespoons (24 g) cornstarch
- 2 tablespoons (16 g) nutritional yeast
- ⅛ teaspoon baking soda
- ⅛ teaspoon fine sea salt
- ¼ cup (60 ml) plain or unsweetened soy or other nondairy milk

Preheat the oven to 350°F (180°C, or gas mark 4). Line two baking sheets with parchment paper or silicone baking mats, such as Silpat.

With an electric mixer, cream together the tamari, oils, and peanut butter.

In a medium-size bowl, whisk together the flours, cornstarch, nutritional yeast, baking soda, and salt.

Stir the dry ingredients into the wet, and add the milk a little at a time until a dough comes together.

Roll out the dough between two pieces of parchment or Silpats, to slightly greater than ⅛ inch (3 mm) thick. Cut out shapes with your favorite cutter about 1 to 2 inches (2.5 to 5 cm) in diameter.

Repeat until you run out of dough, rolling it out again between each batch.

Bake for 12 minutes, until the crackers are light brown on the bottom. If you are using a larger cutter, you might have to adjust the baking time. Let cool on the baking sheets.

Yield: About 40 small crackers, depending on the size of the cookie cutter

Savory Cookies All' Italiana

Bigger than crackers, and just as addictive, these flaky, buttery cookies are almost better than pizza, but not quite as big as the beloved pie, we're afraid.

- **2 tablespoons (16 g) nutritional yeast**
- **¼ teaspoon Italian seasoning or other dried herb of choice**
- **1 tablespoon (20 g) low-sodium white miso**
- **1 tablespoon (15 ml) extra-virgin olive oil**
- **1 clove garlic, grated**
- **1¼ cups (150 g) white whole wheat or whole wheat pastry flour**
- **¼ cup (20 g) old-fashioned oats**
- **1 tablespoon (12 g) raw sugar**
- **1½ teaspoons baking powder**
- **4 tablespoons (56 g) nondairy butter**
- **2 tablespoons (24 g) vegetable shortening**
- **3 tablespoons (45 ml) unsweetened soy or other nondairy milk**

Preheat the oven to 350°F (180°C, or gas mark 4). Line a baking sheet with parchment paper or a silicone baking mat, such as Silpat.

Combine the nutritional yeast, Italian seasoning, miso, oil, and garlic in a small-size bowl. Set aside.

Whisk together the flour, oats, sugar, and baking powder in a large-size bowl.

Cut in the nondairy butter and shortening, and add the nutritional yeast mixture.

Using your fingers or a fork, mix until it is crumbly.

Add the milk, a little at a time, and stir until a dough forms.

Divide into 12 walnut-size, equal portions.

Press down as flat as you want the cookies to be, because they don't spread while baking.

Bake for 12 to 15 minutes, or until golden brown at the very edges. Leave on the sheet for a couple of minutes before transferring to a wire rack to cool.

Yield: 12 cookies

Soy Free

Relish Oat Crackers

If you are among those of us who never know what to do with the relish that sits in the fridge—outside of slapping it onto sandwiches—here's a new way to put it to good use. Rest assured that salsa will be a good substitute for the relish, if the latter is either inaccessible or just not your cup of tea.

1 cup (80 g) old-fashioned oats
¼ cup (30 g) nutritional yeast
1 teaspoon fine sea salt
¼ teaspoon baking powder
¼ cup (28 g) garlic dill relish, or any relish, or even salsa
3 tablespoons (45 ml) extra-virgin olive oil
2 cloves garlic, grated

Preheat the oven to 350°F (180°C, or gas mark 4). Line two baking sheets with parchment paper or silicone baking mats, such as Silpat.

In your food processor, grind the oats into a fine flour.

Add the nutritional yeast, salt, and baking powder, and pulse several times.

Add the relish, olive oil, and garlic, and pulse until the dough starts coming together.

Roll out the dough between two pieces of parchment or Silpats, to a little less than ¼ inch (6 mm) thick. Using a round cookie cutter 1 to 2 inches (2.5 to 5 cm) in diameter, cut out crackers until you run out of dough, rolling it out again between each batch.

Bake the crackers for 14 to 16 minutes, depending on the size and thickness, until they are light golden brown on the bottom.

Slide the parchment paper or Silpat off of the baking sheet, and let cool directly on there.

Yield: About 45 crackers, depending on the size of the cookie cutter

Peanut Butter and Marmite Savory Cookies

Peanut butter and yeast extract spread make for one unbeatable pairing. You will be surprised to find that these cookies have a pleasant cheesy flavor—and you might have to prove they are 100 percent dairy free by exposing the list of ingredients to those with whom you share.

¼ cup (64 g) crunchy or creamy natural peanut butter
¼ cup (60 ml) canola oil
4 teaspoons (32 g) yeast extract spread, such as Marmite
¼ cup plus 2 tablespoons (90 ml) soy or other nondairy milk
1 teaspoon ground cumin
1½ cups (180 g) light spelt flour
½ teaspoon baking powder

Preheat the oven to 375°F (190°C, or gas mark 5). Line a baking sheet with parchment paper or a silicone baking mat, such as Silpat.

Combine the peanut butter, oil, yeast extract spread, milk, and cumin in a large-size bowl, and mix until emulsified.

Sift in the flour and baking powder on top of the wet ingredients; combine with a fork until just mixed. If the dough is too stiff, incorporate the ingredients by kneading quickly.

Shape into a ball.

Roll out the dough to approximately ¼ inch (6 mm) thick, and cut out cookies with a 3-inch (7-cm) round cookie cutter. Repeat until you run out of dough, rolling it out again between each batch.

Place the cookies on the baking sheet and bake for 12 to 14 minutes, or until golden brown on the bottom.

Let cool on a wire rack.

Yield: 12 cookies

Garlic Flatbread Rounds

Need a little something to dip all those yummy dips into? Or maybe you'd like to serve up something a little more unique than regular old garlic bread with your Moroccan Spaghetti (page 178). Try these little guys.

1 envelope (¼ ounce, or 7 g) active dry yeast
1 tablespoon (13 g) granulated sugar or (21 g) agave nectar
1 cup (235 ml) warm water
3 cups (375 g) all-purpose flour
¼ teaspoon salt
¼ cup (60 ml) extra-virgin olive oil
1 tablespoon (15 g) minced garlic
1 tablespoon (2 g) dried parsley or 3 tablespoons (12 g) fresh, chopped

Mix together the yeast, sugar, and warm water. Let stand for 10 minutes.

In a mixing bowl, combine the flour and salt.

Add the olive oil, garlic, and parsley to the yeast mixture.

Add the wet ingredients to the dry and knead until a nice dough ball is formed.

Lightly oil the dough, cover loosely with plastic wrap, and let rise for 1 hour.

Punch down the dough and divide into 16 equal pieces.

Heat a dry, nonstick frying pan or skillet over high heat.

Roll out each piece of dough to ⅛ inch (3 mm) thick, and shape into a round.

Place in the frying pan, 2 or 3 at a time, and cook for about 2 to 3 minutes per side.

Yield: 16 flatbreads

Scarborough Fair Cream Cheese Wontons

You are only allowed to serve these to your peace-loving hippie friends while harmoniously enjoying an evening of libations and Simon and Garfunkel! Just be sure to double-check the ingredients on your wonton wrappers, because most brands contain eggs.

8 ounces (224 g) nondairy cream cheese
1 tablespoon (2 g) dried parsley
1 teaspoon dried sage
2 teaspoons dried rosemary
2 teaspoons dried thyme
20 vegan wonton wrappers
Olive oil, for brushing

Preheat the oven to 350°F (180°C, or gas mark 4).

Mix together the cream cheese, parsley, sage, rosemary, and thyme in a small-size bowl.

Take one wonton wrapper at a time. Brush with olive oil. Place 1 tablespoon (16 g) of cream cheese mixture in the center of the wonton wrapper.

Fold the wrapper closed by bringing each corner into the center and pinching, then twisting closed. Place on a baking sheet and bake for 10 to 12 minutes, until golden.

Let cool for a minute or two before eating, or the melty filling will burn you.

Yield: About 20 wontons

Ginger Soy Tofu Satay with Simple Thai Peanut Dipping Sauce

An extra hot grill will give you those ever sought after grill marks, and grill marks make everything taste better! Using gluten-free tamari makes this dish gluten free.

For the Ginger Soy Marinade:

⅓ cup (80 ml) soy sauce or tamari
⅓ cup (80 ml) rice vinegar
⅓ cup (80 ml) water
1 teaspoon ground ginger

1 block (12 to 16 ounces, or 336 to 448 g) extra-firm tofu, drained and pressed
12 skewers, soaked in water for at least 30 minutes

For the Simple Thai Peanut Dipping Sauce:

½ cup (128 g) peanut butter
½ cup (120 ml) peanut oil
⅓ cup (53 g) chopped scallion (white and green parts)
2 tablespoons (30 ml) soy sauce or tamari
1 teaspoon dried red pepper flakes

To make the marinade: Whisk together the soy sauce, vinegar, water, and ginger and place in a shallow dish or resealable plastic bag.

Slice the tofu lengthwise into 6 pieces, and then cut those pieces in half lengthwise. Place the pieces in the marinade. The tofu should only marinate for about 30 minutes or it will get too salty.

Carefully slide each piece of tofu onto the skewers.

On an indoor grill, a grill pan, or a barbecue, grill each side of the tofu for about 1 to 2 minutes, and then flip it over to the next side. You'll make four turns total.

To make the sauce: Place the peanut butter, oil, scallions, soy sauce, and red pepper flakes in a blender and purée until smooth. Serve alongside the tofu.

Yield: 12 skewers and just over 1 cup (250 g) sauce

Soy Free

Curry Couscous–Stuffed Mushrooms

Did you know mushrooms are an excellent source of riboflavin, potassium, and selenium? They are also low in calories and fat, and the majority of their dry weight is made up of fiber. With more than 3,000 edible varieties to choose from, mushrooms top the list as a favorite in the vegan kitchen. Stuffing mushrooms are white and about 3 inches (7.5 cm) in diameter.

12 stuffing mushrooms

For the mushroom marinade:

3 tablespoons (45 ml) balsamic vinegar
2 tablespoons (30 ml) extra-virgin olive oil

For the filling:

Reserved mushroom stems
2 tablespoons (30 ml) extra-virgin olive oil
1 cup (160 g) diced yellow onion
3 cloves garlic, minced
1½ cups (355 ml) water
1 cup (175 g) dry couscous
1 tablespoon (6 g) yellow curry powder, store-bought or homemade (page 307)
1 tablespoon (2 g) dry parsley flakes
1 teaspoon garam masala, store bought or homemade (page 305)
Salt and pepper, to taste

Preheat the oven to 350°F (180°C, or gas mark 4).

Carefully remove the stems from the mushrooms. Reserve the stems.

To make the marinade: Combine the vinegar and oil. Place the marinade in a shallow baking dish and place the mushrooms in the baking dish "hole" side up. Set aside.

To make the filling: Chop the reserved mushroom stems. Heat the oil in a pan and sauté the chopped mushroom stems, onion, and garlic until fragrant, about 7 to 10 minutes.

Bring the water to a boil in a small-size pot. Add the couscous, reduce the heat to a simmer, and stir until all the water is absorbed. Add the sautéed mixture, curry, parsley, garam masala, salt, and pepper. Mix together well.

Stuff a heaping scoop of couscous mixture into the hollowed-out mushrooms and bake, uncovered, for about 15 minutes.

If you have any leftover couscous mixture, it tastes great on its own as a side dish.

Yield: 12 stuffed mushrooms

Greek Phyllo Samosas

Sweet and savory, these triangular treats are full of vegetables and nuts, which not only flavor, but also contain lots of protein, fiber, and heart-healthy fats.

For the filling:

1 tablespoon (15 ml) olive oil
8 ounces (224 g) button mushrooms, chopped
1 cup (160 g) diced yellow onion
3 cloves garlic, minced
2 ounces (about ½ cup, or 56 g) walnut pieces
½ cup (69 g) cashews, ground into a fine powder
¼ teaspoon cardamom
¼ teaspoon cinnamon
¼ teaspoon paprika
1 teaspoon garam masala, store-bought or homemade (page 309)
¼ cup (30 g) pine nuts
Sea salt and freshly cracked pepper, to taste

Nonstick cooking spray (optional)
1 package (1 pound, or 455 g) vegan frozen phyllo dough, thawed according to package directions
Olive oil, for brushing

To make the filling: Heat the oil in a skillet and add the mushrooms, onion, and garlic, and sauté until fragrant and the mushrooms have shrunk by half.

Add the walnuts, cashew powder, cardamom, cinnamon, paprika, and garam masala to a food processor and pulse a few times, so that the mixture is chopped well, yet still a bit chunky.

Fold in the pine nuts and season to taste with salt and pepper.

Preheat the oven to 350°F (180°C, or gas mark 4).

Prepare a baking sheet by either lining it with parchment or a silicone baking sheet or spraying with nonstick cooking spray.

Prepare a workstation. You will need ample space. If you have a basting brush, now is the time to use it. At your workstation, you will need your brush, a small-size bowl of olive oil, and two damp (not wet) dish towels.

Lay a dish towel flat. Open your package of thawed phyllo and lay the entire stack on the towel. Cover with the other towel.

Take one sheet of phyllo, and brush liberally with olive oil. Take another sheet, stack it on top of the first, and brush with oil as well. Cut the two stacked sheets into three strips lengthwise.

Scoop 2 to 3 tablespoons (30 to 45 g) of filling onto the short end of one of the strips.

Fold from the left corner to the right edge of the strip to form a triangle. Then fold up, then over, then up, then over, until you reach the end of the strip. Brush the entire triangle with olive oil, and place on the prepared baking sheet.

Repeat with the remaining strips.

Bake for 16 to 20 minutes, or until golden brown and flaky.

Yield: 8 to 10 triangles

Inari with Spicy Sushi Sauce

Every recipe for inari (stuffed tofu pockets) we saw online called for store-bought tofu pockets. Not acceptable. This inari is not exactly like the store-bought or sushi bar stuff, but it's yummy and can be made at home without having to find any special ingredients. And the sauce? Killer.

For the rice:

- 1 cup (180 g) dry sushi rice
- 2 cups (470 ml) water
- 1 tablespoon (15 ml) rice wine vinegar
- 1 tablespoon (21 g) agave nectar
- ½ teaspoon salt

For the tofu pockets:

- 1 cup (235 ml) vegetable oil, for frying
- 12 ounces (336 g) extra-firm tofu, drained and pressed
- 1 cup (235 ml) soy sauce
- ¼ cup (60 ml) rice wine vinegar
- ¼ cup (84 g) agave nectar

For the Spicy Sushi Sauce:

- ½ cup (112 g) vegan mayonnaise, store-bought or homemade (page 301 or 302)
- 2 tablespoons (30 ml) sriracha chili sauce
- ¼ teaspoon toasted sesame oil

To prepare the rice: Place the rice, water, vinegar, agave, and salt in a rice cooker. If you don't have a rice cooker, follow the instructions on your package of rice, adding the vinegar and agave to the water.

To make the tofu: In a pot or a deep fryer, pour the oil to a depth of 1 inch (2.5 cm). Heat over high heat. Cut the tofu into 12 to 16 pieces. You want to have rectangles that measure about 2 inches (5 cm) long, 1½ inches (3.8 cm) wide, and ¼ inch (6 mm) thick.

Deep-fry the blocks, three or four at a time, until golden brown, about 5 minutes. Take care that they don't touch in the oil, or they will stick together. Remove from the oil and set on a plate lined with paper towels to drain off any excess oil.

In a wide shallow dish, or a gallon-size resealable plastic bag, mix together the soy sauce, vinegar, and agave. Place the fried tofu in the marinade and let soak for at least 10 minutes, but no longer than 20. Remove from the marinade and place on a plate lined with paper towels to absorb excess moisture.

Carefully cut a slit in the long end of the tofu to create a pocket.

Stuff with the prepared sushi rice.

To make the sauce: Whisk together the mayonnaise, sriracha, and sesame oil.

Drizzle on top of the tofu pockets.

Place any extra sauce in a dish for dipping.

Yield: 12 to 16 pieces

 Under 30 Minutes   Soy Free

Yalanchi Dolmas

What is a dolma? It is a family of stuffed vegetable dishes common in the Middle East. What is a yalanchi dolma? Literally translated, it means false dolma. *In other words, a dolma without meat. Meatless dolmas taste delicious served warm, cold, or at room temperature, which makes them perfect appetizers to make ahead of time and serve at get-togethers. Serve with Tzatziki (page 86) or nondairy yogurt for dipping.*

2 cups (348 g) cooked rice (white, brown, long, short—your choice!)
2 tablespoons (6 g) finely chopped mint leaves
2 tablespoons (30 ml) balsamic vinegar
2 tablespoons (30 ml) lemon juice
2 tablespoons (30 ml) extra-virgin olive oil
½ cup (60 g) finely chopped walnuts
Salt and pepper, to taste
12 grape leaves

In a mixing bowl, combine the rice, mint, vinegar, lemon juice, oil, walnuts, salt, and pepper. Mix until uniform. Your hands will work best for this.

Prepare a clean, flat workspace.

Carefully lay one grape leaf flat. Place about 2 tablespoons (20 g) of mixture in the center of the leaf and wrap up like a little burrito.

Repeat with the remaining 11 leaves.

Yield: 12 dolmas

NOTE

Grape leaves can usually be found in most grocers in the same aisle as the pickles and olives. They will either be in a jar or a can.

Mediterranean "Egg" Rolls

Not your typical appetizer! These little fellows taste really yummy dipped in marinara or hummus.

For the wraps:

1¼ cups (156 g) all-purpose flour
¼ teaspoon salt

¼ teaspoon baking powder
¼ teaspoon baking soda
½ teaspoon garlic powder
½ teaspoon onion powder
½ teaspoon dried parsley
½ teaspoon dried basil
½ cup (120 ml) water

For the filling:

6 ounces (168 g) extra-firm tofu, drained, pressed, and crumbled
¼ cup (40 g) sun-dried tomatoes packed in oil, chopped
1 teaspoon garlic powder
1 teaspoon onion powder
2 tablespoons (15 g) nutritional yeast
½ teaspoon paprika
1 tablespoon (15 ml) extra-virgin olive oil
Salt and pepper, to taste

Olive oil, for brushing

Preheat the oven to 400°F (200°C, or gas mark 6). Prepare a baking sheet by lining with parchment or a silicone baking mat, such as Silpat.

To make the wraps: Mix together the flour, salt, baking powder, baking soda, garlic powder, onion powder, parsley, and basil. Add the water and knead until a nice elastic dough ball forms. Add a little extra water if your dough is too dry, or a little extra flour if it's too sticky. Divide into 8 equal pieces. On a well-floured surface, roll each piece flat, until it resembles a tortilla in size and thickness. Stack between layers of waxed paper and set aside.

To make the filling: Combine all the filling ingredients in a bowl and stir until very well incorporated. Divide into 8 equal portions.

To assemble the rolls, place one portion of the filling in the center of one wrap and roll it up like a little burrito.

Place on the baking sheet, seam side down, and brush lightly with olive oil. Bake for 15 to 20 minutes, or until golden brown.

Serve warm on their own, or with marinara or hummus for dipping.

Yield: 8 rolls

VARIATION

Chopped black olives are a nice addition, as are mushrooms, pine nuts, and fresh basil.

Avocado Spring Rolls

So fresh and healthy! Serve with Sweet and Sour Sauce (page 256) for dipping. These taste best when served right away, but if you need to make them ahead of time, just be sure to store them in the refrigerator and make sure they are not touching, or they will get stuck together. Laying them on a bed of spinach, cabbage, or lettuce will keep them from sticking to the serving dish.

12 large-size dry rice spring roll wrappers
6 ounces (168 g) baby spinach leaves
1 cucumber, seeded and cut into matchsticks
3 avocados, peeled and sliced
2 to 3 cups (216 to 324 g) shredded carrots
6 ounces (168 g) prepared maifun noodles (rice stick noodles)

On an ample flat surface, preferably near the stove, prepare a workstation. Have at hand a shallow pan of hot, but not boiling, water, the rice wrappers, the spinach leaves, the cucumber matchsticks, the sliced avocados, the shredded carrots, and the prepared noodles.

Place a damp dish towel on the flat surface closest to you. Carefully place one rice wrapper in the hot water for about 10 seconds, or until it is soft and pliable. Lay the wrapper flat on the dish towel.

Start by placing a small amount of spinach, about 5 leaves, onto the wrapper, then layer on the cucumber, avocado, carrot, and finally a small handful of noodles. Roll up tightly like a tiny burrito.

Repeat with the remaining 11 wrappers.

Yield: 12 rolls

Gluten Free

Southwestern Tamalliettas

Not quite tamales, these little bite-size nuggets are perfect for entertaining or for snacking on in front of the tube! They taste awesome dipped in Chipotle Ranch Dressing (page 129).

Nonstick cooking spray (optional)
2 cups (240 g) masa harina flour
½ cup (120 ml) canola or other vegetable oil
1 cup (235 ml) vegetable broth
⅓ cup (80 g) nondairy sour cream, store-bought or homemade (page 302)
½ cup (125 g) yellow corn
½ cup (125 g) black beans
¼ cup (16 g) fresh chopped cilantro
1 avocado, sliced
2 chipotle peppers in adobo sauce, diced
½ teaspoon cumin
Salt and pepper, to taste

Preheat the oven to 400°F (200°C, or gas mark 6). Prepare a baking sheet by lining it with parchment or a silicone baking sheet, such as Silpat, or spraying with nonstick cooking spray.

In a mixing bowl, mix all the ingredients together (use your hands) until everything is well incorporated.

Roll about 2 tablespoons of the mixture into balls and place on the baking sheet. Repeat with the remaining mixture.

Bake for 15 to 20 minutes. Let rest for about 5 minutes before serving.

Yield: About 24 balls

Soy Free

Kale Chips

At long last, a snack that doesn't undo your whole day of healthy eating. Be sure to try these chips on top of the Carrot, Squash, and Bean Bisque (page 197), or alongside any of your favorite dishes.

12 ounces (340 g) kale, stems and ribs removed, torn into small pieces, cleaned, and thoroughly spun dry
1 tablespoon (15 ml) extra-virgin olive oil
1 tablespoon (15 ml) white balsamic or apple cider vinegar
1 tablespoon (8 g) nutritional yeast
Pinch fine sea salt

Preheat the oven to 350°F (180°C, or gas mark 4).

In a large-size bowl, toss the kale with the oil, vinegar, yeast, and salt.

Divide the kale between two rimmed baking sheets.

Total baking time could reach 20 minutes, but check after 10 minutes; if the kale doesn't appear to crisp up, increase the temperature to 375°F (190°C, or gas mark 5), and bake for another 10 minutes until crisp.

Yield: 2 servings

Chapter 6

Salads and Salad Dressings

Whether as a great starter or a light lunchtime fare, a healthy salad tossed in a tasty, flavorful dressing is very likely to hit the spot. This chapter is sure to bring your plate from same-old, same-old to colorful, nutritious, and delicious, all in one fell swoop.

Low Fat Soy Free

Ginger- and Sesame-Infused Carrot and Cucumber Salad

Here is a fresh, fast, tangy, and simple salad that will become your go-to summer meal.

2 teaspoons toasted sesame oil
2 teaspoons grated gingerroot
2 cloves garlic, grated
2 teaspoons tamarind paste
2 tablespoons (30 ml) rice vinegar
2 tablespoons (30 ml) water
2 large-size carrots, peeled and shredded
1 English cucumber, cut in half lengthwise and finely sliced into half-moons
1½ teaspoons poppy seeds
1½ teaspoons sesame seeds
2 tablespoons (12 g) finely chopped scallion (optional)
½ teaspoon fine sea salt, to taste

In a large-size saucepan, heat the oil over medium heat, add the ginger and garlic, and cook until fragrant.

Add the tamarind paste, vinegar, and water, and stir until the tamarind is dissolved.

Add the shredded carrots and cook for a couple of minutes.

Place the cucumber half-moons in a large-size bowl, add the carrots and sauce, and toss together.

Sprinkle the poppy seeds, sesame seeds, scallions (if desired), and salt on top.

Chill for 1 hour and stir before serving.

Yield: 2 servings

 Under 30 Minutes  Low Fat  Soy Free

Cilantro Cucumber Salad

This makes a quick, fresh relish that tastes nice on its own or as a tangy, crispy addition to a sandwich. It also tastes great mixed with leftover cold rice or quinoa as a quick lunch.

1 cucumber, thinly sliced and quartered
1 cup (25 g) chopped fresh cilantro
2 tablespoons (30 ml) rice vinegar
Salt and pepper, to taste

In a bowl, mix all the ingredients together. Serve at room temperature or chill before serving.

Yield: 4 small servings

Soy Free

Cucumber, Tomato, and Quinoa Salad

To remove as much unnecessary liquid as you can, sprinkle ½ teaspoon of salt on the sliced cucumber, place in a colander, and let sit for 1 hour. Rinse and drain well.

Using cooled, cooked quinoa is even better in this light and delicious salad, if you have it at hand. Note: 1 cup (170 g) of dry quinoa quadruples once cooked.

4 cups (940 ml) water
1 cup (170 g) uncooked quinoa
½ cup (50 g) finely chopped scallion
2 cloves garlic, grated
1 English cucumber, peeled and thinly sliced
4 Roma tomatoes, diced
1 cup (60 g) chopped fresh curly parsley
⅓ cup (47 g) toasted hazelnuts, halved
6 dried figs, coarsely chopped
3 tablespoons (45 ml) extra-virgin olive oil
2 tablespoons (30 ml) white balsamic vinegar
¼ cup (60 ml) fresh lemon juice
2 teaspoons orange zest
½ teaspoon dried sage
½ teaspoon celery seeds
¼ teaspoon dried marjoram
3 tablespoons (24 g) nutritional yeast (optional)
¼ teaspoon ground black pepper, to taste
¼ teaspoon fine sea salt, to taste

In a medium-size saucepan, bring the water to a boil. Add the quinoa.

Cook over medium heat for 10 minutes, or until the little telltale tail pops up. Drain and set aside.

Combine the remaining ingredients in a very large bowl. Stir in the quinoa.

Serve chilled.

Yield: 6 servings

Soy Free

Raw Kale Salad

Here is a simple, nutritious, and refreshing way to prepare and enjoy the super powerful green veggie that is kale.

¼ cup (60 ml) seasoned rice vinegar
2 tablespoons (30 ml) toasted sesame oil
1 clove garlic, grated
¼ teaspoon ground ginger
Zest of ½ lemon (about 1 teaspoon)
Salt and pepper, to taste
12 ounces (340 g) kale, stems and ribs removed, torn into small pieces, thoroughly cleaned, and spun dry
1½ tablespoons (12 g) sesame seeds (optional)

Combine the vinegar, oil, garlic, ginger, lemon zest, salt, and pepper in a large-size bowl. Add the kale. Toss until the kale is thoroughly coated with the dressing.

Cover with a lid and let the salad marinate overnight in the fridge, to tenderize the kale.

Sprinkle with the sesame seeds upon serving, if desired.

Yield: 4 servings

Pistavocado Rice Salad

It's easy being green with this salad! A great source of fiber, vitamin C, and potassium, avocados are also high in good-for-you monounsaturated fats, so dig into the fruit (yes, it's a fruit!).

2 tablespoons (30 ml) fresh lemon juice
2 tablespoons (30 ml) extra-virgin olive oil
2 tablespoons (30 ml) seasoned rice vinegar
¼ cup (25 g) finely chopped scallion
½ teaspoon cracked black pepper
½ teaspoon fine sea salt
1 tablespoon (3 g) chopped fresh basil
1 tablespoon (4 g) chopped fresh curly parsley
½ teaspoon dried thyme
1 ripe avocado, peeled and mashed
3 cups (474 g) cooked and chilled long-grain white or brown rice
¼ cup (31 g) pistachios, chopped

Combine the lemon juice, oil, vinegar, scallions, pepper, salt, basil, parsley, thyme, and avocado.

Stir in the rice and pistachios.

Serve chilled, preferably the day it is made to avoid oxidation (avocados turn brown quickly).

Yield: 4 servings

Presto Pesto Orzo and Cannellini Salad

Rich in flavor and deliciously refreshing during the summer, this salad could also be made with another shape of pasta, or even rice. Using homemade pesto is the easiest way to ensure that it doesn't contain Parmesan, which store-bought pesto often does. See chapter 4 for some great homemade pesto recipes.

6 tablespoons (96 g) prepared vegan pesto
¼ cup (60 ml) seasoned rice vinegar
¼ cup (40 g) chopped red onion
4 cups (676 g) cooked whole wheat orzo
2 cans (15 ounces, or 425 g each) cannellini beans, drained and rinsed

In a large-size bowl, whisk together the pesto, vinegar, and onion.

Add the orzo and beans, and stir until thoroughly coated.

Serve chilled.

Yield: 6 servings

Taboulleh

Tabouli, tabouleh, or taboulleh—however you spell it, this Middle Eastern dish is simply delicious.

3 cups (705 ml) water
Salt and pepper, to taste
1 cup (176 g) uncooked bulgur wheat
3 cups (144 g) finely chopped parsley
1 large-size cucumber, seeded and diced
1 cup (225 g) seeded and diced tomatoes
¼ cup (12 g) finely chopped mint leaves
¼ to ½ cup (60 to 120 ml) extra-virgin olive oil, to taste
3 tablespoons (45 g) minced garlic
3 tablespoons (45 ml) lemon juice

Add the water to a pot, lightly salt it, and bring to a boil. Add the bulgur wheat, reduce to a simmer, and cook, uncovered, for about 10 minutes, or until all the liquid is absorbed. Set aside.

Place the parsley, cucumber, tomatoes, and mint in a mixing bowl.

In a small-size bowl, combine the oil, garlic, and lemon juice, and mix thoroughly.

Add the cooled bulgur wheat to the cucumber mixture, drizzle the dressing on top, and mix thoroughly.

Serve chilled.

Yield: 6 servings

Millet Salad

Although it contains about as much protein as wheat, while also being a gluten-free grain, millet appears to be a bit of an underdog in most people's kitchens. This salad will hopefully give you a new appreciation for it, and have you put it back in the spotlight, where it belongs.

¼ cup (60 ml) extra-virgin olive oil
¼ cup (60 ml) white wine vinegar
2 tablespoons (30 ml) fresh lemon juice
2 tablespoons (6 g) chopped fresh basil leaves
2 tablespoons (8 g) chopped fresh curly parsley
½ teaspoon fine sea salt
¼ teaspoon ground black pepper, to taste
2 cloves garlic, grated
¼ cup (40 g) chopped red onion
4 cups (696 g) cooked, cooled millet
8 dried apricots, thinly sliced
¼ cup (27 g) chopped pecans
⅔ cup (72 g) grated carrot

Combine the oil, vinegar, lemon juice, basil, parsley, salt, pepper, garlic, and onion in a medium-size bowl.

Add the millet, apricots, pecans, and carrots, and stir until coated with the vinaigrette.

Serve chilled.

Yield: 4 servings

 Low Fat  Soy Free

Jalapeño-Lime Barley Salad

This was the first vegan dish Joni's mom ever made for her. She has been making it ever since. It's really good!

For the salad:

3 cups (705 ml) water
1 cup (184 g) dry pearl barley
½ cup (52 g) seeded and diced cucumber
½ cup (126 g) diced tomato
½ cup (75 g) diced green bell pepper
½ cup (80 g) finely diced red onion

For the dressing:

1 jalapeño pepper, seeded and finely diced
¼ cup (60 ml) fresh lime juice
2 tablespoons (30 ml) extra-virgin olive oil
Salt and pepper, to taste

To make the salad: Bring the water to a boil in a medium-size saucepan, and add the barley. Reduce to a simmer, cover, and cook for 30 to 40 minutes, or until tender and most of the water has been absorbed. Let cool. Add the cucumber, tomato, bell pepper, and onion to the barley.

To make the dressing: Whisk together the dressing ingredients. Drizzle over the salad and toss to coat.

Serve chilled.

Yield: 6 servings

Under 30 Minutes   Gluten Free

Deviled "Egg" Salad

This tastes unbelievably like the real thing.

10 to 12 ounces (280 to 336 g) extra-firm tofu, drained, pressed, and crumbled
2 tablespoons (30 g) prepared yellow mustard
½ cup (120 ml) extra-virgin olive oil
1 teaspoon white miso
1 teaspoon garlic powder
1 teaspoon onion powder
1 teaspoon paprika
¼ teaspoon turmeric
Salt and pepper, to taste (black salt will give it an extra egg-y flavor)

Add all the ingredients to a blender or food processor and purée until very smooth.

Serve on a sandwich, spread on crackers, or make tofu deviled eggs!

Yield: Enough for 4 sandwiches

VARIATIONS

If you are making this for a sandwich filling you can add 3 scallions, chopped, and 1 stalk celery, finely diced.

To make tofu deviled eggs, drain and press an extra-firm block of tofu. Cut it into rectangular blocks about 2 inches (5 cm) long × 1½ inches (3.8 cm) wide × ¾ inch (2 cm) tall. Using a spoon, scoop out a little "bowl" in each block and pipe in the filling. Sprinkle with paprika before serving.

Under 30 Minutes

California Waldorf Salad

This tasty little salad is amazing on its own, but you can also use it as a sandwich filling or toss it with baby spinach for a delicious and easy lunch.

12 to 16 ounces (336 to 448 g) smoked tofu, store-bought or homemade (page 208)
1 cup (160 g) halved red or green grapes
1 cup (99 g) pecans
1 cup (160 g) diced red onion
2 stalks celery, chopped
1 recipe Orange Poppy Seed Dressing (page 129)
Salt and pepper, to taste

Cut the tofu into small ¼-inch (6-mm) cubes. Add to a mixing bowl. Toss together with the grapes, pecans, onion, celery, dressing, and salt and pepper. Serve immediately or keep refrigerated until ready to serve.

Yield: 6 servings

Under 30 Minutes

Edamame "Caviar"

Okay, caviar might be a stretch, but this little salad is so flavorful and delicious, you'll feel like a millionaire! It's also a tasty way to sneak in some heart-healthy fats and proteins, and if you verify that your vinegar is gluten free, this dish is gluten free as well.

1 bag (12 ounces, or 341 g) frozen shelled edamame
2 cloves garlic, minced
¾ cup (120 g) finely diced red onion
¾ cup (120 g) finely diced yellow bell pepper
3 tablespoons (45 ml) extra-virgin olive oil
3 tablespoons (45 ml) canola oil
3 tablespoons (45 ml) rice vinegar
Salt and pepper, to taste

Bring a pot of lightly salted water to a boil. Add the beans to the boiling water and boil for 3 minutes. Drain.

In a mixing bowl, mix together all of the ingredients and toss until well coated.

Refrigerate until ready to serve. Serve chilled.

Yield: 4 servings

Spicy Asian-Inspired Macaroni Salad

Macaroni salad with an Asian flair? A bit wonky in theory, but delicious in your mouth! If macaroni just won't do it for you, feel free to substitute udon, soba, or chow mein noodles. This dish is perfect for potlucks and get-togethers.

For the dressing:

1 cup (224 g) vegan mayonnaise, store-bought or homemade (page 301 or 302)
3 tablespoons (45 ml) sesame oil
3 tablespoons (45 ml) sriracha chili sauce
1 tablespoon (15 ml) rice vinegar
1 teaspoon red pepper flakes

For the salad:

1 pound (455 g) elbow macaroni
1 pound (455 g) broccoli florets, raw or lightly steamed
1 cup (138 g) cashews, raw or toasted
1 cup (108 g) shredded carrot
2 cups (340 g) shelled edamame (cold, but cooked)
Salt and pepper, to taste

To make the dressing: Whisk all the ingredients together, and set aside.

To make the salad: Prepare the pasta according to the package directions. Drain the pasta and rinse under cold water.

Add the broccoli, cashews, carrot, edamame, salt, and pepper, and toss with the dressing. Keep refrigerated until ready to serve.

Yield: 16 side- or 8 main-dish servings

"That" Broccoli Salad

You know the salad. The one everyone's aunt invented and brings to every potluck? Well now you can make it and tell everyone you invented it!

For the nut brittle:

- 1 cup (138 g) raw cashews
- ½ cup (110 g) firmly packed brown sugar
- ¼ cup (84 g) agave nectar
- ¼ teaspoon cayenne pepper

For the dressing:

- 12 ounces (340 g) extra-firm tofu, drained and pressed
- ½ cup (120) canola oil
- 3 tablespoons (45 ml) apple cider vinegar (add more if you like a tangier dressing)
- 2 tablespoons (42 g) agave nectar
- 1 teaspoon onion powder
- 1 teaspoon garlic powder
- ½ teaspoon cayenne pepper
- Salt and pepper, to taste

For the salad:

- 2 pounds (910 g) broccoli florets, raw or lightly steamed
- 1 cup (160 g) diced red onion
- 1 cup (120 g) raisins
- ½ cup (50 g) imitation bacon bits, store-bought or homemade (page 212)

To make the brittle: Preheat the oven to 450°F (230°C, or gas mark 8).

Line a baking sheet with parchment paper.

Spread the cashews in a single layer, leaving plenty of space around the edges.

Mix the brown sugar, agave, and cayenne together in a bowl, then sprinkle on top of the nuts.

Bake for 5 to 7 minutes, until the sugar is bubbling. Keep a close eye on this to prevent burning.

Remove from the oven and place on a wire rack to cool for 10 minutes, then place in the freezer to cool completely.

To make the dressing: Place all the ingredients in a blender and purée until smooth.

To make the salad: In a large-size bowl, toss together the broccoli, onion, raisins, and bacon bits. Drizzle on the dressing and toss to coat.

Serve immediately or store, covered, in the refrigerator until ready to serve. Add the brittle, broken into bite-size pieces, right before serving.

Yield: 10 servings

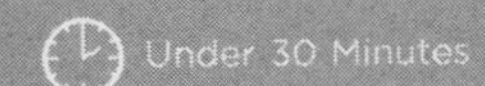
Under 30 Minutes

Gluten Free

Saag Baag

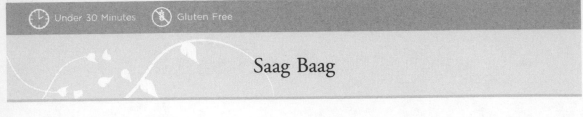

Literally translated, saag *means "leafy green" and* baag *means "garden." This is a tasty, easy little dish that sports sautéed spinach as the leafy green, and onions, garlic, and tofu as the garden from which it sprouts!*

2 tablespoons (30 ml) extra-virgin olive oil
5 ounces (142 g) fresh baby spinach leaves
1 red onion, julienned
2 tablespoons (15 g) minced garlic
10 ounces (280 g) extra-firm tofu, drained and pressed
¼ teaspoon turmeric
¼ teaspoon paprika
3 tablespoons (45 ml) fresh lemon juice
Salt and pepper, to taste

Preheat a pan with the olive oil over medium-high heat. Add the spinach, onion, and garlic. Sauté until the spinach has wilted and the onion and garlic are fragrant, about 5 minutes.

In a bowl, crumble the tofu and add the turmeric and paprika. Add the tofu mixture to the pan and continue to cook for 5 more minutes, stirring constantly.

Transfer back to the bowl and toss with the lemon juice. Season with salt and pepper to taste.

Serve warm or cold.

Yield: 4 servings

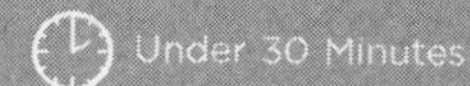

Creamy Curry Coleslaw with Roasted Red Peppers

Quick and tasty, this dish is perfect for your next barbecue as an alternative to a traditional coleslaw. Trying to cut down on fat? Feel free to reduce the amount of mayonnaise.

For the coleslaw:

1 head cabbage, shredded
½ cup (130 g) julienne-sliced fire-roasted red peppers (use jarred, packed in water, or roast your own)
1 cup (108 g) shredded carrot
¼ cup (32 g) sunflower seeds
¼ cup (40 g) raisins or currants

For the dressing:

1 cup (224 g) vegan mayonnaise, store-bought or homemade (page 301 or 302)
3 tablespoons (45 ml) apple cider vinegar
2 tablespoons (12 g) yellow curry powder, store-bought or homemade (page 307)
Salt and pepper, to taste

To make the coleslaw: Add the coleslaw ingredients to a large-size bowl.

To make the dressing: Whisk together the dressing ingredients. Drizzle over the coleslaw and toss to combine.

Keep refrigerated until ready to serve.

Yield: 8 servings

Balsamic Vinaigrette and Marinade

Did you know it is believed that balsamic vinegar naturally helps suppress the appetite and slow down the aging process? Seconds, please. This quick dressing tastes great over baby greens or your favorite salad. It also makes an awesome marinade for portobello mushrooms or your favorite protein.

1 tablespoon (11 g) whole mustard seeds
½ cup (120 ml) extra-virgin olive oil
¼ cup (60 ml) balsamic vinegar
3 tablespoons (63 g) agave nectar
1 tablespoon (15 g) brown or Dijon mustard
Freshly cracked pepper and sea salt, to taste

To toast the mustard seeds, use a dry pan or pot with a tight-fitting lid. Put the seeds in the pan, cover, and turn on the heat to medium-high. Don't go far; it will only take a few seconds for the seeds to start "popping." Once they start popping, turn off the heat—they're done!

Whisk together the toasted mustard seeds, oil, vinegar, agave, mustard, pepper, and salt, and store in an airtight container until ready to use.

Yield: 1 cup (235 ml)

 Under 30 Minutes  Soy Free

Orange Basil Balsamic Vinaigrette

Simple and fresh. Further proof that homemade dressings trump store-bought any day! Prepare this a day ahead of time to let the flavors develop. Toss with baby greens or your favorite green salad.

1 tablespoon (5 g) fresh chopped basil
1 orange, cut into segments, and then into small chunks
½ cup (120 ml) extra-virgin olive oil
¼ cup (60 ml) balsamic vinegar
¼ teaspoon salt
¼ teaspoon freshly cracked pepper

Mix all the ingredients together and store in an airtight container. No need to refrigerate.

Yield: About 1 cup (235 ml)

Creamy Balsamic Dressing

This dressing really adds a kick to an otherwise boring green salad. It is inspired by a creamy garlic dressing served at a little Italian restaurant in Belmont Shores, California. Unfortunately, their version uses beef consommé as a base. Definitely not vegan—until now!

14 ounces (392 g) extra-firm tofu, drained, but not pressed
½ cup (120 ml) extra-virgin olive oil
¼ cup (60 ml) balsamic vinegar
1 tablespoon (8 g) garlic powder
1 tablespoon (8 g) onion powder
Salt and pepper, to taste

Place all the ingredients in a blender and blend until smooth. Keep refrigerated in an airtight container until ready to use. This will keep for about 1 week.

Yield: About 1½ cups (350 ml)

Basic Favorite Dressing

Here is a dressing recipe that is so simple and quick to prepare, it almost makes it embarrassing to share. Double or triple the recipe, depending on the number of people who will partake, and also depending on how the salad ingredients you choose usually absorb dressings.

1 tablespoon (8 g) nutritional yeast
1 tablespoon (15 ml) extra-virgin olive oil
2 tablespoons (30 ml) white balsamic vinegar
1 teaspoon favorite dried herbs, such as thyme, basil, or Italian seasoning

Whisk together all the ingredients at the bottom of your salad bowl. Add the salad ingredients, toss, and serve.

Yield: 1 serving

Under 30 Minutes

Orange Miso Dressing

Citrus fruits have a way of making everything lighter, and this dressing is no exception. Be careful when adding the salt, though, because miso is already packing a punch when it comes to sodium: taste-test before being too generous!

¼ cup (60 ml) fresh orange juice
¼ cup (60 ml) seasoned rice vinegar
2 teaspoons toasted sesame oil
1 tablespoon (21 g) white miso
1 tablespoon (21 g) agave nectar
1 clove garlic, grated
1 teaspoon packed grated gingerroot
1 tablespoon (8 g) black sesame seeds
¼ teaspoon fine sea salt, to taste (optional)

Whisk together the orange juice, vinegar, oil, miso, agave, garlic, gingerroot, sesame seeds, and salt, if desired, in a medium-size bowl.

Serve chilled.

Yield: About ¾ cup (175 ml)

 Under 30 Minutes  Soy Free

Orange Sunflower Dressing

Try dipping steamed broccoli spears in this creamy, deliciously garlicky dressing, or serve it on top of quinoa or rice. As is the case with almost every dressing, the uses are pretty much limitless.

½ teaspoon cumin seeds
½ teaspoon celery seeds
½ teaspoon caraway seeds
¾ cup (180 ml) fresh orange juice
2 tablespoons (30 ml) extra-virgin olive oil
¼ cup (60 ml) apple cider vinegar
1 teaspoon Dijon mustard
¼ cup plus 2 tablespoons (48 g) roasted, salted sunflower seeds
¼ cup (15 g) chopped fresh curly parsley
1 teaspoon coarse sea salt
½ teaspoon ground black pepper, to taste
2 cloves garlic, grated

Place the cumin, celery, and caraway seeds in a small-size saucepan and heat over medium heat for 1 minute, until toasted and fragrant.

Place directly in a blender along with the juice, oil, vinegar, mustard, sunflower seeds, parsley, salt, pepper, and garlic, and blend until smooth.

Serve chilled. Store in the fridge.

Yield: About 2 cups (470 ml)

Under 30 Minutes Gluten Free

Orange Poppy Seed Dressing

Sweet and tangy, this dressing is great for drizzling over mixed fruit and is an essential ingredient for the California Waldorf Salad (page 121).

¾ cup (168 g) plain nondairy yogurt
½ cup (112 g) vegan mayonnaise, store-bought or homemade (page 301 or 302)
½ cup (120 ml) orange juice
1 tablespoon (9 g) poppy seeds

Whisk all the ingredients together and store in an airtight container in the refrigerator until ready to serve.

Yield: About 1½ cups (355 ml)

Under 30 Minutes Gluten Free

Chipotle Ranch Dressing

Cool, fresh, and tangy with a tad bit of heat. This works well as a salad dressing, as a dip, or as a spread for sandwiches. You can use store-bought or homemade mayonnaise and sour cream here; both will yield yummy results.

1 cup (225 g) vegan mayonnaise, store-bought or homemade (page 301 or 302)
½ cup (120 g) nondairy sour cream, store-bought or homemade (page 302)
2 chipotle peppers in adobo sauce, finely diced
½ teaspoon dried parsley
½ teaspoon dried dill
¼ teaspoon garlic powder
¼ teaspoon onion powder
¼ teaspoon ground cumin
⅛ teaspoon salt
⅛ teaspoon black pepper

Mix all the ingredients together until well blended. Store in an airtight container in the refrigerator for up to 2 weeks.

Yield: About 1½ cups (355 ml)

Chapter 7

Soups, Chilis, and Stews

Hearty and filling, a hot bowl of soup, chili, or stew is sure to warm the soul, no matter what the season. Just gather and prepare the ingredients, throw it all into a Dutch oven, and let it cook while you relax and unwind from a busy day.

Low Fat  Gluten Free Soy Free

Cranberry Chili

Get ready for this simple, unusual chili to kick things up. If you're not a fan of spicy stuff, adjust the amount of cayenne pepper to your liking, and/or use regular diced tomatoes instead. Pair it with steamed rice, roasted sweet potatoes, or a big chunk of Mole Bread (page 345).

1 tablespoon (15 ml) extra-virgin olive oil
1⅓ cups (213 g) diced red onion
2 tablespoons (16 g) mild to medium chili powder
¼ teaspoon cayenne pepper, to taste
1 teaspoon ground cumin
1 tablespoon (21 g) agave nectar
2 tablespoons (30 ml) tequila
½ teaspoon coarse sea salt
6 ounces (170 g) fresh or frozen cranberries
1 can (15 ounces, or 425 g) diced tomatoes with jalapeño, including liquid
½ cup (120 ml) water
1 can (15 ounces, or 425 g) cooked red kidney beans, drained and rinsed

In a large-size saucepan, heat the oil over medium-high heat. Add the chopped onion and cook until tender, about 4 minutes, stirring often.

Stir in the chili powder, cayenne, and cumin. Cook for 1 minute, until fragrant.

Add the agave, tequila, and salt, stirring well. Stir in the cranberries and let cook for 5 minutes.

Add the tomatoes, their liquid, and the water. Bring to a low boil, cover with a lid, and reduce the heat to a simmer.

Let simmer for 10 minutes.

Stir in the beans, cover again, and let simmer for another 15 minutes.

If the chili is too liquid for you, let it cook down for another couple of minutes, uncovered.

Yield: 4 small servings

Low Fat Soy Free

Barley Chili

Barley gives a wonderful texture to this spicy chili that will welcome you home when the days are just too cold to be anywhere else but wrapped in a warm blanket.

1 tablespoon (15 ml) extra-virgin olive oil
1 large-size carrot, finely diced
1 large-size zucchini, finely diced
1 cup (160 g) chopped onion
2 large-size cloves garlic, grated
½ teaspoon coarse sea salt, to taste
2 tablespoons (16 g) mild to medium chili powder
1 tablespoon (6 g) ground cumin
¼ teaspoon cayenne pepper, to taste
2 teaspoons dried oregano
1 cup (200 g) uncooked pearl barley, rinsed and drained
3 cups (705 ml) water or vegetable broth
2 tablespoons (33 g) tomato paste
1 can (15 ounces, or 425 g) tomato sauce
1 can (15 ounces, or 425 g) cooked black beans, drained and rinsed

In a large-size saucepan, heat the oil over medium-high heat and add the carrot, zucchini, onion, garlic, and salt.

Cook for 5 minutes over medium heat. Add the chili powder, cumin, cayenne, and oregano, and cook for 1 minute, until fragrant.

Add the barley, and cook for another 2 minutes.

Add the water, tomato paste, and tomato sauce. Stir well. Bring to a boil, cover with a lid, and let simmer for 35 minutes, stirring every now and then and making sure the barley doesn't stick to the saucepan.

Remove the lid, stir in the beans, and let the remaining liquid reduce over low heat, with the pot uncovered, for another 10 minutes, or until the barley is tender and the chili is at your desired consistency.

Yield: 4 large servings

Low Fat

"Chicken" Noodle Soup

This soup is perfect for when you're sick. It's easy to throw together and warming to the soul. And you can use any type of noodle you like; orzo even works well here.

4 cups (940 ml) chicken-flavored vegetable broth, or more if you want a more brothy soup
1 cup (135 g) fresh, frozen, or canned peas
1 cup (135 g) fresh, frozen, or canned corn
6 ounces (170 g) extra-firm tofu, cut into ⅛-inch (6-mm) cubes
6 ounces (170 g) dry udon, soba, or lo mein noodles

Bring the broth to a boil in a medium-size pot. Add the peas, corn, and tofu, and return to a boil. Add the noodles and simmer for 7 to 10 minutes, or until the noodles are tender.

Yield: 4 servings

VARIATION

Carrots make a nice addition to this soup.

Under 30 Minutes

Gluten Free

Soy Free

Coconut Curry Carrot Soup

Cream-based soups need not be off-limits on a vegan diet. Coconut milk is not only creamy and delicious, but it also contains lauric acid, which is found in mother's milk and has been shown to promote brain development and bone health.

2 cups (470 ml) vegetable broth
1 can (14 ounces, or 414 ml) coconut milk
1 pound (455 g) peeled carrots
1 tablespoon (6 g) yellow curry powder, store-bought or homemade (page 307)
1 tablespoon (15 g) minced garlic
Salt and pepper, to taste

Add all the ingredients to a pot and bring to a boil. Reduce to a simmer and simmer until the carrots are nice and tender, about 10 minutes. Using an immersion or a countertop blender, purée until smooth.

Yield: 5 servings

NOTE

If using a countertop blender, let the soup cool slightly before puréeing, so as to avoid a hot-liquid explosion.

Gluten Free

Rustic Potato Leek Soup

This soup is "rustic" because you leave the potato skins on and don't purée it totally smooth. A bit of chunkiness and the earthy brown color from the skins make this a hearty soup that tastes good on its own or as a starter to a meal. Serve in Bread Bowls (page 333) for an extra-special meal.

2 leeks
2 tablespoons (28 g) nondairy butter
2 tablespoons (8 g) finely chopped lemongrass
4 cups (940 ml) vegetable broth
1½ pounds (690 g) russet potatoes
Salt and pepper, to taste

Cut the leeks into ¼-inch (6-mm) slices, using most of the leek, up until it forks off into separate leaves.

Add the butter to a pot and melt over high heat. Add the leeks and lemongrass and sauté until browned, about 2 minutes.

Add the broth, deglaze the pan, and bring to a boil.

Add the potatoes, reduce to a simmer, cover, and simmer for 30 minutes.

Using an immersion or a countertop blender, blend until smooth but still a bit chunky.

Season with salt and pepper.

Yield: 4 servings

NOTE

If using a countertop blender, let the soup cool slightly before puréeing, so as to avoid a hot-liquid explosion.

Coconut Cream of Mushroom Soup

It's almost embarrassing how easy this recipe is. But it really does create super yummy results. Rich, slightly sweet, and certainly earthy, this soup calls for a combination of button and portobello mushrooms, but feel free to use whatever you have on hand.

2 tablespoons (28 g) nondairy butter
8 ounces (227 g) button mushrooms, sliced
8 ounces (227 g) portobello mushroom caps, sliced
2 tablespoons (30 g) minced garlic
2 cans (14 ounces, or 414 ml each) coconut milk
Salt and pepper, to taste
Shredded coconut, for garnish

Melt the butter in a pan and sauté the mushrooms and garlic for 7 to 10 minutes, or until the mushrooms have shrunk in size by about half.

Add the coconut milk and bring to a boil. Reduce to a simmer and simmer for 15 minutes.

Using an immersion or a countertop blender, purée until smooth.

Season with salt and pepper and garnish with the shredded coconut.

Yield: 4 servings

NOTE

If using a countertop blender, let the soup cool slightly before puréeing, so as to avoid a hot-liquid explosion.

Smoky Black Bean Soup

This soup is hearty, smoky, and filling—almost a meal in itself. While it's simmering, relax and read a book as the entire house fills with the smells of a campfire!

1 pound (455 g) dry black beans
2 tablespoons (28 g) nondairy butter
1 cup (160 g) diced yellow onion
1 cup (160 g) diced red onion
2 tablespoons (30 g) minced garlic
Pinch salt
8 cups (1880 ml) water
2 bay leaves
1 tablespoon (7 g) paprika
1 tablespoon (8 g) chili powder
1 tablespoon (8 g) cumin
1 tablespoon (8 g) coriander
2 tablespoons (30 ml) liquid smoke
1 can (15 ounces, or 420 g) diced or stewed tomatoes, with their juice
Nondairy sour cream, store-bought or homemade (page 302), for garnish (optional)
Avocado slices, for garnish (optional)

Rinse, sort, and soak the beans overnight. Rinse and strain the beans.

In a large-size stockpot with a tight-fitting lid, melt the butter over medium-low heat. Add the onions and garlic and a pinch of salt. Sweat the vegetables until fragrant and translucent, 10 to 15 minutes.

Add the water, bay leaves, paprika, chili powder, cumin, coriander, beans, liquid smoke, and tomatoes with their juice, and stir well.

Bring to a boil, then reduce to a simmer. Cover and let simmer for 1½ to 2 hours, stirring every once in a while and checking the beans for tenderness. If your pot lets out a lot of steam while it's covered you may have to add more water to prevent burning.

Fish out the bay leaves and discard before serving. Serve garnished with sour cream and/or avocado slices, if desired. Freeze any leftovers.

Yield: 8 servings

Southwestern Bean and Corn Soup

Lots of corn and beans, plus sweet caramelized onions to balance out the heat of the chipotle, make this a winner in our book! The soymilk is listed as optional; it adds a little bit of creaminess and sweetness to balance the heat. Feel free to substitute with 1 cup (235 ml) water or vegetable broth. If you are sensitive to heat, you can cut the chipotle powder down to ½ teaspoon, though we don't think this is really all that hot!

2 tablespoons (28 g) nondairy butter
1 large-size red onion, roughly chopped or sliced
Pinch salt
2 tablespoons (30 g) minced garlic
1 cup (235 ml) vegetable broth
1 cup (227 g) tomato sauce
½ teaspoon ground cumin
1 teaspoon ground chipotle powder
1 teaspoon ground coriander
1½ cups (375 g) fresh, frozen, or canned corn
1½ cups (390 g) fully cooked pinto or black beans
1 cup (235 ml) plain soy or other nondairy milk (optional)
1 cup (160 g) diced scallion, plus more for garnish
Nondairy sour cream, store-bought or homemade (page 306), for garnish

Melt the butter in a pot over high heat. Add the onion and a pinch of salt, and sauté until caramelized, about 10 minutes, stirring often to prevent burning.

Add the garlic, and sauté 2 to 3 minutes more.

Add the broth, and deglaze the pot.

Add the tomato sauce, cumin, chipotle, and coriander. Bring to a boil, then reduce to a simmer.

Add the corn and beans and simmer for 10 to 15 minutes.

Stir in the soymilk, if using, and return to a boil.

Remove from the heat and stir in the 1 cup scallions.

Serve garnished with additional scallions and nondairy sour cream.

Yield: 4 to 6 servings

Under 30 Minutes

Creamy Tomato Soup

This simple, quickly prepared soup has won over several tomato haters in Celine's family, who, we're happy to report, even ended up licking their bowls clean. Make it even more outstanding by pairing it with Cheezy Quackers (page 97).

1 tablespoon (14 g) nondairy butter
1 tablespoon (15 ml) extra-virgin olive oil
¼ cup (40 g) chopped shallot
2 cloves garlic, grated
4 cups (946 ml) tomato juice
1 can (28 ounces, or 794 g) diced tomatoes, including liquid
4 sun-dried tomatoes packed in oil, drained and finely chopped
1 tablespoon (17 g) tomato paste
2 teaspoons dried basil
1 teaspoon dried thyme
1 dried bay leaf
1 teaspoon fine sea salt, to taste
1 teaspoon ground black pepper, to taste
½ cup (120 g) nondairy sour cream, store-bought or homemade (page 302), or nondairy cream cheese

In a large-size saucepan, melt the butter and oil over medium heat. Add the shallot and garlic and cook for 2 minutes.

Add the tomato juice, diced tomatoes with their juice, chopped sun-dried tomatoes, tomato paste, basil, thyme, bay leaf, salt, and pepper. Bring to a low boil. Cover with a lid and simmer for 15 minutes.

Stir in the sour cream until well blended. Remove from the heat. Remove and discard the bay leaf.

Using an immersion blender or a countertop blender, purée until smooth.

Yield: 4 servings

NOTE

If using a countertop blender, let the soup cool slightly before puréeing, so as to avoid a hot-liquid explosion.

Low Fat   Soy Free

Fig Lentil Soup

Don't let the unusual ingredients keep you from trying this lovely soup: those who tested it went a bit gaga over it. The fig spread lends a subtle sweetness to this heart- and belly-warming dish.

For the fig spread:

1 teaspoon extra-virgin olive oil
1 small-size shallot, finely minced
2 tablespoons (42 g) agave nectar
⅓ cup (80 ml) red wine
1 teaspoon red wine vinegar
½ teaspoon coarse sea salt
½ teaspoon dried rosemary
1 cup (170 g) dried figs, stemmed and quartered
½ cup (100 g) roasted and ground chestnuts

For the soup:

1 tablespoon (15 ml) extra-virgin olive oil
⅔ cup (80 g) chopped celery
1 cup (128 g) chopped carrot
½ cup (80 g) chopped red onion
2 cloves garlic, grated
1 teaspoon coarse sea salt
¼ teaspoon ground white pepper, to taste
1 can (15 ounces, or 425 g) tomato sauce
45 ounces (1.3 l) water
1 tablespoon (17 g) tomato paste
1 cup (190 g) uncooked brown or green lentils, rinsed and drained

To make the spread: In a medium-size saucepan, heat the olive oil over medium heat and cook the shallot until tender and fragrant.

Add the agave, wine, vinegar, salt, and rosemary; bring to a boil.

Add the figs, cover, and let simmer for 10 minutes.

Stir in the ground chestnuts, and set aside.

To make the soup: In a large-size saucepan, heat the oil over medium-high heat; add the celery, carrot, onion, and garlic. Cook for 5 minutes, or until tender.

Add the salt, pepper, tomato sauce, water, tomato paste, and prepared fig spread, stirring well.

Bring to a boil and add the lentils. Cover, lower the heat, and simmer for 20 minutes, or until the lentils are tender. Stir from time to time while the soup is cooking.

Yield: 6 servings

Cumin Carrot Soup

Cumin, carrots, and a subtle orange flavor are natural allies in this healthy soup that demands to be served with a generous spoonful of Parsley Pesto Spread (page 81) or Curried Cauliflower Purée (page 289) swirled into each serving.

1 tablespoon (15 ml) toasted sesame oil
3 tablespoons (30 g) finely chopped shallot
2 cloves garlic, grated
3½ cups (448 g) chopped carrots
1 tablespoon (6 g) ground cumin
1 teaspoon coarse sea salt, to taste
3 cups (705 ml) water
Zest of 1 orange (optional)
Generous spoonfuls Parsley Pesto Spread (page 81) or Curried Cauliflower Purée (page 289)

In a large-size saucepan, combine the oil, shallot, garlic, and carrots. Cook over medium heat for 6 minutes, stirring often. Stir in the cumin powder and salt and cook for 1 minute, or until fragrant.

Stir in the water. Bring to a boil. Cover with a lid and simmer for 20 to 30 minutes, or until the carrots are tender.

Using an immersion or a countertop blender, purée until smooth.

Sprinkle individual servings with the orange zest, if desired. Add a generous scoop of Parsley Pesto Spread.

Yield: 4 servings

NOTE

If using a countertop blender, let the soup cool slightly before puréeing, so as to avoid a hot-liquid explosion.

Split Pea Soup

This classic is sure to return color to your cheeks and happiness to your belly. You can also choose to add the imitation bacon bits after the soup is blended. Try serving this with Peanut Butter Bagels (page 330) or Olive Mini Baguettes (page 338).

- 2 tablespoons (30 ml) toasted sesame or any other oil
- 1 cup (160 g) chopped white onion
- 1 cup (120 g) chopped celery
- 2 cloves garlic, grated
- 1 pound (455 g) dried split peas, rinsed and drained
- 1½ cups (355 ml) dry white wine or more vegetable broth
- 6 cups (1410 ml) low-sodium vegetable broth
- ⅓ cup (42 g) imitation bacon bits, store-bought or homemade (page 216)
- 1½ teaspoons ground pepper, to taste
- 1½ teaspoons liquid smoke
- 1 teaspoon dried rosemary
- 2 dried bay leaves

In a large-size saucepan, heat the oil and cook the onion, celery, and garlic over medium heat, until fragrant and just tender, about 5 minutes.

Stir in the peas. Add the wine, broth, bacon bits, pepper, liquid smoke, and rosemary. Stir well.

Burrow the bay leaves into the soup. Bring to a low boil and cover with a lid. Simmer for 45 minutes, or until the split peas are tender. Add more broth if the soup gets too thick.

Remove and discard the bay leaves. Using an immersion or a countertop blender, purée to the desired consistency, making it as smooth or leaving it as chunky as you like.

Keep in mind that if there are leftovers, the soup will continue to thicken while cooling; you might have to stir in additional liquid upon reheating.

Yield: 6 servings

NOTE

If using a countertop blender, let the soup cool slightly before puréeing, so as to avoid a hot-liquid explosion.

Tahini Miso Potato Soup

Miso, or fermented soybean paste, is a wonderful flavor enhancer, which is far from being its only appeal: it is also rich in protein and vitamin B_{12}. However, it can contain quite a lot of sodium, so choose a low-sodium version, if such a thing is a concern for you. Keep in mind that a little goes a long way, and there's no need to add extra salt when miso is used.

1 tablespoon (15 ml) extra-virgin olive oil
6 sweet potatoes, peeled, washed, and cut into large chunks
4 baby potatoes, scrubbed and cut into large chunks
2 cloves garlic, grated
1 teaspoon packed grated gingerroot
¾ cup (120 g) chopped red onion
2 tablespoons (30 ml) fresh lemon juice
¼ cup (64 g) tahini
2 tablespoons (30 ml) tamari
¼ cup (30 g) nutritional yeast
¼ teaspoon cayenne pepper, to taste
3½ cups (825 ml) water, divided
3 tablespoons (63 g) white miso
2 cups (312 g) frozen spinach

In a large-size saucepan, heat the oil over medium-high heat. Add the potatoes, garlic, ginger, and onion. Cook for 5 minutes, stirring often.

In a large-size measuring cup, whisk together the lemon juice, tahini, tamari, nutritional yeast, cayenne pepper, and 2½ cups (590 ml) of the water.

Add to the vegetables, and bring to a boil. Cover with a lid and let simmer for 15 to 20 minutes. The potatoes should be tender, but still firm.

Whisk together the remaining 1 cup (235 ml) water and the miso. Add to the saucepan along with the spinach, stirring well.

Do not bring back to a boil, or the miso will lose its healthy proprieties. Let simmer for another 5 to 10 minutes, or until the potatoes are to your liking and the soup is heated through.

Using an immersion or a countertop blender, purée until smooth. You can also leave some chunkiness to it by removing some of the soup and only partially blending it.

Yield: 6 servings

Low Fat   Soy Free

Minestrone

This traditional minestrone soup is packed with vitamin-filled veggies, guaranteed to keep your immune system roaring during the colder months. Speaking of colder, this soup freezes beautifully. Stirring a few tablespoons of Simple Cheezy Sauce (page 299) into your bowl makes for a delicious, creamier version if you want to bulk it up even more.

2 tablespoons (30 ml) extra-virgin olive oil
1 cup (160 g) chopped white onion
3 cloves garlic, grated
1 cup (120 g) chopped celery
1 cup (128 g) chopped carrot
1 cup (149 g) chopped green bell pepper
1 cup (118 g) chopped zucchini
1 teaspoon dried oregano
2 teaspoons dried basil
½ teaspoon cayenne pepper, to taste
4 cups (947 ml) vegetable broth
1 can (28 ounces, or 794 g) diced tomatoes, with their juice
1 can (15 ounces, or 425 g) cooked cannellini beans, rinsed and drained
½ cup (112 g) uncooked small pasta, such as stars or alphabets
Salt and pepper, to taste

In a large-size saucepan, combine the oil, onion, garlic, celery, and carrots, and cook over medium-high heat for 4 minutes, stirring often.

Add the bell pepper, zucchini, oregano, basil, and cayenne. Cook for another 4 minutes. Add the broth and tomatoes with their juice.

Bring to a boil, cover with a lid, and let simmer for 10 minutes. Stir in the beans and pasta, and simmer until the pasta is al dente and the veggies are tender, 5 to 10 minutes. Add salt and pepper according to taste, if needed.

Yield: 6 servings

 Low Fat · Gluten Free · Soy Free

Asparagus, Cabbage, and Potato Chowder

Because asparagus is said to help relieve cramping and ease depression, it has been known to help a girl get through that "wonderful" time of the month. Can you think of a better way to see the week through than with a nice hearty soup?

8 cups (1880 ml) vegetable broth
1 pound (455 g) red potatoes
1 pound (455 g) peeled carrots, roughly chopped
12 ounces (336 g) asparagus, cut into 2-inch (5-cm) pieces
1 yellow onion, roughly chopped
2 cloves garlic, roughly chopped
1 teaspoon paprika
1 teaspoon celery seed
1 teaspoon dried dill
¼ cup (30 g) nutritional yeast
1 head cabbage, shredded

Add the broth, potatoes, carrots, asparagus, onion, and garlic to a Dutch oven or large-size soup pot. Cover and bring to a boil. Reduce to a simmer and simmer, covered, for 30 minutes.

Add the paprika, celery seed, dill, and nutritional yeast. Stir.

Using an immersion or a countertop blender, purée until almost smooth. This soup tastes best with a bit of chunkiness.

Stir in the shredded cabbage and simmer for an additional 20 minutes.

Yield: About 10 cups

NOTE

If you're using a countertop blender, let the soup cool slightly before puréeing, to avoid a hot-liquid explosion.

Sweet Potato, Roasted Red Pepper, and Corn Bisque

Dietary fiber, naturally occurring sugars, complex carbohydrates, protein, vitamins A and C, iron, and calcium are just a few reasons sweet potatoes top the list of "good" carbs. It's purely a bonus that these wonder tubers taste great, too! If you like your soup spicy, add an extra chipotle pepper. If you prefer a sweeter bisque, leave out the chipotle and adobo. It's yummy both ways.

- 4 cups (940 ml) vegetable broth
- 1 pound (455 g) sweet potatoes, peeled and cut into chunks
- 6 ounces (168 g) roasted red peppers (packed in water)
- 2 cups (500 g) yellow corn kernels
- 1 white or yellow onion, roughly chopped
- 1 chipotle pepper, packed in adobo sauce (add more if you like it really spicy)
- 1 tablespoon (15 ml) adobo sauce, from the can
- ½ teaspoon black pepper
- 2 cups (470 ml) soy creamer

Combine the broth, sweet potatoes, red peppers, corn, onion, chipotle, adobo, and black pepper in a Dutch oven.

Bring to a boil. Reduce to a simmer. Cover and simmer for about 1 hour, or until most of the moisture has been absorbed. Add the creamer.

Using an immersion or a countertop blender, purée until smooth.

Yield: 6 servings

NOTE

If using a countertop blender, let the soup cool slightly before puréeing, so as to avoid a hot-liquid explosion.

Carrot, Squash, and Bean Bisque

Enjoy this creamy, filling bisque sprinkled with Kale Chips (page 111)! Once the squash is roasted (see page 83 for instructions), it comes together in no time. The garbanzo beans help thicken the bisque and also add protein, making this a complete meal.

1 tablespoon (15 ml) peanut oil
2 cloves garlic, grated
1⅓ cups (144 g) grated carrot (about 2 large)
3 cups (705 ml) water
3 pounds (1.4 kg) butternut squash, roasted, cubed
2 tablespoons (30 ml) mirin or white wine
2 tablespoons (42 g) white miso
2 tablespoons (30 ml) tamari
1 tablespoon (15 ml) seasoned rice vinegar
1 tablespoon (15 ml) toasted sesame oil
1 tablespoon (6 g) grated gingerroot
1 cup (164 g) cooked garbanzo beans, drained and rinsed

In a large-size saucepan, heat the oil over medium-high heat, and add the garlic and carrot. Cook for 2 to 3 minutes, or until the garlic is fragrant. Stir often.

Stir in the water and butternut squash cubes. Bring to a boil. Lower the heat to medium, and cook, uncovered, for 5 minutes.

In a bowl, whisk together the mirin, miso, tamari, vinegar, oil, and ginger.

Lower the heat to a simmer, and stir in the mirin mixture. Stir in the garbanzo beans.

Cover with a lid, and let simmer for 15 minutes.

Using an immersion or a countertop blender, purée until smooth.

Yield: 4 servings

NOTE

If using a countertop blender, let the soup cool slightly before puréeing, so as to avoid a hot-liquid explosion.

Green Cauliflower Masala

If you cannot find green cauliflower at the market, use romanesco or white cauliflower instead. This spicy vegetable dish is especially outstanding when served alongside Crispy Tofu Fries (page 205). But good old brown rice and fried tofu would work perfectly too, if you're pressed for time.

1 pound (455 g) green cauliflower, trimmed, cleaned, and cut into florets
1½ cups (355 ml) unsweetened soy or other nondairy milk
1 recipe garam masala, store-bought or homemade (page 305)
2 teaspoons fine sea salt
4 cloves garlic, grated
¼ cup (64 g) tahini
2 tablespoons (15 g) chickpea flour

Cover the cauliflower with water in a large-size saucepan, bring to a boil, and cook until fork-tender, 10 to 15 minutes.

In the meantime, whisk together the milk, garam masala, salt, garlic, tahini, and flour in a large-size bowl.

Drain the cauliflower, return to the saucepan, and pour the sauce on top.

Coarsely mash the cauliflower, and let the mixture thicken over medium heat, about 2 minutes.

Yield: 4 servings

Low Fat Gluten Free Soy Free

Chickpea Masala

The amount of water in this recipe is so the red lentils retain some texture, but if you like yours a bit mushier, increase the water and cooking time for them to turn out the way you prefer. Serve with a side of steamed kale and a few slices of ripe avocado.

1 tablespoon (15 ml) extra-virgin olive oil
1½ cups (240 g) chopped red onion
3 cloves garlic, grated
1 tablespoon (6 g) grated gingerroot
1 teaspoon ground cumin
1 teaspoon ground coriander
2 teaspoons garam masala, store-bought or homemade (page 305)
½ teaspoon dry mustard
¼ teaspoon cayenne pepper, to taste
1 teaspoon coarse sea salt, to taste
1 cup (192 g) uncooked red lentils, rinsed
1 can (15 ounces, or 425 g) diced tomatoes, including liquid
1 can (15 ounces, or 425 g) cooked garbanzo beans, drained and rinsed
½ cup (120 ml) water, or more if needed
Sprinkle of fresh lemon juice (optional)

In a large-size saucepan, heat the oil over medium-high heat and add the onion, garlic, and ginger. Lower the heat to medium and cook until fragrant, about 3 minutes.

Add the cumin, coriander, garam masala, mustard, cayenne, salt, and lentils. Cook and stir for 1 minute.

Add the tomatoes and their juice, the beans, and the water. Increase the heat a bit to get things going again, cover with a lid, lower the heat, and simmer for 15 minutes. Stir occasionally, and add more liquid if it starts sticking to the bottom of the pan, or if the lentils aren't to your liking when the 15 minutes have gone by.

Sprinkle with the lemon juice, if desired, upon serving.

Yield: 4 small servings

Spicy Gumbo Z'Herbes

Wait. Stop. Don't call the Creole police! We've thrown all of the rules out the window in this gumbo. We've used filé, okra, and roux (the horror!), and we certainly didn't use nine different greens. What we did, however, was come up with a wonderfully flavorful—albeit not entirely traditional—gumbo that really hits the spot. Don't forget to serve it over plain white rice to keep at least some of the tradition going.

2 tablespoons (28 g) nondairy butter
1 large-size red or yellow onion, roughly chopped
1 green bell pepper, cored, seeded, and roughly chopped
3 stalks celery, roughly chopped
6 cups (1410 ml) vegetable broth
1 tablespoon dulse granules (ground seaweed)
1 tablespoon (6 g) Old Bay seasoning
1 tablespoon (6 g) garlic powder
1 tablespoon (6 g) onion powder
1 teaspoon ground black pepper
1 to 2 teaspoons cayenne pepper, to taste
1 pound (455 g) frozen sliced okra
8 ounces (227 g) shredded cabbage
4 ounces (112 g) baby spinach leaves
1 tablespoon (4 g) filé powder
Salt, to taste

For the roux:
½ cup (120 ml) canola or other vegetable oil
½ cup (112 g) all-purpose flour

Heat the butter in a saucepan over medium-high heat, then add the onion, bell pepper, and celery; cook until fragrant, translucent, and beginning to brown, 7 to 10 minutes.

To make the roux: While the veggies are sautéing you can make the roux. In a large-size stockpot or Dutch oven, heat the oil over medium-high heat. Add the flour and whisk vigorously. Continue to whisk until the roux turns golden brown, then reddish brown, then chocolate brown. This can take up to 10 minutes.

Add the sautéed veggies to the roux, then slowly add the vegetable broth. Stir well.

Add the dulse, Old Bay, garlic powder, onion powder, ground black pepper, and cayenne. Stir well.

Add the okra, cabbage, and spinach.

Cover and bring to a boil. Uncover, reduce to a simmer, and simmer for 20 minutes.

Remove from the heat and stir in the filé powder. Add salt to taste.

Serve over rice.

Yield: 8 generous servings

NOTE

Filé powder is a seasoning made from the dried, ground leaves of the sassafras tree. It is widely available in the spice or gourmet section of most large supermarkets.

VARIATION

Looking for a "sausage" gumbo? Eliminate the cabbage and spinach and add 2 chopped tomatoes along with any of the fauxsages (pages 196 to 200), chopped.

Red Jambalaya

Enjoy this spicy Creole take on the usually Cajun jambalaya version: the main difference between the two is that Creole jambalaya uses tomatoes and Cajun jambalaya uses only broth.

2 tablespoons (28 g) nondairy butter
4 stalks celery, chopped
1 green bell pepper, cored, seeded, and diced
2 cups (320 g) diced yellow onion
2 teaspoons Old Bay seasoning
1 pound (455 g) frozen sliced okra
1 can (15 ounces, or 425 g) diced tomatoes, with their juices
1 can (15 ounces, or 425 g) tomato sauce
2 teaspoons cayenne pepper
2 teaspoons ground black pepper
1 teaspoon dried oregano
½ teaspoon dried thyme
2 dried bay leaves
2 cups (470 ml) vegetable broth
2 cups (270 g) uncooked long grain white rice

In a large-size stockpot or Dutch oven, melt the butter over medium-high heat.

Add the celery, bell pepper, onion, and Old Bay. Cook until fragrant, translucent, and slightly browned.

Add the okra, tomatoes with their juice, tomato sauce, cayenne pepper, black pepper, oregano, thyme, and bay leaves. Cook for 5 more minutes.

Stir in the broth and rice and bring to a boil.

Reduce to a simmer, cover, and simmer for 25 to 30 minutes, or until the rice is tender, stirring occasionally to prevent scorching.

Remove and discard the bay leaves before serving.

Yield: 8 servings

 Low Fat  Gluten Free  Soy Free

Roasted Eggplant Ragout with Cannellini Beans and Sweet Potatoes

Don't scoff at this dish if you are usually not too keen on eggplant! This recipe might just be the one to change your mind. Roasting the vegetable and giving it time to absorb the flavors takes it from "blah" to being absolutely worth the preparation time.

1 eggplant, halved, each half quartered lengthwise
2 tablespoons (30 ml) extra-virgin olive oil, divided
1 teaspoon coarse sea salt
4 small-size sweet potatoes, peeled and cubed into bite-size pieces
¼ cup (40 g) chopped shallot
2 cloves garlic, grated
2 tablespoons (12 g) grated gingerroot
1½ teaspoons ground cumin
1½ teaspoons dried basil
¼ teaspoon cayenne
Black pepper, to taste
1 can (15 ounces, or 425 g) diced tomatoes, including liquid
1 cup (235 ml) water
1 can (15 ounces, or 425 g) cooked cannellini beans, drained and rinsed

Preheat the oven to 400°F (200°C, or gas mark 6). Have a large-size rimmed baking sheet handy.

Brush the eggplant with 1 tablespoon (15 ml) of the oil and sprinkle with salt. Roast for 20 minutes, or until tender.

In a large-size saucepan, heat the remaining 1 tablespoon (15 ml) of oil over medium heat. Stir in the potatoes, shallot, garlic, and ginger. Cook for 5 minutes, stirring often. Meanwhile, cut the roasted eggplant into bite-size pieces.

Stir in the cumin, basil, cayenne, and pepper. Cook for 1 more minute, until fragrant.

Stir in the eggplant, the tomatoes and their juice, and the water. Bring to a boil, cover, lower the heat, and let simmer for 20 minutes.

Stir in the beans. Cover and let simmer for another 10 minutes, or until the potatoes are tender.

Yield: 4 servings

Gluten Free   Soy Free

Parsnippity Stew

The aroma of this healthy stew as it cooks will have you tap your foot impatiently until dinnertime. Serve alongside (nondairy) buttered chunks of Pumpkin Yeast Bread (page 347).

1 tablespoon (15 ml) extra-virgin olive oil
6 parsnips, peeled, cleaned, and chopped into slightly larger than bite-size pieces
6 carrots, peeled, cleaned, and chopped into slightly larger than bite-size pieces
2 white potatoes, brushed clean and chopped into slightly larger than bite-size pieces
3 cloves garlic, grated
¼ cup (40 g) chopped shallot
¼ cup (60 ml) white wine
1 tablespoon (6 g) medium to mild curry powder, store-bought or homemade (page 307)
1 teaspoon coarse sea salt, to taste
Cracked black pepper, to taste
1 can (14 ounces, or 414 ml) coconut milk
½ cup (122 g) pumpkin purée
2 dried bay leaves
1 tablespoon (15 g) tamarind paste, diluted in 1 tablespoon (15 ml) water

In a large-size saucepan, heat the oil over medium heat. Add the parsnips, carrots, potatoes, garlic, and shallot, and cook for 5 minutes.

Add the white wine, and cook for another 2 to 3 minutes.

Add the curry, salt, pepper, coconut milk, pumpkin, and enough water to cover the vegetables, stirring to combine. Add the bay leaves, burrowing them among the veggies.

Cover with a lid, reduce the heat, and simmer for 15 minutes.

Remove and discard the bay leaves, and stir in the tamarind. Let simmer for another 5 to 10 minutes, or until the veggies are tender.

Yield: 4 servings

Disco Stew

Packed with as many sumptuous flavors as a disco ball has colored lights, this stew is destined to grace your table over and over again—especially during the winter months. Add chunks of fried Laurel and Hardy Peanut Fauxsages (page 197) to make it a complete meal.

1 tablespoon (15 ml) extra-virgin olive oil
½ cup (80 g) chopped red onion
3 cloves garlic, grated
9 potatoes, scrubbed clean, unpeeled, and cut into 1 × ½-inch (2.5 × 1.3-cm) cubes
4 large-size carrots, peeled and cut into ½-inch (1.3-cm) half-moons
1 tablespoon (8 g) mild to medium chili powder
½ teaspoon coarse sea salt
2 tablespoons (33 g) tomato paste
2 tablespoons (44 g) blackstrap or regular molasses
2 tablespoons (30 ml) vegan Worcestershire sauce
2 tablespoons (30 ml) fresh lemon juice
¼ cup (60 g) Dijon mustard
¼ cup (64 g) crunchy or creamy natural peanut butter
2 teaspoons dried thyme
2 dried bay leaves
1 cup (235 ml) lager beer
1 cup (235 ml) coconut milk
2 cups (267 g) frozen peas

In a large-size saucepan, heat the oil over medium heat, and add the onion, garlic, potatoes, and carrots. Cook for 8 minutes. Add the chili powder and salt, stirring to coat. Cook for another minute. Stir in the tomato paste, and cook for another minute.

In a small-size bowl, whisk together the molasses, Worcestershire sauce, lemon juice, mustard, peanut butter, and thyme.

Stir the mixture into the saucepan. Add the bay leaves, beer, and coconut milk. Cover, and let cook over medium-low heat for 40 minutes, stirring occasionally. Once the potatoes are fork-tender, stir in the peas and heat through for 5 to 10 minutes, or until the liquid is mostly absorbed. Remove and discard the bay leaves.

Yield: 6 servings

Ethiopian Wat

Traditional wat, a thick stew, comes in many forms, from chicken, beef, or lamb to vegetarian preparations. Generally, they all have a few things in common: lots of onions, berbere spice, and a seemingly large amount of butter or oil. From there, things can go in a million different delicious directions.

½ cup plus 2 tablespoons (150 ml) extra-virgin olive oil, divided
2 red onions, roughly chopped
Pinch salt
½ recipe (1 pound, or 455 g) Baked Berbere Seitan (page 217)
1½ pounds (672 g) russet potatoes
8 cups (1880 ml) beef-flavored vegetable broth or plain veggie broth
2 cups (224 g) sliced carrots
1 cup (190 g) dry red or green lentils
½ teaspoon freshly cracked black pepper
1 cup (184 g) uncooked long grain rice
Injeera, for serving (optional)

Heat 2 tablespoons (30 ml) of the olive oil in a Dutch oven over medium heat. Add the onions and the salt. Let them sweat for 15 to 20 minutes, stirring occasionally.

While the onions are cooking, chop the seitan and potatoes into bite-size chunks, and set aside.

Add the remaining ½ cup (120 ml) oil to the onions and deglaze the pot.

Add the broth and bring to a boil.

Add the seitan, carrots, potatoes, lentils, and pepper. Return to a boil, reduce to a simmer, cover, and simmer for 30 minutes.

Stir in the rice, cover, and simmer an additional 20 minutes, or until the rice is tender. Serve on its own or with injera (a sourdough flatbread) for scooping.

Yield: 8 servings

VARIATION

You can make the wat without the seitan; simply add one full recipe of the Berbere Spice Blend (page 306) at the same time you add the potatoes and carrots.

Chapter 8

Pasta, Grains, and Potatoes

Who said grains have to be boring? With savory sauces and inventive preparations, taunt your taste buds and your tummy with these delicious delights, from Rosemary White-Wine Roasted Potatoes to Quinoa with Hazelnut Parsley Pesto. Or revisit your favorite comfort foods with classics like Mac and Sleaze, Twice-Baked Potatoes, and Stuffed Ravioli.

Under 30 Minutes · Gluten Free · Soy Free

Ginger Curry Potatoes

Hot, hot, hot! Be sure to use the type of curry paste or powder that is best suited to the amount of heat you're able to handle.

2 tablespoons (30 ml) coconut or peanut oil
1 pound (455 g) baby Yukon potatoes, scrubbed clean, unpeeled, and cut into small cubes, fries, or wedges
1 tablespoon (15 g) green curry paste
½ teaspoon ground ginger
1 clove garlic, grated
2 tablespoons (30 ml) water

In a large-size frying pan, heat the oil over medium-high heat. Add the potatoes and cook until golden brown, about 10 minutes, stirring often and lowering the heat if needed.

In a small-size bowl, whisk together the curry, ginger, garlic, and water.

Add the curry mixture on top of the potatoes and let cook until the sauce coats the potatoes and cooks down a bit. Continue cooking until the potatoes are fork-tender.

Yield: 4 servings

Rosemary White-Wine Roasted Potatoes

You'll be happy to know that these flavorful potatoes stay perfectly tender and delicious, unlike some other roasted potato recipes you might have tried in the past.

2 cloves garlic, grated
½ teaspoon ground pepper, to taste
1 teaspoon coarse sea salt
1 teaspoon dried rosemary, crumbled
¼ cup (60 ml) dry white wine
1 tablespoon (15 ml) white wine vinegar
1 tablespoon (15 g) Dijon mustard
2 tablespoons (30 ml) extra-virgin olive oil
1¼ pounds (567 g) baby Yukon potatoes, scrubbed clean, unpeeled, and halved
1 red onion, cut into wedges

Preheat the oven to 400°F (200°C, or gas mark 6). Combine the garlic, pepper, salt, rosemary, wine, vinegar, mustard, and oil in an 8-inch (20-cm) square baking dish, stirring to combine.

Stir in the potatoes and onion.

Cover with foil, and bake for 30 minutes.

Remove the foil and stir the potatoes. Bake for an additional 20 to 25 minutes, or until the potatoes are golden brown and fork-tender.

Yield: 4 servings

Au Gratin Potatoes

Comfort food in its purest form. Leaving on the tater skins or not is up to you. You can use any old potato for this one, including russets, baby reds, Yukon golds, or baby Dutch yellows.

1¾ pounds (790 g) potatoes, sliced ⅛-inch (3 mm) thick
12 ounces (340 g) extra-firm tofu, drained and pressed
¼ cup (30 g) nutritional yeast
¼ cup (45 g) sesame oil
½ cup (110 g) soy creamer
2 tablespoons (15 g) cornstarch
2 tablespoons (40 g) white or yellow miso
1 tablespoon (10 g) garlic powder
1 tablespoon (10 g) onion powder
1 tablespoon (2 g) paprika
Pinch turmeric
Salt and pepper, to taste
Bread crumbs, for topping (optional)

Preheat the oven to 350°F (180°C, or gas mark 4).

Rinse the sliced potatoes in cold water to prevent discoloration, drain, and set aside.

Add the tofu, yeast, oil, creamer, cornstarch, miso, garlic powder, onion powder, paprika, turmeric, salt, and pepper to a blender and blend until smooth. In a bowl, combine the potatoes and the sauce, and then spread evenly in an 8 × 8-inch (20 × 20-cm) square baking dish. Sprinkle the top with bread crumbs, if desired.

Bake, covered with foil, for 45 minutes. Remove the foil and bake for an additional 30 minutes. Let rest for about 10 minutes before serving.

Yield: 6 servings

VARIATION

These potatoes lend themselves well to the addition of green vegetables. Steamed kale, broccoli, asparagus, or peas all make nice additions. Mix in the vegetables at the same time you mix the sauce with the potatoes.

Twice-Baked Potatoes

These are rich and decadent. If you have leftover filling, it tastes yummy on its own in a bowl!

8 russet potatoes
¼ cup (56 g) nondairy butter
¼ cup (30 g) nutritional yeast
½ cup (120 ml) plain nondairy creamer
1 cup (240 g) nondairy sour cream, store-bought or homemade (page 302)
Salt and pepper, to taste

Preheat the oven to 350°F (180°C, or gas mark 4).

Bake the potatoes, unwrapped, for about 1 hour, or until fork-tender.

Remove from the oven, and increase the oven temperature to 450°F (230°C, or gas mark 8).

Cut the potatoes in half lengthwise. Hollow out 8 of the halves, leaving about ¼ inch (6 mm) of flesh around the edge. Place the scooped-out flesh in a mixing bowl. Hollow out the remaining 8 halves completely, placing the flesh in the bowl and discarding the skins.

Combine the potato flesh, butter, yeast, creamer, sour cream, salt, and pepper like you are making mashed potatoes. You can do this with a hand masher or with a hand mixer. The smoother you get your mixture, the fancier you can make the tops.

Using a piping bag and your largest star tip, pipe the mixture into huge mounds inside the hollowed-out halves. If you don't have a piping bag, you can snip the corner off of a sandwich bag, or easier yet, you can simply spoon the mixture in and scrape the top with a fork to make decorative ridges.

Bake for 15 minutes, or until the tops are just beginning to brown.

Yield: 8 servings

Gluten Free Soy Free

Spicy Frites

Be sure to dry the potatoes thoroughly after washing, so they will crisp up nicely. (Another way to ensure extra crispness is to have the baking sheet preheat at the same time the oven does.) Peeling the potatoes is up to you; as long as the skin is scrubbed clean, there's no problem with leaving it on.

- 3 russet potatoes, scrubbed clean, cut into ½-inch-thick (1.3-cm) fries, and patted dry with paper towels
- 2 tablespoons (30 ml) peanut oil
- ½ teaspoon coarse sea salt, to taste, plus extra for serving
- ¼ teaspoon cayenne pepper, to taste
- 1 teaspoon garam masala, store-bought or homemade (page 305)
- Juice of ½ a lime, for serving

Preheat the oven to 425°F (220°C, or gas mark 7). Place a large-size rimmed baking sheet in the oven while it preheats.

Toss the fries in a large-size bowl together with the oil, salt, cayenne, and garam masala.

Spread the fries on the baking sheet, and bake for 25 to 30 minutes, until golden brown and crispy, checking every 10 to 15 minutes to make sure they don't burn.

Sprinkle with the lime juice and extra salt upon serving.

Yield: 2 servings

Mustard and Spinach Smashed Potatoes

Add some green to them taters! Spinach is rich in vitamins A, C, K, folate, riboflavin, and, of course, iron.

- 2½ pounds (1140 g) red potatoes
- 1 pound (455 g) spinach (frozen works well here)
- 3 tablespoons (35 g) stone-ground mustard
- ¼ cup (60 g) nondairy sour cream, store-bought or homemade (page 306)
- ¼ cup (56 g) nondairy butter
- Salt and pepper, to taste

Cut the potatoes into chunks. Leave the skin on or peel, your choice. Boil in salted water until fork-tender.

While the potatoes are boiling, prepare the spinach. If using frozen spinach, cook according to the package instructions. If using fresh, cook down in a large-size pot until reduced to about 3 cups. Drain and set aside.

Drain the potatoes and return to the pot.

Add the cooked spinach, mustard, sour cream, butter, salt, and pepper and mash until the desired consistency is reached.

Yield: 6 servings

Whiskey Sweet Potato Mash

This is quite a departure from traditional mashed potatoes. You won't be cooking off any of the whiskey here, so reserve this for your adults-only meals (or just omit the whiskey).

1 pound (455 g) sweet potatoes
1 pound (455 g) red or russet potatoes
½ cup (110 g) brown sugar
¼ cup (60 ml) pure maple syrup
¼ cup (56 g) nondairy butter
¼ cup (60 g) nondairy sour cream, store-bought or homemade (page 302)
¼ cup (60 ml) whiskey
Pinch cinnamon
Salt, to taste
¼ cup (50 g) toasted pecans

Peel the potatoes and boil until fork-tender.

Add the brown sugar, maple syrup, butter, sour cream, whiskey, cinnamon, and salt and mash until smooth. Some lumps are okay.

Fold in the pecans.

Yield: 4 large servings

 Under 30 Minutes

Kale Pesto Pasta

Kale is one of the most nutritionally generous leafy greens there is, with its high amounts of vitamins (A, C, and K) and calcium, so be sure to incorporate it into your meals as often as you can. Prepare the pesto while the pasta is cooking, and have a delicious and nutritious meal ready on the table in no time at all.

2 cups (220 g) whole wheat elbow macaroni
1 recipe Kale Pesto (page 294)
¼ cup (60 g) nondairy cream cheese
2 tablespoons (16 g) sesame seeds
2 tablespoons (16 g) nutritional yeast
¼ teaspoon ground black pepper, to taste

Cook the pasta in a medium-size saucepan, following the package directions, but aiming for the lowest cooking time.

Reserve 2 tablespoons (30 ml) of pasta water, drain the pasta, and set the colander with the pasta aside.

In the same saucepan, stir in the pesto, cream cheese, sesame seeds, nutritional yeast, pepper, and reserved pasta water. Transfer the pasta back to the saucepan. Let simmer for 5 minutes, to let the kale cook a bit and heat through.

Yield: 2 large servings

Under 30 Minutes  

Quinoa Pilaf

This versatile, protein-rich pilaf can be served warm, as a side dish, or chilled as a salad. Enjoy it with chopped radicchio, baby spinach, cherry tomatoes, and Crispy Tofu Fries (page 205), for extra crunch.

1 cup (168 g) uncooked quinoa, rinsed and drained
2 tablespoons (30 ml) extra-virgin olive oil
2 tablespoons (30 ml) fresh lemon juice
1 teaspoon fine sea salt, to taste
¼ to ½ teaspoon ground black pepper or cayenne pepper, to taste
1 teaspoon turmeric
1 clove garlic, grated
1 teaspoon grated gingerroot
½ teaspoon ground cumin
½ cup (80 g) mix of chopped dried dates, cherries, and raisins
Handful toasted slivered almonds
Handful chopped fresh parsley
1 carrot, peeled, washed, and grated

Fill a medium-size saucepan with water and bring to a boil. Add the quinoa and cook, uncovered, over medium-high heat for 10 minutes.

Drain and set aside, fluffing with a fork every now and then to let the steam escape and prevent further cooking.

In a large-size bowl, whisk together the oil, lemon juice, salt, pepper, turmeric, garlic, ginger, and cumin.

Stir in the quinoa and dried fruit. Decorate with the almonds, parsley, and carrot.

Yield: 2 large servings

Leek, Bean, and Rice Medley

If you could have a meal that is both comfort food and good for you at the same time, wouldn't you jump at the chance? Rejoice! Packed with a wonderful texture and surprising flavor combinations, this rice medley will keep you full for hours, and have you long for the eventual leftovers to come.

1 tablespoon (15 ml) extra-virgin olive oil
2 cloves garlic, grated
½ cup (80 g) uncooked wild rice, rinsed
¾ cup (140 g) uncooked long grain brown rice, rinsed
2½ cups (590 ml) water
1 teaspoon coarse sea salt, divided
1 can (15 ounces, or 425 g) cooked cannellini beans, drained and rinsed
⅓ cup (33 g) pecan halves, broken in half
2 tablespoons (28 g) nondairy butter
2 cups (178 g) chopped leeks (about 2 leeks)
1 large-size tomato, chopped
4 fresh basil leaves, cut into a chiffonade
1 tablespoon (15 ml) vegan Worcestershire sauce
1 tablespoon (15 ml) fresh lemon juice (optional)

Place the oil, garlic, and both types of rice in a large-size saucepan. Toast for a couple of minutes over medium-high heat, until fragrant.

Add the water and ½ teaspoon of the salt, bring to a boil, cover, and let simmer for about 45 minutes, or until the water is absorbed and the rice is tender.

Add the beans and pecans; heat for a minute or two. Set aside.

In a separate large-size skillet, melt the nondairy butter; add the leeks and remaining ½ teaspoon salt. Cook for 5 minutes, or until the leeks are wilted.

Add the tomato, basil, and Worcestershire. Let cook for 2 to 3 more minutes, then pour onto the rice, beans, and pecans.

Stir and heat through. Sprinkle with the lemon juice, if desired, before serving.

Yield: 4 servings

Low Fat

Eggplant, Lentil, and Rice Pilaf

The eggplant is peeled to ensure extreme creaminess in this dish. Serve with a side of your favorite steamed greens. For a version made with brown rice, precook the rice for 20 to 30 minutes before adding it in.

1 tablespoon (15 ml) peanut oil
1 large-size eggplant, peeled and cut into thin, bite-size pieces
1 teaspoon coarse sea salt
2 cloves garlic, grated
¼ cup (40 g) chopped shallot
1 tablespoon (6 g) grated gingerroot
1 teaspoon garam masala, store-bought or homemade (page 305)
1 teaspoon ground cumin
¼ teaspoon cayenne pepper, to taste
½ cup (96 g) uncooked red lentils, rinsed
½ cup (93 g) uncooked long grain white rice, rinsed
2½ cups (590 ml) water
1 tablespoon (15 ml) tamari or soy sauce
2 tablespoons (30 g) tamarind paste

In a large-size skillet, heat the oil. Stir in the eggplant and salt. Cook over medium-high heat for about 10 minutes, until the eggplant has browned up a little and is tender.

Stir in the garlic, shallot, and ginger. Cook for 2 minutes.

Stir in the garam masala, cumin, cayenne, drained lentils, and rice. Cook for 1 minute.

Stir in the water, tamari, and tamarind. Bring to a boil.

Cover with a lid, and let simmer over low to medium heat until the rice is tender and the water is absorbed, 20 to 22 minutes, stirring occasionally.

Let stand for a few minutes before serving.

Yield: 4 small servings

Balsamic Rice and Orzo Pilaf

This is the perfect dish to bring to a potluck or get-together. It doesn't have any "weird vegan" ingredients, so even your father-in-law won't be afraid to try it, plus it tastes good hot or cold.

5 cups (1175 ml) vegetable broth
¼ cup plus 1 tablespoon (75 ml) extra-virgin olive oil, divided
2 cups (368 g) uncooked long grain rice (brown or white)
2 cups (470 ml) water
1 cup (160 g) uncooked orzo
2 tablespoons (30 g) minced garlic
10 to 15 fresh basil leaves, tightly packed, then cut into a chiffonade
½ cup (60 g) toasted pine nuts
¼ cup (60 ml) balsamic vinegar
6 to 8 sun-dried tomatoes packed in oil, chopped
Salt and pepper, to taste

Bring the broth to a boil in a medium-size pot. Add 1 tablespoon (15 ml) of the olive oil and the rice. Reduce to a simmer, cover, and simmer for 20 to 30 minutes.

Add the water, return to a boil, add the orzo, cover, and boil for about 7 more minutes.

Uncover and let stand until all the moisture has been absorbed, 5 to 10 minutes.

Mix in the garlic, basil, pine nuts, vinegar, remaining ¼ cup oil, sun-dried tomatoes, salt, and pepper and serve.

Yield: 6 servings

Dirty Red Beans and Rice

Here's a recipe for some good old dirty rice, with some red beans thrown in for good measure. Enjoy with Red Jambalaya (page 151) or any dish that doesn't mind a little Southern flair!

2 tablespoons (30 ml) extra-virgin olive oil
1 green bell pepper, cored, seeded, and diced
1 cup (160 g) finely diced yellow onion
3 stalks celery, chopped
Pinch salt
2¾ cups (650 ml) vegetable broth
¼ cup (60 ml) soy sauce
1½ cups (270 g) uncooked long grain white rice
1 can (15 ounces, or 425 g) red beans, drained but not rinsed

In a saucepan or pot with a tight-fitting lid, heat the oil over medium heat.

Add the bell pepper, onion, celery, and salt. Cover and cook for about 15 minutes, or until very fragrant and reduced in volume by almost half. The onions should look translucent and the vegetables slightly browned.

Add the broth and soy sauce and deglaze the pot.

Bring to a boil.

Add the rice, return to a boil, and then reduce to a simmer.

Cover and simmer for about 20 minutes, or until most of the moisture has been absorbed. Stir in the beans, heat through, and enjoy!

Yield: 6 to 8 servings

Coconut Rice with Sugar Snap Peas

This creamy, tangy rice makes a great lunch or a wonderful addition to a nice Thai-inspired meal. Enjoy warm or cold.

1 can (14 ounces, or 414 ml) full-fat coconut milk
14 ounces (414 ml) water
2 cups (360 g) uncooked sushi rice
3 tablespoons (45 ml) lime juice
½ teaspoon salt
½ cup (8 g) fresh cilantro leaves
6 ounces (170 g) raw sugar snap peas, cut in half

Add the coconut milk, water, and uncooked rice to a saucepan or pot with a tight-fitting lid and bring to a boil.

Immediately reduce the heat to low, cover, and simmer for 20 minutes, or until most of the moisture has been absorbed. Try not to remove the lid while simmering.

Remove from the heat, uncover, and stir in the lime juice, salt, and cilantro leaves.

Fold in the raw sugar snap peas.

Yield: 6 servings

Veggie Fried Rice

Nothing pairs better with a Chinese-style meal than veggie fried rice. This is basically some plain white rice all dressed up with veggies and spices, and if you so fancy, a bit of chopped tofu. As always, fresh veggies are best, but use frozen if necessary.

¼ cup (60 ml) canola or other vegetable oil for stir-frying, divided
1 cup (67 g) green peas
½ cup (54 g) shredded carrot
½ cup (68 g) yellow corn kernels
½ cup (35 g) thinly sliced button mushrooms
½ cup (60 g) chopped celery
4 ounces (112 g) extra-firm tofu, chopped into small cubes (optional)
1 teaspoon salt
½ teaspoon ground aniseed or fennel
⅛ teaspoon Chinese five-spice powder, store-bought or homemade (page 307)
4 cups (630 g) fully cooked long grain white rice, preferably cold
2 tablespoons (30 ml) soy sauce or tamari
½ cup (60 g) chopped scallion

In a wok or very large frying pan, heat 2 tablespoons (30 ml) of the oil over high heat.

Add the peas, carrot, corn, mushrooms, celery, and tofu, if using.

Stir in the salt, aniseed, and five-spice powder.

Stir-fry for about 2 minutes. Remove the vegetables from the wok and set aside.

Heat the remaining 2 tablespoons (30 ml) oil, and stir-fry the rice for about 2 minutes.

Add the soy sauce, cooked vegetable mixture, and scallion and toss and cook for 2 more minutes.

Remove from the heat and serve hot.

Yield: 4 large servings

Quinoa with Hazelnut Parsley Pesto

If you aren't a fan of Brussels sprouts, use any other green vegetable, such as kale, bok choy, or spinach.

For the pesto:

¼ cup (34 g) hazelnuts, toasted (see note)
2 cloves garlic, grated
2 tablespoons (30 ml) fresh lemon juice
1 teaspoon coarse sea salt
1½ cups (90 g) fresh curly parsley
¼ cup (60 ml) extra-virgin olive oil

For the quinoa:

4 cups (940 ml) water
1 cup (168 g) uncooked quinoa, rinsed and drained

For the sprouts:

1 tablespoon (15 ml) canola oil
¼ cup (40 g) chopped white onion
10 Brussels sprouts, trimmed, cleaned, and quartered
1 tablespoon (15 ml) fresh lemon juice
½ teaspoon coarse sea salt
1 tablespoon (15 ml) sherry wine or water, if needed

To make the pesto: In a food processor, blend the hazelnuts into a meal.

Add the garlic, lemon juice, salt, and parsley, and process for 1 minute. Drizzle in as much oil as needed to get a paste, and process until well combined, scraping the sides occasionally.

To make the quinoa: Bring the water to a boil in a medium-size saucepan. Stir in the quinoa and cook over medium heat, uncovered, for 10 minutes. Drain the quinoa, and combine with the pesto in a large-size bowl. Set aside.

To make the sprouts: In a large-size saucepan, heat the oil and cook the onion over medium heat until translucent, about 4 minutes.

Stir in the Brussels sprouts, lemon juice, and salt. Cook until tender, 6 to 8 minutes.

Deglaze the pan with the sherry, if the sprouts stick to the pan.

Add to the quinoa pesto. Serve warm.

Yield: 2 large servings

NOTE

To toast the nuts, preheat the oven to 350°F (180°C, or gas mark 4), and place the hazelnuts on a rimmed baking sheet in a single layer. Bake for 10 to 15 minutes, or until lightly colored. Wrap in a kitchen towel and leave covered for about a minute, to steam. Rub with the towel to remove as much of the skin as possible. Let cool.

Mac and Sleaze

This simple pasta dish may not contain "real" cheese, but it is deliciously comforting nonetheless.

8 ounces (227 g) whole-grain pasta of choice (penne, rotini, macaroni)

For the topping:

1 cup (80 g) whole wheat panko or other bread crumbs
½ teaspoon fine sea salt
1 teaspoon Italian seasoning
2 tablespoons (30 ml) extra-virgin olive oil

For the sauce:

1 cup (120 g) nutritional yeast
2 tablespoons (16 g) arrowroot powder or any other flour
1 teaspoon garlic powder
1 teaspoon fine sea salt
1 teaspoon chili powder
2 cups (470 ml) water or unsweetened soy or other nondairy milk, for creamier and richer results
1 tablespoon (16 g) tahini
2 tablespoons (28 g) nondairy butter
1 teaspoon yellow mustard (optional)

Preheat the oven to 375°F (190°C, or gas mark 5). Have ready an 8-inch (20-cm) square baking dish.

Cook the pasta following the package directions. Drain, but reserve ¼ cup (60 ml) of the pasta water in case the pasta needs extra liquid after being combined with the sauce later.

To make the topping: Combine all the ingredients in a medium-size bowl, stirring with a fork until the panko is coated with the oil. Set aside.

To make the sauce: Place the yeast, arrowroot, garlic powder, salt, chili powder, water, and tahini in a medium-size saucepan. Whisk to combine. Cook over medium-high heat, whisking constantly, until the sauce thickens. Whisk in the butter and mustard, if using. Place the sauce and cooked pasta in the baking pan, stirring to combine. If the sauce is too thick, add the reserved pasta water, a little at a time.

Sprinkle the topping over the pasta. Cover with foil.

Bake, covered, for 20 minutes. Remove the foil and bake for 10 more minutes, or until the topping is golden brown. Let stand for 10 minutes before serving, to let it firm up.

Yield: 4 servings

Under 30 Minutes

Cheater Mac and Cheese

Don't have the time to make the full-blown Mac and Sleaze (page 171)? Enter Cheater Mac and Cheese, a quick, easy, cheater recipe for a creamy, delicious bowl of kid-friendly mac.

1 pound (455 g) elbow macaroni
½ cup (120g) nondairy sour cream, store-bought or homemade (page 302)
½ cup (112 g) nondairy butter
½ cup (60 g) nutritional yeast
2 tablespoons (36 g) white or yellow miso
2 teaspoons paprika
2 teaspoons garlic powder
1 teaspoon ground mustard
Salt and pepper, to taste

Prepare the pasta according to the package directions. Drain and return the pasta to the pot. Add the sour cream, butter, yeast, miso, paprika, garlic powder, mustard, salt, and pepper, and mix together well. Done!

Yield: 6 servings

Creamy Barley-sotto

If you are the proud owner of black truffle oil, this deliciously earthy and refined dish is begging for you to make good use of it by drizzling some on your plate upon serving.

3 cups (705 ml) water or vegetable broth, or a combination of the two
½ cup (90 g) uncooked pearl barley, rinsed
1 tablespoon (15 ml) extra-virgin olive oil
1 clove garlic, grated
1 tablespoon (10 g) chopped shallot
1 pound (455 g) green asparagus, cut on the diagonal into 1-inch (2.5-cm) pieces
1 tablespoon (15 ml) fresh lemon juice
6 dried shiitake mushrooms, soaked in warm water for 30 minutes until hydrated, excess water gently squeezed out, and thinly sliced
¼ cup (28 g) drained and thinly sliced oil-packed sun-dried tomatoes
½ teaspoon grated nutmeg
½ teaspoon black pepper, to taste
½ teaspoon fine sea salt, to taste
½ teaspoon dried thyme
¼ cup (60 ml) soy creamer or unsweetened nondairy milk
Black truffle oil or more extra-virgin olive oil, to drizzle upon serving

Bring the water to a boil in a large-size saucepan. Add the barley, cover with a lid, and cook for 40 minutes, or until the barley is tender. Drain and set aside.

In a large-size saucepan, heat the oil over medium-high heat. Cook the garlic and shallot for 2 minutes, stirring often. Stir in the asparagus. Cook for 5 minutes, then stir in the lemon juice. Cook for another 5 minutes, or until tender.

Stir in the cooked barley, mushrooms, and tomatoes. Add the nutmeg, pepper, salt, and thyme. Cook for 1 minute, or until fragrant. Add the creamer and cook until the liquid is mostly absorbed, stirring often.

Serve hot, with a few droplets of black truffle oil sprinkled on top.

Yield: 2 large servings

MexiQuinoa

This is a healthy alternative to traditional Spanish rice and makes a great accompaniment to all of your favorite Mexican dishes. It tastes great as a hot dish, but it is even better the next day after all of the flavors have really melded together!

4 cups (940 ml) water
2 cups (336 g) dry quinoa
2 cups (420 g) yellow corn kernels
1 can (15 ounces, or 420 g) black beans (pinto would work well, too), drained and rinsed
1 can (4 ounces, or 112 g) nacho-style sliced jalapeño peppers, drained
1 cup (235 ml) chunky salsa
2 tablespoons (30 ml) extra-virgin olive oil
1 tablespoon (15 ml) lemon or lime juice
¼ teaspoon ground cumin
1 teaspoon garlic powder
1 teaspoon onion powder
1 teaspoon red pepper flakes
1 teaspoon dried oregano or 1 tablespoon (4 g) fresh
Salt and pepper, to taste

Optional Toppings:

½ cup (75 g) diced bell pepper
½ cup (80 g) finely diced red onion
¼ cup (16 g) finely chopped cilantro
½ cup (126 g) seeded and diced tomatoes

In a saucepot, bring the water to a boil. Add the quinoa, return to a boil, then reduce the heat and cook, covered, for 10 to 12 minutes, or until all the water has been absorbed and the quinoa "tails" have unfurled.

Remove from the heat. Fluff with a fork, cover, and let sit for another 10 minutes.

While the quinoa is cooling, combine all the other ingredients in a large-size bowl.

When the quinoa is ready, mix it into the other ingredients. Serve with toppings, if desired.

Yield: 12 servings

Pumpkin Spinach Ravioli

If you don't have a pasta roller, no problem! All you need is a flat surface and a rolling pin. These taste great topped with the Garlic and Sage Cashew Cream Sauce (page 296).

For the dough:

2 cups (334 g) semolina flour, plus more for dusting
Pinch salt
1 cup (235 ml) water

For the filling:

1 can (15 ounces, or 420 g) spinach, drained
1 can (15 ounces, or 420 g) solid-pack pure pumpkin purée
½ cup (120 g) vegan cream cheese
½ teaspoon garlic powder
½ teaspoon ground sage
Salt and pepper, to taste

To make the dough: In a mixing bowl, combine the flour and salt, add the water, and knead into a nice soft, but firm, elastic dough ball, about 5 minutes.

Divide into 4 equal pieces. Leave in the bowl, cover the bowl with a dish towel, and let rest for about 30 minutes.

After the dough has rested, dust your rolling surface with flour.

Flatten one of the pieces and roll it out with a rolling pin. Roll it out very thin, to 1⁄16 inch (1.5 mm).

Take the sheet of pasta dough and lay it on a dish towel on a flat surface. Cover with another dish towel. Repeat with the remaining 3 pieces. It is okay to stack the pasta sheets on top of one another. They should be pretty dry after rolling, and not too sticky. If they are too sticky, dust in between the sheets with additional semolina flour.

To make the filling: In a mixing bowl, combine all the filling ingredients.

Bring a pot of salted water to a boil.

To make the raviolis, lay one sheet of pasta dough on a flat surface. Using approximately a 3-inch (7.5-cm) circular cookie cutter or a pint glass, cut as many circles as possible from the sheet. Stack the circles, and reserve the remaining dough. Repeat with the remaining sheets. Your goal is 60 or more circles, which is enough to make 30 ravioli. If needed, you can reroll the remaining dough after cutting the circles.

Once all of the circles are cut, spoon about 1 tablespoon (15 g) of the filling into the center of one circle.

Top with another circle, and use a fork to seal the edges.

Drop 3 or 4 ravioli into the boiling water. Boil for 3 to 5 minutes, then remove from the water with a slotted spoon. Return the water to a boil. Add 3 or 4 more ravioli, and cook as before, repeating until all the ravioli are cooked.

Serve warm, topped with your favorite pasta sauce or the Garlic and Sage Cashew Cream Sauce (page 300). White sauces taste much better than reds with this one.

Yield: About 30 ravioli

Garlic and Herb Gnocchi

These soft, billowy potato dumplings do not take long to prepare and taste wonderful right out of the pot. Plus they're a great project for kids!

1 pound (455 g) red potatoes
2 tablespoons (30 ml) extra-virgin olive oil
1 cup (125 g) all-purpose flour, plus more for dusting
½ teaspoon dried basil or 1 tablespoon (3 g) finely chopped fresh
1 teaspoon garlic powder
1 teaspoon onion powder
Salt and pepper, to taste

Preheat the oven 400°F (200°C, or gas mark 6).

Prick a few holes in the potatoes with the tines of a fork and bake, uncovered, for 1 hour. Remove from the oven and let cool completely.

Scoop out the flesh of the potatoes and place in a mixing bowl. Discard the skins.

Add the olive oil and mash the potatoes until there are as few lumps as possible.

Add the flour, basil, garlic powder, onion powder, salt, and pepper. Knead until a nice soft dough forms. Depending on the moisture of the potatoes, you may need a little more or a little less flour.

Turn out onto a well-floured surface. Divide into 4 equal pieces.

Roll each piece into a rope about 8 inches (20 cm) long.

Cut each rope into 12 equal pieces.

From here, you can freeze the gnocchi to use at a later date by placing them in a single layer on a baking sheet and freezing until solid, then transferring them to an airtight storage container.

Or you can cook them fresh. Bring a pot of water to a full boil. Add the gnocchi, about 12 at a time, being careful not to overcrowd them, and boil until they float to the top of the water.

Serve immediately, topped with your favorite pasta sauce, or lightly sauté in a bit of olive oil and sprinkle with salt and pepper.

Yield: 48 gnocchi, or 4 servings

VARIATION

Red potatoes work well for gnocchi because of their soft, creamy texture, but if you cannot find reds, russets, Yukons, or fingerlings will work just as well. For a heavier, more dumpling-like gnocchi, you can also peel the potatoes and cut them into chunks. Boil until fork-tender, then drain and return to the pot or a mixing bowl and let cool completely. Once cooled, proceed as directed.

Whole Wheat Pumpkin Gnocchi

Gnocchi with a twist! The sweetness of the pumpkin adds a nice flavor dimension here. These gnocchi taste wonderful lightly sautéed in a little olive oil or nondairy butter, served alone with a little salt and pepper, or topped with the Garlic and Sage Cashew Cream Sauce (page 296).

1 pound (455 g) red potatoes
2 tablespoons (30 g) extra-virgin olive oil
½ cup (122 g) solid-pack pure pumpkin purée
1½ to 2 cups (180 to 240 g) whole wheat pastry flour, plus more for dusting
1 teaspoon ground sage
Pinch nutmeg
Salt and pepper, to taste

Peel the potatoes and cut into chunks. Boil until fork-tender. Drain and return to the pot or a mixing bowl.

Add the olive oil and pumpkin and mash the potatoes until there are as few lumps as possible. Let cool completely.

Add the flour, sage, nutmeg, salt, and pepper. Knead until a nice soft dough forms. Depending on the moisture of the potatoes, you may need a little more or a little less flour.

Turn out onto a well-floured surface. Divide into 6 equal pieces.

Roll each piece into a rope about 8 inches (20 cm) long.

Cut each rope into 12 equal pieces.

From here, you can freeze the gnocchi to use at a later date by placing them in a single layer on a baking sheet and freezing until solid, then transferring them to an airtight storage container.

Or you can cook them fresh. Bring a pot of water to a full boil. Add the gnocchi, about 12 at a time, being careful not to overcrowd them, and boil until they float to the top of the water.

Sauté in a little olive oil or nondairy butter until crisped. Serve immediately.

Yield: 72 gnocchi, or 6 servings

Under 30 Minutes   Soy Free

Moroccan Spaghetti

Here's a delightfully spicy twist on a type of pasta that's typically prepared "Italian-style," but is really much more versatile than it gets credit for.

1 tablespoon (15 ml) peanut oil
½ cup (80 g) diced red onion
2 cloves garlic, grated
1 zucchini, quartered and chopped
1 red bell pepper, diced
¼ cup (40 g) raisins
2 teaspoons ground cumin
2 teaspoons paprika
1 teaspoon ground ginger
Pinch ground cinnamon
1 can (15 ounces, or 425 g) tomato sauce
1 can (15 ounces, or 425 g) cooked garbanzo beans, drained and rinsed
4 ounces (130 g) whole wheat spaghetti, broken lengthwise into 3 pieces
1 cup (235 ml) water
½ teaspoon fine sea salt, to taste
Handful roasted peanuts, for garnish (optional)

In a large-size pot, heat the oil and add the onion, garlic, zucchini, bell pepper, and raisins. Cook for 4 minutes.

Add the cumin, paprika, ginger, and cinnamon, stir, and cook for 1 minute, until fragrant.

Pour in the tomato sauce and beans, stir in the spaghetti, and add the water to cover the pasta. Sprinkle with the salt.

Stir well, cover, and let simmer over medium-high heat for 10 minutes, checking and stirring occasionally to make sure there's enough liquid and that it doesn't stick to the bottom of the pot.

Remove the lid and let cook for another 5 minutes, until the pasta is al dente and the liquid is absorbed; the end result shouldn't be a soup. On the other hand, add more water or even broth if the pasta isn't cooked to your taste just yet.

Sprinkle with the peanuts upon serving, if desired.

Yield: 4 servings

Under 30 Minutes

Tofu Caprese Pasta

This spin on the traditional Caprese salad boasts heart-healthy olive oil, an extra boost of protein from the tofu, and some zip from the fresh tomatoes and basil. Enjoy this dish warm or cold, or simply make it without the pasta and enjoy over crostini, or toasted bread.

1 pound (455 g) pasta (penne rigate works well)
12 ounces (336 g) extra-firm tofu, drained and pressed
1 cup (180 g) diced Roma tomatoes
20 leaves fresh basil, tightly packed, then cut into a chiffonade
2 tablespoons (30 g) minced garlic
¼ cup (60 ml) extra-virgin olive oil
Salt and pepper, to taste

Cook the pasta in salted water according to the package directions.

While the pasta is cooking, chop the tofu into tiny, tiny cubes, about ¼ inch (6 mm) maximum. Combine the tofu, tomatoes, basil, garlic, olive oil, salt, and pepper in a mixing bowl. Drain the pasta, toss with the sauce, and enjoy!

Yield: 8 side- or 4 main-dish servings

 Under 30 Minutes 

Israeli Couscous with Curry, Cashews, and Currants

Israeli couscous, otherwise known as pearl couscous or maftoul, *resembles tiny white peas and is a bit larger and more pearl-like than regular couscous. It is also a bit more toothsome and perfect for all types of exotic preparations, such as this one.*

2 cups (470 ml) water, salted to taste
1 cup (173 g) dry Israeli couscous
¼ cup (60 ml) extra-virgin olive oil
¼ cup (36 g) currants
¼ cup (35 g) cashew pieces
1 tablespoon (2 g) dried parsley or 3 tablespoons (12 g) fresh
1 teaspoon yellow curry powder, store-bought or homemade (page 307)
Salt and pepper, to taste

Bring the salted water to a boil. Add the couscous, reduce to a simmer, cover, and cook for 8 to 10 minutes, stirring often to prevent scorching, or until the water is absorbed. Fluff with a fork. Stir in the oil, currants, cashews, parsley, curry powder, salt, and pepper.

Yield: About 2½ cups (4 side- or 2 main-dish servings)

Chapter 9

Casseroles and Savory Pies and Tarts

Sophisticated comfort food, ahoy! From classic favorites such as Shepherd's Pie (but with a Latin twist) to slightly more unexpected dishes such as Lentil Tarts in Tahini Crust, this chapter will inspire you to create one-dish meals that truly satisfy.

Soy Free

Caramelized Onion Tart with Sweet Potato Sage Crust

This is a deliciously refined tart that takes far less work and time than you might think. The leftover "sprinkles" are also scrumptious liberally sprinkled on salads, soups, and stews.

For the crust:

½ cup (128 g) sweet potato purée, at room temperature
¼ cup (60 ml) water, heated to 100°F (38°C)
2 tablespoons (30 ml) canola oil, plus more for coating
1 tablespoon (21 g) agave nectar
1 cup (120 g) white whole wheat flour or regular whole wheat flour, plus more for dusting
¾ cup (90 g) light spelt flour
1 teaspoon dried sage
⅛ teaspoon cayenne pepper
⅛ teaspoon ground nutmeg
1 teaspoon fine sea salt
1 teaspoon bread machine yeast

For the caramelized onions:

3 tablespoons (45 ml) peanut oil
2 softball-size red onions, cut into rings, then into half-moons
2 large-size shallots, thinly sliced
4 cloves garlic, grated
½ teaspoon coarse sea salt, to taste

For the Parmesan-like sprinkles:

2 tablespoons (16 g) roasted, salted sunflower seeds
2 tablespoons (18 g) sesame seeds
2 tablespoons (16 g) nutritional yeast
½ teaspoon coarse sea salt
1 teaspoon dried sage

To make the crust: In a medium-size bowl, combine the sweet potato purée, water, oil, and agave.

In a large-size bowl, combine the flours, sage, cayenne pepper, nutmeg, salt, and yeast.

Stir the flour mixture into the sweet potato mixture.

Transfer to a lightly floured surface and knead for 8 to 10 minutes, or until the dough is smooth and pliable, adding more flour if the dough is too wet. Shape into a ball.

Lightly coat a large-size bowl with oil, add the dough, and turn the dough to coat. Cover tightly with plastic wrap, and let rise until doubled, 60 to 90 minutes. While the dough is rising, make the caramelized onions and sprinkles.

To make the onions: Place all the onion ingredients in a large-size, shallow saucepan. Cook for about 20 minutes over medium-low heat, or until the onions are caramelized and brown. Set aside.

To make the sprinkles: Place all the sprinkle ingredients in a coffee grinder or a food processor. Blend until pulverized into a fine powder. Set aside.

Twenty or 30 minutes before the dough is done rising, preheat the oven to 400°F (200°C, or gas mark 6). Have a large-size rimless baking sheet handy, as well as a large-size piece of parchment or silicone baking mat, such as Silpat.

Punch down the dough, and roll it into an 8 × 10-inch (20 × 25-cm) rectangle directly on the parchment or Silpat.

Sprinkle (all, or most of them, depending on your taste) the onions on top first, then add some of the sprinkles, to taste.

Bake for 18 minutes, or until the edges of the crust are golden brown.

Serve with a nice salad of mixed greens.

Yield: 6 servings

Balsamic Onion and Potato-Topped Focaccia

As if the herbed focaccia weren't enough, the rich béchamel, starchy potatoes, and sweet and tangy balsamic caramelized onions make this savory tart irresistible.

For the focaccia:

1 envelope (¼ ounce, or 7 g) active dry yeast
1 teaspoon evaporated cane juice or granulated sugar
½ cup (120 ml) water, heated to 100°F (38°C)
1 cup (120 g) whole wheat pastry flour
1 cup (125 g) all-purpose flour
2 tablespoons (16 g) onion powder
1 tablespoon (2 g) dried basil
½ teaspoon salt
½ teaspoon freshly cracked pepper
Olive oil, for coating

For the potatoes:

1 pound (455 g) potatoes
Nonstick cooking spray

For the onions:

2 tablespoons (30 ml) extra virgin olive oil
1 large-size red onion, sliced into rings
Pinch salt
¼ cup (60 ml) balsamic vinegar
2 tablespoons (30 g) minced garlic
2 tablespoons (30 ml) extra-virgin olive oil
1 recipe Béchamel Sauce (page 298)

To make the focaccia: Mix together the yeast, cane juice, and warm water in a medium-size bowl. Let proof for about 10 minutes; it should foam and bubble up. If it doesn't, start over again because your yeast might not be fresh.

In a large-size bowl, combine the flours, onion powder, basil, salt, and pepper. Add the yeast mixture and begin to knead. If the dough is too dry, add more water, 1 tablespoon (15 ml) at a time, until you can incorporate all of the flour. Knead for about 5 minutes, until you get a soft, elastic, uniform dough ball. Lightly coat the ball with oil, cover lightly with plastic wrap, and let rise for 45 minutes to 1 hour.

To make the potatoes: Use whatever kind of potatoes you like. Red ones cook faster than russets, so your end result will be creamier. Also, it's up to you whether or not to peel the potatoes. I almost always leave the skins on. If you have a mandolin-type slicer, set it on a very thin setting and use it! If not, just use a sharp knife, cutting the thinnest slices you can. After all the slicing is done, make sure you rinse the potatoes in cold water to prevent discoloration.

Preheat the oven to 350°F (180°C, or gas mark 4) and prepare a glass 9 × 13-inch (23 × 33-cm) baking dish by lightly greasing or spraying with nonstick cooking spray.

To make the onions: In a large-size frying pan, heat the oil over medium heat. Add the onion and salt and sauté until translucent and beginning to brown, 5 to 7 minutes. Add the vinegar and continue to cook for 2 to 3 more minutes, tossing to coat. Remove from the heat.

Punch down the dough. Press the dough into the baking dish, making sure you get it into the corners, and make lots of dimples in the surface with your fingers. Using a fork, poke holes all over the surface of the dough.

Spread the minced garlic all over the top of the dough, then drizzle with the olive oil. Layer the potatoes to completely cover and spread the béchamel sauce all over the potatoes. Top with the balsamic caramelized onions.

Bake for 1 hour, or until the potatoes are fork-tender and the edges are beginning to brown. Let cool before slicing and serving.

Yield: 8 pieces

Lentil Tart with Tahini Crust

Rich in flavor and healthy fiber, this crusty tart is perfect for all occasions, from fancy dinners to meals on the go. Serve with mixed greens drizzled with a simple dressing on the side, and meet your daily veggie intake requirements without even breaking a sweat.

Nonstick cooking spray

For the crust:

3 tablespoons (48 g) tahini
¼ teaspoon fine sea salt
1¼ cups (150 g) light spelt flour
¼ cup plus 1 tablespoon (75 ml) water

For the filling:

4 cups (940 ml) water
1 cup (192 g) uncooked brown or red lentils
1 tablespoon (15 ml) extra-virgin olive oil
1 red bell pepper, finely diced
¼ cup (40 g) finely chopped red onion
2 cloves garlic, grated or finely minced
½ teaspoon ground black or white pepper, to taste
1 teaspoon coarse sea salt
2 teaspoons garam masala, store-bought or homemade (page 305)
1 teaspoon ground cumin
¼ teaspoon cayenne pepper, to taste
½ teaspoon turmeric
½ teaspoon ground coriander
½ cup (123 g) tomato sauce
1 tablespoon (17 g) tomato paste
1 tablespoon (21 g) agave nectar

Preheat the oven to 375°F (190°C, or gas mark 5). Lightly coat an 8-inch (20-cm) pie plate with nonstick spray.

To make the crust: In a stand mixer or food processor, combine the tahini, salt, and flour. Add the water, 1 tablespoon (15 ml) at a time, until a dough forms.

Shape into a disk. Roll out the crust and transfer to the prepared pie plate. Lightly prick the crust across the bottom to prevent air bubbles. Set aside.

To make the filling: Bring the water to a boil in a medium-size saucepan. Add the lentils and cook for 25 minutes if using brown lentils, 15 minutes if using red lentils, or until tender to preference. Drain, and set aside.

In a large-size saucepan, heat the oil over medium-high heat. Cook the bell pepper, onion, and garlic for 4 minutes, or until tender.

Stir in the black pepper, salt, garam masala, cumin, cayenne, turmeric, and coriander, and cook for 1 minute, or until fragrant.

Stir in the tomato sauce, tomato paste, agave, and cooked lentils. Lower the heat, cover with a lid, and let simmer for 5 minutes.

Pour the lentil filling into the prepared crust and level the top with a spatula. Bake for 40 minutes, or until the edges of the crust are golden and the filling is set. Let stand for 15 minutes before slicing and serving.

Yield: One 8-inch (20-cm) tart

Spicy Chorizo Veggie Pie

It's all salsa, all the time, with this pie that makes reaching your daily quota of vegetables sound more like a treat than ever before. Control the amount of heat by picking the appropriate salsa. And if you just can't get enough of the spicy stuff, or have people with different heat tolerance levels joining you at the table, go with a mild salsa and set some extra hot sauce on the table upon serving.

For the crust:

¼ cup (60 ml) water, heated to 100°F (38°C)
1¼ teaspoons active dry yeast
1 tablespoon (21 g) agave nectar
2½ cups (300 g) bread flour, plus more for dusting
1 teaspoon fine sea salt
½ cup (120 g) salsa, store-bought or homemade (page 83)
1 tablespoon plus ½ teaspoon (18 ml) canola oil, divided

For the filling:

1 teaspoon canola oil
6 ounces (170 g) store-bought soy chorizo or 1 recipe Seitan Chorizo Crumbles (page 209)
2 cloves garlic, grated
¼ cup (40 g) chopped white onion
2 teaspoons ground cumin
⅔ cup (90 g) frozen corn
⅔ cup (90 g) frozen green peas
1 cup (240 g) salsa, store-bought or homemade (page 81)
Drizzle of hot sauce, such as Tabasco, for serving

To make the crust: In a small-size bowl, combine the water, yeast, and agave. Let proof for about 10 minutes: it should foam and bubble up. If it doesn't, start over again because your yeast might not be fresh.

In a large-size bowl, stir together the flour, salt, salsa, and 1 tablespoon (15 ml) of the oil.

Stir the proofed yeast into the flour mixture. Transfer to a lightly floured surface and knead for 8 to 10 minutes, or until the dough is smooth and pliable, adding more flour if the dough is too sticky. Shape into a ball.

Lightly coat a large-size bowl with the remaining ½ teaspoon oil. Turn the dough around to coat, cover, and let rise for 90 minutes, or until doubled in size. Prepare the filling while the dough is rising.

To make the filling: In a large-size saucepan, heat the oil. Crumble the soy chorizo into the pan, and add the garlic, onion, and cumin. Cook over medium heat until lightly browned, about 4 minutes.

Add the corn, peas, and salsa. Simmer for 6 minutes.

Preheat the oven to 375°F (190°C, or gas mark 5). Line a baking sheet with parchment paper or a silicone baking mat, such as Silpat.

Punch down the dough, and roll it out into an 8 × 10-inch (20 × 25-cm) rectangle directly on the parchment or Silpat.

Spread the filling evenly on top; let rest for at least 20 minutes, while the oven is preheating.

Bake for 24 minutes, or until the edges of the crust are golden brown.

Drizzle with hot sauce, if desired, upon serving.

Yield: 4 servings

Curry Cashew Tofu Bake

Rich and full of warmth, this casserole is truly comfort food. We suggest topping it with a recipe of Garlic and Sage Cashew Cream Sauce (page 296) for extra goodness.

1 can (15 ounces, or 450 ml) full-fat coconut milk
1 tablespoon (6 g) yellow curry powder, store-bought or homemade (page 307)
8 ounces (224 g) mushrooms, chopped
12 ounces (340 g) extra-firm tofu, drained, pressed, and crumbled
2 tablespoons (16 g) cornstarch mixed with 2 tablespoons (30 ml) water to make a slurry
Nonstick cooking spray (optional)
2 cups (250 g) all-purpose flour
2 tablespoons (16 g) vegetable broth powder
1 tablespoon (8 g) garlic powder
Salt and pepper, to taste
1 tablespoon (15 ml) coconut or other vegetable oil, for sautéing
1 can (15 ounces, or 425 g) garbanzo beans, drained and rinsed
1 yellow or white onion, diced
4 cloves garlic, minced
¼ cup (35 g) ground raw cashews
¼ cup (30 g) nutritional yeast
¼ teaspoon paprika

In a large-size skillet, bring the coconut milk and curry powder to a boil. Reduce to a simmer. Add the mushrooms and crumbled tofu. Cover and simmer for about 15 minutes, then uncover and cook for another 10 minutes.

Slowly add the cornstarch slurry, mix well, and cook for 3 to 5 more minutes, or until thickened. Remove from the heat, and let cool.

Preheat the oven to 350°F (180°C, or gas mark 4). Prepare an 8-inch (20-cm) square casserole dish, either by lightly oiling or by spraying lightly with nonstick spray.

In a mixing bowl, mix together the flour, veggie broth powder, garlic powder, salt, and pepper. Add the flour mixture to the coconut curry tofu mixture and knead together until a sticky dough forms. Set aside.

In a skillet, heat the oil and sauté the beans, onion, and garlic for 5 to 7 minutes, or until just beginning to brown.

Spread the dough in the bottom of the dish, pressing into the corners. Layer the bean and onion mixture on top of the dough. Sprinkle the ground cashews all over the top, then the nutritional yeast, and finally, the paprika.

Bake, covered with foil, for 20 to 25 minutes, then uncover and bake for an additional 10 minutes to brown the top. Remove from the oven, and let cool for about 10 minutes before serving.

Yield: 6 servings

Tempeh Spinach Rustic Pie

This flavorful and protein-packed healthy pie may look mighty fancy and time-consuming, but in reality it takes less than an hour to put together. Dazzle your guests by serving it alongside a simple plate of arugula leaves and slices of oranges dressed with a drizzle of extra-virgin olive oil and white balsamic vinegar.

For the filling:

- 2 teaspoons orange zest (from about 2 oranges)
- ½ cup (120 ml) freshly squeezed orange juice (from about 2 oranges)
- 2 tablespoons (40 g) all-fruit orange marmalade
- 1 tablespoon (15 ml) toasted sesame oil
- 2 tablespoons (30 ml) soy sauce
- 3 cloves garlic, grated
- ½ teaspoon red pepper flakes, to taste (optional)
- 2 teaspoons ground ginger
- 8 ounces (227 g) tempeh, crumbled
- 1 tablespoon (15 ml) peanut oil
- 2 cups (380 g) frozen chopped spinach

For the crust:

- 3 tablespoons (48 g) tahini
- ¼ teaspoon fine sea salt
- 1¼ cups (150 g) light spelt flour
- ¼ cup plus 1 tablespoon (75 ml) freshly squeezed orange juice (from about 1 orange)

To make the filling: In a medium-size bowl, whisk together the zest, juice, marmalade, sesame oil, soy sauce, garlic, red pepper flakes, if using, and ginger. Stir in the tempeh.

Marinate in the fridge for 30 minutes, stirring once halfway through.

Heat the oil in a large-size saucepan. Cook the marinated tempeh, along with the marinade, over medium heat until it browns up, about 8 minutes. Add the spinach and cook until heated through, about 5 minutes.

Preheat the oven to 375°F (190°C, or gas mark 5). Line a rimless baking sheet with parchment paper or a silicone baking mat, such as Silpat.

To make the crust: In a stand mixer or food processor, combine the tahini, salt, and flour. Add the orange juice, 1 tablespoon (15 ml) at a time, until a dough forms.

Shape into a disk. Roll out the dough to approximately 11 × 10 inches (28 × 25 cm), a little over ⅛ inch (3 mm) thick.

Transfer to the prepared baking sheet.

Place the filling on top of the prepared crust, leaving about 1 inch (2.5 cm) from the edges; the filling will pile up high. Level the filling, and fold the edges of the pie crust up to form a wall of sorts, leaving some of the filling visible.

Bake for 25 to 30 minutes, or until the top of the crust is golden brown.

Let stand for 10 minutes before slicing and serving.

Yield: 6 servings

Enchilada Casserole

Easy to toss together and throw in the oven, this hot, hearty meal is less than an hour away—and most of that time is bake time!

Nonstick cooking spray
6 to 8 flour or corn tortillas
2 cups (470 ml) enchilada sauce, store-bought or homemade (page 288), divided
2 recipes Seitan Chorizo Crumbles (page 209) or 12 ounces (340 g) store-bought soy chorizo, divided
2 cups (320 g) diced onion
1 recipe Nutty Cheese, Mexican variation (page 88) or 12 ounces (340 g) Mexican-flavored vegan cheese
2 ounces (56 g) sliced or chopped black olives
8 to 10 slices jarred nacho-style jalapeño slices (optional)
Nondairy sour cream, store-bought or homemade (page 302), for garnish (optional)
Chopped scallion, for garnish (optional)

Preheat the oven to 400°F (200°C, or gas mark 6).

Spray a glass 8-inch (20-cm) square baking dish with nonstick spray.

Begin to layer all the ingredients, starting with a single layer of tortillas on the bottom. (You can cut your tortillas into strips about 2 to 3 inches [5 to 7.5 cm] wide so that you can put straight edges against the sides of the baking dish.) Then add about ¼ cup (60 ml) of sauce, more tortillas, chorizo crumbles, onion, tortillas, more sauce, some of the cheese, more tortillas, more sauce, more crumbles, more cheese—you get the picture.

When you get to the top, finish with a whole tortilla, a bit more sauce, and a crumbling of cheese, olives, and jalapeños, if using.

Bake for 20 to 25 minutes, or until the cheese begins to brown. Remove from the oven and let sit for about 10 minutes before cutting and serving.

Garnish with the sour cream and scallion, if desired.

Yield: 6 servings

Tuna-Less Casserole

Although hijiki doesn't taste exactly like tuna, it certainly does give this casserole the flavor of the sea—but in a more tasty and animal-friendly way.

1 pound (455 g) pasta (such as bow ties or spirals)
2 tablespoons (8 g) dried hijiki seaweed
6 ounces (168 g) extra-firm tofu, drained, pressed, and crumbled
6 ounces (168 g) plain soy tempeh, crumbled
½ cup (68 g) peas
½ cup (68 g) corn kernels
½ cup (112 g) nondairy butter, melted
½ cup (120 ml) soy or other nondairy milk
¼ cup (30 g) nutritional yeast
2 tablespoons (16 g) all-purpose flour
1 teaspoon garlic powder
1 teaspoon onion powder
1 teaspoon Old Bay seasoning
1 teaspoon paprika
¼ teaspoon black pepper
½ cup (40 g) panko bread crumbs

Preheat the oven to 400°F (200°C, or gas mark 6).

Cook the pasta in salted water according to the package directions. (Once the water begins to boil, remove 1 cup [235 ml] for reconstituting the hijiki.) Once the pasta is ready, strain and return to the pot.

Add the dried hijiki to the reserved cup of boiling water. Cover and allow to reconstitute for about 10 minutes.

Add the hijiki, along with the water, tofu, tempeh, peas, corn, butter, milk, nutritional yeast, flour, garlic powder, onion powder, Old Bay seasoning, paprika, and pepper, and mix well.

Transfer to an 8-inch (20-cm) square baking dish and top with the bread crumbs.

Bake for 20 to 25 minutes, or until the bread crumbs begin to brown.

Yield: 6 servings

Mexican Shepherd's Pie

Another traditional favorite with a Latin twist! Masa harina is a finely ground corn flour that is traditionally used in making corn tortillas.

For the potatoes:

- 2 pounds (910 g) russet potatoes, peeled
- ½ cup (120 g) nondairy sour cream, store-bought or homemade (page 302)
- 2 tablespoons (28 g) nondairy butter
- ½ teaspoon ground cumin
- ½ teaspoon ground coriander
- ½ teaspoon garlic powder
- ½ cup (32 g) chopped scallion

For the crust:

- 2 cups (228 g) masa harina
- 1 cup (235 ml) veggie broth
- ½ cup (120 ml) canola oil
- ½ teaspoon chili powder

- 1 recipe MexiMeat (page 213)
- 1¼ cups (280 g) enchilada sauce, store-bought or homemade (page 288)
- Garnishes: sour cream, salsa, avocado, fresh cilantro (optional)

To make the potatoes: In a large-size pot, boil the potatoes in enough water to cover. Cook until fork-tender. Strain and return to the pot. Add the sour cream, butter, cumin, coriander, and garlic powder. Mash until smooth. Stir in the scallion. Set aside.

To make the crust: Combine all the ingredients in a medium-size bowl and mix well. Press evenly into a 9 × 13-inch (23 × 33-cm) greased casserole dish.

Spread the MexiMeat evenly over the crust.

Pour the enchilada sauce evenly over the MexiMeat.

Spread the potatoes evenly over the top.

Bake for 25 to 30 minutes. Let stand for about 5 minutes before serving. Serve on its own or garnish with additional sour cream, salsa, avocado, and fresh cilantro, if desired.

Yield: 8 servings

Chili and Cornbread Pie

Chili and cornbread in one dish? Dinner doesn't get much better than that.

For the chili:

1 can (15 ounces, or 425 g) kidney beans, drained
1 can (15 ounces, or 425 g) pinto beans, drained
1 can (15 ounces, or 425 g) tomato sauce
1 cup (180 g) diced yellow onion
1 cup (100 g) TVP granules
2 tablespoons (15 g) chili powder, to taste
2 tablespoons (15 g) smoked paprika
1 tablespoon (6 g) garlic powder
½ teaspoon black pepper

For the cornbread topping:

1 cup (125 g) all-purpose flour
¾ cup (105 g) yellow cornmeal
1 tablespoon (12 g) baking powder
1 teaspoon salt
1 cup (235 ml) plain soy or other nondairy milk
3 tablespoons (63 g) agave nectar
2 tablespoons (28 g) nondairy butter, melted
¼ cup (60 ml) canola or other vegetable oil
Equivalent of 2 beaten eggs (a flax egg, Ener-G, and Bob's Red Mill all work well here)
1 cup (250 g) yellow corn kernels

Preheat the oven to 350°F (180°C, or gas mark 4). Have ready a glass 8-inch (20-cm) square baking dish.

To make the chili: Mix together all the chili ingredients and pour into the bottom of the baking dish.

To make the cornbread topping: In a mixing bowl, combine the flour, cornmeal, baking powder, and salt.

In a separate bowl, combine the milk, agave, melted butter, oil, and egg replacer.

Add the wet ingredients to the dry and combine. Fold in the corn.

Carefully spread the cornbread mixture evenly over the chili mixture.

Bake for 45 minutes to 1 hour, or until the cornbread is golden brown and cooked through.

Yield: 4 servings

Spinach Quiche

It's hard to believe there are no eggs or cheese in this wonderful quiche! You can choose to bake it without the crust, if you'd rather keep it lower in carbs and calories (and gluten free). For an even fancier presentation, try baking the filling alone in individual greased ramekins. The crustless ramekins will need to spend 30 minutes in the oven.

Nonstick cooking spray

For the crust:

2 cups (240 g) light spelt flour
¼ cup plus 2 tablespoons (96 g) creamy natural peanut butter
½ teaspoon fine sea salt
1 tablespoon (21 g) agave nectar (optional)
½ cup (120 ml) unsweetened almond or other nondairy milk

For the filling:

1 pound (455 g) firm or extra-firm silken tofu
2 tablespoons (28 g) nondairy butter
2 tablespoons (16 g) nutritional yeast
3 tablespoons (30 g) brown rice or any flour
2 tablespoons (24 g) ground toasted almonds
½ teaspoon fine sea salt, to taste
¼ teaspoon ground black pepper
¼ teaspoon ground nutmeg
¼ teaspoon turmeric
½ teaspoon baking powder
½ teaspoon garlic powder
1 teaspoon dried minced onion
2 cups (380 g) frozen chopped spinach, thawed, squeezed dry

Preheat the oven to 375°F (190°C, or gas mark 5). Lightly coat an 8-inch (20-cm) or 9-inch (23-cm) pie plate with nonstick cooking spray.

To make the crust: Combine the flour, peanut butter, and salt in a food processor. Pulse a few times to combine. Add the agave, if using, and the milk, a little at a time, until a dough forms.

Roll out as thinly as possible and fit to the pie plate. Prick the crust with a fork to prevent air bubbles. Set aside.

To make the filling: Combine the tofu, butter, yeast, flour, almonds, salt, pepper, nutmeg, turmeric, baking powder, garlic powder, and minced onion in a food processor.

Blend until smooth, scraping the sides occasionally. Add the spinach, and pulse just a few times to combine. Pour the filling into the prepared crust.

Bake for 40 minutes, or until the edges of the crust are golden brown and the filling is set.

Let stand for 10 minutes on a wire rack before slicing and serving.

Yield: 6 servings

Chapter 10

Faux Meats

Although there's absolutely nothing wrong with digging into a big bowl of rice and beans to get a complete protein, you might find yourself craving something a bit more involved and refined every now and then. The rich flavors and amazing textures of tofu, seitan, and tempeh in this chapter will provide you with just that, and leave you wondering why meat was ever even on the menu.

A word about our fauxsages: if you do a search for "Seitan O'Greatness" on the Internet, you will find a hundred fantastic recipes using the baked-in-foil method. We based ours on the method posted by the user Lachesis on a forum at Post Punk Kitchen (www.theppk.com).

Apple Sage Fauxsage

Recreate your very own Oktoberfest by serving slices of this sausage alongside a generous serving of fresh sauerkraut, steamed whole potatoes, and a cold glass of quality beer.

1 cup (144 g) vital wheat gluten flour
¼ cup (30 g) nutritional yeast
1 teaspoon fine sea salt
1 tablespoon (2 g) dried ground sage
2 teaspoons dried minced onion
¼ teaspoon grated nutmeg
¼ teaspoon ground cinnamon
2 tablespoons (30 ml) walnut or canola oil
1 tablespoon (15 ml) pure maple syrup
½ cup (120 ml) apple juice
4 ounces (113 g) unsweetened applesauce

Preheat the oven to 325°F (170°C, or gas mark 3).

In a large-size bowl, whisk together the wheat gluten, yeast, salt, sage, onion, nutmeg, and cinnamon.

In a medium-size bowl, whisk together the oil, syrup, juice, and applesauce.

Pour the wet ingredients into the dry, stir with a spoon, then start combining with your hands and knead for a couple of minutes. Let rest for 5 minutes.

Roll into a log. Wrap in foil, twisting the ends tightly closed.

Bake for 90 minutes. Flip the wrapped sausage halfway through the cooking time so that it doesn't brown up too much on the bottom.

Carefully remove the foil and let cool. Store in the fridge or freezer.

Yield: 1 large-size sausage

Laurel and Hardy Peanut Fauxsages

The rather intriguing name for these fauxsages comes from the fact that we added too much liquid to the very first batch, resulting in rather misshapen shapes—some long and thin, others rather stocky. If you chop them into bite-size pieces, and crisp them up in a pan for use on salads, tacos, and chilis, though, no one will know the difference!

2 cups (288 g) vital wheat gluten flour
1½ tablespoons (11 g) paprika
⅓ cup (40 g) nutritional yeast
2 teaspoons fine sea salt
2 cups (470 ml) water
½ cup (128 g) creamy or crunchy natural peanut butter

Preheat the oven to 325°F (170°C, or gas mark 3).

In a large-size bowl, whisk together the wheat gluten, paprika, yeast, and salt.

In a medium-size bowl, whisk together the water and peanut butter until emulsified.

Pour the wet ingredients into the dry, stir with a spoon, then start combining with your hands and knead for a couple of minutes. Let rest for 5 minutes.

Divide the dough into 2 equal portions, and roll into logs. Wrap each sausage in foil, twisting the ends tightly closed.

Bake for 90 minutes. Flip the wrapped sausages halfway through the cooking time so that they don't brown up too much on the bottom.

Carefully remove the foil and let cool. Store in the fridge or freezer.

Yield: 2 large-size sausages

Pumpkin Fauxsage

Here's an autumnal version of the dense, protein-packed seitanic sausage that tastes amazing on its own, as well as added to stews, pizzas, and sandwiches.

1½ cups (216 g) vital wheat gluten flour
¼ cup (30 g) nutritional yeast
1 teaspoon paprika
2 teaspoons dried sage
1 teaspoon dried oregano
½ teaspoon ground white pepper, to taste
2 teaspoons dried minced onion or 1 teaspoon onion powder
¼ teaspoon cayenne pepper, to taste
¼ teaspoon grated nutmeg
1 tablespoon (12 g) Sucanat or 1 tablespoon (15 ml) pure maple syrup
¾ cup (180 ml) vegetable broth
¼ cup plus 2 tablespoons to ½ cup (92 to 122 g) pumpkin purée, depending on thickness
2 tablespoons (30 ml) walnut or canola oil

Preheat the oven to 325°F (170°C, or gas mark 3).

In a large-size bowl, whisk together the wheat gluten, yeast, paprika, sage, oregano, white pepper, onion, cayenne pepper, nutmeg, and Sucanat.

In a medium-size bowl, whisk together the broth, ¼ cup plus 2 tablespoons pumpkin, and oil.

Pour the wet ingredients into the dry, stir with a spoon, then start combining with your hands and knead for a couple of minutes. If the preparation is too dry, incorporate the remaining 2 tablespoons (30 g) pumpkin purée. Let rest for 5 minutes.

Roll into a log. Wrap in foil, twisting the ends tightly closed.

Bake for 90 minutes. Flip the wrapped sausage halfway through the cooking time so that it doesn't brown up too much on the bottom.

Carefully remove the foil and let cool. Store in the fridge or freezer.

Yield: 1 large-size sausage

Apple Curry Fauxsage

This particular version will be a perfect addition to Asian-inspired dishes. Crisp it up in a dry or slightly oiled skillet, and sprinkle on top of your favorite stir-fries for a tasty protein boost.

1¼ cups (180 g) vital wheat gluten flour
¼ cup (30 g) nutritional yeast
½ teaspoon ground cumin
1 teaspoon fine sea salt
1 tablespoon dried basil
4 ounces (113 g) unsweetened applesauce
2 tablespoons (30 ml) canola oil
⅔ cup (160 ml) water
1 tablespoon (15 g) green curry paste
1 tablespoon (15 ml) pure maple syrup

Preheat the oven to 325°F (170°C, or gas mark 3).

In a large-size bowl, whisk together the wheat gluten, yeast, cumin, salt, and basil.

In a medium-size bowl, whisk together the applesauce, oil, water, curry paste, and syrup until combined.

Pour the wet ingredients into the dry, stir with a spoon, then start combining with your hands and knead for a couple of minutes. Let rest for 5 minutes.

Roll into a log. Wrap in foil, twisting the ends tightly closed.

Bake for 90 minutes. Flip the wrapped sausage halfway through the cooking time so that it doesn't brown up too much on the bottom.

Carefully remove the foil and let cool. Store in the fridge or freezer.

Yield: 1 large-size sausage

Ham Fauxsage

The flavor is sweet and smoky, like a Black Forest ham—minus the dead pig! This works well in the frittatas (page 54), thinly sliced as a sandwich meat, or cut into thin rounds and used as a pizza topping.

½ cup (60 g) garbanzo or fava bean flour
½ cup (72 g) vital wheat gluten flour
½ cup (120 ml) water or veggie broth
¼ cup (60 ml) canola or vegetable oil
2 tablespoons (14 g) packed brown sugar
2 tablespoons (15 g) nutritional yeast
1½ tablespoons (24 g) tomato paste
½ to 1 teaspoon liquid smoke, to taste
½ teaspoon black pepper
¼ teaspoon salt

Preheat the oven to 350°F (180°C, or gas mark 4).

In a mixing bowl, mix together all the ingredients until a nice goopy mixture forms. Let rest for 5 minutes.

Roll into a log. Wrap in foil, twisting the ends tightly closed.

Place on a baking sheet, seam side down, and bake for about 45 minutes, or until nice and firm.

Let cool before unwrapping. Store in an airtight container in the refrigerator for up to 1 week, or freeze indefinitely.

Yield: 1 large-size sausage

Independence Day Wieners

Why should your bun be filled only with lettuce and mustard while everyone else is gorging on hot dogs at the next Fourth of July barbecue? Now you can get your dog on too, without having to hunt down expensive, sodium-packed tofu dogs from the local health food store!

2 cups (288 g) vital wheat gluten flour
1 cup (120 g) whole wheat pastry flour
2 tablespoons (14 g) smoked paprika
1 teaspoon garlic powder
1 teaspoon onion powder
½ teaspoon turmeric
1½ cups (355 ml) water
½ cup (120 ml) canola or vegetable oil
¼ cup (60 ml) soy sauce or tamari
¼ cup (84 g) brown rice syrup or agave nectar
2 tablespoons (33 g) tomato paste
1 tablespoon (15 ml) liquid smoke

Preheat the oven to 350°F (180°C, or gas mark 4).

Mix together the flours, paprika, garlic powder, onion powder, and turmeric.

In a separate bowl, whisk together the water, oil, soy sauce, syrup, tomato paste, and liquid smoke.

Add the wet ingredients to the dry and mix until uniform. Your mixture will be wet, not at all like a bread dough.

Divide the dough into 8 to 12 pieces, depending on how large you like your wieners.

Tear off 8 to 12 pieces of aluminum foil, about 6 × 12 inches (15 × 30 cm).

Form each piece of dough into a sausage shape and place near the long edge of the foil.

Roll up the foil and twist the ends tight.

Place the seam side down on a baking sheet and bake for 30 to 40 minutes, or until firm.

Remove from the oven and let cool before unwrapping.

Enjoy as you would any hot dog.

Yield: 8 to 12 wieners

Oktoberfest Wieners

Local German beer garden not serving up vegan brats this year? Das ist okay—make your own!

2 cups (288 g) vital wheat gluten flour
¼ cup (30 g) nutritional yeast
1 tablespoon (6 g) garlic powder
1 tablespoon (6 g) onion powder
1 tablespoon (4 g) dried parsley or 3 tablespoons (12 g) fresh
1 teaspoon ground black pepper
1 cup (235 ml) vegetable broth
½ cup (71 g) sauerkraut
¼ cup (60 ml) canola or vegetable oil

Preheat the oven to 350°F (180°C, or gas mark 4).

Mix together the wheat gluten, yeast, garlic and onion powders, parsley, and black pepper.

In a separate bowl, whisk together the vegetable broth, sauerkraut, and oil.

Add the wet ingredients to the dry and mix until uniform. Your mixture will be wet, not at all like a bread dough. If your mixture is too dry, add a bit more veggie broth.

Divide the dough into 8 to 12 pieces, depending on how large you like your wieners.

Tear off 8 to 12 pieces of aluminum foil, about 6 × 12 inches (15 × 30 cm).

Form each piece of dough into a sausage shape and place near the long edge of the foil.

Roll up the foil and twist the ends tight.

Place seam side down on a baking sheet and bake for 30 to 40 minutes, or until firm.

Remove from the oven and let cool before unwrapping.

Enjoy as you would any hot dog.

Yield: 8 to 12 wieners

Black Bean Grillers

The all-important backyard barbecue often leaves vegetarians, and vegans alike, out of the fun. Veggie burgers are a great alternative to the standard carnivorous fare, but many of them can't stand up to the grill. Barbecue sauce and black beans make this a hearty, grill-worthy burger.

1 cup (100 g) TVP granules
1 cup (235 ml) water
1 tablespoon (15 ml) soy sauce
1 can (15 ounces, or 425 g) black beans, drained and rinsed
½ cup (72 g) vital wheat gluten flour
¼ cup (60 ml) barbecue sauce, plus more for basting
1 tablespoon (15 ml) liquid smoke
½ teaspoon black pepper
2 tablespoons (32 g) creamy natural peanut butter

Reconstitute the TVP by mixing it with the water and soy sauce in a microwave-safe bowl, covering tightly with plastic wrap, and microwaving on high for 5 minutes. Alternatively, you can pour boiling water over the TVP and soy sauce, then cover and let stand for 10 minutes.

Add the beans, wheat gluten, ¼ cup (60 ml) barbecue sauce, liquid smoke, pepper, and peanut butter to the reconstituted TVP once it is cool enough to handle. Mush it together with your hands until it is uniform and most of the beans are mashed up.

Form into 6 patties.

Grill these babies up on the barbecue, brushing with the additional barbecue sauce as you go, about 5 minutes per side. Alternatively, these can be pan-fried in a bit of oil, then topped with additional barbecue sauce.

Yield: 6 burgers

Beefy Bacon Burgers

This beefy burger is quite tasty, holds together on the grill, tastes great barbecued or pan-fried, uses up some of those homemade Imitation Bacon Bits (page 212), and serves up well on a toasted bun smothered in vegan mayo.

1 cup (100 g) TVP granules
1 cup (235 ml) water
2 tablespoons (30 ml) steak sauce
1 tablespoon (15 ml) liquid smoke
¼ cup (60 ml) canola or other vegetable oil
⅓ cup (85 g) creamy natural peanut butter
½ cup (72 g) vital wheat gluten flour
½ cup (50 g) imitation bacon bits, store-bought or homemade (page 212)
¼ cup (30 g) nutritional yeast
1 tablespoon (7 g) paprika
1 tablespoon (6 g) garlic powder
1 teaspoon ground black pepper

Reconstitute the TVP by either mixing together the TVP, water, steak sauce, and liquid smoke in a microwave-safe bowl, covering tightly with plastic wrap, and microwaving on high for 5 minutes, or alternatively pour boiling water over the TVP, steak sauce, and liquid smoke, then cover and let stand for 10 minutes.

Add the oil and peanut butter to the TVP mixture.

In a mixing bowl, mix together the wheat gluten, bacon bits, yeast, paprika, garlic powder, and black pepper.

Add the TVP mixture to the flour mixture and knead until well incorporated. Cover and let stand for 20 minutes.

Form into 4 to 6 patties and prepare as desired. If grilling, grill for 5 to 7 minutes per side. If panfrying, use a smidge of oil and fry for 3 to 5 minutes per side.

For a firmer texture, try baking at 350°F (180°C, or gas mark 4) for about 20 minutes and then panfrying.

Yield: 4 to 6 patties

Gluten Free

Crispy Tofu Fries

These crispy fries taste delicious served with Green Cauliflower Masala (page 148) or simply dipped into good-quality ketchup.

12 ounces (340 g) extra-firm tofu, drained, simmered, cut into 14 fries, and patted dry (see note)
1 tablespoon (15 ml) peanut oil
1 teaspoon fine sea salt
1 tablespoon (6 g) mild to medium curry powder (optional)
1 teaspoon dried basil (optional)
1 tablespoon (21 g) agave nectar (optional)

Preheat the oven to 400°F (200°C, or gas mark 6). Have a large-size rimmed baking sheet handy.

Coat the tofu with the oil, salt, and curry powder, basil, and agave, if using.

Bake for 25 minutes, then flip the tofu over. Bake for another 25 minutes, or until the fries are extra crispy.

Yield: 2 to 4 servings

NOTE

To simmer, cover the tofu with water in a medium-size saucepan, bring to a boil, and let simmer for 5 minutes. Drain well, then pat dry if necessary.

Thai Tofu

Enjoy this delicious tofu with steamed greens such as broccoli greens, bok choy, or kale, and over rice or rice noodles.

¼ cup (60 ml) vegetable broth or water
1½ teaspoons cornstarch
1½ tablespoons (24 g) crunchy or creamy natural peanut butter
1 teaspoon hot chili oil
1½ teaspoons Sucanat
1½ teaspoons seasoned rice vinegar
1 tablespoon (15 ml) tamari
1 tablespoon (15 ml) peanut oil
8 ounces (227 g) super-firm or extra-firm tofu, pressed, drained, and cubed

In a small-size bowl, whisk together the broth and cornstarch until dissolved. Add the peanut butter, chili oil, Sucanat, vinegar, and tamari; it will look a bit unmanageable at this point.

In a skillet, heat the peanut oil over medium-high heat, add the tofu, and cook until golden and crispy on every side, about 8 minutes.

Pour the peanut butter sauce on top, lower the heat to medium, and cook until the tofu is coated and the sauce has thickened, about 2 minutes.

Yield: 2 servings

VARIATION

Sesame fans may want to try replacing the peanut butter with tahini instead, for equally delicious results, but be sure to increase the amount of Sucanat to 1 tablespoon (12 g) instead, because tahini has a tendency to be a touch more bitter than peanut butter, depending on whether the seeds are hulled or not.

Under 30 Minutes

Curried Tofu Sandwich Filling

This simple and tasty filling can also be used as a dip for crackers, or even enjoyed plain.

¼ cup (56 g) vegan mayonnaise, store-bought or homemade (page 301 or 302)
2 tablespoons (30 ml) white balsamic vinegar
1½ tablespoons (9 g) mild curry powder
¼ teaspoon ground black pepper or pinch cayenne pepper, to taste
½ teaspoon fine sea salt
¼ cup (40 g) raisins
¼ cup (38 g) granulated or coarsely chopped peanuts
2 tablespoons (12 g) chopped scallion (optional)
12 ounces (340 g) extra-firm tofu, drained, simmered, cooled, and crumbled (see note)

In a medium-size bowl, combine the mayonnaise, vinegar, curry, pepper, salt, raisins, peanuts, and scallion, if using.

Add the crumbled tofu and stir until well combined.

Chill before serving. Use as a sandwich filling or as a side dish.

Yield: 2 to 4 servings

NOTE

To simmer the tofu, cover the tofu with water in a medium-size saucepan, bring to a boil, and let simmer for 5 minutes. Drain well, then pat dry if necessary.

Oven-Smoked Tofu, Three Ways

Don't you wish you had all the time in the world? Time to spend all day in the backyard, sipping lemonade and smoking tofu in the wood-fired smoker? Well, let's face it, we simply don't have that leisure, and most of us don't even have smokers. Although not quite as authentic as the real thing, oven-smoked tofu can come out quite lovely, and with the amount of food-grade planks and papers available these days, it's pretty easy as well. No access to planks or papers? That's okay, too. There's even a way to do it without the wood.

For each type, you will need 1 block (any size) of extra-firm tofu, drained and pressed, then sliced into "steaks" about ¼-inch (6 mm) thick.

Plank-smoked:

1 food-safe cedar plank

Paper-smoked:

6 to 10 pieces cedar paper

Liquid-smoked:

1 cup (235 ml) water
2 tablespoons (30 ml) tamari or soy sauce
2 tablespoons (30 ml) liquid smoke

Preheat the oven to 250°F (125°C, or gas mark ½).

For plank-smoked tofu: Soak the plank in warm water for about 1 hour. Place the tofu steaks evenly spaced on the plank. Cover the entire plank loosely with aluminum foil to create a steam tent. Bake for 2 hours.

For paper-smoked tofu: Preheat the oven to 250°F (125°C, or gas mark ½). Soak the papers in warm water for 10 to 15 minutes. Wrap each tofu steak in paper and place seam side down directly on the oven rack or on a baking sheet. Bake for 2 hours.

For liquid-smoked tofu: Preheat the oven to 250°F (125°C, or gas mark ½).

Mix together the water, tamari, and liquid smoke in a shallow baking dish or pan that is large enough for a single layer of tofu steaks. Place the tofu steaks in the dish and bake, uncovered, for 2 hours.

Yield: 10 to 12 tofu steaks (depending on the size of your block)

Under 30 Minutes

Seitan Bacon Crumbles

These crumbles are not only mighty tasty, but they're also very quick to prepare, making it easy for you to enjoy a nutritious meal even after a long day at work. You'll know what to say if anyone wonders how you get your protein if you don't eat meat.

½ cup (72 g) vital wheat gluten flour
2 tablespoons (16 g) nutritional yeast
1 teaspoon pure maple syrup
2 tablespoons (30 ml) soy sauce
1 teaspoon liquid smoke
1 teaspoon ketchup
1 tablespoon (15 ml) peanut oil
2 tablespoons (30 ml) water

In a medium-size bowl, combine the wheat gluten and yeast.

Stir in the syrup, soy sauce, liquid smoke, ketchup, oil, and water. Use your fingertips to crumble.

Fry in a large-size saucepan over medium-high heat for 8 minutes, or until browned up.

Yield: 1¼ cups (156 g)

Under 30 Minutes

Seitan Chorizo Crumbles

Our testers cannot stop swooning over this one! Good news is that even non-vegan chorizo connoisseurs fell in love with this animal friendly version.

½ cup (72 g) vital wheat gluten flour
2 tablespoons (16 g) nutritional yeast
½ teaspoon fine sea salt
1 teaspoon ground cumin
¼ teaspoon cayenne pepper
½ teaspoon paprika
2 teaspoons mild to medium chili powder
½ teaspoon dried minced onion or ¼ teaspoon onion powder
2 tablespoons (30 ml) water
2 tablespoons (30 ml) apple cider vinegar
2 tablespoons (34 g) ketchup
1 tablespoon (15 ml) canola oil

In a medium-size bowl, combine the wheat gluten, yeast, salt, cumin, cayenne, paprika, chili powder, and onion.

Stir in the water, vinegar, ketchup, and oil. Use your fingertips to crumble.

Fry in a large-size saucepan over medium-high heat for 8 minutes, or until browned up.

Yield: 1¼ cups (156 g)

 Under 30 Minutes

Asian-Inspired Seitan Crumbles

These would be especially great if used in Asian-inspired dishes. The hot chili oil gives them just a little hint of heat.

If you are sensitive to vinegar, replace 1 tablespoon (15 ml) of it with the same quantity of water.

½ cup (72 g) vital wheat gluten flour
2 tablespoons (16 g) nutritional yeast
¼ teaspoon ground ginger
2 tablespoons (30 ml) water
2 tablespoons (30 ml) rice vinegar
2 tablespoons (30 ml) soy sauce
½ teaspoon hot chili oil
½ teaspoon toasted sesame oil

In a medium-size bowl, combine the wheat gluten, yeast, and ginger.

Stir in the water, vinegar, soy sauce, and oils. Use your fingertips to crumble.

Fry in a large-size saucepan over medium-high heat for 8 minutes, or until browned up.

Yield: 1¼ cups (156 g)

 Under 30 Minutes

Basic Seitan Crumbles

This version is great to have around when you need the protein but don't want the flavor to overwhelm whatever you're serving the crumbles with.

½ cup (72 g) vital wheat gluten flour
¼ cup (30 g) nutritional yeast
1 clove garlic, grated
1 tablespoon (15 ml) extra-virgin olive oil
1 tablespoon (15 ml) vegan Worcestershire sauce
3 tablespoons (51 g) organic ketchup
2 tablespoons (30 ml) water

In a medium-size bowl, combine the wheat gluten and yeast.

Stir in the garlic, oil, Worcestershire sauce, ketchup, and water. Use your fingertips to crumble.

Fry in a large-size saucepan over medium-high heat for 8 minutes, or until browned up.

Yield: 1¼ cups (156 g)

Crispy Seitan Bacon

It's not always easy to find meatless bacon strips, so here's an amazing version that will make your BLTs worth your while, all over again.

½ cup (128 g) cooked cannellini beans, drained and rinsed
1 teaspoon canola oil
¼ cup (36 g) vital wheat gluten flour
¼ cup (20 g) whole wheat panko or other bread crumbs
3 tablespoons (45 ml) soy sauce
2 tablespoons (16 g) nutritional yeast
2 tablespoons (30 ml) pure maple syrup
1 tablespoon (15 ml) liquid smoke
1 tablespoon (17 g) tomato paste
1 clove garlic, grated

Blend all the ingredients in a food processor until the preparation is smooth and pastelike. Scrape the sides occasionally.

Preheat the oven to 375°F (190°C, or gas mark 5). Line a baking sheet with parchment paper or a silicone baking mat, such as Silpat.

Scoop up about 1½ tablespoons (30 g) of seitan paste, and pat down in the shape of bacon strips, spreading the paste as thinly as possible.

Bake for 15 minutes, or until brown and crispy, turning once halfway through the baking time.

If you have leftovers, fry them in a pan for a few seconds to make them crispy again.

Yield: 12 to 16 strips

Imitation Bacon Bits

Homemade beats store-bought ANY day of the week. No hydrogenated fats or weird chemicals. Plus, they are so easy to whip up in just a few minutes, so you can have bacon-y goodness whenever you want it! Sprinkle on top of baked potatoes, in tofu scrambles, or anywhere you would use bacon bits.

2 tablespoons (30 ml) liquid smoke
1 scant cup (205 ml) water
1 cup (100 g) TVP granules
¼ teaspoon salt
A few drops red food coloring (optional)
3 tablespoons (45 ml) canola or other vegetable oil

To a measuring cup add the liquid smoke, then fill to get 1 cup (235 ml) water.

In a microwave-safe dish, mix together the liquid smoke water, TVP, and salt. Cover tightly with plastic wrap and microwave on high for 5 minutes. (Alternatively, bring the water to a boil, add to the TVP, liquid smoke, and salt, then cover and let stand for 10 minutes.)

Carefully remove the wrap. Stir in the food coloring, if using.

Preheat a frying pan with the oil. Add the reconstituted TVP to the pan and toss to make sure it all gets coated with oil. Panfry to desired crispness, stirring often, about 10 minutes. You don't necessarily want to "brown" them, but rather dry them out.

Let cool completely before transferring to an airtight container. Store in the refrigerator. These should last at least a week, but probably much longer.

Yield: About 1 cup (80 g)

MexiMeat

This meatless substitute is excellent for all of your Mexican dishes. It's great in tacos, burritos, nachos, quesadillas, and especially the Very Veggie Shepherd's Pie (page 226)!

- 1 cup (100 g) TVP granules
- 2 tablespoons (14 g) paprika
- 1 teaspoon ground cumin
- 1 teaspoon evaporated cane juice or granulated sugar
- 1 teaspoon garlic powder
- 1 teaspoon onion powder
- ½ teaspoon cayenne powder
- ½ teaspoon chili powder
- ½ teaspoon chipotle powder
- ½ teaspoon salt
- 1 cup (235 ml) water or vegetable broth
- ¼ cup (60 ml) canola oil

In a microwave-safe bowl, combine the TVP, paprika, cumin, cane juice, garlic powder, onion powder, cayenne, chili powder, chipotle, and salt. Add the water, cover tightly with plastic wrap, and microwave for 6 to 8 minutes on high. (Alternatively, bring the water to a boil, add to the TVP and spices, cover, and let stand for 10 minutes.) Carefully remove from the microwave, remove the plastic, and mix in the oil.

Yield: About 2 cups (200 g)

Meat-Free BBQ Riblets

The amount of barbecue sauce used in these delicious strips is to your preference. Please note that the strips are delicious on their own too, or as a meat substitute in sandwiches.

1 teaspoon canola oil
1 cup (144 g) vital wheat gluten flour
1 tablespoon (7 g) paprika
3 tablespoons (24 g) nutritional yeast
1 teaspoon onion powder
¼ cup (64 g) creamy natural peanut butter or tahini
1 cup (235 ml) water
½ cup (136 g) barbecue sauce, more if needed, to taste

Preheat the oven to 350°F (180°C, or gas mark 4). Lightly brush a rimmed baking sheet with the oil.

Combine the wheat gluten, paprika, yeast, and onion powder in a large-size bowl.

Stir in the peanut butter and water.

Divide into 6 equal portions. Form 6 strips, and place them on the prepared baking sheet.

Bake for 30 minutes, flipping them over halfway through the cooking time.

Brush both sides of the strips with a generous amount of barbecue sauce, then bake for an additional 10 minutes.

Yield: 6 riblets

Barbecue "Beef" Sandwiches

These sammies are great to serve in the summertime, or when you have people over for a casual gathering. Serve on a crusty French roll topped with a mountain of Creamy Curry Coleslaw (page 125).

For the seitan:

1½ cups (216 g) vital wheat gluten flour
½ cup (60 g) whole wheat flour
¼ cup (30 g) nutritional yeast
1 cup (160 g) diced yellow onion
½ cup (120 ml) water
¼ cup (60 ml) steak sauce
2 tablespoons (33 g) tomato paste
1 tablespoon (15 g) prepared Dijon mustard

For the barbecue broth:

2 cups (470 ml) vegetable broth
½ cup (110 g) packed brown sugar
2 tablespoons (14 g) paprika
2 tablespoons (16 g) onion powder
2 tablespoons (16 g) garlic powder
1 tablespoon (7 g) black pepper
1 teaspoon cayenne powder
1 teaspoon liquid smoke
1 teaspoon ground cumin

4 crusty French rolls

To make the seitan: In a mixing bowl, combine the wheat gluten, whole wheat flour, and yeast.

In a separate bowl, combine the onion, water, steak sauce, tomato paste, and mustard.

Add the wet ingredients to the dry and knead together.

Let stand for 20 minutes.

To make the broth: Combine all the broth ingredients in a pot and bring to a boil.

Divide the seitan dough into 4 pieces and drop into the boiling broth.

Reduce to a simmer, cover, and simmer for about 30 minutes, or until most of the moisture is absorbed, stirring often so the seitan does not stick to the bottom of the pot.

Remove from the heat. Cut the rolls in half. Using a fork, pull apart the "beef" and pile onto the rolls.

Yield: 4 sandwiches

Traditional Boiled Seitan

Fear not the boiled seitan! With a little elbow grease, you can create a large batch of homemade seitan that will store for weeks! This one results in a fairly neutral, beefy-type seitan. The yield works very well in most recipes calling for seitan.

For the boiling broth:

- 10 cups (2350 ml) water
- 2 cups (470 ml) soy sauce
- 10 cloves garlic, chopped in half
- 5 whole bay leaves
- 3 2-inch (5-cm) pieces fresh gingerroot, peeled and chopped into chunks

For the seitan dough:

- 1 cup (144 g) vital wheat gluten flour
- 5 cups (600 g) whole wheat flour
- 2½ cups (588 ml) water
- ½ cup (32 g) fresh chopped parsley
- 3 scallions, whites only, finely chopped
- 1 teaspoon garlic powder
- 1 teaspoon onion powder
- 1 to 3 teaspoons freshly cracked pepper, to taste

To make the broth: Combine all the broth ingredients in a pot and bring to a simmer while preparing the dough.

To make the dough: In a large-size mixing bowl, combine the wheat gluten and flour, then slowly add the water to form a stiff dough. Knead the dough about 70 times. You can do it right in the bowl. Let it rest for 20 minutes.

After resting, take the dough, still in the bowl, to the sink and cover with water. Knead the dough until the water becomes milky, then empty the bowl and repeat. Do this 10 to 12 times. By the tenth or twelfth time, the dough will feel and look like the consistency of brains, but the water will still be a little milky.

After the last rinse, add the parsley, scallion, garlic powder, onion powder, and pepper. Mix thoroughly by hand.

Divide the dough in half. Place one piece of dough in the center of a large-size piece of cheesecloth and roll in tightly into a log shape. Tie the ends to secure. Repeat with the other piece.

Place both seitan logs in the broth and simmer for 90 minutes.

Remove from the broth and set on a plate to cool. Remove from the cheesecloth. If the cheesecloth is sticking, run it under some water and it should come off easily.

You can store it in the refrigerator in foil or in a plastic container. To keep it really moist, place some of the broth in the container. The seitan keeps in the fridge for about 2 weeks, or in the freezer indefinitely.

Yield: About 4 pounds (1820 g)

Baked Berbere Seitan

Most Ethiopian cuisine is based on the berbere spice mix. This seitan is perfect for the Ethiopian Wat (page 155) or simply sliced and panfried and served up with lentils and rice or your favorite green vegetable.

1 recipe Berbere Spice Blend (page 306)
2 cups (288 g) vital wheat gluten flour
1 cup (120 g) chickpea flour
1 cup (235 ml) water
½ cup (120 ml) extra-virgin olive oil
2 tablespoons (30 ml) tomato paste
2 tablespoons (30 ml) steak sauce

In a mixing bowl, combine the spice blend, wheat gluten, and flour. In a separate bowl, combine the water, oil, tomato paste, and steak sauce.

Add the wet ingredients to the dry and knead for 5 minutes, or until well incorporated. Let stand for 20 minutes to rest.

Preheat the oven to 350°F (180°C, or gas mark 4).

Divide the dough in half. Roughly shape each piece into a log about 6 inches (15 cm) long and 3 inches (7.5 cm) in diameter.

Place each log in the center of a sheet of aluminum foil and roll the foil around it. Twist the ends tight.

Bake, seam side down, for 1 hour. Let cool before unwrapping. Store in an airtight container in the refrigerator for up to a week, or freeze indefinitely.

Yield: About 2 pounds (910 g)

Grilled Tempeh in Kickin' Onion Marinade

Who says a vegan can't enjoy a barbecue?

4 cloves garlic
1 large-size yellow onion, roughly chopped
1 cup (235 ml) soy sauce or tamari
3 dried jalapeño peppers, with seeds (if you can't find dried, fresh will work, but remove the seeds)
¼ cup (60 ml) apple cider vinegar
1 teaspoon ground cumin
Freshly cracked pepper, to taste
8 ounces (224 g) plain soy tempeh, cut into 4 equal pieces

Combine the garlic, onion, soy sauce, jalapeño peppers, vinegar, cumin, and pepper in a food processor and process until well incorporated but still chunky.

Place the tempeh in a shallow dish or resealable plastic bag and pour the marinade over the tempeh. Let marinate for a few hours.

Remove the tempeh from the marinade, reserving any leftover marinade.

If grilling on a barbecue, choose an area with a medium-high flame. Place the tempeh on the grill, cook for 5 to 7 minutes, then turn and cook for 5 to 7 minutes longer. Serve with the reserved marinade.

To bake in the oven, preheat the oven to 450°F (230°C, or gas mark 8). Place the tempeh and any reserved marinade in an ovenproof baking dish and bake, uncovered, for 10 to 12 minutes.

Yield: 4 servings

Protein, Quick! Mini Seitan Bites

Are you in dire need of some protein? You can whip up a batch of these without having to wait for hours to get your snack on. Although the seitan bites are tasty as is, add-ins, such as olives, nuts, pieces of roasted red pepper, and steamed broccoli, are also delicious. Or spread some sauce on top, such as Curried Cauliflower Purée (page 289).

Nonstick cooking spray
½ cup (72 g) vital wheat gluten flour
¼ cup (30 g) nutritional yeast
2 tablespoons (20 g) brown rice flour
½ teaspoon garlic powder
1 teaspoon Italian seasoning
½ teaspoon fine sea salt
¾ cup (180 ml) unsweetened soy or other nondairy milk
2 tablespoons (32 g) tahini

Preheat the oven to 375°F (190°C, or gas mark 5). Lightly coat 6 standard muffin cups with spray.

Combine the wheat gluten, yeast, flour, garlic powder, Italian seasoning, and salt in a medium-size bowl.

Stir in the milk and tahini until well combined. If you choose to incorporate any add-ins, do so now.

Divide the batter equally among the muffin cups.

Bake for 20 minutes, until the seitan bites are light golden brown and firm to the touch.

Yield: 6 seitan bites

Chapter 11

Main Dishes

Make room for the star of the meal! Delve into a chapter full of tempting main courses and dishes that are worthy of taking center stage on your holiday or any-day table.

Butternut Squash Hummus White Lasagna

Although a bit labor-intensive, this wonderful pasta dish is absolutely worth the trouble. We recommend you prepare the components separately, so it will seem like a less-imposing task.

For the béchamel:

2 tablespoons (28 g) nondairy butter
1 clove garlic, grated
¼ teaspoon ground nutmeg
⅛ teaspoon paprika
½ teaspoon fine sea salt
¼ teaspoon ground white or black pepper, to taste
¼ cup (30 g) light spelt flour
2 cups (470 ml) soy creamer or unsweetened nondairy milk

8 lasagne noodles, prepared according to package directions
½ recipe Curried Butternut Squash Hummus (page 83)
1 recipe Nutty Cheese (page 88)

To make the béchamel: In a medium-size saucepan over medium heat, cook the butter and garlic for 1 minute, until fragrant.

Add the nutmeg, paprika, salt, and pepper. Cook for 1 minute. Stir in the flour and cook for a few seconds. Whisk in the soy creamer. Cook and whisk until thickened. Set aside.

Preheat the oven to 375°F (190°C, or gas mark 5).

A quick note before assembling the lasagna: be sure to keep some béchamel to apply on the very top of the lasagna. You will have 4 layers of pasta in all, so divide each ingredient accordingly.

Place a little béchamel on the bottom of an 8-inch (20-cm) square baking dish. Top with 2 lasagne noodles, a layer of hummus, and a layer of Nutty Cheese, and repeat until you run out of ingredients, ending with a layer of béchamel.

Cover with a piece of foil. Bake for 20 minutes. Remove the foil, and bake for another 15 minutes, or until golden brown on top.

Let stand for at least 15 minutes before serving, so that the portions don't fall apart when cut.

Yield: 4 servings

Red "Meat" Lasagna

Longing for that meaty red lasagna you grew up on? Full of ricotta cheese and red sauce oozing with ground sausage? This version is much easier on the waistline, but certainly not short on flavor.

1 recipe "Meaty" Marinara (page 290)
12 lasagne noodles, prepared according to package directions
1 recipe Tofu Ricotta (page 303)
2 tablespoons (15 g) nutritional yeast
2 tablespoons (14 g) ground cashews or walnuts

Preheat the oven to 375°F (190°C, or gas mark 5).

A quick note before assembling the lasagna: be sure to keep some sauce and ricotta to apply on the very top of the lasagna. You will have 4 layers of pasta in all, so divide each ingredient accordingly.

In a square 8-inch (20-cm) or 9-inch (23-cm) baking dish, place a thin layer of sauce, add 3 noodles in a single layer, add another layer of sauce, then a layer of Tofu Ricotta and another layer of noodles, and repeat until you run out of ingredients, ending with a layer of ricotta and sauce. Sprinkle with the nutritional yeast and cashews.

Bake, uncovered, for 30 to 40 minutes, or until the top is beginning to brown and your noodles are nice and tender.

Let stand for at least 15 minutes before serving, so that the portions don't fall apart when cut.

Yield: 6 servings

Mushroom Lasagna

No red sauce here. Just purely rich, earthy mushrooms and creamy goodness. You can use any type or combination of mushrooms for this recipe, even though the recipe calls for buttons.

2 tablespoons (28 g) nondairy butter
2 tablespoons (30 g) minced garlic
1 pound (454 g) sliced button mushrooms
2 cups (470 ml) unsweetened soy or other nondairy milk
¼ cup (30 g) nutritional yeast
1 tablespoon (2 g) dried basil
¼ teaspoon ground black pepper
Salt, to taste
½ cup (63 g) all-purpose flour mixed with ½ cup (135 ml) water to make a slurry
12 lasagne noodles, prepared according to package directions
1 recipe Tofu Ricotta (page 303)

Preheat the oven to 350°F (180°C, or gas mark 4). Have ready an 8-inch (20-cm) square baking dish.

In a frying pan or cast-iron skillet, melt the butter over medium-high heat. Add the garlic and mushrooms and sauté for 5 to 7 minutes, or until the mushrooms have reduced in size by about half.

Add the milk, yeast, basil, pepper, and salt.

Bring to a boil and reduce to a simmer. Simmer, uncovered, for 15 minutes.

Slowly stir in the flour slurry and stir to thicken. Remove from the heat.

A quick note before assembling the lasagna: be sure to keep some mushroom sauce and ricotta to apply on the very top of the lasagna. You will have 4 layers of pasta in all, so divide each ingredient accordingly.

Place a very thin layer of mushroom sauce in the bottom of the dish. Lay 3 noodles across the bottom, then a layer of mushroom sauce, then a layer of ricotta. Repeat until you run out of ingredients, ending with a final thin layer of sauce and a sprinkling of ricotta.

Bake, covered, for 25 minutes, then uncover and bake for an additional 15 minutes.

Let stand for at least 15 minutes before serving, so that the portions don't fall apart when cut.

Yield: 6 servings

Eggplant Lasagna

This lasagna uses thinly sliced pieces of eggplant instead of noodles, making this a gluten-free lasagna! Use your favorite marinara sauce here, or use the "Meaty" Marinara (page 290), omitting the TVP altogether.

2¼ cups (510 g) marinara sauce
2 eggplants, sliced ⅛ inch (3 mm) thick
40 large-size leaves fresh basil
1 recipe Tofu Ricotta (page 303)
6 Roma tomatoes, sliced ⅛ inch (3 mm) thick

Preheat the oven to 350°F (180°C, or gas mark 4). Have ready a 9 × 13-inch (23 × 33-cm) baking dish.

A quick note before assembling the lasagna: you will have 4 layers in all, so divide each ingredient accordingly.

Place a very thin layer of sauce in the bottom of the dish.

Place a single layer of eggplant slices over the sauce.

Place a thin layer of sauce over the eggplant.

Place about 10 leaves of basil on top of the sauce.

Sprinkle with a layer of ricotta.

Add a single layer of tomatoes over the ricotta.

Repeat until you have 4 complete layers.

Bake, covered with aluminum foil, for 30 minutes.

Remove the foil and bake for an additional 20 minutes.

Let stand for at least 15 minutes before serving, so that the portions don't fall apart when cut.

Yield: 12 servings

Very Veggie Shepherd's Pie

This is a filling and comforting one-pot meal that is chock-full of vegetable goodness to keep your immune system raring to go during the cold winter months.

4 small-size russet potatoes, scrubbed clean, peeled if desired, and cubed small
2 tablespoons (28 g) nondairy butter, plus an extra ½ teaspoon for coating dish
⅓ cup (80 ml) unsweetened almond or other nondairy milk
1 teaspoon fine sea salt, divided
½ teaspoon ground black pepper, divided
¾ cup (165 g) Kale Pesto (page 294)
⅓ cup (39 g) chopped walnuts
4 cups (940 ml) water
1 cup (192 g) uncooked red lentils, rinsed and drained
1 tablespoon (15 ml) extra-virgin olive oil
¼ cup (40 g) chopped red onion
2 cloves garlic, grated
1⅓ cups (160 g) chopped zucchini
1 cup (180 g) chopped fresh tomato
4 leaves fresh basil, minced
2 tablespoons (33 g) tomato paste
1 cup (185 g) Fu-ttage Cheese (page 85)

Place the cubed potatoes in a large-size saucepan, cover with water, bring to a boil, and cook until very tender, 15 to 20 minutes. Drain and return to the saucepan.

Add the 2 tablespoons (28 g) butter, milk, ½ teaspoon of the salt, and ¼ teaspoon of the pepper and mash until the potatoes are rather smooth. Add the pesto and walnuts and stir to combine. Set aside.

Bring the water to a boil in a medium-size saucepan. Add the lentils. Cook until tender, 15 to 20 minutes. Drain and set aside.

Preheat the oven to 375°F (190°C, or gas mark 5). Lightly coat an 8-inch (20-cm) square baking dish with the remaining ½ teaspoon butter.

In a large-size saucepan, heat the oil over medium heat. Cook the onion, garlic, zucchini, tomato, remaining ½ teaspoon salt, and remaining ¼ teaspoon pepper over medium heat until the zucchini browns, about 6 minutes.

Stir in the basil, tomato paste, cooked lentils, and Fu-ttage Cheese. Let simmer for another 2 minutes.

Spread the zucchini and lentil mixture in the bottom of the baking dish. Top with the kale pesto potatoes, spreading in an even layer.

Cover with foil and bake for 20 minutes. Remove the foil, and bake for another 15 minutes.

Let stand for at least 15 minutes before serving, so that the portions don't fall apart when cut.

Yield: 4 servings

Veggie Curry Feast

Here is a simple, affordable, and healthy dish that is perfect for cold winter nights when you need something tasty and that can be prepared in no time, especially if you have leftover cooked broccoli from a previous meal.

1 tablespoon (15 ml) peanut oil
¼ cup (40 g) chopped shallot
2 cloves garlic, grated
1 tablespoon (6 g) grated gingerroot
1 tablespoon (6 g) curry powder
1 teaspoon turmeric
2 teaspoons garam masala, store-bought or homemade (page 305)
2 teaspoons dried basil
½ teaspoon coarse sea salt
1½ cups (355 ml) coconut milk
1 tablespoon (15 ml) tamari or soy sauce
1 head cauliflower, cleaned and chopped small
1 can (15 ounces, or 425 g) cooked garbanzo beans, drained and rinsed
1 head broccoli, trimmed and steamed until tender
Handful toasted slivered almonds, for garnish (optional)

In a large-size saucepan, heat the oil over medium-high heat. Cook the shallot, garlic, and ginger over medium heat until fragrant, about 2 minutes.

Stir in the curry, turmeric, garam masala, basil, and salt. Cook for another minute.

Stir in the coconut milk and tamari. Bring to a boil. Add the cauliflower, cover with a lid, and let simmer for 15 minutes, or until tender.

Coarsely mash the cauliflower; stir in the beans and broccoli, and let simmer for another 5 minutes.

Garnish with the slivered almonds, if desired.

Yield: 4 servings

Gluten Free

Nutty Stuffed Veggies

Choose eggplants, tomatoes, or bell peppers to use as healthy vessels for a gloriously spicy sauce that will delight your senses and tickle your taste buds.

Nonstick cooking spray or 1 teaspoon nondairy butter or any oil, for coating baking dish
2 medium-size eggplants or 8 large-size tomatoes or 4 large-size bell peppers
1 pound (455 g) extra-firm tofu, drained and patted dry
1 medium-size Granny Smith or other tart apple, peeled, cored, and quartered
2 cloves garlic, grated
¼ cup (40 g) chopped shallot
¼ cup (15 g) fresh curly parsley
1½ cups (246 g) cooked wild rice
1 can (14 ounces, or 414 ml) coconut milk
1 can (15 ounces, or 425 g) diced tomatoes, drained
¼ cup (64 g) creamy or crunchy natural peanut butter
2 teaspoons agave nectar
1 tablespoon (6 g) curry powder
½ teaspoon turmeric
¼ teaspoon cayenne pepper
1 teaspoon fine sea salt
½ teaspoon ground black pepper
2 teaspoons dried basil
1 tablespoon (15 ml) extra-virgin olive oil

Preheat the oven to 400°F (200°C, or gas mark 6). Lightly coat a 9 × 13-inch (23 × 33-cm) baking dish with spray.

If using eggplant: cut in half, place on a lightly oiled baking sheet, and roast for 15 minutes, or until the flesh is partially tender. Cool for a few minutes until it is possible to scoop out the flesh, then chop it up into small pieces, and set aside; you will add it to the tofu mixture a bit later.

If using tomatoes: carefully cut a slice off the top, scoop out the flesh, chop the flesh into small pieces, and set aside; you will add it to the tofu mixture a bit later.

If using bell peppers: carefully cut in half, remove the seeds, and rinse.

Combine the tofu, apple, garlic, shallot, and parsley in a food processor. Blend until just coarsely chopped. Transfer to a large-size bowl, add the wild rice, and stir to combine.

Combine the coconut milk, diced tomatoes, peanut butter, agave, curry powder, turmeric, cayenne, salt, pepper, and basil in the food processor. Blend until perfectly smooth.

In a large-size saucepan over medium heat, combine the oil, tofu mixture, and half of the coconut sauce. Add the flesh of the eggplant or tomato, if using. Simmer for 8 minutes.

Place the veggie shells in the prepared baking dish. Fill with the tofu mixture. Drizzle the remaining half of the coconut sauce on top of the filling. If using tomatoes, place the previously sliced top on the filling.

Cover tightly with foil. Bake for 20 minutes, remove the foil, and bake for another 10 to 20 minutes, or until the veggies are tender. Serve hot.

Yield: 4 servings

Potato-Stuffed Portobellos

Meaty portobellos stuffed with creamy mashed potatoes? Seconds, please. The combination of baby red and baby gold potatoes gives these a really creamy texture. Of course, you can always substitute another type of potato if these are not available.

1 pound (455 g) baby red potatoes, with skins
1 pound (455 g) baby gold potatoes, with skins
½ cup (120 ml) extra-virgin olive oil
½ cup (120 ml) soy sauce
4 large-size portobello mushroom caps
1 cup (235 ml) plain soy creamer or soymilk
¼ cup (56 g) nondairy butter
¼ cup (30 g) nutritional yeast
1 cup (160 g) diced scallion
1 teaspoon garlic powder
1 teaspoon paprika
¼ teaspoon ground cumin
¼ teaspoon chili powder
Salt and pepper, to taste

Add the potatoes to a large-size pot of salted water and bring to a boil. Boil until fork-tender, then drain and return to the pot.

Preheat the oven to 375°F (190°C, or gas mark 5).

Place the olive oil and soy sauce in the bottom of a 9 x 13-inch (23 x 33-cm) baking dish.

Remove the stems and gills from the portobello caps. Place the mushrooms, top side down, in the dish.

Add the creamer, butter, nutritional yeast, scallion, garlic powder, paprika, cumin, chili powder, salt, and pepper to the potatoes.

Using a hand masher, mash until fairly smooth, but a little bit chunky.

Spoon an equal amount of potatoes into each mushroom.

Bake for 30 minutes or until the tops are beginning to brown.

Yield: 4 servings

Carciofi Farciti (Italian Stuffed Artichokes)

Serve with warm marinara or vegan mayonnaise (page 301 or 302) and lemon juice for dipping the leaves once all of the stuffing has been gobbled up.

- 2 large-size artichokes
- 1 cup (235 ml) vegetable broth

For the filling:

- 3 tablespoons (45 ml) extra-virgin olive oil, divided
- 1 cup (160 g) diced red onion
- 8 ounces (227 g) baby bella or button mushrooms, chopped
- 1 tablespoon (15 g) minced garlic
- ½ cup plus 2 tablespoons (165 ml) water
- ½ cup (86 g) dry couscous
- 6 sun-dried tomatoes packed in oil, chopped
- 2 tablespoons (6 g) finely chopped fresh basil or 2 teaspoons dried
- 2 tablespoons (30 ml) balsamic vinegar

- ¼ cup (30 g) pine nuts
- Salt and freshly cracked pepper, to taste

Prepare the artichokes by first removing the top one-third of the leaves, then remove the stem. Using kitchen shears, cut off the pointy tips of each of the remaining leaves. Set flat on its bottom and open up the top. Remove all of the inner purple flowers, all the way to the "hairy" parts. Use one large outer leaf to press into the center and prevent the hairs from getting into the stuffing. Alternatively, you can spend the extra time to get way down in there and dig out the coveted heart.

Bring a large-size pot of water to a boil. Place the prepared artichokes in the boiling water, cover, and boil for 10 minutes. Drain.

Preheat the oven to 450°F (230°C, or gas mark 8). Pour the broth into a small-size baking dish.

To make the filling: In a skillet or frying pan over medium-high heat, heat 2 tablespoons (30 ml) of the oil and sauté the onion, mushrooms, and garlic until fragrant and translucent, 5 to 7 minutes. Remove from the heat.

Bring the water to a boil, add the couscous, remove from the heat, cover, and let stand for 5 minutes.

Add the couscous, sun-dried tomatoes, basil, and balsamic vinegar to the sautéed mixture.

Stuff the mixture into the center of the artichokes, as well as in between the leaves. Sprinkle the tops with the pine nuts, salt, and pepper.

Place the artichokes in the baking dish and bake for 15 to 20 minutes, or until the pine nuts begin to brown.

Yield: 2 stuffed artichokes

Chorizo Tacos with Chunky Roasted Veggie Salsa

Sprinkling some of your favorite animal-friendly cheese, along with a nice dollop of nondairy sour cream, on top of these tacos will turn you into your friends and family's favorite person ever when you invite them over for Mexican Food Night. What is it, you say? You don't have Mexican Food Nights yet? Consider this recipe your incentive to get with the program. You'll thank us later!

1 pound (455 g) cherry or grape tomatoes
1 green bell pepper, seeded and quartered
½ large-size lemon
1 large-size red onion, cut into 8 chunks
4 cloves garlic, peeled and left whole
2 tablespoons (30 ml) extra-virgin olive oil
1 teaspoon coarse sea salt
12 ounces (340 g) store-bought soy chorizo, casings removed, crumbled, or 2 recipes Seitan Chorizo Crumbles (page 209)
⅓ cup (5 g) fresh cilantro or (20 g) curly parsley
6 burrito-style flour tortillas

Preheat the oven to 400°F (200°C, or gas mark 6). Have ready a large-size rimmed baking sheet.

Combine the tomatoes, bell pepper, lemon, onion, and garlic on the baking sheet.

Drizzle the oil and sprinkle salt on top. Mix it all in with your hands, making sure every inch of the veggies gets coated. Place the lemon cut side down on the sheet.

Bake for 20 minutes, or until the tomatoes look deflated. Check once while the veggies are baking, to make sure nothing burns.

In the meantime, place the soy chorizo in a skillet, and brown it over medium heat, about 8 minutes. Set aside.

Crush the roasted garlic with the flat of a knife; add to a food processor along with three-fourths of the tomatoes, the onion, and the cilantro, and squeeze the lemon over all.

Pulse several times, leaving the salsa somewhat chunky.

Cut the bell pepper into large chunks; place some on a fresh, warm tortilla. Top with a few remaining whole tomatoes, the salsa, and some chorizo. Repeat with the remaining 5 tortillas.

Yield: 6 tacos

VARIATION

Add 1 cup (155 g) fresh pineapple chunks or a couple of peeled, pitted, and chopped ripe peaches while roasting the veggies, for a delicious fruity salsa version.

Baked Chimichangas

It's hard to believe how chicken-like the tofu tastes here, even though it's prepared with four simple ingredients. So quick to put together, and with scrumptious results, this is a meal you can definitely plan even for busy weeknights.

For the cheesy salsa:

1 tablespoon (8 g) arrowroot powder or any flour
¼ cup (30 g) nutritional yeast
½ teaspoon fine sea salt
½ cup (120 ml) soy creamer or unsweetened nondairy milk
1 tablespoon (16 g) tahini
1 cup (240 g) your favorite salsa

For the filling:

1 tablespoon (15 ml) peanut oil
1 pound (455 g) extra-firm or super-firm tofu, pressed and torn into bite-size pieces
½ teaspoon fine sea salt
1 tablespoon (8 g) nutritional yeast
1 clove garlic, grated
1 cup (172 g) cooked black beans or any beans

6 burrito-style flour tortillas
1 tablespoon (15 ml) extra-virgin olive oil, for brushing tortillas
Hot sauce, for serving
Nondairy sour cream, store-bought or homemade (page 302), for serving

To make the cheesy salsa: In a medium-size saucepan, combine the arrowroot powder, nutritional yeast, and salt. Whisk in the creamer and tahini.

Cook over medium heat, whisking constantly, just until it begins to thicken. Stir in the salsa. Set aside.

Preheat the oven to 375°F (190°C, or gas mark 5). Line a rimmed baking sheet with parchment paper or a silicone baking mat, such as Silpat.

To make the filling: In a large-size skillet, heat the oil over medium-high heat and cook the tofu for 5 minutes. Add the salt and nutritional yeast, and cook for another 5 minutes, or until browned.

Stir in the cheesy salsa, garlic, and beans.

Divide the filling equally among the tortillas. Fold them up like burritos. Lightly brush the tops with oil.

Place seam side down on the prepared baking sheet and bake for 18 minutes.

Serve with a dash of hot sauce or a spoonful of nondairy sour cream.

Yield: 6 chimichangas

Stuffed Chiles

For a complete Mexican meal, serve these up with some warm tortillas, Spanish rice, and refried beans (page 282).

- 2 large-size green chiles (such as Anaheims or poblanos)
- 1 cup (160 g) diced red onion
- 6 ounces (170 g) extra-firm tofu, drained, pressed, and crumbled
- 6 ounces (170 g) seitan, diced
- 2 tablespoons (30 ml) extra-virgin olive oil
- ¼ cup (60 g) nondairy cream cheese or plain soy or other nondairy yogurt
- 1 tablespoon (18 g) mellow white or yellow miso (optional)
- 2 tablespoons (36 g) taco seasoning, store-bought or homemade (page 306)
- Sour cream, store-bought or homemade (page 302); salsa; or enchilada sauce, store-bought or homemade (page 288), for serving

Preheat the oven to 425°F (220°C, or gas mark 7). Prepare a baking sheet by lining with parchment or a silicone baking mat, such as Silpat.

Cut a slit in the chiles lengthwise, from top to bottom, and reach in to pull out the seeds and core. Rinse under water to remove any stray seeds. If you enjoy a spicier meal, reserve some of the seeds to mix in with the filling.

In a mixing bowl, combine the onion, tofu, seitan, oil, cream cheese, miso, if using, and taco seasoning, and mush together with your hands until all the ingredients are well incorporated.

Stuff half of the mixture into each of the chiles.

Bake, uncovered, for 30 minutes, or until slightly browned and tender. Serve with sour cream, your favorite salsa, or enchilada sauce.

Yield: 2 stuffed chiles

Chiles Rellenos

A traditional chile relleno consists of a large chile stuffed with cheese and pork, then dipped in an egg batter and fried. That doesn't seem very fitting for a vegan! The chickpea flour used in this batter lends an egglike texture, and with the growing availability of nondairy versions of products such as cream cheese, the relleno is ours! Serve on their own, or top with Enchilada Sauce (page 288).

4 large-size green chiles (such as Anaheims or poblanos)
1 cup (227 g) nondairy cream cheese
6 ounces (170 g) store-bought soy chorizo or ½ recipe MexiMeat (page 213)
1 cup (120 g) chickpea flour
1 teaspoon ground cumin
1 teaspoon garlic powder
1 teaspoon dried oregano
Salt and pepper, to taste
1 cup (235 ml) soy creamer or nondairy milk
Canola or other vegetable oil, for frying

Preheat the oven to 350°F (180°C, or gas mark 4).

Roast the whole chiles on a baking sheet for 30 minutes, until soft. Let cool.

Remove the stems. Cut a slit in the chiles lengthwise, from top to bottom, and reach in to pull out the seeds and core. Rinse under water to remove any stray seeds. Lay flat and set aside.

Mix together the cream cheese and soy chorizo.

Place one-fourth of the mixture in each of the peppers and fold closed.

In a shallow dish, large enough for the peppers, mix together the chickpea flour, cumin, garlic powder, oregano, salt, and pepper. Add the creamer and mix until smooth.

Pour the oil to a depth of ¼ inch (6 mm) in the bottom of a large-size frying pan or cast-iron skillet and heat over high heat.

Carefully dip each pepper into the chickpea batter to coat, and transfer to the frying pan.

Panfry each side for 2 to 3 minutes, or until golden and crispy.

Transfer to a paper towel–lined plate to absorb excess oil.

Yield: 4 chiles rellenos

Black Bean, Corn, and Roasted Chile Quesadilla

Enjoy this traditional Mexican finger food served up with nondairy sour cream, salsa, and guacamole.

2 large-size green chiles (such as Anaheims or poblanos)
1 can (15 ounces, or 425 g) black beans, drained and rinsed
½ cup (68 g) yellow corn kernels
8 ounces (227 g) Nutty Cheese, Mexican variation (page 88), or your favorite nondairy cheese, cut into small pieces
½ cup (13 g) chopped fresh cilantro leaves
4 ounces (112 g) nondairy cream cheese
6 (8-inch, or 20-cm) flour tortillas

Preheat the oven to 350°F (180°C, or gas mark 4).

Roast the whole chiles on a baking sheet for 30 minutes. Let cool.

Cut off the stems and remove the seeds. Cut into thin strips.

In a mixing bowl, mix together the chile strips, beans, corn, cheese, cilantro, and cream cheese, using your hands to mash everything together.

Spread one-sixth of the mixture onto half of one tortilla and fold the other half over the top.

Repeat with the remaining 5 tortillas.

Cook one of three ways:

Lay all 6 quesadillas flat on a baking sheet in a single layer and bake for 15 minutes at 350°F (180°C, or gas mark 4), flipping them halfway through.

Panfry in a very hot, dry pan until slightly browned, about 2 to 3 minutes per side.

For a crispier tortilla, panfry in a very hot pan in a smidge of nondairy butter for 2 to 3 minutes per side.

Yield: 6 servings

Veggie Enchiladas

Yet another dish to serve on your newly dedicated Mexican Food Night! These enchiladas taste great served up with a dollop of nondairy sour cream, a few slices of ripe avocado, and a sprinkling of fresh cilantro leaves. If jalapeños are a bit too spicy for you, but you'd still like to add a little heat, try sprinkling on diced fire-roasted chiles instead.

Nonstick cooking spray
2 tablespoons (30 ml) extra-virgin olive oil
8 ounces (227 g) mushrooms, sliced
1 red bell pepper, cored, seeded, and diced
2 cups (320 g) diced yellow onion
1 tablespoon (15 g) minced garlic
¼ teaspoon ground cumin
¼ teaspoon dried oregano
¼ teaspoon ground black pepper
12 corn tortillas
1 pound (455 g) refried beans, store-bought or homemade (page 282)
12 ounces (340 g) Nutty Cheese, Mexican variation (page 88), or your favorite nondairy cheese, grated or chopped, divided
2 cups (470 ml) enchilada sauce, store-bought or homemade (page 288)
2 ounces (56 g) black olives, sliced or diced
20 slices jarred nacho-style jalapeño chiles (optional)

Preheat the oven to 350°F (180°C, or gas mark 4). Coat a 9 × 13-inch (23 × 33-cm) baking dish with nonstick spray.

In a frying pan or cast-iron skillet, heat the olive oil over medium-high heat.

Add the mushrooms, bell pepper, onion, and garlic. Sauté for 10 to 12 minutes.

Stir in the cumin, oregano, and black pepper. Remove from the heat and set aside.

To the center of a tortilla add about 3 tablespoons (45 g) beans, ¼ cup (45 g) of the veggie mixture, and ½ ounce (14 g) of the cheese.

Roll up the tortilla and place seam side down in the baking dish. Repeat with the remaining tortillas.

Spread the enchilada sauce evenly over the top of the rolled-up enchiladas.

Sprinkle the remaining 6 ounces (170 g) cheese evenly over the sauce. Sprinkle the olives over the cheese. Sprinkle the jalapeños, if using, over the olives.

Bake for 30 minutes, or until bubbly and cooked through.

Yield: 12 enchiladas

Under 30 Minutes

Fajita Pitas

Sizzling fajitas are high up on the list of aroma perfection! Using whole wheat pita adds an extra healthy boost to an already healthy meal. These taste especially great when drizzled with Chipotle Ranch Dressing (page 129) and topped off with Salsa Fresca (page 81).

2 teaspoons chili powder
1 teaspoon salt
1 teaspoon paprika
1 teaspoon granulated sugar
½ teaspoon onion powder
¼ teaspoon garlic powder
¼ teaspoon cayenne pepper
¼ teaspoon cumin
1 red bell pepper, cored, seeded, and cut into strips
1 green bell pepper, cored, seeded, and cut into strips
1 large-size red onion, cut julienne style
2 large-size portobello caps, stems removed and cut into strips
1 pound (455 g) seitan, store-bought or homemade (page 216), cut into thin strips
2 tablespoons (30 ml) canola or other vegetable oil, for frying
2 tablespoons (30 ml) soy sauce or tamari
4 whole wheat pita, cut in half to make 8 pita pockets

In a small-size bowl, combine the chili powder, salt, paprika, sugar, onion powder, garlic powder, cayenne pepper, and cumin.

In a large-size mixing bowl, combine the bell peppers, onion, mushrooms, and seitan. Add the seasoning mix and toss to coat.

Heat the oil in a large-size skillet or wok over high heat. Add the veggie-seitan mixture and stir-fry for 10 to 12 minutes, constantly tossing, until the vegetables are tender and aromatic.

Add the soy sauce, toss to coat, and cook 2 to 3 minutes longer.

Stuff an equal amount into each pita pocket and serve hot.

Yield: 8 servings

Traditional Tamales

Afraid to tackle homemade tamales? Don't be. We've broken it down into easy steps. If you don't have a steamer, a large-size pasta pot with a removable strainer works well for this. And be creative with the fillings! You can make a variety, including those listed below.

36 corn husks, soaked in warm water at least 2 hours

For the masa:

8 cups (1.88 L) vegetable broth
2 pounds (900 g) masa harina flour (Maseca instant masa flour works well here)
3 tablespoons (21 g) each paprika, chili powder, and garlic powder
3 tablespoons (54 g) salt
1 tablespoon (18 g) cumin seeds
2 cups (470 ml) corn oil

Options for the filling:

- 1 recipe MexiMeat (page 213) mixed with about ¼ cup (60 g) nondairy cream cheese
- 1 recipe Nutty Cheese (page 88)
- 3 or 4 diced chipotle chiles in adobo mixed with ½ cup (120 g) nondairy sour cream, store-bought or homemade (page 302)
- Mixed vegetables
- Jalapeños and tomatoes
- Salsa

To make the masa: Warm the vegetable broth over low heat. Put the masa in a very large mixing bowl. Mix the paprika, chili powder, garlic powder, salt, and cumin seeds into the flour until well incorporated.

Add the corn oil to the masa and spice mixture. Slowly add the broth, about 1 cup (235 ml) at a time. Work the mixture with your hands to make a dough. If it is too dry, add enough warm water to get it to the consistency of thick peanut butter. If it is too thin, add a little more masa.

Have a workstation set up with your fillings within easy reach. Remove the husks from the water and carefully separate them. Stack them on a damp kitchen towel where they are well within reach.

Spread the masa from the center all the way to one long edge of the husk. Leave enough space to roll up and fold over the pointy end.

Add about 2 to 3 tablespoons (30 to 45 g) of filling to the center of the masa. Roll up the tamale, starting from the side where the masa goes all the way to the edge, then fold the pointy end under. We like to tie a little bow on ours using a thin strip of husk (so cute), but it is not necessary.

Stack the tamales in tight to the steamer basket until it is full, then place it upright in the larger pot.

Place enough water in the bottom of the pot so that it does not touch the tamales. Place the lid on the steamer. Bring it to a boil, reduce the heat to a simmer, and steam for 2 to 3 hours. Remember to check the water level every once in a while so that the pot does not boil dry, and add more water if necessary.

After 2 hours of steaming, remove one tamale and place it on a plate to cool for 5 minutes. Unwrap it and test for doneness. It should be its own "unit" and not mushy or runny. If it is not done, continue to steam for another 15 to 30 minutes, and then retest.

Remove the tamales from the pot, place on a tray to cool, and enjoy, or place in resealable plastic bags to freeze. You can freeze tamales for up to a year.

Yield: 36 tamales

Pumpkin Cranberry Tamales

These are definitely not your typical tamales. They are on the sweet side and make a nice accompaniment to other savory main dishes. As with all tamales, these take a few hours to make, but most of that is steam time. For the corn husks, be sure to use the real thing and not the reusable plastic tamale wrappers; it is key to giving the tamale the flavor it deserves after all your hard work. You'll also need a large-size steamer with a lid. If you don't have a steamer, a large-size pasta pot with a removable strainer works well for this.

30 corn husks

For the filling:

4 cups masa harina flour (Maseca instant masa flour works well)
2 cans (15 ounces, or 425 g each) solid-pack pure pumpkin purée
1 cup (235 ml) canola oil
½ cup (110 g) packed brown sugar
¼ cup (84 g) pure maple syrup or pure agave nectar
1 tablespoon (15 ml) pure vanilla extract
1 tablespoon (7 g) ground cinnamon
1 teaspoon ground nutmeg
1 teaspoon ground cloves
1 cup (122 g) dried cranberries

Soak the corn husks in warm water for about 2 hours to soften them and make them more pliable.

To make the filling: In a large-size bowl, mix all the filling ingredients together, using your hands, until well incorporated. The consistency should be that of thick peanut butter. If it is too thick, add a little more oil; if it is too thin, add a little more masa.

Using one husk at a time, open it up with the pointy side pointing away from you. Add about ¼ cup (45 g) of the filling to the center of the husk. Roll up the tamale and fold over the pointy end. Repeat with the remaining tamales.

Remove the inside basket of the steamer, lay it on its side, stack the tamales in tight until it is full, then place it upright in the larger pot.

Place enough water in the bottom of the steamer so that it does not touch the tamales. Place the lid on the steamer. Bring it to a boil, reduce the heat to medium-low, and steam for 2 to 3 hours. Remember to check the water level every once in a while so that the pot does not boil dry, and add more water if necessary.

After 2 hours of steaming, remove one tamale, place it on a plate to cool for 5 minutes, unwrap it, and test for doneness. It should be its own "unit" and not mushy or runny. If it is not done, continue to steam for another 15 to 30 minutes, and then retest.

Remove the tamales from the pot, place on a tray to cool, and enjoy, or place in resealable plastic bags to freeze. You can freeze tamales for up to a year.

Yield: 30 tamales

Peruvian Tamales

These tamales have a completely different flavor than that of traditional tamales. The use of banana leaves instead of corn husks adds to the depth of flavor. Banana leaves can usually be found in the frozen section of Latin markets. Thaw in the refrigerator for about a day before using.

1 package (1 pound, or 455 g) banana leaves

For the masa:

- 3 pounds (1362 g) masa harina (Maseca instant masa works well here)
- 2 dried ancho chile pods, ground into a powder
- 2 tablespoons (14 g) garlic powder
- 2 tablespoons (14 g) onion powder
- 1 tablespoon (18 g) salt
- 6 cups (1410 ml) vegetable broth
- 3 cups (705 ml) canola oil
- 1 cup (235 ml) coconut milk

For the filling:

- 10 ounces (284 g) diced tomatoes
- 6 ounces (170 g) diced mango
- 6 ounces (170 g) diced pineapple
- 6 ounces (170 g) diced sweet potato
- 1 can (15 ounces, or 425 g) black beans, drained and rinsed
- 1 can (15 ounces, or 425 g) crushed tomatillos

Unfold the banana leaves and cut into twenty 10-inch (25-cm) squares. Rinse under cool water and set aside.

To make the masa: Mix together all the masa ingredients until a thick paste is formed.

To make the filling: Mix all the filling ingredients together in a bowl.

Place 1 square of banana leaf on a flat surface. Spread 6 ounces (170 g) of the masa to the center of the edge of the leaf closest to you, leaving a few inches on either side.

Add ¼ cup (45 g) of the filling on top of the masa, near the edge closest to you.

Roll up the tamale like a burrito, folding in the edges as you roll. If you choose, tie the tamale closed with a strip of banana leaf. Repeat with the remaining tamales.

Remove the inside basket of the steamer, lay it on its side, stack the tamales in tight until it is full, then place it upright in the larger pot.

Place enough water in the bottom of the steamer so that it does not touch the tamales. Place the lid on the steamer. Bring it to a boil, reduce the heat to medium-low, and steam for 2 to 3 hours. Remember to check the water level every once in a while so that the pot does not boil dry, and add more water if necessary.

After 2 hours of steaming, remove one tamale, place it on a plate to cool for 5 minutes, unwrap it, and test for doneness. It should be its own "unit" and not mushy or runny. If it is not done, continue to steam for another 15 to 30 minutes, and then retest.

Remove the tamales from the pot, place on a tray to cool, and enjoy. Serve them up with a healthy dollop of Argentinian Tomatillo and Roasted Green Chile Chimichurri (page 292) for an added punch of fresh Latin flavor.

Yield: 20 tamales

Festivus Loaf

Even non-veggies will love this yummy main dish at your next holiday get-together! Serve with Green Bean Almondine (page 269) and Whiskey Sweet Potato Mash (page 162) for a really traditional meal.

2 cups (288 g) vital wheat gluten flour
2 cups (240 g) chickpea flour
2 cups (240 g) whole wheat pastry flour
5 cups (1175 ml) vegetable broth, divided
1 recipe Sun-Dried Tomato Pesto (page 91)
2 recipes Traditional Bread Dressing (page 272), divided

Preheat the oven to 350°F (180°C, or gas mark 4).

In a large-size bowl, combine the wheat gluten and flours, and then slowly add the vegetable broth. Start with 2 cups (470 ml) and add more, a little bit at a time, if needed, using no more than 1 more cup (235 ml).

Knead together until a nice smooth dough ball is formed. Knead for 5 more minutes, and then cover and set aside to rest for 20 minutes.

After the dough has rested, roll it out on a well-floured surface, trying to keep a rectangular shape about 12 × 18 inches (30.5 × 46 cm).

Spread the pesto evenly all over the dough.

Sprinkle on half of the dressing.

Starting at the short end, roll up the dough.

Pour the remaining 2 cups (470 ml) vegetable broth into a 9 × 13-inch (23 × 33-cm) baking dish, then place the loaf in the center of the dish.

Add the remaining half of the dressing all around the loaf.

Place in the oven and bake for 90 minutes, basting with the broth every 15 minutes or so.

Yield: 8 servings

Granny's Meatloaf

Beware of the amazing smells that will be coming out of the oven while this is baking. Neighbors, neighbor's kids, and neighbor's neighbors will be banging down your door asking, "What's for dinner?" Serve with mashed potatoes and greens for a traditional Sunday night meal.

3 cups (288 g) TVP granules
2½ cups (590 g) vegetable broth or water
2 tablespoons (30 ml) soy sauce or tamari
2 tablespoons (30 ml) extra-virgin olive oil
2 cups (320 g) diced yellow onion
2 cloves garlic, minced
1 teaspoon ground black pepper
1 tablespoon (8 g) garlic powder
1 tablespoon (8 g) onion powder
½ teaspoon cumin
1 cup (272 g) organic ketchup, plus extra for basting
1½ cups (216 g) vital wheat gluten flour

Preheat the oven to 350°F (180°C, or gas mark 4). Have ready a baking sheet lined with parchment or a silicone baking mat, such as Silpat.

Reconstitute the TVP in one of two ways: 1) mix together the TVP granules, vegetable broth, and soy sauce in a microwave-safe bowl, cover tightly with plastic wrap, and microwave on high for 5 to 6 minutes or 2) mix together the TVP and soy sauce, bring the vegetable broth to a boil, pour over the TVP, cover, and let stand for 10 minutes. Set aside.

In a frying pan or cast-iron skillet, heat the olive oil and sauté the onion and garlic until translucent and just beginning to brown, about 7 to 10 minutes.

Combine the pepper, garlic powder, onion powder, cumin, ketchup, wheat gluten, and sautéed onion and garlic mixture and stir into the reconstituted TVP. Mix well.

Use your hands and knead the mixture together. Make sure everything is well incorporated.

At this point you can proceed with the mixture as is or place half of the mixture in the food processor and process until it is the consistency of paste. Then mix the two portions back together, very well, with your hands. The point of this step is to get your meatloaf to stick together better when you slice it. TVP is crumbly, and when you slice your loaf, if you want perfect slices, use this method. If you don't mind crumbly meatloaf, you can skip this step. It tastes the same either way, and we have done it both ways with great results.

Form the mixture into a large loaf shape.

Place in the center of the baking sheet and "paint" on a thin layer of ketchup.

Bake for 20 minutes.

Remove from the oven and brush on another layer of ketchup.

Return to the oven and bake for an additional 25 minutes. Your loaf should be firm and the ketchup dark and sticky.

Let stand for 10 minutes before slicing.

Yield: 8 servings

Seitan en Croûte

A juicy, savory seitan wrapped in a flaky pastry crust . . . need we say more?

- 2 cups (288 g) vital wheat gluten flour
- 1 cup (120 g) whole wheat flour
- ¼ cup (30 g) nutritional yeast
- 1 teaspoon dried parsley flakes, plus extra for sprinkling
- 1 teaspoon paprika, plus extra for sprinkling
- 1 teaspoon garlic powder
- ½ teaspoon black pepper
- 1 cup (235 ml) beef-flavored vegetable broth (or plain vegetable broth)
- ½ cup (120 ml) extra-virgin olive oil
- ¼ cup (60 ml) soy sauce or tamari
- 3 tablespoons (50 g) tomato paste
- 1 tablespoon (15 g) prepared stone-ground mustard
- 2 teaspoons liquid smoke
- 1 package (1 pound, or 455 g) vegan frozen puff pastry

Preheat the oven to 350°F (180°C, or gas mark 4). Have ready a baking sheet lined with parchment or a silicone baking mat, such as Silpat.

In a large-size mixing bowl, combine the wheat gluten, wheat flour, nutritional yeast, parsley, paprika, garlic powder, and pepper.

In a separate bowl, mix together the broth, oil, soy sauce, tomato paste, mustard, and liquid smoke.

Add the wet ingredients to the dry and knead together until well incorporated and a moist dough forms. Let rest for 20 minutes.

Thaw the puff pastry according to the package instructions.

Form the mixture into a loaf (similar to a meat loaf shape) and place in the center of the baking sheet.

Bake, uncovered, for 35 minutes. Remove from the oven and let cool slightly, to allow the loaf to reabsorb its juices.

Increase the oven temperature to 375°F (190°C, or gas mark 5).

Cover the loaf entirely with one of the pastry sheets, tucking the edges underneath the loaf.

Slice another sheet into 10 even strips for weaving. Weave the strips, on the diagonal, across the top of the loaf (like the top of an apple pie!). Tuck loose ends under the loaf.

Sprinkle a little paprika and parsley on top for color.

Return to the oven and bake for an additional 20 to 25 minutes, or until the pastry is fluffy and golden brown.

Yield: 1 loaf (about 8 servings)

Apricot-Glazed Roast

This versatile roast tastes great as the main course alongside some Mustard and Spinach Smashed Potatoes (page 161) and Balsamic Roasted Asparagus with Pearl Onions (page 275). Or, believe it or not, this roast makes a mean taco! Slice a few thin slices and serve in a crispy corn tortilla, along with some avocado, and topped with Chipotle Ranch Dressing (page 129).

For the Apricot Glaze:

10 ounces (284 g) apricot jam
½ cup (168 g) agave nectar
½ cup (60 ml) extra-virgin olive oil
1 tablespoon (15 g) stone-ground mustard
Salt and pepper, to taste

2 cups (288 g) vital wheat gluten flour
2 cups (240 g) whole wheat pastry flour
¼ cup (30 g) nutritional yeast
1 teaspoon ground black pepper
1 cup (235 ml) water
1 cup (160 g) finely diced white or yellow onion
¼ cup (60 ml) soy sauce or tamari
6 dried apricots, cut into small pieces
10 to 15 fresh basil leaves, cut into a chiffonade
2 cloves garlic, minced

To make the glaze: Whisk together all the glaze ingredients. Divide into 2 equal portions and set aside.

Preheat the oven to 350°F (180°C, or gas mark 4). Line a baking sheet with parchment or a silicone baking mat, such as Silpat.

In a large-size mixing bowl, mix together the wheat gluten, flour, yeast, and pepper.

Separately mix together half of the glaze, the water, onion, soy sauce, apricots, basil, and garlic.

Add the wet ingredients to the dry and knead together until well incorporated.

Form into a loaf and place in the center of the baking sheet.

Brush on a thick layer of the remaining glaze, reserving enough for a second brushing of glaze halfway through the baking.

Bake, uncovered, for 30 minutes.

Remove from the oven and increase the heat to 400°F (200°C, or gas mark 6).

Brush on the remaining glaze and bake for an additional 30 minutes.

Yield: 8 servings

Colcannon

Here's an animal-friendly version of the budget-conscious, deliciously simple traditional Irish dish of the same name. Feel free to substitute leek for the onion, if you prefer a subtler flavor. Kale would also make a pleasant and nutrient-packed alternative to cabbage.

1 tablespoon (15 ml) canola oil
½ cup (80 g) chopped white onion
36 ounces (1 kg) russet potatoes, scrubbed clean, peeled if desired, and cubed
4 cups (280 g) shredded green cabbage
¼ cup (60 ml) unsweetened almond or other nondairy milk
3 tablespoons (42 g) nondairy butter
¼ teaspoon ground nutmeg
½ teaspoon ground black pepper
1 teaspoon coarse sea salt
2 cloves garlic, grated
2 recipes Seitan Bacon Crumbles (page 209) or Crispy Seitan Bacon (page 211), crumbled

In a large-size saucepan, combine the oil and onion. Cook for 2 minutes over medium heat. Stir in the potatoes and cook for 2 minutes. Cover with water. Bring to a boil, and cook for 12 minutes.

Add the cabbage to the boiling pot of potatoes and cook for another 8 minutes, or until the potatoes are tender. Drain, and return to the saucepan.

Add the milk, butter, nutmeg, pepper, salt, and garlic. Mash until the potatoes reach the desired consistency. Stir in the bacon crumbles.

Serve hot.

Yield: 4 servings

Soy Free

Eggplant Marinara Pizza

This dish is a bit more time-consuming than it would be to pop a ready-made, frozen pizza into the oven, but the fancy look and amazing flavor make the preparation absolutely worth your while. If you'd rather have only one pizza, halve the crust recipe, and just use half of the marinara sauce, and enjoy the rest served with pasta, potatoes, or rice.

For the crust:

- 4 cups (480 g) white whole wheat, regular whole wheat, or bread flour
- 2 teaspoons fine sea salt
- 1 tablespoon (12 g) bread machine yeast
- 1 tablespoon (12 g) raw sugar
- ½ cup (60 g) nutritional yeast
- ½ teaspoon black pepper
- ¼ cup (60 ml) extra-virgin olive oil
- 3 cloves garlic, grated
- 1½ cups (355 ml) water
- ½ teaspoon canola oil, to coat bowl

For the marinara:

- 1 tablespoon (15 ml) extra-virgin olive oil
- 2 cloves garlic, grated
- 1 cup (160 g) chopped red onion
- 1 teaspoon dried thyme
- 1 teaspoon dried oregano
- 1½ teaspoons dried basil
- 1 teaspoon fine sea salt
- ½ teaspoon ground black pepper
- 1 eggplant, peeled if desired, finely diced
- 2 cans (15 ounces, or 425 g each) fire-roasted or regular diced tomatoes, including juice
- 2 tablespoons (33 g) tomato paste
- ⅓ cup (44 g) black olives, sliced

To make the crust: Combine the flour, salt, bread machine yeast, sugar, nutritional yeast, and pepper in a large-size bowl. Stir in the olive oil, the garlic, and a little of the water at a time until a dough forms.

Transfer to a lightly floured surface and knead for 8 to 10 minutes, until the dough is smooth and pliable, adding more flour, a little at a time, if the dough is too wet. Shape into a ball.

Lightly coat a large-size bowl with the canola oil. Turn the dough to coat, cover, and let rise for 90 minutes. While the dough is rising, prepare the marinara.

To make the marinara: In a large-size saucepan, combine the oil, garlic, onion, thyme, oregano, basil, salt, pepper, and eggplant. Cook over medium-high heat for 5 minutes, until the onion is tender and the eggplant is a little brown, stirring often.

Stir in the diced tomatoes with their juice, tomato paste, and olives. Lower the heat, cover partially, and let simmer for 8 to 10 minutes, until the eggplant is very tender.

Preheat the oven to 400°F (200°C, or gas mark 6). Prepare 2 large-size baking sheets and 2 large-size pieces of parchment or silicone baking mats, such as Silpat.

Punch down the dough and divide into 2 equal portions. Press each one down with your hands directly onto the parchment into large circles about ¼ inch (6 mm) thick.

Spread half of the eggplant marinara onto each crust.

Bake for 18 to 20 minutes, or until the edges of the crusts are golden brown.

Yield: 2 pizzas

White Pizza

This pizza is something you might order at a fancy pizzeria, if there were any fancy pizzerias that served vegan white pizza. It makes enough for two 10-inch (25-cm) pizzas, so if you'd like, feel free to cut the recipe in half.

1 recipe Cast-Iron Deep Dish Pizza Dough (page 333)
20 whole leaves fresh basil
1 recipe Béchamel Sauce, garlic and basil variation (page 298)
½ white onion, sliced into julienne
6 ounces (170 g) smoked tofu, store-bought or homemade (page 208), cut into thin strips

Preheat the oven to 450°F (230°C, or gas mark 8). Prepare 2 large-size baking sheets and 2 large-size pieces of parchment or silicone baking mats, such as Silpat.

Roll out the dough into two 10-inch (25-cm) crusts.

On each, layer 10 whole basil leaves.

Add half of the béchamel to each, spreading evenly over the basil.

Sprinkle half of the onions on each.

Top each with half of the smoked tofu.

Bake for about 10 minutes, or until the crust is nice and golden.

Yield: 2 pizzas

Gluten Free

Rosemary Apple Potato Rösti

A traditional potato dish from Switzerland, comparable to hash browns, this cheap and filling meal is also quick and easy to prepare. For best results, use chilled cooked potatoes. Simply shock them in cold water after 15 minutes of boiling time, and place them in the fridge overnight.

- 26 ounces (750 g) russet potatoes, scrubbed clean, peeled if desired
- Nonstick cooking spray or extra nondairy butter, for the pie plates
- 2 Fuji or other tart apples, peeled if desired, quartered, and cored
- 1 red onion, quartered
- 2 tablespoons (30 ml) peanut oil
- 2 tablespoons (28 g) nondairy butter
- 1½ teaspoons dried rosemary
- 1 teaspoon coarse sea salt
- ½ teaspoon ground black pepper

Place the potatoes in a large-size saucepan. Cover with water, bring to a boil, and cook for 15 minutes, or until barely tender. Drain well.

Preheat the oven to 400°F (200°C, or gas mark 6). Lightly grease two 9-inch (23-cm) pie plates.

In a food processor, shred the potatoes, apples, and onion.

In a large-size saucepan, heat the oil and butter. Add the rosemary, salt, and pepper.

Add the shredded potatoes, apples, and onion. Cook for 8 minutes over medium-high heat, stirring often.

Firmly press down the potato mixture into one of the pie plates. Bake for 15 minutes.

Flip the rösti over carefully into the second pie plate. Bake for another 15 minutes, or until golden brown on top.

Leave in the plate to set for a few minutes before serving.

Yield: 4 servings

VARIATION

Enjoy with Seitan Bacon Crumbles (page 209) or Crispy Seitan Bacon (page 211) for extra yum factor. Please note that this addition would turn the dish into a non-gluten-free one.

Gluten Free

Mamou's Stuffed Tomatoes

This super simple recipe goes way back to the days when Celine and her family didn't even know there was such a thing as veganism. The whole family agrees that this is not only its healthiest, but also its tastiest incarnation by far.

½ teaspoon olive oil, for coating dish
4 medium-size tomatoes
2 cloves garlic, grated
1 teaspoon fine sea salt, plus more to taste
¼ cup (15 g) packed mixture of equal amounts chopped fresh parsley, basil, and thyme
¼ cup (40 g) chopped red onion
¾ cup (100 g) pressed and coarsely crumbled extra-firm tofu
1½ cups (237 g) fully cooked long grain white or (293 g) brown rice
¼ teaspoon ground black pepper, plus more to taste
2 tablespoons (28 g) nondairy butter

Preheat the oven to 375°F (190°C, or gas mark 5). Lightly coat the bottom of an 8-inch (20-cm) square baking dish with oil.

Slice off the top from each tomato.

Scoop out the flesh and juice and place in a large-size bowl. Cut off and discard the tougher parts of the tomato and add the garlic.

Sprinkle a little salt inside each tomato shell and place them in the baking dish.

Blend the herbs and onion in a food processor. Add the tofu and pulse two or three times; you want it to still have some texture, not be completely mashed. Stir into the tomato mixture, along with the rice and more salt and pepper to taste.

Divide the stuffing among the tomatoes, and place the tomato tops back on top of each one. Top each tomato with 1½ teaspoons of butter.

Bake for 35 to 40 minutes, or until the tomatoes appear a little wrinkly and are tender to the fork.

Yield: 4 stuffed tomatoes

Baked Eggplant Parmesan

If you end up having leftover coating, don't discard it! It makes an awesome coating for fried tofu or seitan cutlets. Just dip a piece of tofu or seitan into coconut or soymilk, then into the coating, then back into the milk, then back into the coating (double dredge), and panfry in plenty of oil, or simply sprinkle it on top of spaghetti!

1 large-size eggplant
1 cup (80 g) panko-style bread crumbs
½ cup (60 g) walnut pieces, ground into a powder
¼ cup (30 g) nutritional yeast
1 tablespoon (2 g) dried basil
1 tablespoon (8 g) garlic powder
Salt and freshly cracked pepper, to taste
Olive oil, for brushing
2 Roma or hothouse tomatoes, thinly sliced

Preheat the oven to 350°F (180°C, or gas mark 4). Prepare a baking sheet by lining with parchment or a silicone baking mat, such as Silpat.

Slice the eggplant into ½-inch-thick (1.3-cm) slices. You can peel the eggplant or leave it unpeeled. If you decide to leave it unpeeled, the coating won't stick to the skin on the edges, but you will still have plenty of coating on the flesh.

In a bowl, mix together the bread crumbs, walnuts, nutritional yeast, basil, garlic powder, and salt and pepper.

Brush both sides of a piece of eggplant liberally with olive oil and then coat in the panko mixture. Place on the baking sheet. Top with a slice of tomato. Repeat with the remaining pieces. Top with more salt and pepper to taste.

Bake for 25 to 30 minutes.

Serve on its own or with your favorite marinara sauce.

Yield: About 10 pieces, depending on the size of your eggplant

Soy Free

Multigrain Pilaf

Chock-full of all the grains you can think of (well, at least lots of them) and forming a complete protein by combining whole grains with beans, this pilaf goes extremely well with a simple side of panfried bell peppers of various colors.

1 tablespoon (15 ml) melted coconut oil
½ cup (80 g) chopped red onion
4 cloves garlic, grated
1 tablespoon (6 g) garam masala, store-bought or homemade (page 305)
½ teaspoon caraway seeds
½ teaspoon ground coriander
½ teaspoon ground ginger
¼ teaspoon cayenne pepper
1 teaspoon coarse sea salt
⅓ cup (53 g) raisins (optional)
½ cup (70 g) uncooked brown lentils, rinsed
½ cup (90 g) uncooked pearl barley, rinsed
½ cup (80 g) uncooked long grain brown rice, rinsed
½ cup (80 g) uncooked wild rice, rinsed
3 cups (705 ml) vegetable or tomato juice
3 cups (705 ml) water or vegetable broth
½ cup (84 g) uncooked quinoa, rinsed
1 can (15 ounces, or 425 g) black beans, drained and rinsed
1 can (15 ounces, or 425 g) kidney beans, drained and rinsed
Handful of Chili Roasted Peanuts (page 96), for serving

In a large-size saucepan, combine the oil, onion, garlic, garam masala, caraway seeds, coriander, ginger, and cayenne. Cook over medium heat for 2 minutes, until fragrant.

Stir in the salt, raisins (if using), lentils, barley, and rices. Cook for 2 minutes.

Add the juice and water, and bring to a boil. Lower the heat to medium-low, cover with a lid, and cook for 35 minutes, stirring twice during the process.

Add the quinoa and beans, cover again, and let cook for another 15 minutes: you want to see the little "tail" on the quinoa to know it is thoroughly cooked.

Remove the lid and let simmer longer if there is still a lot of liquid, to let it reduce. If the grains aren't tender by then and all the liquid is gone, add extra water or broth, and cook until tender.

Sprinkle with the roasted peanuts upon serving.

Yield: 6 servings

Cauliflower Pasta Crisp

Here is a creamy and nutritious cholesterol-free alternative to the beloved flavorful baked pasta dishes of days gone by. Choose the amount of pasta based on whether you prefer just a little pasta with your sauce or vice versa.

For the cauliflower sauce:

1 head cauliflower (about 2 pounds, or 907 g), trimmed, cleaned, and separated into small florets
1 tablespoon (15 ml) extra-virgin olive oil
4 cloves garlic, grated
½ cup (50 g) chopped scallion
¼ cup (64 g) tahini
1 tablespoon (6 g) ground cumin
1 teaspoon paprika
¼ teaspoon cayenne pepper
1 teaspoon fine sea salt
2 teaspoons brown rice or other flour
1½ cups (355 ml) unsweetened soy or other nondairy milk

For the topping and the pasta:

1 cup (120 g) walnuts
¼ cup (30 g) nutritional yeast
2 teaspoons lemon zest
1 teaspoon dried thyme
½ teaspoon ground pepper
1 teaspoon coarse sea salt
1 cup (80 g) whole wheat panko or other bread crumbs
2 tablespoons (30 ml) extra-virgin olive oil
1 teaspoon nondairy butter, to coat dish
12 ounces to 1 pound (340 to 455 g) uncooked whole-grain rotini pasta

To make the cauliflower sauce: Place the cauliflower florets in a large-size saucepan and cover with water. Bring to a boil, and cook until the florets are tender, about 10 minutes. Drain well.

In a medium-size saucepan, cook the oil, garlic, and scallion over medium heat for about 2 minutes, until fragrant.

Add the tahini, cumin, paprika, cayenne, salt, and flour. Cook for 1 minute.

Whisk in the milk and cook, just until it begins to thicken.

Combine the florets and sauce in a blender, or use an immersion blender, and purée until smooth.

To make the topping and pasta: Blend the nuts, nutritional yeast, zest, thyme, pepper, and salt in a food processor until a coarse meal forms.

In a medium-size bowl, combine the resulting coarse meal with the bread crumbs. Using a fork, coat the bread crumbs with the oil.

Preheat the oven to 350°F (180°C, or gas mark 4). Lightly coat a 9 × 13-inch (23 × 33-cm) baking dish with butter.

Cook the pasta according to package directions until just al dente, scooping out some of the cooking water to thin out the sauce if it needs it. Drain and return to the pot.

Stir the cauliflower sauce into the pasta, adding some of the extra liquid if it is too thick.

Pour into the baking dish, sprinkle the bread crumb topping over evenly, and bake for 15 minutes, until the topping is golden brown.

Let stand for at least 15 minutes before serving.

Yield: 4 to 6 servings, depending on amount of pasta used

Crispy Coconut Tempeh Nuggets

These little nuggets are a great alternative to coconut shrimp or chicken nuggets. Serve with good old ketchup for dipping.

1 pound (455 g) plain soy tempeh
½ cup (120 ml) coconut milk
½ cup (56 g) coconut flour
½ cup (60 g) unsweetened coconut flakes
½ cup (120 ml) coconut oil
Salt and pepper, to taste

Have ready a paper towel–lined plate.

Cut the tempeh into 1-inch (2.5-cm) "nuggets."

In a shallow bowl, mix together the coconut milk, flour, and coconut flakes.

In a frying pan or cast-iron skillet, heat the coconut oil over high heat.

Coat each nugget in the flour mixture and panfry until golden on all sides.

Transfer to the paper towel–lined plate to absorb the excess oil. Sprinkle with salt and pepper.

Yield: 2 servings

Seitan Poppers

Jalapeño poppers, beware. These little bite-size nuggets of deep-fried spicy delight are coming after you! Dare to dip them into the Hot and Spicy Buffalo Sauce (page 291), or opt for a cooler ranch dressing.

For the seitan patties:

1 cup (144 g) vital wheat gluten flour
½ cup (60 g) whole wheat pastry flour
1 tablespoon (7 g) chili powder
1 tablespoon (7 g) paprika
1 teaspoon ground cumin
1 teaspoon black pepper
½ cup (120 ml) canola or other vegetable oil, plus more for frying
¼ cup (60 ml) soy sauce or tamari
¼ cup (60 ml) water
4 ounces (112 g) Nutty Cheese, Mexican variation (page 88), or your favorite vegan cheese, cut into small pieces
12 to 24 jarred slices nacho-style jalapeño chiles, to taste

For the batter:

1 cup (125 g) all-purpose flour
½ teaspoon paprika
½ teaspoon salt
½ teaspoon ground black pepper
1 cup (235 ml) beer

To make the seitan: In a large-size bowl, combine the wheat gluten, flour, chili powder, paprika, cumin, and black pepper. Add the ½ cup (120 ml) canola oil, soy sauce, and water. Knead into a uniform ball. Divide into 12 equal pieces and form into small patties.

Place a bit of cheese and 1 or 2 slices of jalapeño, according to your taste, in the center of a patty. Wrap the seitan around the filling and form into a mini log. Repeat with the remaining patties and set aside.

In a large-size flat-bottomed pan or cast-iron skillet, pour the canola oil to a depth of ¼ inch (6 mm) and heat over high heat. If you have a deep fryer, this would be a great time to use it.

To make the batter: Mix together the flour, paprika, salt, and pepper. Stir in the beer until fairly smooth.

Dip each popper into the batter and then transfer to the pan to fry. Fry each side for about 3 minutes, or until golden and crispy.

Transfer to a plate lined with paper towels to absorb the excess oil.

Yield: 12 poppers

Moo Goo Gai Pan

Why order takeout when you can make your own? This is a very straightforward, easy-to-prepare dish. If you are sensitive to salt, use low-sodium soy sauce or tamari. This dish is easily made gluten free by choosing gluten-free soy sauce and vinegar.

2 tablespoons (30 ml) sesame oil
8 ounces (227 g) mushrooms, sliced
5 ounces (140 g) bamboo shoots, sliced
5 ounces (140 g) water chestnuts, sliced
1 ounce (28 g) fresh gingerroot, minced or grated
2 tablespoons (30 g) minced garlic
Pinch salt
⅓ cup (80 ml) water
⅓ cup (80 ml) soy sauce or tamari
⅓ cup (80 ml) rice wine vinegar
2 tablespoons (16 g) cornstarch, mixed with ¼ cup (60 ml) water to make a slurry

Preheat the sesame oil in a wok, or your largest frying pan, over high heat.

Add the mushrooms, bamboo shoots, water chestnuts, ginger, garlic, and salt. Stir-fry until the mushrooms have reduced in size by about half, 10 minutes.

Stir in the water, soy sauce, and vinegar. Bring to a boil.

Slowly stir in the cornstarch slurry and remove from the heat. Continue to stir until a nice thick sauce has formed. Serve alone or over sticky rice.

Yield: 4 servings

Sweet and Sour Tofu

Reminiscent of traditional food-court fare, this recipe is sure to satisfy your sweet and sour cravings. This is also a great dipping sauce for the Avocado Spring Rolls (page 110).

For the Sweet and Sour Sauce:

¾ cup (180 ml) pineapple juice
2 tablespoons (30 ml) rice wine vinegar
2 tablespoons (25 g) granulated sugar
2 tablespoons (34 g) organic ketchup
2 tablespoons (30 ml) soy sauce
¼ teaspoon salt
1 teaspoon red pepper flakes (optional)
1 tablespoon (8 g) cornstarch, dissolved in ¼ cup (60 ml) water to make a slurry

For the tofu:

½ cup (68 g) all-purpose flour
Salt and pepper, to taste
Vegetable oil, for frying
12 ounces (340 g) extra-firm tofu, drained and pressed

To make the sauce: Combine the juice, vinegar, sugar, ketchup, soy sauce, salt, and red pepper flakes, if using, in a pot and bring to a boil. Reduce to a simmer and simmer for 10 minutes. Stir in the cornstarch slurry and remove from the heat. Set aside, or keep warm on very low heat until the tofu is ready.

To make the tofu: Combine the flour, salt, and pepper in a shallow dish. Preheat a frying pan with about ¼ inch (6 mm) of oil.

Cut the tofu into small triangles by first cutting the tofu into strips, then cutting each strip in half, then cutting each half in half again, on the diagonal. Dip each triangle into the flour mixture to coat and place in the frying pan. Fry on each side for 3 to 5 minutes, remove from the pan, and place directly into the pot of sauce to coat.

Serve on its own or over sticky rice.

Yield: 4 servings

Veggie Chow Mein

Yet another take-out dish to make-in! Feel free to add other vegetables here, such as sugar snap peas, mung bean sprouts, edamame, or baby corn.

1 package (6 ounces, or 170 g) chow mein noodles
2 tablespoons (30 ml) sesame oil
8 ounces (227 g) broccoli florets
1 cup (110 g) shredded or (122 g) sliced carrots
½ cup (56 g) cashew pieces
1 tablespoon (12 g) grated fresh gingerroot
2 tablespoons (30 ml) peanut oil
12 ounces (340 g) extra-firm tofu, drained and pressed
¼ cup (60 ml) soy sauce or tamari
1 tablespoon (8 g) sesame seeds

Prepare the noodles according to the package directions, drain, cover, and set aside.

Using a wok or a large-size frying pan, heat the sesame oil over high heat. Add the broccoli, carrots, cashews, and ginger. Stir-fry for 5 to 7 minutes. Add the peanut oil.

Cut the tofu into small cubes and add to the wok. Continue to cook for 5 more minutes, tossing often.

Add the soy sauce, sesame seeds, and then the noodles. (Rinse the noodles under water if they are sticky before adding them to the wok.)

Toss to coat and cook for 5 minutes longer, stirring continuously.

Yield: 8 side- or 4 main-dish servings

Lemon Herb Coconut Tofu with Udon

Creamy and flavorful, this Asian fusion dish is wonderful served up warm, but even tastes yummy cold the next day.

1 package (10 ounces, or 280 g) udon noodles
12 ounces (340 g) extra-firm tofu, drained and pressed
1 can (14 ounces, or 414 ml) coconut milk
3 tablespoons (45 ml) fresh lemon juice
½ cup (32 g) finely chopped scallion
7 tablespoons (21 g) chopped fresh chives
3 tablespoons (18 g) finely chopped fresh basil or 1 tablespoon (2 g) dried
1 tablespoon (3 g) fresh dill or 1 teaspoon dried
1 tablespoon (4 g) finely chopped fresh parsley or 1 teaspoon dried
¼ teaspoon yellow curry powder, store-bought or homemade (page 307)
Salt and pepper, to taste

Cook the udon in lightly salted water according to the package directions.

While the udon is boiling, cut the tofu into bite-size triangles and set aside.

To another pot, add the coconut milk, lemon juice, scallion, chives, basil, dill, parsley, and curry powder. Bring to a boil. Reduce to a simmer.

Add the tofu and simmer, uncovered, for 10 minutes.

Drain the udon and add to the sauce. Toss to coat. Add salt and pepper to taste.

Yield: 8 servings

Tofu Marsala

Cooking with wine brings out the gourmet in all of us. This herb and mushroom tofu serves up wonderfully with a side of Sesame Garlic Wilted Kale (page 279).

- ¼ cup (31 g) all-purpose flour
- ½ teaspoon salt
- ¼ teaspoon ground black pepper
- ½ teaspoon dried oregano
- 20 ounces (570 g) extra-firm tofu, drained and pressed, cut into 4 "steaks"
- ¼ cup (56 g) nondairy butter or (60 ml) extra-virgin olive oil
- 8 ounces (227 g) button mushrooms, sliced
- ½ cup (120 ml) Marsala wine
- ¼ cup (60 ml) cooking sherry

Mix together the flour, salt, pepper, and oregano in a small-size bowl.

Coat the tofu steaks in the flour mixture.

In a large-size frying pan or cast-iron skillet, melt the butter over medium heat.

Add the tofu and sauté until lightly browned, 3 to 5 minutes, then flip.

Add the mushrooms, wine, and sherry. Cover and cook for 10 minutes, turning halfway through and checking occasionally to prevent the tofu from sticking to the bottom of the pan.

Yield: 4 servings

Ginger Lime Tofu

This recipe calls for tofu, but feel free to experiment with all kinds of proteins, such as tempeh and seitan, with this marinade. It is bright and fresh and lends itself wonderfully to the grill.

¼ cup (60 ml) lime juice
¼ cup (60 ml) extra-virgin olive oil
3 tablespoons (18 g) finely grated fresh gingerroot
2 tablespoons (30 ml) soy sauce or tamari
12 to 15 ounces (340 g to 425 g) extra-firm tofu, drained, pressed, and cut into 4 "steaks"

Whisk together the lime juice, olive oil, ginger, and soy sauce.

Place the tofu steaks in a shallow dish or resealable plastic bag and pour the marinade over the tofu. Let marinate for at least 1 hour or up to overnight.

Remove the tofu from the marinade and reserve the leftover marinade.

If grilling on a barbecue, choose an area on the grill with a medium-high flame, place the tofu on the grill, and cook for 5 to 7 minutes before turning. Cook an additional 5 to 7 minutes on the other side.

If a barbecue is unavailable, you can bake this in the oven.

Preheat the oven to 450°F (230°C, or gas mark 8).

Place the marinated tofu, as well as any reserved marinade, in a glass, oven-safe baking dish. Bake, uncovered, for 10 to 12 minutes.

Spoon any leftover marinade on top before serving.

Yield: 4 servings

Veggie Tofu Bake

This dish is a wonderful way to introduce someone to tofu. Because it is crumbled, the texture resembles ricotta or feta cheese, so it seems a little less intimidating for first-timers.

For the tofu:

20 ounces (570 g) extra-firm tofu, drained and pressed
¼ cup (30 g) nutritional yeast
¼ cup (60 ml) extra-virgin olive oil
½ cup (32 g) finely chopped fresh parsley
Salt and pepper, to taste

For the veggies:

8 ounces (227 g) thinly sliced carrot coins
8 ounces (227 g) broccoli florets
8 ounces (227 g) green peas
8 ounces (227 g) yellow corn kernels
8 ounces (227 g) sliced water chestnuts
2 tablespoons (15 g) minced garlic
¼ cup (60 ml) soy sauce or tamari
¼ cup (60 ml) extra-virgin olive oil
Salt and pepper, to taste

Preheat the oven to 350°F (180°C, or gas mark 4). Have ready a 9 × 13-inch (23 × 33-cm) baking dish.

To make the tofu: In a mixing bowl, crumble the tofu until it resembles ricotta cheese.

Add the nutritional yeast, olive oil, parsley, salt, and pepper.

Spread half of the mixture evenly all over the bottom of the baking dish, pressing into place to form a sort of crust. Set aside the remaining tofu mixture.

To make the veggies: In a large-size mixing bowl, toss together the vegetables with the garlic, soy sauce, olive oil, salt, and pepper. Spread evenly over the tofu base.

Sprinkle the remaining half of the tofu on top of the veggies.

Bake for 35 minutes, or until the top is beginning to brown and the carrots are tender.

Yield: 8 servings

Monte Cristo Reuben

A Monte Cristo is a fried ham or turkey sandwich using French toast as the bread. A Reuben is a toasted sandwich filled with corned beef and sauerkraut. This sandwich brings together the best of both! It tastes especially wonderful with a schmear of Curry Aioli (page 304).

1 cup (235 ml) unsweetened soy or other nondairy milk
¼ cup (31 g) all-purpose flour
Pinch paprika
Pinch dill
Salt and pepper, to taste
Oil, for frying
8 slices stale (or firm) sandwich bread
1 pound (455 g) seitan, cut into thin strips
1 cup (240 g) sauerkraut, drained
1 red onion, sliced into julienne
Favorite sandwich spread (optional)

Mix together the milk, flour, paprika, dill, salt, and pepper in a shallow dish.

In a frying pan or cast-iron skillet, heat about 2 tablespoons (30 ml) of oil over high heat.

Dip a piece of bread into the batter and panfry for 2 to 3 minutes per side, or until golden. Repeat with the remaining pieces, adding oil as needed.

Once all of the bread is cooked, add a little more oil to the pan and panfry the seitan strips, along with the sauerkraut and onion.

Add equal amounts of the seitan mixture to each of 4 slices of bread, top with the other 4 bread slices, and serve with your favorite sandwich spread, if desired.

Yield: 4 sandwiches

Chapter 12

Side Dishes

Is a main dish not enough to satisfy your ravenous appetite? Or maybe you are looking to prepare a quicker, lighter meal instead? These healthy, delicious, and nutritious concoctions will be the perfect answer to what your heart and tummy both desire.

 Gluten Free Soy Free

Roasted Butternut Squash with Caramelized Onion, Garlic, and Fennel

The licorice-y note fennel brings to this dish is quite distinct and contrasts nicely with the onions and garlic in this unique twist on roasted squash.

1 butternut squash, peeled, cored, and cut into bite-size chunks
2 yellow onions, roughly chopped
1 full head garlic, cloves peeled and cut in half
1 bulb fennel, roughly chopped
Salt and pepper, to taste
Extra-virgin olive oil, for drizzling

Preheat the oven to 350°F (180°C, or gas mark 4).

Toss together the squash, onion, garlic, and fennel in a shallow baking dish or baking sheet. Sprinkle with the salt and pepper and drizzle with the olive oil.

Bake for about 1 hour, or until fork-tender, tossing halfway through the cooking time.

Yield: 4 servings

 Under 30 Minutes  Gluten Free

Curried Apple Sprouts

This spicy side dish comes together very quickly, giving you plenty of time to whip up a batch of Crispy Seitan Bacon (page 211) to serve alongside it! Keep in mind, though, that the latter would make this meal a non-gluten-free one.

¼ cup (56 g) nondairy butter
4 cloves garlic, grated
1 tablespoon (2 g) dried sage
2 teaspoons mild to medium curry powder, store-bought or homemade (page 307)
1 teaspoon coarse sea salt, plus extra for sprinkling
2 Fuji or other tart apples, cored, quartered, and shredded
¼ cup (40 g) chopped red onion
1 pound (455 g) Brussels sprouts, trimmed, cleaned, and thinly sliced in a food processor
Ground pepper or crushed chili pepper, optional, to taste

In a large-size saucepan, cook the butter, garlic, sage, curry powder, and 1 teaspoon salt for 1 minute over medium heat.

Stir in the apples and onion and cook for 2 minutes.

Stir in the sprouts and cook until tender, about 4 minutes.

Sprinkle a little extra sea salt and pepper or chili pepper on the plates upon serving, if desired.

Yield: 4 servings

Cannellini All' Italiana

This dish is a nutritious and filling meal that is so flavorful you might be making a single serving out of the whole recipe. If you aren't quite that brave, serve alongside simple steamed brown rice and Roasted Garlic Steamed Broccoli (page 274).

2 tablespoons (30 ml) extra-virgin olive oil
½ cup (80 g) chopped red onion
4 cloves garlic, grated
2 cans (15 ounces, or 425 g each) cannellini beans, drained and rinsed
2 jars (9 ounces, or 255 g each) roasted red bell peppers, drained and chopped
½ cup (68 g) green olives, left whole if small, or roughly chopped if larger
2 tablespoons (33 g) tomato paste
2 teaspoons dried oregano
½ cup (120 ml) water or vegetable broth
1 teaspoon fine sea salt
½ teaspoon ground black pepper

In a medium-size saucepan, heat the oil over medium heat and cook the onion and garlic until fragrant and tender, about 4 minutes.

Add the beans, peppers, olives, tomato paste, oregano, water, salt, and pepper. Bring to a boil, cover, lower the heat, and simmer for 30 minutes, stirring occasionally.

Yield: 4 servings

 Gluten Free Soy Free

Orangér Than Thou Carrot Coins

Does it get any more orange and beta-carotene happy than this? We think not. You might find yourself having to adjust the cooking time, depending on the diameter of the carrots, and how thin you manage to slice them.

2 tablespoons (30 ml) melted coconut oil
4 cloves garlic, grated
2 teaspoons cumin seeds
1 teaspoon ground coriander
1 teaspoon ground ginger
1 teaspoon mild to medium curry powder, store-bought or homemade (page 307)
2 teaspoons coarse sea salt
10 carrots, trimmed, peeled, and thinly sliced into coins (in a food processor or with a mandolin)
1 cup (235 ml) fresh orange juice

In a large-size saucepan, heat the coconut oil over medium heat and cook the garlic, cumin, coriander, ginger, curry powder, and salt for 2 minutes, until fragrant.

Stir in the carrots and cook for 2 minutes.

Add the juice and bring to a boil. Cover partially, and cook over medium heat for 10 to 15 minutes, stirring occasionally, until the carrots are tender and the liquid has reduced.

Yield: 4 large servings

Green Bean Almondine (with a twist)

Traditional green bean almondines simply call for green beans sautéed in butter and tossed with blanched almonds. Boring! We added mushrooms, onions, garlic, and, as an option, imitation bacon bits.

1 pound (455 g) fresh green beans
3 cups (705 ml)
2 tablespoons (28 g) nondairy butter
8 ounces (227 g) sliced mushrooms
1 cup (160 g) diced yellow onion
2 tablespoons (30 g) minced garlic
¼ cup (25 g) slivered or sliced almonds
¼ cup (25 g) imitation bacon bits, store-bought or homemade (page 212, optional)
Salt and pepper, to taste

Trim the ends off the green beans.

In your largest frying pan, add the water and bring to a boil (you can add a pinch of salt to the water, if you choose). Add the beans and boil for 3 minutes. Remove from the heat, drain, and set aside.

Reheat the pan and add the butter. Heat over high heat. When the butter has melted, add the mushrooms, onion, and garlic. Sauté until the mushrooms have reduced in size by half, about 7 minutes.

Add the almonds and bacon bits, if using. Cook for 2 more minutes.

Add the green beans. Toss to coat, and cook 3 to 5 more minutes. Season with salt and pepper.

Yield: 4 servings

Cannellini, Tempeh, and Couscous Bake

Creaminess from the beans, protein from the tempeh, and texture from the couscous: this trifecta of vegan staples makes a lovely side dish alongside some green veggies and a nice protein main course.

8 ounces (227 g) plain soy tempeh, crumbled
1 can (15 ounces, or 420 g) cannellini beans, drained and rinsed
1 cup (227 g) tomato sauce
1 cup (173 g) uncooked couscous
1 cup (124 g) shredded yellow zucchini
1 cup (124 g) shredded green zucchini
¼ cup (60 ml) extra-virgin olive oil
10 leaves fresh basil
2 tablespoons (30 g) minced garlic
Salt and pepper, to taste

Preheat the oven to 350°F (180°C, or gas mark 4).

Add all the ingredients to a food processor and blend until uniform but still a little chunky.

Roll out 2 pieces of foil, about 12 inches (30 cm) long. Divide the mixture in half and place in the center of each piece of foil. Roll up the foil, and twist the ends together to tighten.

Bake for 1 hour. Let cool, then transfer to a bowl and fluff with a fork.

Yield: 8 servings

Greek Stuffing

Try this Mediterranean version of a traditional dressing at your next holiday get-together. The cinnamon gives this savory stuffing a unique and lovely flavor.

2½ cups (400 g) uncooked wild rice blend
2 cubes (9 g each) vegetable bouillon or 1 tablespoon (6 g) powdered
¼ cup (60 ml) extra-virgin olive oil, divided
1½ pounds (680 g) seitan, diced or 1 recipe Basic Seitan Crumbles (page 210)
2 cups (320 g) diced yellow onion
6 cloves garlic, minced
4 teaspoons (9 g) ground cinnamon
1 cup (120 g) golden raisins
¼ cup (66 g) tomato paste
1 cup (120 g) toasted pine nuts
2 teaspoons fine sea salt
1 teaspoon freshly cracked black pepper

Prepare the rice according to the package directions, adding the bouillon cubes to the water.

In a separate pan, heat 1 tablespoon (15 ml) of the olive oil and cook the seitan over medium-high heat for 5 to 7 minutes, or until browned and beginning to crisp.

Add 2 more tablespoons (30 ml) of the olive oil to a large-size pan or wok and sauté the onion and garlic over medium-high heat for 5 to 7 minutes, or until the onions are translucent and the garlic is fragrant. Reduce the heat, add the seitan, cinnamon, raisins, tomato paste, pine nuts, salt, and pepper, mix well, and remove from the heat.

After the rice is fully cooked, add to the sautéed ingredients along with the remaining 1 tablespoon (15 ml) olive oil and combine.

Yield: 10 servings

Traditional Bread Dressing

This recipe is an awesome way to use up leftover or not-so-fresh bread you may have lingering around in the bread box. It is also a crucial ingredient for the Festivus Loaf (page 241), and is an all-around great bread dressing recipe.

8 to 10 slices bread or 8 cups (227 g) bread cubes
6 tablespoons (84 g) nondairy butter, divided
1 large-size onion, roughly chopped
3 stalks celery, roughly chopped
1¾ cups (415 ml) vegetable broth

To make the bread cubes, cut the stale bread into small squares. No stale bread? It's okay. You can cut fresh bread, set it in a single layer on a baking sheet, and let it sit out, uncovered, overnight. No time to wait for stale bread overnight? Place it in the oven at 225°F (110°C, or gas mark ¼), uncovered, for about 1 hour.

Preheat the oven to 350°F (180°C, or gas mark 4). Have ready a 9-inch (23-cm) square glass baking dish.

Heat 2 tablespoons (28 g) of the butter over medium heat and sauté the onion and celery for 5 to 7 minutes, or until fragrant and translucent.

Melt the remaining 4 tablespoons (56 g) butter.

Place the bread cubes, celery and onion mixture, melted butter, and vegetable broth in a mixing bowl and toss together until well combined.

If you are using this dressing to stuff something, such as the Festivus Loaf (page 241), stop here and proceed with the directions for that recipe.

Transfer to the baking dish and bake, uncovered, for 40 to 45 minutes, or until the top begins to brown.

Yield: 6 servings

Chorizo, Cranberry, and Cornbread Stuffing

Everyone knows that cranberries are traditional with a holiday meal . . . but chorizo? This unusual stuffing combines tradition with delicious!

1 recipe Sweet Skillet Cornbread (page 326)
½ cup (61 g) dried cranberries
12 ounces (340 g) soy chorizo, casings removed, crumbled, or 2 recipes Seitan Chorizo Crumbles (page 209)
1 cup (160 g) diced yellow or red onion
1 teaspoon cayenne pepper
½ cup (120 ml) vegetable broth
Salt and pepper, to taste

Preheat the oven to 400°F (200°C, or gas mark 6). Have ready a 9-inch (23-cm) square baking dish.

Into a mixing bowl, crumble the cornbread.

Add the cranberries, soy chorizo, onion, and cayenne pepper and mix well, using your hands.

Add the vegetable broth and toss to coat. Season with salt and pepper.

Transfer to the baking dish and bake, uncovered, for 30 minutes, or until the top begins to brown.

Yield: 6 servings

Sweet Glazed Baby Carrots

This is a great way to serve carrots at a holiday meal. This preparation also works quite nicely with sweet potato chunks.

1 pound (455 g) peeled baby carrots
¼ cup (55 g) packed brown sugar
2 tablespoons (30 ml) pure maple syrup
2 tablespoons (28 g) nondairy butter, melted

Preheat the oven to 350°F (180°C, or gas mark 4).

In an oven-safe dish with a lid, toss together the carrots, brown sugar, maple syrup, and butter.

Cover and bake for 1 hour, or until the carrots are fork-tender.

Yield: 4 servings

Gluten Free Soy Free

Roasted Garlic Steamed Broccoli

This simple and flavorful dish boasts the antioxidant power of garlic, heart-healthy fats from olive oil, and calcium-rich broccoli. Prepare the broccoli to your preferred tenderness.

20 cloves garlic, peeled (about 2 full heads)
6 tablespoons (90 ml) extra-virgin olive oil, divided
Sea salt, to taste
1 pound (455 g) broccoli florets

Preheat the oven to 350°F (180°C, or gas mark 4).

Place the garlic cloves in the center of a 10-inch (25-cm) square piece of aluminum foil. Add 2 tablespoons (30 ml) of the olive oil and a pinch of salt. Bring the corners of the foil to meet and twist together to form a closed pouch.

Bake the garlic for 30 minutes.

Meanwhile, steam the broccoli to your desired tenderness.

Toss together the broccoli, roasted garlic, remaining 4 tablespoons (60 ml) olive oil, and sea salt to taste.

Yield: 4 servings

Soy Free

Roasted Lima Beans

Here's a simple and effective preparation for those sweet little beans we call lima.

1 pound (455 g) lima beans, fresh, frozen, or canned
1 red onion, sliced into julienne
2 tablespoons (30 g) minced garlic
2 tablespoons (30 ml) extra-virgin olive oil
2 tablespoons (30 ml) balsamic vinegar
Salt and pepper, to taste

Preheat the oven to 350°F (180°C, or gas mark 4). Line a baking sheet with aluminum foil (makes cleanup a snap).

In a bowl, toss together all the ingredients to coat and spread evenly on the baking sheet.

Bake for 20 to 25 minutes, or until the lima beans are tender and the onions are translucent and beginning to brown.

Yield: 4 servings

Under 30 Minutes Soy Free

Balsamic Roasted Asparagus with Pearl Onions

This tasty preparation for asparagus will wow your friends and family with its simplicity.

¼ cup (60 ml) extra-virgin olive oil
¼ cup (60 ml) balsamic vinegar
1 tablespoon (15 g) minced garlic
1 pound (455 g) fresh asparagus spears
10 ounces (284 g) pearl onions, peeled
Salt and pepper, to taste

Preheat the oven to 400°F (200°C, or gas mark 6). Line a baking sheet with parchment or aluminum foil (makes cleanup a snap).

Whisk together the oil, vinegar, and garlic.

Add the asparagus and onions and toss to coat. Place in a single layer on the baking sheet. Season with salt and pepper.

Bake for 20 minutes, or until the asparagus is cooked to your desired tenderness. The stalks should be tender yet still firm, and the onions should be soft and translucent.

Yield: 4 servings

Under 30 Minutes

Soy Free

Spring Beans in Raspberry Sauce

Are you ready to get your beans on? This ridiculously pink cold bean salad is perfect for get-togethers or as an easy side dish on warm summer afternoons—no cooking required!

1 can (15 ounces, or 425 g) kidney beans
1 can (15 ounces, or 425 g) garbanzo beans
1 can (15 ounces, or 425 g) cut green beans
1 can (15 ounces, or 425 g) butter beans
1 can (15 ounces, or 425 g) cannellini beans
1 cup (125 g) raspberries, fresh or frozen
½ cup (120 ml) canola or other vegetable oil
¼ cup (60 ml) apple cider vinegar
1 tablespoon (15 g) minced garlic
5 leaves fresh basil
Salt and pepper, to taste

In a colander or strainer, empty the contents of all of the canned beans; rinse and drain. Shake off the excess water and transfer to a large-size bowl.

Add the raspberries, oil, vinegar, garlic, basil, salt, and pepper to a blender and purée until frothy and pink.

Pour the raspberry sauce over the beans and toss to coat.

Serve cold or at room temperature.

Yield: 8 servings

Roasted Harvest Vegetables in Garlic Sauce

Autumn brings out the squash in all of us! This roasted veggie medley is a perfect substitute for plain old mashed or baked potatoes.

½ cup (112 g) sliced carrot coins
½ cup (112 g) chopped red onion
1 medium-size butternut squash, chopped
8 ounces (227 g) baby red potatoes, halved
¼ cup (60 ml) extra-virgin olive oil
1 teaspoon garlic powder
½ teaspoon ground sage
¼ teaspoon ground black pepper
Salt, to taste

Preheat the oven to 350°F (180°C, or gas mark 4). Have ready a rimmed baking sheet lined with parchment or aluminum foil.

In a mixing bowl, toss together all the ingredients to coat.

Arrange in a single layer on the baking sheet, cover with foil, and bake for 50 minutes to 1 hour, or until the veggies are fork-tender.

Yield: 4 servings

 Gluten Free  Soy Free

Garlic and Mustard Roasted Brussels Sprouts

Even if you don't care for Brussels sprouts, give these a try. The marinade is so flavorful you will totally forget you are eating this high-protein, high-fiber, calcium-rich mini cabbage!

¼ cup (60 ml) extra-virgin olive oil
¼ cup (84 g) agave nectar
2 tablespoons (30 g) stone-ground mustard
2 tablespoons (30 g) minced garlic
1 pound (455 g) Brussels sprouts

Preheat the oven to 350°F (180°C, or gas mark 4). Have ready a rimmed baking sheet lined with parchment or aluminum foil.

In a mixing bowl, whisk together the olive oil, agave, mustard, and garlic.

Add the Brussels sprouts and toss to coat. Spread evenly on the baking sheet in a single layer.

Bake, uncovered, for 30 minutes, or until fork-tender.

Yield: 4 servings

Sweet and Spicy Edamame with Mandarin Oranges

Sweet and spicy is always a delicious combination. This side dish tastes great with Asian-inspired main courses, such as Thai Tofu (page 206).

1 pound (455 g) shelled edamame
1 can (15 ounces, or 425 g) mandarin oranges in light syrup
1 red bell pepper, cored, seeded, and diced
¼ cup (60 ml) soy sauce or tamari
¼ cup (60 ml) extra-virgin olive oil
1 tablespoon (15 g) red pepper flakes

Add all the ingredients to a pot and bring to a boil.

Reduce to a simmer and cook, uncovered, for 20 minutes, or until the beans are fork-tender.

Yield: 6 servings

Creamed Corn

Corn is good. Creamed corn is better. Creamed corn with garlic, onions, and red peppers?

Simply the best.

2 tablespoons (28 g) nondairy butter
1 cup (160 g) diced onion
1 tablespoon (15 g) minced garlic
¼ cup (31 g) all-purpose flour
1½ cups (355 ml) unsweetened soy or other nondairy milk
1 cup (227 g) yellow corn kernels
1 cup (227 g) white corn kernels
1 red bell pepper, cored, seeded, and diced
Salt and pepper, to taste

Add the butter to a pot and melt over medium heat.

Add the onion and garlic, reduce the heat to low, cover, and cook for 12 to 15 minutes, until translucent, fragrant, and beginning to brown.

Add the flour and stir until fully incorporated.

Add the milk and stir until smooth.

Turn up the heat to medium-high and bring to a boil. As soon as it begins to boil, stir in the corn and bell pepper. Stir until completely heated through.

Add salt and pepper to taste.

Yield: 4 servings

Creamed Spinach

Craving comfort food? What says it better than creamed spinach? Enjoy this take on a classic alongside your favorite protein and Twice-Baked Potatoes (page 160) for a real down-home comfort meal.

2 tablespoons (28 g) nondairy butter
1 cup (160 g) diced onion
1 tablespoon (15 g) minced garlic
¼ cup (31 g) all-purpose flour
1½ cups (355 ml) unsweetened soy or other nondairy milk
1 pound (455 g) frozen cut leaf spinach
Salt and pepper, to taste

Add the butter to a pot and melt over medium heat.

Add the onion and garlic, reduce the heat to low, cover, and cook for 12 to 15 minutes, until translucent, fragrant, and beginning to brown.

Add the flour and stir until fully incorporated.

Add the milk and stir until smooth. Turn up the heat to medium-high and bring to a boil. As soon as it begins to boil, stir in the frozen spinach.

Stir until the spinach is completely heated through.

Add salt and pepper to taste.

Yield: 4 servings

 Under 30 Minutes

Creamy Boiled Leeks

This creamy, savory side dish tastes wonderful alongside a "meaty" protein, such as Seitan en Croûte (page 243), or as a topping for a nice crusty Little Baguette (page 335).

2 tablespoons (28 g) nondairy butter
10 ounces (284 g) chopped leeks, white and light green parts only
2 cups (235 ml) vegetable broth
¼ cup (31 g) all-purpose flour mixed with ¼ cup (60 ml) water to make a slurry
Salt and pepper, to taste

Add the butter to a pot and melt over medium heat.

Add the leeks, and cook for 12 to 15 minutes, stirring often. Add the broth and deglaze the pot.

Bring to a boil, and then reduce to a simmer.

Add the flour slurry and stir to thicken. Simmer, uncovered, for 5 to 7 minutes to reduce and thicken a bit more. Add the salt and pepper to taste.

Remove from the heat and let stand, uncovered, for 10 minutes, to continue to thicken, before serving.

Yield: 4 servings

Gluten Free

Chili Lime Corn with Smoked Tofu

Simple and flavorful with a spicy kick, this Latin-inspired dish is quick and easy to throw together and works well as a side to any Mexican meal. To make this a lunch or light supper, simply mix with some rice and beans for a completely balanced meal.

- 1 pound (455 g) yellow corn kernels, fresh, frozen, or canned
- 6 ounces (170 g) extra-firm tofu, drained and pressed (Oven-Smoked Tofu [page 208], cut into very small cubes, works nicely here)
- 1 red bell pepper, cored, seeded, and diced
- 1 fresh lime, thinly sliced
- 3 scallions, chopped
- 2 tablespoons (30 ml) fresh lime juice
- 2 tablespoons (30 ml) extra-virgin olive oil
- 1 teaspoon cayenne pepper

Preheat the oven to 400°F (200°C, or gas mark 6).

Toss all the ingredients together in a mixing bowl. Line a baking sheet with foil.

Spread evenly on the baking sheet.

Bake for 20 minutes, or until the corn is tender and the edges of the lime slices are beginning to curl and brown.

Yield: 4 to 6 servings

Under 30 Minutes

Gluten Free

Soy Free

Sesame Garlic Wilted Kale

With all of the health benefits we get from kale, it's a wonder we don't cook it more often. This super quick and super simple preparation for this calcium-, fiber-, and vitamin C–rich green veggie is not only easy but delicious as well. To easily remove kale leaves from the stem, use a pair of kitchen shears and cut along the center stem to remove the leaves.

- 2 tablespoons (30 ml) extra-virgin olive oil
- 2 tablespoons (30 g) minced garlic
- 12 ounces (340 g) kale, stems and ribs removed
- 2 tablespoons (16 g) sesame seeds

Heat the olive oil over medium-high heat. Add the garlic and kale leaves. Cook, tossing constantly, because kale will wilt rather quickly, for 2 to 3 minutes, or until it is soft and pliable and reduced in size by about three-fourths.

Remove from the heat and stir in the sesame seeds.

Yield: 4 servings

Fried Zucchini

When french fries or onion rings just won't do, these little zukes come to the rescue. Serve with marinara sauce for dipping.

2 or 3 zucchini
1 cup (125 g) all-purpose flour
½ teaspoon paprika
½ teaspoon cayenne
½ teaspoon parsley flakes
Salt and pepper, to taste
Vegetable oil, for frying

Slice the zucchini into thin disks.

Place the flour, paprika, cayenne, parsley, salt, and pepper in a resealable plastic bag and toss to mix.

In a large-size frying pan or cast-iron skillet, pour the oil to about a depth of ¼ inch (6 mm) and heat over high heat to 350° to 375°F (180° to 190°C), or until a drop of water or a bit of flour sizzles immediately upon contact.

Add the sliced zucchini to the bag, about 10 slices at a time, and shake until each piece is nicely coated.

Add the floured zucchini to the hot oil, and fry for 1 to 2 minutes per side. Make sure you don't overcrowd the pan.

Remove the zucchini slices from the oil, and place them on a plate lined with a kitchen towel or paper towels to drain off the excess oil.

Place them back in the bag for a fresh coating of the flour mixture.

Meanwhile, add a little bit more oil to the pan and let it return to temperature.

For the second fry, cook them a little longer on each side, to get that yummy golden brown color.

After the second fry, it's back to the draining plate.

Repeat with the remaining zucchini slices.

Serve nice and hot.

Yield: 4 servings

Barbecue Baked Beans

Looking for something besides potato salad and corn on the cob to serve at your next barbecue? Try these beans. Sweet and smoky and full of flavor, these beans will fool even the toughest meat eaters into thinking there's bacon fat in there somewhere!

- 2 tablespoons (28 g) nondairy butter
- 1 cup (160 g) diced yellow onion
- 1 tablespoon (15 g) minced garlic
- 1 can (15 ounces, or 425 g) tomato sauce
- ½ cup (110 g) packed brown sugar
- 2 tablespoons (40 g) grape jelly
- 2 teaspoons liquid smoke
- 2 tablespoons (30 g) stone-ground mustard
- 1 can (15 ounces, or 425 g) pinto beans, drained and rinsed
- 1 can (15 ounces, or 425 g) black beans, drained and rinsed
- 1 can (15 ounces, or 425 g) red beans, drained and rinsed
- Salt and pepper, to taste

In a saucepan, melt the butter over medium heat.

Add the onion and garlic and cook for 10 minutes, or until fragrant and transluscent.

Add the tomato sauce, brown sugar, jelly, liquid smoke, and mustard. Stir.

Add the beans and stir to combine. Bring to a boil, reduce to a simmer, cover, and simmer for 15 minutes.

Uncover, reduce the heat to low, and cook an additional 10 minutes, or until thickened. Season with salt and pepper.

Yield: 8 servings

Refried Beans

What would Mexican Food Night be without beans? You can use black or pinto here, depending on your mood. This recipe calls for canned beans. If you like to cook your beans from scratch, you'll need 3½ cups (800 g) of fully cooked beans plus ½ cup (120 ml) of the cooking liquid.

2 tablespoons (28 g) nondairy butter
2 cups (320 g) diced yellow onion
1 tablespoon (15 g) minced garlic
½ teaspoon ground cumin
½ teaspoon smoked paprika
½ teaspoon dried oregano
2 cans (15 ounces, or 425 g each) pinto or black beans, with liquid

In a frying pan or cast-iron skillet, melt the butter over high heat.

Add the onion and garlic and sauté until nice and brown, 3 to 5 minutes.

Stir in the cumin, paprika, and oregano. Cook for 1 minute longer.

Add the beans with their liquid and reduce the heat to medium-low.

Simmer, uncovered, for 15 minutes, stirring occasionally.

Remove from the heat and mash with a hand potato masher, or a fork, to your desired chunkiness.

Yield: 6 servings

Vegetable Fritters

Try serving these instead of plain potatoes or tater tots. It's a tasty way to add some veggies to a normally starch-based side dish.

1 cup (124 g) grated zucchini
1 cup (125 g) grated potatoes, rinsed under cool water and drained
½ cup (50 g) grated carrots
½ cup (67 g) green peas
2 cups (250 g) all-purpose flour
¾ cup (170 g) nondairy plain yogurt
¼ cup (60 ml) canola or other vegetable oil, plus more for frying
¼ cup (60 ml) plain soy or other nondairy milk
¼ teaspoon paprika
¼ teaspoon cayenne pepper
Salt and pepper, to taste

Add the shredded zucchini, potatoes, carrots, peas, flour, yogurt, ¼ cup (60 ml) oil, milk, paprika, cayenne, salt, and pepper to a mixing bowl and mix together until well incorporated. Your mixture should be wet, like a very thick pancake batter.

Pour the oil into a frying pan to about a depth of ¼ inch (6 mm) and heat over high heat.

Spoon the batter into the pan to make 6 fritters. Fry for 5 to 7 minutes, until the edges start to turn brown, then flip and cook for 5 to 7 minutes longer.

Yield: 6 fritters

Chapter 13

Sauces and Condiments

If you are looking for tasty sauces and condiments that will take your pasta, potatoes, and other dishes from "blah" to "hallelujah!" or if you find it impossible to locate an affordable and fresh spice mix at the store, we're happy to announce you need not worry anymore. This chapter offers a lot of options to meet the needs of the most discerning palates and people who prefer their pasta and other dishes covered with a lot of creamy goodness and mind-blowing spiciness.

Under 30 Minutes  Low Fat  Gluten Free

Smoky Pumpkin Marinara

If you are feeling lazy, but still would rather prepare your own marinara instead of twisting open a jar of store-bought sauce, this recipe is here to help. You may very well find yourself eating it with a spoon before it even makes it to the pasta!

1 teaspoon extra-virgin olive oil
¼ cup (40 g) chopped red onion
1 clove garlic, grated
1 can (15 ounces, or 425 g) tomato sauce
½ cup (122 g) pumpkin purée
1 teaspoon dried basil
¼ teaspoon liquid smoke
1 teaspoon fine sea salt
¼ teaspoon ground black pepper
1 teaspoon mild to medium chili powder

In a medium-size saucepan, heat the oil over medium-high heat and cook the onion and garlic until fragrant and tender, about 3 minutes.

Stir in the tomato sauce, pumpkin purée, basil, liquid smoke, salt, pepper, and chili powder. Lower the heat and simmer, covered, for 10 minutes.

Serve with your favorite pasta.

Yield: About 3 cups (750 g)

 Under 30 Minutes

Creamy Pumpkin Almond Sauce

So quick to throw together, this tasty and creamy sauce goes well with pasta, rice, potatoes, and steamed veggies.

1 cup (235 ml) soy creamer or unsweetened nondairy milk (add 1 teaspoon cornstarch if using nondairy milk)
¾ cup (183 g) pumpkin purée
¼ cup (64 g) almond butter
2 tablespoons (16 g) nutritional yeast
1½ teaspoons all-purpose seasoning or a combination of your favorite dried herbs, such as basil and thyme
1 teaspoon fine sea salt
¼ teaspoon ground black pepper
2 cloves garlic, grated (optional)

In a medium-size saucepan, combine all the ingredients and cook over medium-high heat until it just starts to bubble. Lower the heat and simmer, covered, for 10 minutes.

Yield: About 2½ cups (615 g)

Coconut Peanut Sauce

This flavorful sauce is perfectly creamy and rich; use it on steamed veggies, rice, or pasta.

1 teaspoon peanut oil
2 tablespoons (20 g) chopped shallot
2 cloves garlic, grated
1 teaspoon ground ginger
1 tablespoon (6 g) curry powder, store-bought or homemade (page 307)
2 teaspoons ground cumin
1 teaspoon dried cilantro
1 tablespoon (8 g) arrowroot powder
1 can (14 ounces, or 414 ml) light coconut milk, divided
⅓ cup (85 g) crunchy natural peanut butter
2 tablespoons (30 ml) tamari or reduced-sodium soy sauce
2 tablespoons (42 g) agave nectar
¼ cup (60 ml) vegetable broth or water

In a medium-size saucepan over medium heat, heat the oil and cook the shallot and garlic until tender and fragrant, about 2 minutes.

Lower the temperature and stir in the ginger, curry powder, cumin, and cilantro. Cook for another minute, until fragrant.

Combine the arrowroot powder with 2 ounces (60 ml) of the coconut milk and stir until dissolved. Add to the saucepan, then add the remaining 12 ounces (354 ml) coconut milk, peanut butter, tamari, agave, and broth.

Bring to a boil, whisking occasionally. Lower the temperature to medium and cook until thickened and reduced a bit, about 10 minutes.

Yield: About 3 cups (750 g)

Under 30 Minutes

Sun-Dried Tomato Sauce

This healthy, protein-rich, pink-hued sauce is perfect served on top of steamed veggies or baked potatoes, as well as stirred into pasta or rice.

12 ounces (340 g) firm silken tofu, drained
½ cup (55 g) drained sun-dried tomatoes (packed in oil)
⅓ cup (13 g) chopped fresh basil
2 tablespoons (30 ml) extra-virgin olive oil
2 tablespoons (30 ml) white balsamic or white wine vinegar
2 tablespoons (32 g) almond butter
1 can (15 ounces, or 425 g) diced tomatoes, drained
¼ teaspoon ground black pepper
3 cloves garlic, grated
1 tablespoon (20 g) white miso

Place all the ingredients in a food processor and blend until smooth. Transfer to a saucepan and cook over medium heat for a few minutes until just heated through.

Yield: About 3 cups (705 ml)

Enchilada Sauce

Now you can make it from scratch! Serve with Veggie Enchiladas (page 236), tacos, saucy burritos, Enchilada Casserole (page 188), or any of your favorite Mexican dishes.

¼ cup (28 g) chili powder
1 tablespoon (7 g) paprika
1 teaspoon garlic powder
1 teaspoon cumin
¼ teaspoon chipotle powder
¼ teaspoon instant espresso powder
3 tablespoons (45 ml) canola or other vegetable oil
2 tablespoons (16 g) all-purpose flour
1 can (15 ounces, or 425 g) tomato sauce
1½ cups (355 ml) vegetable broth

Combine the chili powder, paprika, garlic powder, cumin, chipotle powder, and espresso powder in a small-size bowl. Set aside.

In a medium-size saucepan, heat the oil over medium-high heat.

Add the flour and stir until smooth, bubbly, and just beginning to brown.

Stir in the spice mixture. Add the tomato sauce and broth and stir to combine.

Bring to a simmer, cover, and simmer for 15 minutes.

Yield: 2½ cups (615 g)

Curried Cauliflower Purée

This purée deserves its own superhero costume, because it just knows no boundaries: stir it into Cumin Carrot Soup (page 141), serve it with Protein, Quick! Mini Seitan Bites (page 219), or simply enjoy it on its own, with a side of quinoa, brown rice, or whatever grain you love the most.

Play around with the amount of curry paste, or choose a different sort of curry to match your preference when it comes to heat levels.

1 head cauliflower, trimmed, cleaned, and separated into florets
1½ cups (355 ml) unsweetened almond or other nondairy milk
1½ tablespoons (23 g) green curry paste
¼ teaspoon turmeric
1 tablespoon (15 ml) tamari or soy sauce
2 tablespoons (32 g) crunchy natural peanut butter
¼ cup (40 g) raisins
2 cloves garlic, grated
1 teaspoon coarse sea salt

Place the cauliflower in a large-size saucepan and cover with water. Bring to a boil, and cook until tender, about 10 minutes. Drain well.

Combine the cauliflower with the milk, curry paste, turmeric, tamari, peanut butter, raisins, garlic, and salt in a blender, or use an immersion blender, and purée until smooth. Serve hot.

Yield: About 5 cups (1225 g)

Low Fat

"Meaty" Marinara

This sauce is great on pasta and in the Red "Meat" Lasagna (page 223). The TVP gives it a great meaty texture, as well as a hefty punch of protein, that is incredibly realistic. Although this recipe is not labeled gluten free, it can be if you purchase soy-based, gluten-free TVP.

2 cans (14 ounces, or 395 g each) diced tomatoes, no salt added, with their juice
1 cup (227 g) tomato sauce
¾ cup (170 g) tomato paste
1 tablespoon (2 g) dried basil or 3 tablespoons (9 g) chopped fresh
1 tablespoon (13 g) granulated sugar
1 tablespoon (22 g) molasses
2 tablespoons (30 ml) extra-virgin olive oil
6 cloves garlic, minced
1 cup (160 g) finely diced white or yellow onion
1¼ cups (120 g) TVP granules

Place the diced tomatoes with their juice, tomato sauce, tomato paste, basil, sugar, and molasses in a large-size stockpot. Bring to a simmer over medium-low heat.

Meanwhile, in a skillet, heat the olive oil and sauté the garlic and onion until the garlic is fragrant and the onions are translucent, about 10 minutes. Add the garlic and onion to the pot. Cover and continue to simmer for 20 more minutes. Uncover and simmer for 10 more minutes. Stir in the TVP, cover, and let sit for 10 minutes.

Yield: 6 cups (1470 g)

Gluten Free Soy Free

Orange Chipotle Barbecue Sauce

Oh, so sweet! But wait, what's that kick? Ohhh, the smoky chipotle has emerged from the sweetness to leave your tongue warm . . . not burning. This recipe calls for a strange ingredient—grape jelly! Please, don't use jam, but jelly. This is Joni's Gramma Jo's secret ingredient. She uses it in all of her barbecue sauces, even store-bought ones.

2 tablespoons (30 g) extra-virgin olive oil
1 yellow onion, roughly chopped
1 tablespoon (15 g) minced garlic
3 cups (680 g) tomato sauce
¾ cup (170 g) tomato paste
½ cup (120 ml) fresh orange juice
½ cup (110 g) firmly packed brown sugar
¼ cup (80 g) grape jelly
2 tablespoons (12 g) ground chipotle powder

In a stockpot or Dutch oven, heat the olive oil over medium-high heat. Add the onion and garlic and sauté until translucent, fragrant, and just beginning to brown.

Add the tomato sauce, tomato paste, juice, brown sugar, jelly, and chipotle powder and stir to combine. Bring to a simmer. Cover, reduce the heat to medium-low, and simmer for 20 minutes.

Remove from the heat and serve as you would any barbecue sauce.

If not using right away, place in an airtight container and store in the fridge. The sauce will last for about a week in the fridge, or freeze for later use.

Yield: About 4 cups (1000 g)

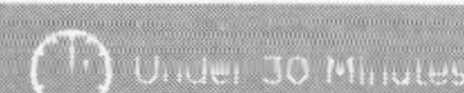

Under 30 Minutes

Hot and Spicy Buffalo Sauce

Sure, anyone can throw some Tabasco in melted butter and call it buffalo sauce, but for us, this does not a tasty, spicy buffalo sauce make. Use this sauce on the Meat-Free BBQ Riblets (page 218) or as a dip for your favorite chicken-free nuggets. We also think it tastes great as a dipping sauce with the Seitan Poppers (page 254).

1 cup (224 g) vegan mayonnaise, store-bought or homemade (page 301 or 302)
¼ cup (60 ml) sriracha chili sauce
1 tablespoon (15 g) prepared yellow mustard
2 tablespoons (28 g) nondairy butter, melted
½ teaspoon ground black pepper

Whisk together all the ingredients. Store in the refrigerator in an airtight container. The sauce should last for at least 2 weeks.

Yield: 1½ cups (338 g)

Under 30 Minutes

Secret Sauce

Use this sauce on burgers, as a dip for fries, on sandwiches, or even as a salad dressing!

1 cup (224 g) vegan mayonnaise, store-bought or homemade (page 301 or 302)
¼ cup (61 g) sweet pickle relish
¼ cup (68 g) ketchup
Salt and pepper, to taste

Whisk all the ingredients together and store in an airtight container in the refrigerator until ready to use. It should last for up to 1 week.

Yield: 1½ cups (338 g)

Gluten Free

Tomatillo and Roasted Green Chile Chimichurri

The great green barbecue sauce of Argentina is South America's answer to Italy's pesto. Here we've added a bit of a Southern California kick with the addition of tomatillos and roasted green chiles. Use as a marinade or a sauce over your favorite protein or to top Peruvian Tamales (page 240).

4 large-size green chiles, such as Anaheims or poblanos
1 can (15 ounces, or 425 g) crushed tomatillos
1 cup (235 ml) extra-virgin olive oil
1 bunch fresh parsley, stems removed (about 2 cups, or 112 g)
2 tablespoons (30 g) minced garlic
2 tablespoons (30 g) red pepper flakes
1 tablespoon (2 g) dried oregano
1 tablespoon (7 g) ground paprika
2 teaspoons ground cumin
Salt and pepper, to taste

Preheat the oven to 350°F (180°C, or gas mark 4).

Roast the whole chiles on a baking sheet for 30 minutes, until soft. Remove from the oven and let cool.

Remove the stems and cut a slit lengthwise from top to bottom. Open up and remove the seeds, running under water, if necessary.

Add the roasted chiles, tomatillos, oil, parsley, garlic, red pepper, oregano, paprika, cumin, salt, and pepper to a blender or food processor and purée until smooth.

Yield: 4 cups (900 g)

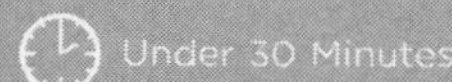

Gaucho Marinade

This easy and versatile, spicy and savory marinade works well on any of your favorite proteins. Use it on tofu, tempeh, seitan, and even vegetables! Simply marinate your protein in this sauce for a few hours before grilling or baking.

½ cup (120 ml) soy sauce or tamari
¼ cup (60 ml) extra-virgin olive oil
¼ cup (60 g) Dijon or brown mustard
2 tablespoons (13 g) freshly ground black pepper

Whisk together all the ingredients and pour over your favorite protein to marinate.

Yield: About 1 cup (235 ml)

Chili Water

This Asian-fusion dipping sauce is a staple on almost every table in Hawaii. Enjoy it with bread, tofu, rice, and pretty much anything that it can be dipped into, poured onto, or mixed into. Sambal chile powder can usually be found in the international food aisle of your supermarket.

⅔ cup (160 ml) rice wine vinegar
2 tablespoons (28 g) firmly packed brown sugar
1 tablespoon (15 ml) minced garlic
1 tablespoon (8 g) sambal chile powder

Add all the ingredients to an airtight container and shake.

Keeps indefinitely in the refrigerator.

1 cup (235 ml)

Under 30 Minutes  Gluten Free Soy Free

Kale Pesto

If you are on the lookout for a new way to enjoy one of the healthiest, calcium-packed green veggies on the planet, then you're going to love this recipe. Be sure to check out the Kale Pesto Pasta (page 162), where the pesto is combined with nondairy cream cheese.

12 ounces (340 g) kale, stems and ribs removed, torn into small pieces, thoroughly cleaned, and spun dry
8 large-size basil leaves
⅔ cup (40 g) fresh curly parsley
3 cloves garlic, grated
1 teaspoon coarse sea salt
¼ teaspoon freshly ground black pepper
¼ cup (60 ml) extra-virgin olive oil, plus more if needed

Chop the kale in a food processor in two batches. Remove the first batch; add it back in once the second batch has been processed.

Combine both batches of kale and the basil, parsley, garlic, salt, and pepper. Drizzle in ¼ cup (60 ml) olive oil and process until it reaches a pastelike consistency, adding extra oil if needed to reach a proper pesto consistency.

Yield: About 2 cups (520 g)

VARIATIONS

Add ¼ cup (34 g) toasted pine nuts, for a fancier version.

If you aren't going to cook the kale pesto in a dish, and fear it will taste "too healthy" if eaten raw, wilt the kale (not spun dry, but still damp from being washed) for a few minutes in a large-size saucepan, before processing it. Rest assured that even skeptical testers fell in love with the raw version of this pesto.

Under 30 Minutes 

Broccoli Pesto

Here's a simple pesto spread that helps you meet your daily quota of fiber, calcium, vitamins, and deliciousness. If using it with pasta, be sure to reserve a little of the pasta cooking liquid to thin the spread, if needed, when combining it with the pasta. Adjust the amount of peppers according to taste; it is moderately spicy.

½ cup (64 g) roasted, salted sunflower seeds
1 head broccoli, trimmed and steamed until tender
1 cup (60 g) fresh curly parsley
Juice of 1 large-size lemon (about 3 tablespoons [45 ml])
2 tablespoons (30 ml) extra-virgin olive oil
2 tablespoons (30 ml) toasted sesame oil
2 cloves garlic, grated
1 teaspoon crushed chile pepper
1 teaspoon coarse sea salt

Process the sunflower seeds in a food processor until finely ground.

Add the broccoli, parsley, lemon juice, oils, garlic, chile pepper, and salt and process until smooth, scraping the sides occasionally.

Stir into pasta dishes, or spread on bread or crackers.

Enjoy warm, at room temperature, or cold.

Yield: About 3 cups (780 g)

Cilantro Pepita Pesto

Here's a fresh Latin twist on an Italian favorite! Serve over pasta, mix with rice, or mix into vegan mayonnaise for an amazing aioli to spread on sandwiches.

2 cups (50 g) fresh cilantro leaves
1 cup (138 g) shelled pepitas (pumpkin seeds)
1 tablespoon (15 g) minced garlic
½ teaspoon paprika
¼ teaspoon cayenne pepper
¾ cup (180 ml) olive oil
Salt and pepper, to taste

Place all the ingredients in a blender and blend until smooth.

Yield: 1½ cups (390 g)

 Under 30 Minutes  Gluten Free  Soy Free

Pistachio Pesto

This nutty, garlicky pesto tastes great poured over pasta or spread on toasty bread.

½ cup (52 g) roasted, salted, and shelled pistachios
1 cup (120 g) raw pine nuts
20 leaves fresh basil
½ cup (120 ml) extra-virgin olive oil
4 cloves garlic
Salt and pepper, to taste

Place all the ingredients in a food processor. Process until smooth.

Heat in a saucepan before serving.

Yield: About 2 cups (520 g)

Garlic and Sage Cashew Cream Sauce

This is a rich, tasty cream sauce that is delicious on pasta. It tastes especially yummy on Pumpkin Spinach Ravioli (page 175).

¼ cup (56 g) nondairy butter
½ cup (120 ml) unsweetened soy or other nondairy milk
½ teaspoon garlic powder or 1 clove garlic, minced
½ teaspoon ground sage
¼ cup (28 g) ground cashews
1 tablespoon (8 g) all-purpose flour
Salt and pepper, to taste

In a small-size saucepan, combine the butter, milk, garlic, and sage. Heat over medium-low heat until completely melted, mixed, and beginning to bubble. Add the cashews and flour. Stir vigorously, then remove from the heat. Add salt and pepper to taste. Serve warm over pasta.

Yield: About 1 cup (235 ml)

Fire-Roasted Red Pepper Cream Sauce

The charred, smoky flavor from a roasted pepper gives this cream sauce quite a zing. If you don't have access to nondairy cream cheese, feel free to substitute it with Tofu Mayo (page 302) or Soymilk Mayo (page 301).

1 red bell pepper
½ cup (112 g) nondairy cream cheese
3 cloves roasted garlic (see page 274 for an easy way to roast garlic)
½ cup (56 g) cashews, ground into a fine powder
¼ cup (60 ml) olive oil
Salt and pepper, to taste

Roast the red pepper in one of two ways: If you have a gas stove, simply lay the pepper over the open flame and roast until charred, turning and repeating on each side. You can also do this on a barbecue grill. If you are stuck with an electric stove, use the oven instead. Lay the pepper directly on the oven rack and roast at 450°F (230°C, or gas mark 8) for 30 minutes. Once the pepper is blackened, let it cool, and then you can remove the charred bits, or leave them on for an extra fire-roasted flavor.

Remove the stem, core, and seeds.

Add the pepper, cream cheese, garlic, cashew powder, oil, salt, and pepper to a blender and blend until smooth.

Heat in a saucepan or in the microwave before using to top pasta, rice, or your favorite protein.

Yield: 1½ cups (370 g)

Under 30 Minutes

Béchamel Sauce

This quick sauce lends rich and decadent results to many a dish. Traditional béchamel calls for a touch of nutmeg for depth of flavor. This sauce works great on pizza or pasta, even tofu. Use it right away, because it tends to separate quickly as it cools.

½ cup (112 g) nondairy butter
¼ cup (31 g) all-purpose flour
1 cup (235 ml) plain nondairy milk
⅛ teaspoon grated nutmeg (optional)
Salt, to taste

In a pot, melt the butter until just beginning to bubble.

Vigorously whisk in the flour until smooth.

Add the milk and continue to whisk until your desired thickness is achieved (about 1 to 2 minutes).

Remove from the heat and add the nutmeg, if using, and salt to taste.

Yield: Just under 1½ cups (355 ml)

VARIATIONS

Garlic and basil: Omit the nutmeg and add 1 teaspoon garlic powder and 1 teaspoon dried basil.

Curry: Omit the nutmeg and add 1 teaspoon curry powder.

Sweet: Leave in the nutmeg and add ½ teaspoon cinnamon and 2 tablespoons (25 g) granulated sugar (great over waffles or cinnamon rolls).

 Under 30 Minutes

Simple Cheezy Sauce

This tasty sauce is great stirred into soups, such as Minestrone (page 144), and quick to whip up when you are looking for a simple way to dress a hot bowl of pasta.

1 cup (120 g) nutritional yeast
2 tablespoons (20 g) brown rice flour
1 teaspoon garlic powder
1 teaspoon fine sea salt
2 cups (470 ml) unsweetened almond or other nondairy milk
1 tablespoon (14 g) nondairy butter
1 teaspoon prepared yellow mustard

Add the nutritional yeast, flour, garlic powder, salt, and milk to a medium-size saucepan and whisk to combine.

Cook over medium-high heat, whisking constantly, until the sauce thickens a bit. Remove from the heat. Stir in the butter and mustard, whisking until melted. Serve immediately, or whisk again before use.

Yield: About 2 cups (470 ml)

Low Fat

Takeout-Style Orange "Chicken" Glaze

This one works well to coat any of your favorite proteins. It goes fabulously over panfried seitan or tofu and swimmingly with Asian-Inspired Seitan Crumbles (page 210).

1½ cups (355 ml) water
2 tablespoons (30 ml) orange juice
¼ cup (60 ml) lemon juice
⅓ cup (80 ml) rice vinegar (in a pinch you can use 2 tablespoons [30 ml] apple cider vinegar)
2½ tablespoons (38 ml) soy sauce
1 tablespoon (6 g) grated orange zest or 1 teaspoon orange extract
1 cup (220 g) firmly packed brown sugar
1 teaspoon minced garlic
½ teaspoon freshly minced gingerroot or ¼ teaspoon powdered
½ teaspoon red pepper flakes
3 tablespoons (24 g) cornstarch mixed with ¼ cup (60 ml) water to make a slurry

Combine the water, orange juice, lemon juice, vinegar, soy sauce, orange zest, brown sugar, garlic, ginger, and red pepper flakes in a saucepan and bring to a boil, stirring occasionally. Reduce the heat to a simmer and slowly add the cornstarch mixture, stirring as it thickens. Lower the heat to keep warm. Toss in your favorite protein to coat.

Yield: About 2½ cups (590 ml)

Soppy (Brown Gravy)

What's soppy? You know, the sauce that you "sop" up with your bread or your last few bites of pasta. This brown gravy gets its flavor from mushrooms and onions, plus a bit of steak sauce for that extra oomph. If you prefer smooth, silky gravy, simply transfer to a blender after it is done and purée until smooth; otherwise, enjoy the big chunks of mushrooms and onions with glee.

2 tablespoons (28 g) nondairy butter
8 ounces (227 g) baby bella or button mushrooms, sliced
1 cup (160 g) diced onion
2 cups (470 ml) beef-flavored vegetable broth or plain vegetable broth
2 tablespoons (30 ml) soy sauce or tamari
2 tablespoons (30 ml) steak sauce
¼ cup (30 g) nutritional yeast
1 teaspoon freshly ground black pepper
1 teaspoon dried parsley
2 to 3 tablespoons (16 to 24 g) all-purpose flour mixed with ¼ cup (60 ml) water to make a slurry

Melt the butter in a frying pan or skillet over medium-high heat.

Add the mushrooms and onion and sauté until the mushrooms have reduced in size by about half.

Add the broth, soy sauce, and steak sauce. Deglaze the pan.

Bring to a boil, then reduce to a simmer. Simmer, uncovered, for 15 minutes.

Stir in the yeast, pepper, and parsley. Continue to simmer for 5 more minutes.

Slowly stir in the slurry. Use 2 tablespoons (16 g) for a thinner gravy or 3 tablespoons (24 g) for a thicker gravy. Stir until the desired thickness is reached. Remove from the heat.

Yield: About 3 cups (705 ml)

Soymilk Mayo

Instead of forking out what can be a rather large sum of money for store-bought mayonnaise, make your own eggless version without even breaking a sweat.

1 cup (235 ml) plain soymilk (use soy here, or your milk might not curdle)
3 tablespoons (45 ml) apple cider vinegar
¼ cup (60 ml) canola oil
¼ teaspoon packed lemon zest
2 teaspoons agave nectar
1 teaspoon dry mustard
½ teaspoon fine sea salt
1 tablespoon (8 g) cornstarch

Combine the soymilk and vinegar in a medium-size microwave-safe bowl; it will curdle and become like buttermilk.

Add the oil, lemon zest, agave, mustard, salt, and cornstarch. With an immersion blender, blend for 1 minute.

Transfer to the microwave and heat for 1 minute; keep a close eye on it to make sure the mixture doesn't bubble up and make a mess in your microwave. Remove from the microwave and blend again.

Return the bowl to the microwave and heat for 1 minute, then blend again.

Heat the mixture for 1 more minute, then let stand to cool.

Once cooled, stir with a fork, because a skin will form. Transfer to an airtight container.

Store in the refrigerator. Stir again before using. Enjoy chilled.

Yield: About 1 cup (225 g)

VARIATION

To make aioli, simply add 1 clove garlic, grated, and ¼ cup (15 g) fresh curly parsley, finely chopped (or a combination of your favorite fresh herbs, such as basil, thyme, and parsley). Add the garlic when first combining the ingredients. Add the parsley when doing the final stirring once cooled.

Under 30 Minutes

Tofu Mayo

There's no need to worry if your local market doesn't carry egg-free mayonnaise. Just whip up some of your own. This recipe works very well as a sandwich spread or in any of the mayonnaise-based dressings in this book. As long as you use gluten-free vinegar, this mayonnaise is indeed gluten free.

7 ounces (198 g) extra-firm tofu, drained and pressed
¼ cup (35 g) raw cashews, ground into a very fine powder
1 tablespoon (15 ml) lemon juice
1 tablespoon (12 g) raw sugar or (21 g) agave nectar
1½ teaspoons prepared brown or Dijon mustard
1 teaspoon apple cider vinegar or rice wine vinegar
½ teaspoon sea salt
6 tablespoons (90 ml) canola oil

Place the tofu, cashew powder, lemon juice, sugar, mustard, vinegar, and salt in a blender and whirl away.

Slowly drizzle in the oil until you get the consistency that you like.

Store refrigerated in an airtight container for up to 2 weeks.

Yield: Almost 2 cups (450 g)

Under 30 Minutes

Tofu Sour Cream

Although nondairy versions of traditional dairy products are becoming more readily available, you may occasionally want to whip up a delicious batch of your own.

7 ounces (198 g) extra-firm tofu, drained well and pressed
¼ cup (28 g) raw cashews, ground into a fine powder
1 tablespoon (15 ml) white rice vinegar
1 tablespoon (15 ml) lemon or lime juice
1 tablespoon (18 g) white miso
1 tablespoon (15 ml) canola oil

Place all the ingredients in a blender or food processor and blend until very, very smooth and creamy. Store refrigerated in an airtight container for up to 1 week.

Yield: About 1½ cups (345 g)

Under 30 Minutes  Gluten Free

Tofu Feta

Make this a day ahead of time, because it is really important to let the flavors develop overnight. Use as you would any feta, on salads, in wraps, in omelets . . .

14 ounces (397 g) extra-firm tofu, drained and pressed
3 tablespoons (45 ml) extra-virgin olive oil
2 tablespoons (30 ml) lemon juice
1 tablespoon (2 g) dried basil or 3 tablespoons (9 g) finely chopped fresh basil
Salt and pepper, to taste

Crumble the tofu into a bowl until it resembles feta.

Add the oil, lemon juice, basil, salt, and pepper and mix together with your hands.

Store refrigerated in an airtight container for up to 1 week.

Yield: About 2½ cups (590 g)

VARIATION

Add 2 tablespoons (17 g) capers for an extra briny feta.

 Under 30 Minutes  Gluten Free

Tofu Ricotta

Use as you would any ricotta, in the Red "Meat" Lasagna (page 223), on pizza, in stuffed manicotti . . .

14 ounces (397 g) extra-firm tofu, drained and pressed
¼ cup (35 g) raw cashews, ground into a fine powder
¼ cup (30 g) nutritional yeast
3 tablespoons (45 ml) extra-virgin olive oil
2 tablespoons (6 g) finely chopped fresh basil or 1 tablespoon (2 g) dried
Salt and pepper, to taste

Crumble the tofu into a bowl until it resembles ricotta.

Add the cashew powder, yeast, oil, basil, salt, and pepper and mix together with your hands.

Store refrigerated in an airtight container for up to 1 week.

Yield: About 2½ cups (590 g)

Curry Aioli

When plain old mayo just won't do, then a nice aioli can really spruce up a sandwich or salad dressing. This one tastes particularly nice on the Monte Cristo Reuben (page 262).

- 7 ounces (198 g) extra-firm tofu, drained and pressed
- ¼ cup (35 g) raw cashews, ground into a very fine powder
- 1 tablespoon (15 ml) lemon juice
- 1 tablespoon (21 g) agave nectar
- 1½ teaspoons prepared brown or Dijon mustard
- 1 teaspoon apple cider vinegar
- ½ teaspoon sea salt
- 1 tablespoon (7 g) ground coriander
- 2 teaspoons chili powder
- 2 teaspoons ground turmeric
- 1 teaspoon ground cumin
- 1 teaspoon black pepper
- 6 tablespoons (90 ml) canola oil

Place the tofu, cashew powder, lemon juice, agave, mustard, vinegar, salt, coriander, chili powder, turmeric, cumin, and black pepper in a blender and whirl away.

Slowly drizzle in the oil until you get the consistency that you like.

Store refrigerated in an airtight container for up to 2 weeks.

Yield: Almost 2 cups (470 ml)

 Under 30 Minutes  Low Fat  Gluten Free  Soy Free

Sweet Pickle-less Relish

Don't you dare call this salsa! This sweet and fresh relish *works wonderfully to add a tropical flare to your hot dogs, burgers, chicken-less salads—anywhere you would use a traditional pickle relish. Okay, we guess you* could *dip some tortilla chips in it, too.*

- 6 ounces (170 g) diced mango
- 5 ounces (140 g) diced pineapple
- 4 ounces (112 g) diced roasted red pepper
- 3 ounces (85 g) diced red onion
- 2 ounces (56 g) diced scallion
- 1 ounce (28 g) chopped fresh cilantro leaves
- 2 tablespoons (30 ml) lemon or lime juice
- 1 tablespoon (13 g) granulated sugar

Toss all the ingredients together and place in an airtight container in the refrigerator until ready to serve.

Yield: About 3 cups (777 g)

 Low Fat  Soy Free

Pickled Fruits and Veggies

These crunchy veggies make a fabulous addition to salads or sandwiches in place of relish, especially when the latter can be hard to find without high-fructose corn syrup.

2¼ cups (270 g) diced celery
1¼ cups (160 g) chopped carrot
½ cup (80 g) chopped red onion
⅔ cup (160 ml) apple cider vinegar
⅓ cup (59 g) chopped dates
⅓ cup (53 g) raisins
1 teaspoon dried thyme
¼ teaspoon ground cinnamon

Combine all the ingredients in a medium-size saucepan. Bring to a boil. Cover, lower the heat, and simmer for 20 minutes. Let cool before using and storing.

Yield: About 4 cups (940 g)

 Under 30 Minutes  Low Fat  Gluten Free  Soy Free

Garam Masala Mix

Use this hot and flavorful spice combination in Green Cauliflower Masala (page 148) and other Indian dishes; since preferences always vary, we recommend trying it as is once, and adjusting the spices to your liking over time. We often like to switch things up by not using peppercorns and increasing the chile pepper to ½ teaspoon instead.

2 tablespoons (10 g) ground coriander
2½ tablespoons (15 g) ground cumin
1 teaspoon ground cardamom or 1 black cardamom pod
½ teaspoon white peppercorns
1 dried bay leaf
¼ teaspoon crushed chile pepper
¼ teaspoon ground cinnamon
¼ teaspoon ground cloves (optional)
¼ teaspoon ground nutmeg

Combine all the ingredients in a coffee grinder. Process until finely ground. Store in an airtight container in a cool, dry place.

Yield: About ¼ cup (25 g)

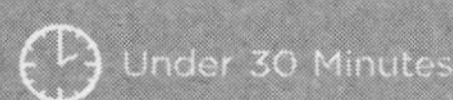 Under 30 Minutes  Low Fat  Gluten Free  Soy Free

Taco Seasoning

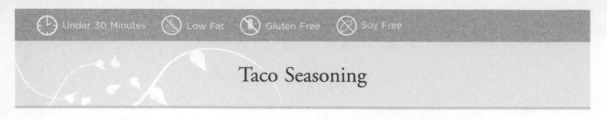

If you don't have, or can't find, a vegan store-bought taco seasoning, it is very simple to make your own.

1 tablespoon (8 g) garlic powder
1 tablespoon (8 g) onion powder
1 tablespoon (13 g) granulated sugar
1 tablespoon (6 g) ground cumin
1 tablespoon (7 g) paprika
2 tablespoons (14 g) chili powder
1½ teaspoons salt

Place all the ingredients in a small-size airtight container and shake vigorously. Two tablespoons of this mix roughly equals one packet of store-bought taco seasoning.

Store in a cool, dry place.

Yield: About ½ cup (60 g)

 Under 30 Minutes  Low Fat  Gluten Free  Soy Free

Berbere Spice Blend

Use this spice blend in seitan, to coat tofu, to add to deep-fryer coatings, or to mix with mayonnaise to make a nice aioli spread for pita or sandwiches.

2 teaspoons whole cumin seeds
4 whole cloves
½ teaspoon black peppercorns
¼ teaspoon whole allspice
1 dried ancho chile pepper, ground into a fine powder (about 2 tablespoons [16 g] powder)
3 tablespoons (21 g) smoked paprika
1 teaspoon ground ginger
¼ teaspoon turmeric
¼ teaspoon cinnamon
1 teaspoon salt

In a dry pan, toast the cumin seeds, cloves, peppercorns, and allspice for 1 to 2 minutes. Be careful not to burn. In a spice grinder or coffee grinder dedicated to spices, grind the whole spices into a powder.

Add the chile powder, paprika, ginger, turmeric, cinnamon, and salt. Mix well.

Store in an airtight container in a cool, dry place.

Yield: About ¼ cup (40 g)

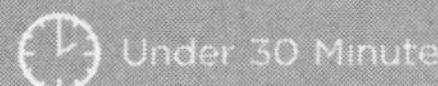

Curry Powder

Sure, it's easy to pick up a bottle of premade curry powder, but if you mix your own, you can adjust the heat to your specific taste!

5 teaspoons (9 g) ground coriander
2 teaspoons chili powder
1 teaspoon ground cumin
1 teaspoon black pepper
1 teaspoon ground turmeric, or more for a strongly yellow-colored type of curry
1 teaspoon five-spice powder, store-bought or homemade (see below)

Mix all the spices together and store in an airtight container in a cool, dry place.

Yield: About ¼ cup (20 g)

Under 30 Minutes

Chinese Five-Spice Powder

The original Chinese five-spice blend was created by ancient Chinese philosophers to balance the yin and yang in food. Some of the original ingredients are very difficult to find, but these everyday spices make an exceptional substitute.

1 tablespoon (6 g) ground cinnamon
1 tablespoon (6 g) ground fennel
4 teaspoons (8 g) ground anise
2 teaspoons ground toasted black peppercorns
½ teaspoon ground cloves

Mix all the spices together and store in an airtight container in a cool, dry place.

Yield: About ¼ cup (20 g)

Chapter 14

Sweet and Savory Quick Breads

Do you ever find yourself wishing for a nice afternoon break that would involve something tastier and daintier than a candy bar that will do nothing for you, or worse, an overly sweetened and caffeinated beverage that will have your blood sugar spike in no time, only to leave you feeling more tired and eager for the end of the day to arrive?

Celebrate teatime with good friends or coworkers by sharing slices of delicious sweet or savory quick breads that teeter on the edge of being called cakes.

We draw the line at wearing white gloves and raising our little finger while doing it, though.

Pumpkin Whiskey Quick Bread

With just a slightly boozy aftertaste, this dense loaf is reminiscent of a good fruitcake, only better for you and tastier too, because of the absence of eggs.

Nonstick cooking spray
¼ cup (60 ml) canola or vegetable oil
¼ cup (60 ml) whiskey
¾ cup (183 g) pumpkin purée
2 teaspoons pure vanilla extract
½ cup (96 g) Sucanat
¼ cup (60 ml) plain soy or other nondairy milk
1½ cups (180 g) whole wheat pastry flour
2 tablespoons (16 g) instant coconut milk powder (optional, check for ingredients if using)
½ teaspoon fine sea salt
1½ teaspoons baking powder
½ teaspoon baking soda
1 tablespoon (8 g) egg replacer powder, such as Ener-G
½ teaspoon ground ginger
2 teaspoons ground cinnamon
¼ cup (40 g) raisins
¼ cup (34 g) candied ginger, finely chopped

Preheat the oven to 350°F (180°C, or gas mark 4). Lightly coat an 8 × 4-inch (20 × 10-cm) loaf pan with spray.

In a medium-size bowl, whisk together the oil, whiskey, pumpkin purée, vanilla, Sucanat, and milk.

In a large-size bowl, sift together the flour, coconut powder, if using, salt, baking powder, baking soda, egg replacer powder, ginger, and cinnamon.

Fold the wet ingredients into the dry, being careful not to overmix. Fold in the raisins and chopped ginger. Pour the batter into the prepared pan.

Bake for 50 minutes, or until a toothpick inserted into the center comes out clean. If the loaf browns up too quickly, loosely cover with a piece of foil.

Place on a wire rack, still in the pan, for about 15 minutes before transferring directly to the rack, and let cool completely before slicing or storing.

Yield: One 8-inch (20-cm) loaf

Cinnamon Quick Bread

Do you want our secret to having a great day? It's simple enough: grab a couple slices of a fragrant, tender loaf made irresistible with cinnamon and sugar. That's all there is to it.

Nonstick cooking spray
2 teaspoons apple cider vinegar
¾ cup (180 ml) plain soymilk (use soy here, or your milk might not curdle)
2½ teaspoons ground cinnamon, divided
8 tablespoons (96 g) Sucanat, divided
½ cup plus ⅓ cup (67 g) ground oats
1 cup (120 g) light spelt flour
1 teaspoon baking powder
½ teaspoon baking soda
1 tablespoon (8 g) cornstarch
¼ teaspoon fine sea salt
2 tablespoons (30 ml) canola oil
1½ teaspoons pure vanilla extract
4 ounces (112 g) unsweetened applesauce

Preheat the oven to 350°F (180°C, or gas mark 4). Lightly coat an 8 x 4-inch (20 x 10-cm) loaf pan with spray.

Combine the vinegar and soymilk in a medium-size bowl; it will curdle and become like buttermilk.

In a small-size bowl, combine 1 teaspoon of the cinnamon with 3 tablespoons (36 g) of the Sucanat: this will be the cinnamon-sugar mixture to be sprinkled into and on top of the loaf. Set aside.

In a large-size bowl, combine the oats, flour, remaining 1½ teaspoons cinnamon, remaining 5 tablespoons (60 g) Sucanat, baking powder, baking soda, cornstarch, and salt.

Add the oil, vanilla, and applesauce to the buttermilk mixture and stir to combine.

Fold the wet ingredients into the dry, being careful not to overmix.

Pour half of the batter into the prepared pan. Sprinkle half of the cinnamon-sugar mixture evenly over the batter. Pour the remaining batter on top. Sprinkle the rest of the cinnamon-sugar mixture evenly over the batter.

Bake for 35 minutes, or until a toothpick inserted into the center comes out clean.

Place on a wire rack, still in the pan, for about 15 minutes before transferring directly to the rack, and let cool completely before slicing or storing.

Yield: One 8-inch (20-cm) loaf

Pecan Raisin Quick Bread

A few slices of a tender loaf that is packed with lovely cinnamon flavor will turn into a well-received break on a cold, busy afternoon when your batteries need to be recharged more efficiently than with a simple cup of tea or coffee.

Nonstick cooking spray
1 tablespoon (15 ml) apple cider vinegar
¾ cup (180 ml) unsweetened soymilk (use soy here, or your milk might not curdle)
1¼ cups (150 g) whole wheat pastry flour
½ cup (96 g) raw sugar
2 teaspoons baking powder
2 teaspoons ground cinnamon
1 tablespoon (8 g) cornstarch
½ cup (80 g) raisins
¼ cup (56 g) nondairy butter, melted and cooled
1 teaspoon pure vanilla extract
½ cup (55 g) chopped pecans

Preheat the oven to 350°F (180°C, or gas mark 4). Lightly coat an 8 x 4-inch (20 x 10-cm) loaf pan with spray.

Combine the vinegar and milk in a medium-size bowl: it will curdle and become like buttermilk.

Place the flour, sugar, baking powder, cinnamon, and cornstarch in a food processor. Blend for a minute or two, until the sugar is finer. Add the raisins and pulse several times, until the raisins are coarsely chopped.

Transfer the dry ingredients to a large-size bowl.

Whisk the melted butter and vanilla into the buttermilk mixture.

Fold the wet ingredients into the dry, being careful not to overmix. Fold in the pecans. Pour the batter into the prepared pan.

Bake for 45 minutes, or until a toothpick inserted into the center comes out clean.

Place on a wire rack, still in the pan, for about 15 minutes before transferring directly to the rack, and let cool completely before slicing or storing.

Yield: One 8-inch (20-cm) loaf

Cocoa-Nut Quick Bread

Heads-up to anyone who used to be addicted to milk chocolate: the coconut and cocoa combination in this flavorful loaf is reminiscent of the milky stuff. Dig in, and see for yourself.

Nonstick cooking spray
1 cup plus 2 tablespoons (135 g) whole wheat pastry flour
⅓ cup (27 g) unsweetened cocoa powder
1 teaspoon baking powder
½ teaspoon baking soda
½ teaspoon fine sea salt
1 cup (93 g) shredded coconut, processed into a fine powder
½ cup (96 g) raw sugar
2 tablespoons (30 ml) canola oil
1 cup (235 ml) plain almond or other nondairy milk
¾ cup (170 g) vanilla soy or other nondairy yogurt
1 teaspoon pure vanilla extract

Preheat the oven to 350°F (180°C, or gas mark 4). Lightly coat an 8 × 4-inch (20 × 10-cm) loaf pan with spray.

In a large-size bowl, sift together the flour, cocoa, baking powder, baking soda, and salt. Whisk in the shredded coconut and sugar.

In a medium-size bowl, whisk together the oil, milk, yogurt, and vanilla.

Fold the wet ingredients into the dry, being careful not to overmix.

Pour the batter into the prepared pan.

Bake for 60 minutes, or until a toothpick inserted into the center comes out clean.

Place on a wire rack, still in the pan, for about 15 minutes before transferring directly to the rack, and let cool completely before slicing or storing.

Yield: One 8-inch (20-cm) loaf

March of the Figs Quick Bread

This scrumptious and healthy loaf is sure to have you and those you'll share it with swoon until the last slice disappears. Choose between Calimyrna, Medjool, or Black Mission figs: whichever kind you can find will work well here.

Nonstick cooking spray
1 cup (120 g) whole wheat pastry flour
¾ cup (90 g) light spelt flour
½ teaspoon baking powder
½ teaspoon baking soda
½ teaspoon fine sea salt
⅓ cup (31 g) almond meal
½ cup (96 g) Sucanat
½ cup (120 g) vanilla soy or other nondairy yogurt
1 cup (235 ml) plain almond or other nondairy milk
1 teaspoon rose water
1 teaspoon pure vanilla extract
⅓ cup (80 ml) vegetable or canola oil
1 cup (170 g) chopped dried figs

Preheat the oven to 350°F (180°C, or gas mark 4). Lightly coat an 8 × 4-inch (20 × 10-cm) loaf pan with spray.

In a large-size bowl, sift together the flours, baking powder, baking soda, and salt. Whisk in the almond meal.

In a medium-size bowl, whisk together the Sucanat, yogurt, milk, rose water, vanilla, and oil.

Fold the wet ingredients into the dry, being careful not to overmix. Fold in the chopped figs.

Pour the batter into the prepared loaf pan.

Bake for 60 minutes, or until a toothpick inserted into the center comes out clean. If you see the loaf brown up too much too soon before being done, cover it loosely with a piece of foil.

Turn the oven off, leaving the loaf in the oven for another 10 minutes.

Place on a wire rack, still in the pan, for about 30 minutes before transferring directly to the rack, and let cool completely before slicing or storing.

Yield: One 8-inch (20-cm) loaf

Lemon Thyme Quick Bread

An unexpected ingredient in a sweet bread recipe, thyme makes a subtly perfect addition to fresh and zesty lemon in this deliciously soft and fragrant loaf.

Nonstick cooking spray
1 cup (240 g) vanilla soy or other nondairy yogurt
⅓ cup (80 ml) canola oil
2 teaspoons pure lemon extract
2 teaspoons lemon zest
1 tablespoon (15 ml) fresh lemon juice
⅔ cup (132 g) granulated sugar
1½ cups (188 g) all-purpose flour
2 teaspoons baking powder
1 teaspoon dried thyme

Preheat the oven to 350°F (180°C, or gas mark 4). Lightly coat an 8 × 4-inch (20 × 10-cm) loaf pan with spray.

In a medium-size bowl, whisk together the yogurt, oil, extract, zest, juice, and sugar until emulsified.

In a large-size bowl, sift together the flour and baking powder. Crumble the thyme between your fingers on top of the flour.

Fold the wet ingredients into the dry, being careful not to overmix.

Pour the batter into the prepared loaf pan.

Bake for 45 to 50 minutes, or until a toothpick inserted into the center comes out clean.

Place on a wire rack, still in the pan, for about 30 minutes before transferring directly to the rack, and let cool completely before slicing or storing.

Yield: One 8-inch (20-cm) loaf

Chocolate Tahini Quick Bread

Here is an unusual pairing that already won over many skeptical palates. With a tender crumb, the smooth chocolate and subtle tahini flavors make beautiful culinary music together in this loaf. Make even more of an impression by spreading a slice with a little peanut butter upon serving.

Nonstick cooking spray
½ cup (40 g) unsweetened cocoa powder
1½ cups (180 g) whole wheat pastry flour
1½ teaspoons baking powder
½ teaspoon baking soda
¼ teaspoon fine sea salt
2 tablespoons (16 g) instant coconut milk powder (optional, check for ingredients if using)
1½ teaspoons ground cinnamon
¼ cup plus 2 tablespoons (96 g) tahini
½ cup plus 2 tablespoons (210 g) agave nectar
½ cup (112 g) unsweetened applesauce
2 teaspoons pure vanilla extract
¾ cup (180 ml) plain soy or other nondairy milk

Preheat the oven to 350°F (180°C, or gas mark 4). Lightly coat an 8 × 4-inch (20 × 10-cm) loaf pan with spray.

In a large-size bowl, sift together the cocoa, flour, baking powder, baking soda, salt, coconut milk powder, if using, and cinnamon.

In a medium-size bowl, combine the tahini, agave, applesauce, vanilla, and milk.

Fold the wet ingredients into the dry, being careful not to overmix.

Pour the batter into the prepared loaf pan.

Bake for 65 minutes, or until a toothpick inserted into the center comes out clean. Loosely cover with foil if the loaf browns up too quickly.

Place on a wire rack, still in the pan, for about 15 minutes before transferring directly to the rack, and let cool completely before slicing or storing.

Yield: One 8-inch (20-cm) loaf

Espresso Chocolate Chip Quick Breads

These rich and sweet quick breads are perfect for gift giving, bake sales, or certainly to enjoy all on your own! Remember to have a nice tall cold glass of soymilk on standby when enjoying these.

Nonstick cooking spray
¾ cup (170 g) plain or vanilla soy yogurt
1 cup (235 ml) canola oil
1 tablespoon (15 ml) pure vanilla extract
1 tablespoon (15 ml) chocolate extract, or more vanilla
2 cups (400 g) granulated sugar
2 tablespoons (44 g) molasses
½ cup (120 ml) coffee-flavored liqueur, such as Kahlúa, store-bought or homemade (page 495)
1 cup (235 ml) vanilla or plain soy or other nondairy milk
½ cup (22 g) instant coffee crystals
3½ cups (438 g) all-purpose flour
1 cup (120 g) whole wheat pastry flour
½ cup (40 g) unsweetened cocoa powder
2 teaspoons baking powder
2 teaspoons baking soda
2 tablespoons (16 g) cornstarch
1 teaspoon salt
1½ cups (264 g) nondairy semisweet chocolate chips

Preheat the oven to 350°F (180°C, or gas mark 4). Spray 6 mini loaf tins with nonstick spray.

In a large-size bowl, mix together the yogurt, oil, vanilla, chocolate extract, sugar, molasses, coffee liqueur, milk, and coffee crystals.

In a separate bowl, sift together the flours, cocoa powder, baking powder, baking soda, cornstarch, and salt.

Fold the dry ingredients into the wet, being careful not to overmix. Fold in the chocolate chips.

Fill the mini loaf tins two-thirds full.

Bake for 35 to 45 minutes, or until a toothpick inserted into the center comes out clean.

Yield: 6 mini loaves

Apple Sage Quick Bread

If you are getting bored of the same old quick bread or muffin components, you will delight in a tasty bread that pairs the tart taste of dried apples with the lovely fragrances of dried sage and nutmeg.

- Nonstick cooking spray
- 1 tablespoon (15 ml) apple cider vinegar
- 1 cup (235 ml) plain soymilk (use soy here, or your milk might not curdle)
- ¾ cup (90 g) light spelt flour
- ¾ cup (90 g) whole wheat pastry flour
- 2 teaspoons baking powder
- ½ teaspoon fine sea salt
- ¼ teaspoon ground nutmeg
- 2 teaspoons dried sage
- ½ cup (96 g) raw sugar
- ¼ cup (60 ml) extra-virgin olive oil
- 2 teaspoons pure vanilla extract
- ½ cup (80 g) dried apple slices, chopped

Preheat the oven to 350°F (180°C, or gas mark 4). Lightly coat an 8 × 4-inch (20 × 10-cm) loaf pan with spray.

Combine the vinegar and soymilk in a medium-size bowl; it will curdle and become like buttermilk.

In a large-size bowl, sift together the flours, baking powder, salt, nutmeg, and sage. Whisk in the sugar.

Add the oil and vanilla to the buttermilk mixture.

Fold the wet ingredients into the dry, being careful not to overmix. Fold in the chopped apple slices.

Pour the batter into the prepared loaf pan. Bake for 40 to 45 minutes, or until a toothpick inserted into the center comes out clean.

Place on a wire rack, still in the pan, for about 15 minutes before transferring directly to the rack, and let cool completely before slicing or storing.

Yield: One 8-inch (20-cm) loaf

Cranberry Nut Quick Bread

A simple cranberry bread with a subtle citrus flavor and a buttery crust, this loaf is sure to be the perfect companion to your teatime ritual. And if you don't have a teatime ritual yet, consider it a good incentive to get one started.

Nonstick cooking spray
1 cup (120 g) whole wheat pastry flour
½ cup (60 g) cornmeal
1½ teaspoons baking powder
½ teaspoon baking soda
½ teaspoon fine sea salt
½ cup (120 ml) vanilla soy or other nondairy milk
¼ cup (60 g) nondairy sour cream or vanilla soy yogurt
2 tablespoons (30 ml) canola oil
¾ cup (144 g) raw sugar
2 teaspoons pure orange extract
1 teaspoon pure vanilla extract
1 cup (63 g) fresh or frozen cranberries
½ cup (56 g) chopped pecans

Preheat the oven to 375°F (190°C, or gas mark 5). Lightly coat an 8 × 4-inch (20 × 10-cm) loaf pan with spray.

In a large-size bowl, whisk together the flour, cornmeal, baking powder, baking soda, and salt.

In a medium-size bowl, whisk together the milk, sour cream, oil, sugar, and extracts.

Fold the wet ingredients into the dry, being careful not to overmix. Fold in the cranberries and pecans.

Pour the batter into the prepared pan.

Bake for 45 to 50 minutes, or until a toothpick inserted into the center comes out clean.

Place on a wire rack, still in the pan, for about 15 minutes before transferring directly to the rack, and let cool completely before slicing or storing.

Yield: One 8-inch (20-cm) loaf

Zucchini Quick Bread

Not too sweet, but strangely buttery, without any added oil or butter. Hmm? Must be magic. Zucchini, banana, and applesauce make this cake very moist and increase the baking time. This makes for a nice firm and crunchy crust on top. Serve warm and spread with jam or nondairy butter for an afternoon or anytime treat.

Nonstick cooking spray
1 banana, mashed
¾ cup (170 g) soy or other nondairy yogurt
½ cup (112 g) unsweetened applesauce
½ cup (168 g) brown rice syrup
2 teaspoons pure vanilla extract
2 cups (240 g) whole wheat pastry flour
½ teaspoon baking powder
½ teaspoon baking soda
½ teaspoon salt
¼ teaspoon ground cinnamon
1 cup (98 g) shredded zucchini
½ cup (60 g) walnut pieces

Preheat the oven to 350°F (180°C, or gas mark 4). Lightly coat an 8 × 4-inch (20 × 10-cm) loaf pan with spray.

In a mixing bowl, mix together the mashed banana, yogurt, applesauce, brown rice syrup, and vanilla.

In a separate bowl, mix together the flour, baking powder, baking soda, salt, and cinnamon.

Fold the wet ingredients into the dry, being careful not to overmix. Fold in the zucchini and walnuts.

Pour the batter into the prepared loaf pan.

Bake for 35 to 45 minutes, or until a toothpick inserted into the center comes out clean.

Place on a wire rack, still in the pan, for about 15 minutes before transferring directly to the rack, and let cool completely before slicing or storing.

Yield: One 8-inch (20-cm) loaf

Peanut Butter Quick Bread

With its pound cake–like good looks, this delicious quick bread gets even better eaten the day after it's baked. If you are feeling particularly sinful, replace the raisins with chocolate chips or chunks. Other dried or even fresh fruit (raspberries, blueberries, even cranberries) would be perfect, too.

Nonstick cooking spray
½ cup (116 g) Soymilk Mayo (page 301) (omit dry mustard, add 2 teaspoons agave nectar, ½ teaspoon lemon zest, let cool completely, and chill for a few hours before using)
½ cup (128 g) creamy or crunchy natural peanut butter
1 cup (235 ml) plain soy or other nondairy milk
⅔ cup (128 g) raw sugar
2 teaspoons pure vanilla extract
1½ cups (180 g) whole wheat pastry flour
2 tablespoons (16 g) cornstarch
2 teaspoons ground cinnamon
1½ teaspoons baking powder
½ teaspoon baking soda
½ teaspoon fine sea salt
¼ cup (34 g) candied ginger, finely chopped, or ⅓ cup (80 g) raisins

Preheat the oven to 350°F (180°C, or gas mark 4). Lightly coat an 8 × 4-inch (20 × 10-cm) loaf pan with spray.

In a medium-size bowl, combine the mayonnaise, peanut butter, milk, sugar, and vanilla until emulsified.

In a large-size bowl, whisk together the flour, cornstarch, cinnamon, baking powder, baking soda, and salt.

Fold the wet ingredients into the dry, being careful not to overmix. Fold in the candied ginger.

Pour the batter into th eprepared pan.

Bake for 60 to 65 minutes, or until a toothpick inserted into the center comes out clean. Loosely cover with foil if it browns up too quickly while baking.

Place on a wire rack, still in the pan, for about 15 minutes before transferring directly to the rack, and let cool completely before slicing or storing.

Yield: One 8-Inch (20-cm) loaf

Blueberry Cornmeal Quick Bread

This succulent loaf demands to be lathered with a thin layer of nondairy butter and all-fruit blueberry jam, to make the life of true blueberry lovers complete.

Nonstick cooking spray
¾ cup (170 g) blueberry soy or other nondairy yogurt
¼ cup (60 ml) canola oil
1 cup (235 ml) plain almond or other nondairy milk
1 teaspoon pure vanilla extract
1½ cups (180 g) whole wheat pastry flour
½ cup (60 g) cornmeal
½ cup (96 g) raw sugar
2 teaspoons baking powder
½ teaspoon fine sea salt
½ cup (55 g) chopped pecans
½ cup (62 g) dried blueberries

Preheat the oven to 350°F (180°C, or gas mark 4). Lightly coat an 8 × 4-inch (20 × 10-cm) loaf pan with spray.

In a medium-size bowl, whisk together the yogurt, oil, milk, and vanilla.

In a large-size bowl, combine the flour, cornmeal, sugar, baking powder, and salt.

Fold the wet ingredients into the dry, being careful not to overmix. Fold in the pecans and blueberries.

Pour the batter into the prepared pan.

Bake for 50 to 60 minutes, or until a toothpick inserted into the center comes out clean.

Place on a wire rack, still in the pan, for about 15 minutes before transferring directly to the rack, and let cool completely before slicing or storing.

Yield: One 8-inch (20-cm) loaf

Banana Chestnut Quick Bread

The combination of bananas, chestnuts, and white chocolate chips lends an irresistible marzipan flavor to this scrumptious bread.

Nonstick cooking spray
3½ ounces (100 g) roasted chestnuts
2 large-size ripe bananas
1 teaspoon pure vanilla extract
¼ cup (60 ml) canola oil
¼ cup (60 ml) soy or other nondairy milk
6 tablespoons (92 g) unsweetened applesauce
½ cup (96 g) raw sugar
1 cup (160 g) brown rice flour
1 cup (120 g) whole wheat pastry flour
1 tablespoon (8 g) arrowroot powder or cornstarch
1 teaspoon baking powder
½ teaspoon baking soda
½ teaspoon fine sea salt
⅓ cup (67 g) nondairy white chocolate chips

Preheat the oven to 350°F (180°C, or gas mark 4). Lightly coat an 8 × 4-inch (20 × 10-cm) loaf pan with spray.

Blend the chestnuts in a food processor until finely ground. Add the bananas, vanilla, oil, milk, applesauce, and sugar. Process until mostly smooth: it's okay if there are small pieces of banana left.

In a large-size bowl, whisk together the flours, arrowroot powder, baking powder, baking soda, and salt.

Fold the wet ingredients into the dry, being careful not to overmix. Fold in the chocolate chips.

Pour the batter into the prepared pan.

Bake for 60 minutes, or until a toothpick inserted into the center comes out clean.

Place on a wire rack, still in the pan, for about 15 minutes before transferring directly to the rack, and let cool completely before slicing or storing.

Yield: One 8-inch (20-cm) loaf

VARIATION

Bake this recipe in 6 jumbo muffin cups instead, decreasing the total baking time to 30 minutes.

Caraway Onion Cornmeal Bread

Caraway and onion appear to be as inseparable as cinnamon and sugar are, to us. We hope you'll think the same too, when you bite into a slice of this hearty loaf that goes especially well with soups and salads.

- Nonstick cooking spray
- 1 tablespoon (15 ml) apple cider vinegar
- 1¾ cups (415 ml) plain soymilk (use soy here, or your milk might not curdle)
- 1 cup (120 g) cornmeal
- 2 cups (240 g) white whole wheat or regular whole wheat flour
- 1 tablespoon (12 g) baking powder
- 1 teaspoon baking soda
- 1 teaspoon fine sea salt
- 2 teaspoons dried minced onion
- 2 teaspoons caraway seeds
- 1 tablespoon (8 g) cornstarch
- ¼ cup (60 ml) canola oil

Preheat the oven to 350°F (180°C, or gas mark 4). Lightly coat an 8 × 4-inch (20 × 10-cm) loaf pan with spray.

Combine the vinegar and soymilk in a medium-size bowl; it will curdle and become like buttermilk.

In a large-size bowl, combine the cornmeal, flour, baking powder, baking soda, salt, dried onion, caraway seeds, and cornstarch.

Stir the oil into the buttermilk mixture.

Fold the wet ingredients into the dry, being careful not to overmix.

Pour the batter into the prepared pan.

Bake for 40 to 45 minutes, or until a toothpick inserted into the center comes out clean.

Place on a wire rack, still in the pan, for about 15 minutes before transferring directly to the rack, and let cool completely before slicing or storing.

Yield: One 8-inch (20-cm) loaf

Soy Free

Beer Bread

Sometimes, you need carbs in bread form without wanting to wait for the dough to rise. Beer bread to the rescue! Although we find that using stout makes for a bolder flavor, feel free to use the one you love the most. Be sure to check that the beer you use is animal-friendly, because isinglass, a substance derived from fish, is often used to clarify beer.

Nonstick cooking spray
1 cup (120 g) bread flour
1 cup (120 g) white whole wheat or regular whole wheat flour
½ cup (60 g) light spelt flour
½ cup (39 g) quick-cooking oats, finely ground
1 tablespoon (12 g) vital wheat gluten flour
1 tablespoon (12 g) raw sugar
1 tablespoon (12 g) baking powder
1½ teaspoons fine sea salt
2 tablespoons (30 ml) canola oil
12 ounces (355 ml) oatmeal stout beer
2 teaspoons caraway seeds (optional)

Preheat the oven to 375°F (190°C, or gas mark 5). Lightly coat an 8 × 4-inch (20 × 10-cm) loaf pan with spray.

In a large-size bowl, whisk together the flours, oats, wheat gluten, sugar, baking powder, and salt. Add the oil and stir with a fork.

Fold in the beer, being careful not to overmix. The dough will be sticky and rather thick, but if it's really impossible to manage, add a few tablespoons of water or extra beer.

Place the batter in the prepared pan. Sprinkle the top with the caraway seeds, if desired.

Bake for 50 to 55 minutes, or until a toothpick inserted into the center comes out clean.

Place on a wire rack, still in the pan, for about 15 minutes before transferring directly to the rack, and let cool completely before slicing or storing.

Yield: One 8-inch (20-cm) loaf

VARIATIONS

Use ½ cup (60 g) dark rye flour or any other flour in place of the oats.

If you have a muffin top pan, this recipe makes 6 individual portions; bake for 20 to 25 minutes.

Sweet Skillet Cornbread

Whether you are making this cornbread to accompany a big bowl of chili or as the base of the Chorizo, Cranberry, and Cornbread Stuffing (page 273), the addition of the melted butter to the bottom of the pan will give a nice buttery crust to the bottom and to the edges. Mmm.

This cornbread is baked in a cast-iron skillet. A 10-inch (25-cm) size is perfect. If you don't have a skillet, a round, nonstick baking pan will work as well.

1 tablespoon (14 g) nondairy butter
1 cup (125 g) all-purpose flour
¾ cup (90 g) cornmeal
3 tablespoons (36 g) raw sugar
2½ teaspoons baking powder
1 teaspoon salt
Equivalent of 2 eggs (Ener-G works great here)
1 cup (235 ml) plain soy or other nondairy milk
¼ cup (60 ml) canola or other vegetable oil
1 cup (250 g) yellow corn kernels

Preheat the oven to 400°F (200°C, or gas mark 6).

Add the butter to an oven-safe skillet. Place in the oven for a few minutes to melt the butter. Remove from the oven and swirl the butter all around the bottom of the skillet.

In a mixing bowl, mix together the flour, cornmeal, sugar, baking powder, and salt.

In a separate bowl, mix together the egg replacer, milk, and oil. Add the wet ingredients to the dry, being careful not to overmix. Fold in the corn.

Add the batter to the skillet.

Bake for 20 to 25 minutes, or until a toothpick inserted into the center comes out clean.

Yield: 8 servings

VARIATION

Fold in ½ cup (61 g) dried cranberries or blueberries at the same time as the corn for a tart twist on an old classic.

Chapter 15

Sweet and Savory Yeast Breads

If you have found yourself spending countless moments checking labels at the bread aisle of the supermarket, only to come to the conclusion that most loaves contain whey, honey, or other animal-based ingredients, we are happy to bring you this great piece of news: baking your own bread is absolutely not as scary or time-consuming as you might have been told or assumed in the past. All it takes is a little practice for you to conquer the yeast beast, and you will soon find yourself artfully preparing loaves that are far fresher, healthier, and tastier than any store-bought bread you've ever enjoyed before.

There is no doubt that fresh bread is best enjoyed on baking day, but if you don't get to savor the fruit of your labor all at once, simply toast or reheat it in the oven for a few minutes, to bring its fresh flavor back to life.

Chapter note: Remember to have the ingredients at room temperature for best results, or heated to 100°F (38°C) when mentioned in the recipe. If your home is on the cold side, give a rising boost to your dough by preheating the oven at its lowest setting for 50 seconds, switching it off, and letting the dough rise in there.

Also, note that you can test all breads for doneness by inserting an instant-read thermometer into the center; the temperature needs to be between 190° and 200°F (88° and 93°C).

Remember to check out chapter 1 for ingredients, substitutions, and various other baking tips!

Soy Free

Pesto Bagels

These bagels add a perfect garlicky touch to your sandwiches, turning them into indispensable partners to your lunch break from this point forward. Your coworkers or schoolmates will be pesto-green with envy.

¼ cup (64 g) prepared vegan pesto
¾ cup (180 ml) water, heated to 100°F (38°C)
1 cup (120 g) bread flour
1 cup (120 g) white whole wheat or regular whole wheat flour
1 tablespoon (9 g) vital wheat gluten flour
1 tablespoon (12 g) Sucanat
1 teaspoon fine sea salt
¾ teaspoon bread machine yeast
½ teaspoon canola oil, to coat bowl

In a medium-size bowl, combine the pesto and water.

In a large-size bowl, combine the flours, wheat gluten, Sucanat, salt, and yeast.

Stir the wet ingredients into the dry.

Transfer to a lightly floured surface and knead for 8 to 10 minutes, until the dough is smooth and pliable, adding more flour, a little at a time, if the dough is too wet. Shape into a ball.

Lightly coat a large-size bowl with oil and turn the dough around to coat. Cover tightly with plastic wrap, and let rise until doubled, 60 to 90 minutes.

Punch down the dough. Divide it into 4 equal portions and shape into balls.

Let rest for 10 minutes.

Flatten with your palm, insert your thumb in the center, and twirl the dough around it until the hole reaches about 1½ inches (3.8 cm) in size.

Let the bagels rest for 5 minutes.

In the meantime, bring water to a boil in a large-size saucepan.

Preheat the oven to 400°F (200°C, or gas mark 6). Prepare a large-size baking sheet with parchment paper or a silicone baking mat, such a Silpat, or grease it with a little oil.

Once the bagels have rested, place 2 bagels at a time in the saucepan, and let boil for 1 minute in all, flipping them over after 30 seconds; try to avoid having them get too close to one another. They should sink, and then rise after a few seconds. Don't worry if they don't sink—it'll work out just fine.

Scoop out the bagels with a slotted spoon. Place on the prepared baking sheet. Repeat until all the bagels have been boiled.

Bake for 22 minutes, or until the bagels are golden brown and sound hollow when the bottom is tapped. Let cool on a wire rack.

Yield: 4 large bagels

 Soy Free

Peanut Butter Bagels

By preparing bagels yourself, you know which ingredients are used and how fresh they are, and you also have the pride of having baked something wonderful from scratch, making you all the more deserving to have a big bite.

½ cup (128 g) creamy natural peanut butter
1 cup plus 1 tablespoon (250 ml) water, heated to 100°F (38°C)
3 cups (360 g) white whole wheat or regular whole wheat flour
1 teaspoon fine sea salt
2 tablespoons (24 g) Sucanat
2 teaspoons bread machine yeast
½ teaspoon canola oil, to coat bowl

In a medium-size bowl, combine the peanut butter and water.

In a large-size bowl, combine the flour, salt, Sucanat, and yeast.

Stir the wet ingredients into the dry.

Transfer to a lightly floured surface and knead for 8 to 10 minutes, until the dough is smooth and pliable, adding more flour, a little at a time, if the dough is too wet. Shape into a ball.

Lightly coat a large-size bowl with oil and turn the dough around to coat. Cover tightly with plastic wrap, and let rise until doubled, 60 to 90 minutes.

Punch down the dough. Divide it into 4 equal portions and shape into balls.

Let rest for 10 minutes.

Cut each piece in half and roll into balls. Flatten with your palm, insert your thumb in the center, and twirl the dough around it until the hole reaches about 1½ inches (3.8 cm) in size.

Let the bagels rest for 5 minutes.

In the meantime, bring water to a boil in a large-size saucepan.

Preheat the oven to 400°F (200°C, or gas mark 6). Prepare a couple of large-size baking sheets with parchment paper or a silicone baking mat, such a Silpat, or grease them with a little oil.

Once the bagels have rested, place 2 bagels at a time in the saucepan, and let boil for 1 minute in all, flipping them over after 30 seconds; try to avoid having them get too close to one another. They should sink, and then rise after a few seconds. But don't worry if they don't sink—it'll work out just fine.

Scoop out the bagels with a slotted spoon. Place on the prepared baking sheets. Repeat until all bagels have been boiled.

Bake for about 20 minutes, one sheet at a time, until the bagels are golden brown and sound hollow when the bottom is tapped. Let cool on a wire rack.

Yield: 8 bagels

VARIATION

Add ⅓ cup (59 g) nondairy semisweet chocolate chips or (53 g) raisins to the dough after the first 4 minutes of kneading, and incorporate by kneading another 4 to 6 minutes.

Pumpkin Bagels

These are a perfect breakfast item that will be made over-the-top delectable if you add dried fruit, nuts, or, dare we say it, chocolate chips to the dough.

¾ cup (183 g) pumpkin purée
⅔ cup (160 ml) plain soymilk, heated to 100°F (38°C)
1 tablespoon (14 g) nondairy butter, softened
3 cups (360 g) white whole wheat or regular whole wheat flour
1 tablespoon (9 g) vital wheat gluten flour
2 tablespoons (24 g) Sucanat
1½ teaspoons fine sea salt
1¾ teaspoons bread machine yeast
1 teaspoon ground cinnamon (optional)
¼ cup (40 g) raisins, nondairy semisweet chocolate chips, or chopped pecans (optional)
½ teaspoon canola oil, to coat bowl

In a medium-size bowl, combine the pumpkin purée, soymilk, and butter.

In a large-size bowl, combine the flour, wheat gluten, Sucanat, salt, yeast, and cinnamon, if using.

Stir the wet ingredients into the dry. If using raisins or other add-ins, knead the dough by itself for 4 minutes, add the raisins, and incorporate by kneading for another 4 to 6 minutes.

Transfer to a lightly floured surface and knead for 8 to 10 minutes, until the dough is smooth and pliable, adding more flour, a little at a time, if the dough is too wet. Shape into a ball.

Lightly coat a large-size bowl with oil and turn the dough around to coat. Cover tightly with plastic wrap, and let rise until doubled, 60 to 90 minutes.

Punch down the dough. Divide it into 4 equal portions and shape into balls.

Let rest for 10 minutes.

Cut each piece in half and roll into balls. Flatten with your palm, insert your thumb in the center, and twirl the dough around it until the hole reaches about 1½ inches (3.8 cm) in size.

Let the bagels rest for 5 minutes.

In the meantime, bring water to a boil in a large-size saucepan.

Preheat the oven to 400°F (200°C, or gas mark 6). Prepare a couple of large-size baking sheets with parchment paper or a silicone baking mat, such a Silpat, or grease them with a little oil.

Once the bagels have rested, place 2 bagels at a time in the saucepan, and let boil for 1 minute in all, flipping them over after 30 seconds; try to avoid having them get too close to one another. They should sink, and then rise after a few seconds. Don't worry if they don't sink—it'll work out just fine.

Scoop out the bagels with a slotted spoon. Place on the prepared baking sheet. Repeat until all the bagels have been boiled.

Bake for about 20 minutes, one sheet at a time, until the bagels are golden brown and sound hollow when the bottom is tapped. Let cool on a wire rack.

Yield: 8 bagels

Cast-Iron Deep Dish Pizza Dough and Bread Bowls

Whether you are craving a big old deep dish pizza or a hearty bowl of thick soup, this will become your go-to recipe.

1 envelope (¼ ounce, or 7 g) active dry yeast
1 teaspoon granulated sugar
½ cup (120 ml) warm water
2 cups (250 g) all-purpose flour
½ cup (72 g) vital wheat gluten flour
½ teaspoon salt
½ cup (120 ml) water
3 tablespoon (45 ml) extra-virgin olive oil, divided
¼ cup (60 ml) melted nondairy butter, for brushing (bread bowls only)

Mix together the yeast, sugar, and warm water. Let stand for 10 minutes.

In a mixing bowl, mix together the flours and salt.

Add the yeast mixture, water, and 1 tablespoon (15 ml) of the olive oil.

Turn out onto a lightly floured surface and knead the dough for 10 minutes, adding more all-purpose flour if it is too wet, or more water if it is too dry, a little bit at a time. Your goal is a soft, elastic dough ball that is easy to handle and not sticky.

Divide in half and roll each piece into a ball. Brush with the remaining 2 tablespoons (30 ml) olive oil, cover with plastic wrap, and let rise for 1 hour.

To make the pizza crusts: Preheat the oven to 450°F (230°C, or gas mark 8).

Punch down the dough, knead for 2 to 3 minutes, and roll out into 2 pizza crusts.

Cover with your favorite toppings and bake for about 10 minutes, or until the crust is a nice golden brown.

To make the bread bowls: Preheat the oven to 400°F (200°C, or gas mark 6).

Cut a few crisscross slits across the top of the dough balls.

Bake for 15 minutes, remove from the oven, and brush liberally with the melted butter. Return to the oven and bake for 5 minutes longer, or until golden brown.

Remove from the oven and let sit for about 5 minutes to cool. Carefully cut a circle out of the top to create a bowl.

Yield: Two 10-inch (25-cm) crusts or 2 bread bowls

Spelt Loaf

Tender and especially perfect for sandwiches, you won't believe how easy this gigantic golden brown and fluffy loaf is to prepare. The dough will be sticky, so although we tried to avoid making "stand mixer only" bread recipes, we definitely recommend using one in this case.

½ cup (120 ml) plain soymilk, heated to 100°F (38°C) (use soy here, or your milk may not curdle)
1 teaspoon apple cider vinegar
2 cups (240 g) light or whole spelt flour
¼ cup (36 g) vital wheat gluten flour
2½ tablespoons (13 g) ground oats
½ teaspoon fine sea salt
2 tablespoons (24 g) raw sugar
2 teaspoons bread machine yeast
1 tablespoon (15 ml) canola oil
¼ cup (60 ml) water

Prepare a large-size baking sheet with parchment paper or a silicone baking mat, such a Silpat.

Combine the soymilk and vinegar in a medium-size bowl; it will curdle and become like buttermilk.

In the bowl of your stand mixer, fitted with the dough hook, combine the flour, wheat gluten, oats, salt, sugar, and yeast.

Add the oil and water to the buttermilk mixture.

Stir the wet ingredients into the dry. Be aware that the dough will be sticky! Let the machine knead for 6 minutes, until the dough comes together. Shape into a ball.

Place the dough on the prepared baking sheet.

Slightly dampening your hands with water to help with the stickiness, shape the dough into a log, about 8 inches (20 cm) in length. Sprinkle with a little flour, so that the plastic wrap doesn't stick while the dough rests.

Loosely cover with a piece of plastic wrap, and let rise for 45 minutes.

Preheat the oven to 375°F (190°C, or gas mark 5).

Remove the plastic wrap. Bake for 20 to 25 minutes, or until the loaf sounds hollow when the bottom is tapped.

Turn off the oven, and leave the loaf in there for another 5 minutes.

Let cool completely before slicing.

Yield: 1 approximately 8-inch (20-cm) loaf

Little Baguettes

You might find these baguettes quickly becoming an indispensable accessory to your sandwiches. Enjoy them the day they're baked, when they've had just enough time to cool down, so that they remain crispy and delicious.

¾ cup (180 ml) unsweetened soy or other nondairy milk, heated to 100°F (38°C)
2 tablespoons (28 g) nondairy butter, softened
1 cup (120 g) white whole wheat or regular whole wheat flour
1 cup (120 g) bread flour
2 tablespoons (18 g) vital wheat gluten flour
2 tablespoons (24 g) Sucanat
1 teaspoon fine sea salt
1½ teaspoons bread machine yeast
½ teaspoon canola oil, to coat bowl
¼ cup (60 ml) boiling water
1½ teaspoons baking soda

In a medium-size bowl, combine the milk and butter.

In a large-size bowl, combine the flours, wheat gluten, Sucanat, salt, and yeast.

Stir the wet ingredients into the dry.

Transfer to a lightly floured surface and knead for 8 to 10 minutes, until the dough is smooth and pliable, adding more flour, a little at a time, if the dough is too wet. Shape into a ball.

Lightly coat a large-size bowl with oil and turn the dough around to coat. Cover tightly with plastic wrap, and let rise until doubled, 60 to 90 minutes.

Prepare a large-size baking sheet with parchment paper or a silicone baking mat, such a Silpat, or grease with a little oil.

Punch down the dough. Divide into 2 equal portions and shape into baguettes, placing them on the prepared baking sheet.

Combine the boiling water and baking soda. Brush on the tops and sides of the baguettes.

Loosely cover with plastic wrap and let rise for another 40 minutes.

Preheat the oven to 375°F (190°C, or gas mark 5).

Remove the plastic wrap. Bake for 16 minutes, until the baguettes are golden brown and sound hollow when the bottom is tapped. Let cool on a wire rack.

Yield: 2 small baguettes

Soy Free

Garlicky Whole Wheat Baguette

Chewy, tasty, crusty goodness, ahoy. Go the extra mile and dip slices into olive oil and balsamic vinegar for a fancy appetizer that will rival anything you've ever had at a restaurant.

¾ cup (180 ml) water, heated to 100°F (38°C)
1 tablespoon (21 g) agave nectar
2 cloves garlic, grated
2 teaspoons bread machine yeast
1 teaspoon fine sea salt
2 tablespoons (18 g) vital wheat gluten flour
¼ cup (30 g) nutritional yeast
2 cups (240 g) white whole wheat or regular whole wheat flour
½ teaspoon canola oil, to coat bowl
1 tablespoon (15 ml) extra-virgin olive oil
1 teaspoon dried basil

In a medium-size bowl, combine the water, agave, and garlic.

In a large-size bowl, combine the bread machine yeast, salt, wheat gluten, nutritional yeast, and flour.

Stir the wet ingredients into the dry.

Transfer to a lightly floured surface and knead for 8 to 10 minutes, until the dough is smooth and pliable, adding more flour, a little at a time, if the dough is too wet. Shape into a ball.

Lightly coat a large-size bowl with the canola oil and turn the dough around to coat. Cover tightly with plastic wrap, and let rise until doubled, 60 to 90 minutes.

Prepare a large-size baking sheet with parchment paper or a silicone baking mat, such a Silpat, or grease with a little oil.

Punch down the dough. Shape into a 10-inch (25-cm) baguette. Place on the prepared baking sheet.

Preheat the oven to 400°F (200°C, or gas mark 6).

Combine the olive oil and basil. Brush the baguette with the oil mixture. Sprinkle a little flour on top. Cover with plastic wrap, and let rise for 30 minutes.

Remove the plastic wrap. Bake for 20 minutes, until the baguette is golden brown and sounds hollow when the bottom is tapped. Let cool on a wire rack.

Yield: One 10-inch (25-cm) baguette

Fu-ttage Cheese Mini Baguettes

Put the protein-packed Fu-ttage Cheese (page 85) to excellent use by incorporating it into these delicious, crunchy mini baguettes that still manage to taste amazing the next day.

½ cup (90 g) Fu-ttage Cheese (page 85)
½ cup (120 ml) water, heated to 100°F (38°C)
2 tablespoons (30 ml) extra-virgin olive oil
1 tablespoon (12 g) raw sugar
½ teaspoon fine sea salt
2 teaspoons bread machine yeast
½ teaspoon dried minced onion
2 tablespoons (18 g) vital wheat gluten flour
2 cups (240 g) white whole wheat or regular whole wheat flour
1 cup (160 g) brown rice flour, divided
½ teaspoon canola oil, to coat bowl
Nonstick cooking spray

In a medium-size bowl, combine the Fu-ttage Cheese, water, olive oil, sugar, and salt.

In a large-size bowl, combine the yeast, onion, wheat gluten, whole wheat flour, and ½ cup (80 g) of the brown rice flour.

Stir the wet ingredients into the dry.

Transfer to a lightly floured surface and knead for 8 to 10 minutes, until the dough is smooth and pliable, adding the remaining ½ cup (80 g) brown rice flour if the dough is too wet. Shape into a ball.

Lightly coat a large-size bowl with the canola oil and turn the dough around to coat. Cover tightly with plastic wrap, and let rise until doubled, 60 to 90 minutes.

Preheat the oven to 375°F (190°C, or gas mark 5). Lightly coat an 8-inch (20-cm) square baking pan with nonstick cooking spray.

Punch down the dough. Divide into 4 equal pieces. Flatten each piece into a small rectangle, rolling each of them up tightly into the shape of a baguette.

Place in the prepared baking pan. Cover with plastic wrap, and let rise for 30 minutes.

Remove the plastic wrap. Bake for 24 minutes, until the baguettes are golden brown and sound hollow when the bottom is tapped. Let cool on a wire rack.

Yield: 4 mini baguettes

Olive Mini Baguettes

Do you love anything that tastes like pesto? You're in luck! These baguettes are unbeatable when enjoyed almost straight out of the oven, given just enough time to handle them without burning your fingers or palate.

1 cup (134 g) black olives
½ cup (120 ml) water, heated to 100°F (38°C)
2 tablespoons (30 ml) extra-virgin olive oil
1 tablespoon (21 g) agave nectar
Zest and juice of ½ lemon
1 clove garlic, grated
1 teaspoon fine sea salt
2 cups (240 g) light spelt flour
1 cup (120 g) white whole wheat or regular whole wheat flour, divided
2 teaspoons Italian seasoning
2 teaspoons bread machine yeast
½ teaspoon canola oil, to coat bowl

In a medium-size bowl, using an immersion blender, or in a countertop blender, purée the olives, water, olive oil, agave, lemon zest, lemon juice, garlic, and salt; it doesn't have to be perfectly smooth.

In a large-size bowl, combine the spelt flour, ½ cup (60 g) of the whole wheat flour, seasoning, and yeast.

Stir the wet ingredients into the dry.

Transfer to a lightly floured surface and knead for 8 to 10 minutes, until the dough is smooth and pliable, adding the remaining ½ cup (60 g) whole wheat flour, as necessary, if the dough is too wet. Shape into a ball.

Lightly coat a large-size bowl with the canola oil and turn the dough around to coat. Cover tightly with plastic wrap, and let rise until doubled, 60 to 90 minutes.

Line a rimless baking sheet with parchment paper or a silicone baking mat, such as Silpat.

Punch down the dough. Divide into 6 equal portions. Shape into mini baguettes, about 8 inches (20 cm) long, and place on the prepared baking sheet. Cover with plastic wrap, and let rise for 30 minutes.

Preheat the oven to 375°F (190°C, or gas mark 5).

Remove the plastic wrap. Bake for 18 to 20 minutes, until the baguettes are golden brown and sound hollow when the bottom is tapped. Let cool on a wire rack.

Yield: 6 mini baguettes

Sesame Fauxcaccia

Reminiscent of a tasty peanut noodle sauce—without the noodles, obviously, but with flour and yeast instead—this bread is addictive: you will have a hard time stopping yourself from repeatedly reaching into the bread basket as soon as it's placed on the table.

½ cup (120 ml) fresh orange juice, heated to 100°F (38°C)
¼ cup (64 g) creamy natural peanut butter
2 cloves garlic, grated
1 tablespoon (15 ml) tamari or soy sauce
2 tablespoons (30 ml) unseasoned rice vinegar
1 teaspoon toasted sesame oil
1 tablespoon (21 g) agave nectar
1 teaspoon ground ginger
1½ teaspoons crushed chile peppers
1 cup (120 g) white whole wheat or regular whole wheat flour
1¼ cups (150 g) light spelt flour, divided
2 teaspoons bread machine yeast
½ teaspoon canola oil, to coat bowl
1 tablespoon (15 ml) warm water
1 tablespoon (8 g) sesame seeds
Coarse sea salt, for topping (optional)

In a medium-size bowl, combine the orange juice, peanut butter, garlic, tamari, vinegar, sesame oil, agave, ginger, and chile peppers.

In a large-size bowl, combine the whole wheat flour, 1 cup (120 g) of the spelt flour, and yeast.

Stir the wet ingredients into the dry.

Transfer to a lightly floured surface and knead for 8 to 10 minutes, until the dough is smooth and pliable, adding the remaining ¼ cup (30 g) spelt flour, as necessary, if the dough is too wet. Shape into a ball.

Lightly coat a large-size bowl with the canola oil and turn the dough around to coat. Cover tightly with plastic wrap, and let rise until doubled, 60 to 90 minutes.

Line a rimless baking sheet with parchment paper or a silicone baking mat, such as Silpat.

Punch down the dough. Roll it out directly onto the parchment paper into a rectangle about 8 × 10 inches (20 × 25 cm) and ½ inch (1.3 cm) thick.

Lightly brush with the warm water and sprinkle the sesame seeds and salt, if using, on top.

Cover with plastic wrap, and let rise for 30 minutes.

Preheat the oven to 375°F (190°C, or gas mark 5).

Remove the plastic wrap. Bake for 16 to 20 minutes, until the bread is golden brown and sounds hollow when the bottom is tapped. Let cool on a wire rack.

Yield: One 8 × 10-inch (20 × 25-cm) bread

Spelt Pesto Bread

For the garlic fans out there who prefer to eat their grain in spelt form, this bread was made with them in mind.

1 cup (235 ml) water, heated to 100°F (38°C)
⅓ cup (85 g) prepared vegan pesto
3 cups (360 g) light spelt flour, plus extra if needed
¼ cup (36 g) vital wheat gluten flour
2 tablespoons (24 g) Sucanat
1½ teaspoons fine sea salt
2 teaspoons bread machine yeast
½ teaspoon canola oil, to coat bowl

In a medium-size bowl, combine the water and pesto.

In a large-size bowl, combine the 3 cups (360 g) flour, wheat gluten, Sucanat, salt, and yeast.

Stir the wet ingredients into the dry.

Transfer to a lightly floured surface and knead for 8 to 10 minutes, until the dough is smooth and pliable, adding more flour, a little at a time, if the dough is too wet. Shape into a ball.

Lightly coat a large-size bowl with the oil and turn the dough around to coat. Cover tightly with plastic wrap, and let rise until doubled, 60 to 90 minutes.

Line a baking sheet with parchment paper or a silicone baking mat, such as Silpat.

Punch down the dough. Divide into 4 equal parts. Shape into loaves. Place on the prepared baking sheet, loosely covering with plastic wrap. Let rise for 45 minutes.

Preheat the oven to 375°F (190°C, or gas mark 5).

Remove the plastic wrap. Bake for 20 minutes, until the loaves are golden brown and sound hollow when the bottom is tapped. Let cool on a wire rack.

Yield: 4 small loaves

Potato Bread

Pick your favorite tuber to make this bread! The results will be equally outstanding, especially when paired with walnuts that are packed with omega-3s, or sunflower seeds, which happen to be rich in vitamin E.

½ cup (120 ml) water, heated to 100°F (38°C)
1 tablespoon (22 g) blackstrap or regular molasses
1 teaspoon active dry yeast
1½ cups (180 g) bread flour, plus extra for sprinkling
1½ cups (180 g) white whole wheat or regular whole wheat flour
1 teaspoon fine sea salt
½ cup (128 g) sweet potato purée or mashed potatoes of any kind
1 tablespoon (15 ml) canola oil, plus an extra ½ teaspoon, to coat bowl
½ cup (64 g) roasted, salted sunflower seeds or (59 g) chopped walnuts

In a medium-size bowl, combine the water, molasses, and yeast. Let stand for about 10 minutes; it should foam and bubble up. If it doesn't, start all over again because your yeast might not be fresh.

In a large-size bowl, combine the flours and salt. Add the sweet potato purée or mashed potatoes and 1 tablespoon (15 ml) oil to the yeast mixture.

Stir the wet ingredients into the dry.

Transfer to a lightly floured surface and knead for 6 minutes, incorporate the seeds or walnuts, and knead for another 2 to 4 minutes, until the dough is smooth and pliable, adding more flour, a little at a time, if the dough is too wet. Shape into a ball.

Lightly coat a large-size bowl with the remaining ½ teaspoon oil. Turn the dough around to coat, cover, and let rise for 90 minutes.

Line a baking sheet with parchment paper or a silicone baking mat, such as Silpat.

Punch down the dough. Divide into 2 equal portions. Shape each into an approximately 8-inch (20-cm) loaf. Place on the prepared baking sheet.

Sprinkle the loaves with a little bread flour. Loosely cover with plastic wrap, and let rise for another 30 minutes.

Preheat the oven to 400°F (200°C, or gas mark 6).

Remove the plastic wrap. Bake for 24 minutes, or until the loaves are golden brown and sound hollow when the bottom is tapped. Let cool on a wire rack.

Yield: Two 8-inch (20-cm) loaves

Dijon Thyme Bread

Reminiscent of sourdough bread, with a pleasant thyme flavor as an added bonus, this soft flavorful bread is especially great for sandwiches.

¾ cup (180 ml) water, heated to 100°F (38°C)
1 tablespoon (21 g) agave nectar
1½ teaspoons active dry yeast
1¼ cups (150 g) bread flour
1¼ cups (150 g) white whole wheat or regular whole wheat flour
2 teaspoons dried thyme
1 teaspoon fine sea salt
¼ cup (60 g) Dijon mustard, at room temperature
2 tablespoons (30 ml) extra-virgin olive oil
½ teaspoon canola oil, to coat bowl
Nonstick cooking spray

In a medium-size bowl, combine the water, agave, and yeast. Let stand for about 10 minutes; it should foam and bubble up. If it doesn't, start all over again because your yeast might not be fresh.

In a large-size bowl, combine the flours, thyme, and salt. Add the mustard and olive oil to the yeast mixture.

Stir the wet ingredients into the dry.

Transfer to a lightly floured surface and knead for 8 to 10 minutes, until the dough is smooth and pliable, adding more flour, a little at a time, if the dough is too wet. Shape into a ball.

Lightly coat a large-size bowl with the canola oil. Turn the dough around to coat, cover, and let rise for 90 minutes.

Lightly coat an 8 × 4-inch (20 × 10-cm) loaf pan with spray.

Punch down the dough. Press down into the prepared pan.

Loosely cover with plastic wrap, and let rise for another 60 minutes.

Preheat the oven to 375°F (190°C, or gas mark 5).

Remove the plastic wrap. Bake for 26 to 28 minutes, or until the loaf is golden brown and sounds hollow when the bottom is tapped. Let cool on a wire rack.

Yield: One 8-inch (20-cm) loaf

Hodgepodge o' Flours Bread

Although this soft and sturdy loaf doesn't seem to make up its mind when it comes to which flour it wants to be prepared with, you can rest assured that it will be perfect to use for sandwiches.

1¼ cups (295 ml) water
2 tablespoons (30 ml) extra-virgin olive oil
2 tablespoons (42 g) agave nectar
1 teaspoon pure maple extract
1 cup (120 g) bread flour
1 cup (120 g) white whole wheat or regular whole wheat flour
½ cup (60 g) dark rye flour
½ cup (60 g) light spelt flour
3 tablespoons (22 g) wheat germ
1 tablespoon (9 g) vital wheat gluten flour
2 tablespoons (23 g) instant soymilk powder (optional)
1½ teaspoons fine sea salt
2 teaspoons bread machine yeast
½ teaspoon canola oil, to coat bowl
Nonstick cooking spray

In a medium-size bowl, combine the water, olive oil, agave, and maple extract.

In a large-size bowl, combine the flours, wheat germ, wheat gluten, soymilk powder, if using, salt, and yeast.

Stir the wet ingredients into the dry.

Transfer to a lightly floured surface and knead for 8 to 10 minutes, until the dough is smooth and pliable, adding more flour, a little at a time, if the dough is too wet. Shape into a ball.

Lightly coat a large-size bowl with the canola oil. Turn the dough around to coat, cover, and let rise for 90 minutes, until doubled in size.

Lightly coat an 8 × 4-inch (20 × 10-cm) loaf pan with spray.

Punch down the dough. Press down into the prepared pan.

Loosely cover with plastic wrap, and let rise for another 60 minutes.

Preheat the oven to 375°F (190°C, or gas mark 5).

Remove the plastic wrap. Bake for 30 to 35 minutes, or until the loaf sounds hollow when the bottom is tapped. Let cool on a wire rack.

Yield: One 8-inch (20-cm) loaf

Agave Bread

You will have a hard time believing that this sweet, light, and fluffy bread is made of 100 percent whole grain, but the proof is in the pudding. Or rather, in the bread.

1 cup (235 ml) soy or other nondairy milk, heated to 100°F (38°C)
¼ cup (84 g) agave nectar
2 tablespoons (28 g) nondairy butter, softened
3 cups (360 g) white whole wheat or regular whole wheat flour, divided
2 teaspoons bread machine yeast
1 teaspoon fine sea salt
½ teaspoon canola oil, to coat bowl
Nonstick cooking spray

In a medium-size bowl, combine the milk, agave, and butter.

In a large-size bowl, combine 2½ cups (300 g) of the flour, yeast, and salt.

Stir the wet ingredients into the dry.

Transfer to a lightly floured surface and knead for 8 to 10 minutes, until the dough is smooth and pliable, adding the remaining ½ cup (60 g) flour, a little at a time, if the dough is too wet. Shape into a ball.

Lightly coat a large-size bowl with oil and turn the dough around to coat. Cover tightly with plastic wrap, and let rise until doubled, 60 to 90 minutes.

Lightly coat an 8 x 4-inch (20 x 10-cm) loaf pan with spray.

Punch down the dough. Press down into the prepared pan.

Loosely cover with plastic wrap, and let rise for another 60 minutes.

Preheat the oven to 375°F (190°C, or gas mark 5).

Remove the plastic wrap. Bake for 15 minutes, then cover with a piece of foil, because baked goods that contain agave nectar tend to brown up quickly.

Bake for another 10 to 15 minutes, or until the loaf sounds hollow when the bottom is tapped. Let cool on a wire rack.

Yield: One 8-inch (20-cm) loaf

Mole Bread

This wonderfully spicy bread is perfect alongside a big bowl of chili, or with nondairy butter or any sort of nut butter lathered on top for a different kind of breakfast.

1 cup (235 ml) soy or other nondairy milk or water, heated to 100°F (38°C)
2 tablespoons (30 ml) canola oil, plus an extra ½ teaspoon, to coat bowl
1 tablespoon (22 g) blackstrap or regular molasses
2 tablespoons (14 g) mild to medium chili powder
1 tablespoon (6 g) ground cumin
1 tablespoon (5 g) unsweetened cocoa powder
½ teaspoon cayenne pepper
½ teaspoon crushed chile peppers
½ teaspoon ground cinnamon
1½ cups (180 g) bread flour
1½ cups (180 g) white whole wheat or regular whole wheat flour
1 teaspoon fine sea salt
2 teaspoons bread machine yeast
Nonstick cooking spray

In a medium-size bowl, combine the milk, 2 tablespoons (30 ml) oil, molasses, chili powder, cumin, cocoa powder, cayenne, chile peppers, and cinnamon.

In a large-size bowl, combine the flours, salt, and yeast.

Stir the wet ingredients into the dry.

Transfer to a lightly floured surface and knead for 8 to 10 minutes, until the dough is smooth and pliable, adding more flour, a little at a time, if the dough is too wet. Shape into a ball.

Lightly coat a large-size bowl with the remaining ½ teaspoon oil and turn the dough around to coat. Cover tightly with plastic wrap, and let rise until doubled, 60 to 90 minutes.

Lightly coat an 8 × 4-inch (20 × 10-cm) loaf pan with spray.

Punch down the dough. Press down into the prepared pan.

Loosely cover with plastic wrap, and let rise for another 60 minutes.

Preheat the oven to 375°F (190°C, or gas mark 5).

Remove the plastic wrap. Bake for 30 minutes, or until the loaf sounds hollow when the bottom is tapped. Let cool on a wire rack.

Yield: One 8-inch (20-cm) loaf

Dried Fruit Rum Bread

A fruity loaf with a subtle rum flavor, this fluffy bread is perfect for breakfast or as a satisfying afternoon snack.

¾ cup (120 g) raisins and dried tart cherries
¼ cup (60 ml) dark rum, heated to 100°F (38°C)
½ cup (120 ml) plain soymilk, heated to 100°F (38°C) (use soy here, or the milk might not curdle)
½ teaspoon apple cider vinegar
2 cups (240 g) white whole wheat or regular whole wheat flour
½ teaspoon fine sea salt
2 tablespoons (24 g) raw sugar
2 teaspoons bread machine yeast
1 tablespoon (15 ml) canola oil, plus an extra ½ teaspoon, to coat bowl
Nonstick cooking spray
2 tablespoons (40 g) all-fruit orange spread
1½ teaspoons water

In a small-size bowl, soak the dried fruit in the rum for 1 hour, stirring once halfway through.

Combine the soymilk and vinegar in a medium-size bowl; it will curdle and become like buttermilk.

In a large-size bowl, combine the flour, salt, sugar, and yeast.

Stir the 1 tablespoon (15 ml) canola oil and dried fruit and rum mixture into the buttermilk mixture.

Stir the wet ingredients into the dry.

Transfer to a lightly floured surface and knead for 8 to 10 minutes, until the dough is smooth and pliable, adding more flour, a little at a time, if the dough is too wet. Shape into a ball.

Lightly coat a large-size bowl with the remaining ½ teaspoon oil and turn the dough around to coat. Cover tightly with plastic wrap, and let rise until doubled, 60 to 90 minutes.

Lightly coat an 8 × 4-inch (20 × 10-cm) loaf pan with spray.

Punch down the dough. Press down into the prepared pan.

Loosely cover with plastic wrap, and let rise for another 45 minutes.

Preheat the oven to 400°F (200°C, or gas mark 6).

Combine the orange spread and water in a small bowl.

Remove the plastic wrap. Lightly brush the orange spread mixture on top of the loaf. Bake for 30 minutes, or until the loaf sounds hollow when the bottom is tapped. Let cool on a wire rack.

Yield: One 8-inch (20-cm) loaf

Pumpkin Yeast Bread

Wonderful to use for sandwiches, or simply toasted and lathered with nondairy butter and jam, this slightly orange-colored bread is sure to be an all-around crowd-pleaser.

⅔ cup (160 ml) soy or other nondairy milk or water, heated to 100°F (38°C)
¾ cup (183 g) pumpkin purée
2 tablespoons (30 ml) canola oil, plus an extra ½ teaspoon, to coat bowl
2 tablespoons (42 g) agave nectar
1½ cups (180 g) bread flour
1½ cups (180 g) white whole wheat or regular whole wheat flour
1 teaspoon fine sea salt
2 teaspoons bread machine yeast
Nonstick cooking spray

In a medium-size bowl, combine the milk, pumpkin purée, 2 tablespoons (30 ml) oil, and agave.

In a large-size bowl, combine the flours, salt, and yeast.

Stir the wet ingredients into the dry.

Transfer to a lightly floured surface and knead for 8 to 10 minutes, until the dough is smooth and pliable, adding more flour, a little at a time, if the dough is too wet. Shape into a ball.

Lightly coat a large-size bowl with the remaining ½ teaspoon oil. Turn the dough around to coat, cover, and let rise for 90 minutes, until doubled in size.

Lightly coat an 8 × 4-inch (20 × 10-cm) loaf pan with spray.

Punch down the dough. Press down into the prepared pan.

Loosely cover with plastic wrap, and let rise for another 60 minutes.

Preheat the oven to 375°F (190°C, or gas mark 5).

Remove the plastic wrap. Bake for 15 minutes, then cover with a piece of foil, because baked goods that contain agave nectar tend to brown up quickly.

Bake for another 15 minutes, or until the loaf sounds hollow when the bottom is tapped. Let cool on a wire rack.

Yield: One 8-inch (20-cm) loaf

Garlic Rolls

These rolls are quite a step up from your everyday garlic bread and make a nice addition to any meal.

2 envelopes (¼ ounce, or 7 g each) active dry yeast
2 teaspoons granulated sugar
½ cup (120 ml) warm water
2 cups (250 g) all-purpose flour
¼ cup (36 g) vital wheat gluten flour
1 tablespoon (8 g) garlic powder
½ teaspoon salt
½ cup (120 ml) water
¼ cup (60 ml) olive oil, plus extra, for brushing
1 recipe Easy Garlic Spread for Bread (page 91)

In a small bowl, combine the yeast, sugar, and warm water and let stand for 10 minutes; it should foam and bubble up. If it doesn't, start all over again because your yeast might not be fresh.

In a mixing bowl, mix together the flour, wheat gluten, garlic powder, and salt. Add the yeast mixture, water, and ¼ cup (60 ml) olive oil. Knead until a nice elastic dough forms. Add a little extra flour if your dough is too sticky, or a little more water if it is too dry. Form into a ball.

Transfer to a plate. Brush lightly with olive oil, cover loosely with plastic wrap, and let rise for 1 hour.

Preheat the oven to 400°F (200°C, or gas mark 6). Have ready a 9 × 13-inch (23 × 33-cm) glass baking dish.

Punch down the dough. On a flat floured surface, press out the dough into a rectangle about 9 × 12 inches (23 × 30.5 cm), using your hands.

Spread the garlic spread all over, leaving about ½ inch (1.3 cm) border on both of the long edges.

Starting at the long edge, roll up. When you get to the end, crimp the dough to seal.

Using a serrated knife, cut the rolled-up dough into 12 equal pieces.

Place, cut side up, equally spaced in the baking dish.

Bake for 15 to 20 minutes, or until golden brown. Let rest to soak up the juices for about 5 minutes before serving.

Yield: 12 rolls

Blooming Onion Rolls

These tasty onion rolls will surprise you with their amazing, almost croissant-like texture.

- 2 tablespoons (28 g) nondairy butter
- 1 tablespoon (7 g) caraway seeds
- ½ cup (50 g) chopped Mexican onion or scallion, white and pale green parts
- ¾ cup (180 ml) water, heated to 100°F (38°C)
- ½ teaspoon fine sea salt
- 1 teaspoon raw sugar
- 2⅓ cups (280 g) white whole wheat or regular whole wheat flour, divided
- 1½ teaspoons bread machine yeast
- ½ teaspoon canola oil, to coat bowl
- ¼ cup (60 ml) warm water, for brushing top
- Coarse sea salt, for sprinkling

In a small-size saucepan over medium heat, melt the butter, add the caraway seeds and onion, and cook for 5 minutes, until the onions are tender. Combine with the hot water in a small-size bowl.

In a large-size bowl, combine the salt, sugar, 2 cups (240 g) of the flour, and yeast.

Stir the wet ingredients into the dry.

Transfer to a lightly floured surface and knead for 8 to 10 minutes, until the dough is smooth and pliable, adding the remaining ⅓ cup (40 g) flour, a little at a time, if the dough is too wet. Shape into a ball.

Lightly coat a large-size bowl with oil. Turn the dough around to coat, cover, and let rise for 90 minutes, until doubled in size.

Have 2 pieces of parchment paper or 2 silicone baking mats, such as Silpat, at hand.

Punch down the dough, and flatten it directly onto a piece of parchment into a rectangle approximately 14 × 12 inches (36 × 30 cm) and ¼ inch (6 mm) thick.

Cut lengthwise (with a plastic knife, to spare the Silpat!) into six 14 × 2-inch (36 × 5-cm) strips. Roll each strip like you would cinnamon rolls, not too tightly. Place on the extra parchment paper; repeat with each strip.

Lightly brush with the warm water and sprinkle with the coarse salt. Transfer the parchment paper to a large-size baking sheet. Loosely cover with plastic wrap, and let rise for 40 minutes.

Preheat the oven to 375°F (190°C, or gas mark 5).

Remove the plastic wrap. Bake for 16 minutes, or until the rolls sound hollow when the bottom is tapped. Let cool on a wire rack.

Yield: 6 rolls

Soy Free

Peanut and Spice Rolls

Especially suited to serve with savory foods, such as chili, these rolls have a wonderful texture, and the dough is so fun to play with that you might find yourself reluctant to stop kneading it. Don't say we didn't warn you!

1 cup (235 ml) water, heated to 100°F (38°C)
1 tablespoon (22 g) blackstrap molasses
1½ teaspoons active dry yeast
2 cups (240 g) white whole wheat or regular whole wheat flour
1 cup (120 g) bread flour
1 teaspoon fine sea salt
1 tablespoon (6 g) ground cumin
½ teaspoon ground ginger
¼ teaspoon cayenne pepper
¼ cup (64 g) crunchy natural peanut butter
½ teaspoon canola oil, to coat bowl

In a medium-size bowl, combine the water, molasses, and yeast. Let stand for about 10 minutes; it should foam and bubble up. If it doesn't, start over because your yeast might not be fresh.

In a large-size bowl, combine the flours, salt, cumin, ginger, and cayenne.

Add the peanut butter to the water and yeast mixture.

Stir the wet ingredients into the dry.

Transfer to a lightly floured surface and knead for 8 to 10 minutes, until the dough is smooth and pliable, adding more flour, a little at a time, if the dough is too wet. Shape into a ball.

Lightly coat a large-size bowl with oil. Turn the dough around to coat, cover, and let rise for 90 minutes, until doubled in size.

Punch down the dough and divide into 6 equal portions. Shape into rolls. Place on a piece of parchment paper or a silicone baking mat, such as Silpat.

Loosely cover with plastic wrap, and let rise for another 45 minutes.

Preheat the oven to 375°F (190°C, or gas mark 5). Have a baking sheet handy.

Remove the plastic wrap. Place the piece of parchment on the baking sheet. Bake for 24 minutes, or until the rolls are golden brown and sound hollow when the bottom is tapped. Let cool on a wire rack.

Yield: 6 rolls

Soy Free

Parsley Pesto Bread Rolls

These soft and savory bread rolls are amazing eaten plain or served alongside a nice bowl of soup or a heaping plate of fresh salad, but they would also be perfect used as burger or sandwich rolls.

½ cup (120 ml) water, heated to 100°F (38°C)
1 tablespoon (21 g) agave nectar
2 teaspoons active dry yeast
1½ cups (180 g) bread flour, divided
1½ cups (180 g) white whole wheat or regular whole wheat flour, divided
1½ teaspoons fine sea salt
¾ cup (165 g) Parsley Pesto Spread (page 81)
2 tablespoons (30 ml) canola oil, plus ½ teaspoon, to coat bowl

In a medium-size bowl, combine the water, agave, and yeast. Let stand for about 10 minutes; it should foam and bubble up. If it doesn't, start over because your yeast might not be fresh.

In a large-size bowl, combine 1¼ cups (150 g) of the bread flour, 1¼ cups (150 g) of the whole wheat flour, and the salt.

Stir the pesto spread and 2 tablespoons (30 ml) oil into the yeast mixture.

Stir the wet ingredients into the dry.

Transfer to a lightly floured surface and knead for 8 to 10 minutes, until the dough is smooth and pliable, adding the remaining ¼ cup (30 g) bread flour and remaining ¼ cup (30 g) whole wheat flour, a little at a time, if the dough is too wet. Shape into a ball.

Lightly coat a large-size bowl with the remaining ½ teaspoon oil. Turn the dough around to coat, cover, and let rise for 90 minutes, until doubled in size.

Punch down the dough and divide into 6 equal portions. Shape into rolls. Place on a piece of parchment paper or a silicone baking mat, such as Silpat.

Loosely cover with plastic wrap, and let rise for another 45 minutes.

Preheat the oven to 375°F (190°C, or gas mark 5). Have a baking sheet handy.

Remove the plastic wrap. Place the piece of parchment on the baking sheet, and bake for 24 minutes, or until the rolls are golden brown and sound hollow when the bottom is tapped. Let cool on a wire rack.

Yield: 6 rolls

Salsa Bread Rolls

Here's a smaller batch of crispy rolls, perfect to enjoy after being given at least half an hour to cool down a bit, lest palates get burned. Their spiciness depends on the salsa you choose.

½ cup (120 g) prepared salsa
¼ cup (60 ml) water, heated to 100°F (38°C)
1 tablespoon (15 ml) canola oil
1 tablespoon (15 ml) agave nectar
1 cup (120 g) white whole wheat or regular whole wheat flour
⅔ cup (80 g) bread flour
⅓ cup (40 g) cornmeal
2 tablespoons (18 g) vital wheat gluten flour
1 scant teaspoon fine sea salt
1¼ teaspoons bread machine yeast
½ teaspoon canola oil, to coat bowl
Almond or other nondairy milk, for brushing tops

In a medium-size bowl, combine the salsa, water, oil, and agave.

In a large-size bowl, combine the flours, cornmeal, wheat gluten, salt, and yeast.

Stir the wet ingredients into the dry.

Transfer to a lightly floured surface and knead for 8 to 10 minutes, until the dough is smooth and pliable, adding more flour, a little at a time, if the dough is too wet. Shape into a ball.

Lightly coat a large-size bowl with oil. Turn the dough around to coat, cover, and let rise for 90 minutes, until doubled in size.

Punch down the dough and divide into 4 equal portions. Shape into rolls or mini baguettes. Place on a piece of parchment paper or a silicone baking mat, such as Silpat.

Loosely cover with plastic wrap, and let rise for another 30 minutes.

Preheat the oven to 375°F (190°C, or gas mark 5). Have a baking sheet handy.

Remove the plastic wrap. Brush each roll with a little milk and place the piece of parchment on the baking sheet. Bake for 22 to 24 minutes, or until the rolls are golden brown and sound hollow when the bottom is tapped. Let cool on a wire rack.

Yield: 4 rolls or mini baguettes

Tahini Bread Rolls

These tender rolls, which are perfect to use as large burger buns, come out with a shiny crust without even having to add any sort of wash to it. The tahini and its (healthy) fat are working their magic here.

1 cup (235 ml) water, heated to 100°F (38°C)
1 tablespoon (21 g) agave nectar
1½ teaspoons active dry yeast
1½ cups (180 g) bread flour
1½ cups (180 g) white whole wheat or regular whole wheat flour
1 teaspoon fine sea salt
½ cup (128 g) tahini
½ teaspoon canola oil, to coat bowl

In a medium-size bowl, combine the water, agave, and yeast. Let stand for about 10 minutes; it should foam and bubble up. If it doesn't, start all over again because your yeast might not be fresh.

In a large-size bowl, combine the flours and salt.

Stir the tahini into the yeast mixture.

Stir the wet ingredients into the dry.

Transfer to a lightly floured surface and knead for 8 to 10 minutes, until the dough is smooth and pliable, adding more flour, a little at a time, if the dough is too wet. Shape into a ball.

Lightly coat a large-size bowl with oil and turn the dough around to coat. Cover tightly with plastic wrap, and let rise until doubled, 60 to 90 minutes.

Punch down the dough and divide into 6 equal portions. Shape into rolls. Place on a piece of parchment paper or a silicone baking mat, such as Silpat, on top of a baking sheet.

Loosely cover with plastic wrap, and let rise for another 45 minutes.

Preheat the oven to 375°F (190°C, or gas mark 5).

Remove the plastic wrap. Bake for 24 minutes, or until the rolls are golden brown and sound hollow when the bottom is tapped. Let cool on a wire rack.

Yield: 6 rolls

Low Fat

Soy Free

Beer Rolls

So light and fluffy, and with just a subtle beer flavor, these rolls need to be prepared with flat beer: simply open a bottle of the stuff, and let it stand for at least an hour at room temperature. You could also simply use last night's party leftovers, if you have them.

¾ cup (180 ml) flat beer
⅓ cup (80 ml) water, heated to 100°F (38°C)
1 tablespoon (14 g) nondairy butter, softened
1½ cups (180 g) bread flour
1½ cups (180 g) white whole wheat or regular whole wheat flour
2 tablespoons (18 g) vital wheat gluten flour
¾ teaspoon fine sea salt
1 tablespoon (12 g) Sucanat
1¾ teaspoons bread machine yeast
½ teaspoon canola oil, to coat bowl

In a medium-size bowl, combine the beer, water, and butter.

In a large-size bowl, combine the flours, wheat gluten, salt, Sucanat, and yeast.

Stir the wet ingredients into the dry.

Transfer to a lightly floured surface and knead for 8 to 10 minutes, until the dough is smooth and pliable, adding more flour, a little at a time, if the dough is too wet. Shape into a ball.

Lightly coat a large-size bowl with oil and turn the dough around to coat. Cover tightly with plastic wrap, and let rise until doubled, 60 to 90 minutes.

Punch down the dough and divide into 12 equal portions. Shape into rolls. Place on 2 pieces of parchment paper or silicone baking mats, such as Silpat, on top of 2 baking sheets.

Loosely cover with plastic wrap, and let rise for another 45 minutes.

Preheat the oven to 375°F (190°C, or gas mark 5).

Remove the plastic wrap. Bake for 13 minutes, or until the rolls are golden brown and sound hollow when the bottom is tapped. Let cool on a wire rack.

Yield: 12 small rolls

Poppy Lemon Bread Rolls

Soft, lemony, and delicious, these not-too-sweet rolls are demanding you spread some jam on them. Obey the rolls!

- 6 ounces (170 g) vanilla soy or other nondairy yogurt
- ½ cup (120 ml) soy or other nondairy milk
- 2 tablespoons (28 g) nondairy butter
- 1 tablespoon (21 g) agave nectar
- 2½ tablespoons (23 g) poppy seeds, divided
- 1 teaspoon pure lemon extract
- 2 teaspoons lemon zest
- 1 cup (120 g) light spelt flour
- 2 cups (240 g) white whole wheat or regular whole wheat flour, divided
- 2 teaspoons bread machine yeast
- 1 teaspoon fine sea salt
- ½ teaspoon canola oil, to coat bowl
- 2 tablespoons (30 ml) water

In a small-size saucepan, combine the yogurt, milk, butter, and agave. Heat over medium heat until the mixture reaches 100°F (38°C). Stir in 2 tablespoons (18 g) of the poppy seeds, the extract, and the zest. Set aside.

In a large-size bowl, combine the spelt flour, 1 cup (120 g) of the whole wheat flour, yeast, and salt.

Stir the wet ingredients into the dry.

Transfer to a lightly floured surface and knead for 8 to 10 minutes, until the dough is smooth and pliable, adding the remaining 1 cup (120 g) flour, a little at a time, if the dough is too wet. Shape into a ball.

Lightly coat a large-size bowl with oil and turn the dough around to coat. Cover tightly with plastic wrap, and let rise until doubled, 60 to 90 minutes.

Punch down the dough and flatten it directly onto a piece of parchment or a silicone mat into a rectangle of approximately 14 × 12 inches (36 × 30 cm) and ¼ inch (6 mm) thick.

Cut lengthwise (with a plastic knife, to spare the Silpat!) into six 14 × 2-inch (36 × 5-cm) strips. Roll each strip like you would cinnamon rolls, not too tightly. Place on the extra parchment paper or Silpat; repeat with each strip.

Lightly brush with the water and sprinkle with the remaining ½ tablespoon poppy seeds. Loosely cover with plastic wrap, and let rise for 30 minutes.

Preheat the oven to 375°F (190°C, or gas mark 5).

Remove the plastic wrap. Bake for 16 to 20 minutes, or until the rolls are golden brown and sound hollow when the bottom is tapped. Let cool on a wire rack.

Yield: 6 rolls

Almond Spelt Sweet Rolls

You will have a hard time resisting these sconelike, buttery rolls that are surrounded with a crunchy sweet and subtle citrus-flavored topping!

For the rolls:

- ⅔ cup (160 ml) soy or other nondairy milk, heated to 100°F (38°C)
- 3 tablespoons (63 g) agave nectar
- 2 tablespoons (28 g) nondairy butter, softened
- ⅓ cup (32 g) finely ground toasted almonds
- ½ teaspoon fine sea salt
- 1 teaspoon pure almond extract
- 2½ cups (300 g) light spelt flour
- 1½ teaspoons bread machine yeast
- ⅓ cup (53 g) raisins, chopped
- ½ teaspoon canola oil, to coat bowl

For the dipping mixture:

- 3 tablespoons (45 ml) extra-virgin olive or canola oil
- 3 tablespoons (36 g) raw sugar
- 2 teaspoons orange zest

Nonstick cooking spray

To make the rolls: In a medium-size bowl, combine the milk, agave, butter, ground almonds, salt, and almond extract.

In a large-size bowl, combine the flour and yeast.

Stir the wet ingredients into the dry.

Transfer to a lightly floured surface and knead for 4 minutes. Incorporate the raisins and knead for another 4 to 6 minutes, until the dough is smooth and pliable, adding more flour, a little at a time, if the dough is too wet. Shape into a ball.

Lightly coat a large-size bowl with oil and turn the dough around to coat. Cover tightly with plastic wrap, and let rise until doubled, 60 to 90 minutes.

To make the dipping mixture: Combine the oil, sugar, and orange zest in a small-size bowl.

Lightly coat a 9 × 13-inch (23 × 33-cm) baking pan with nonstick cooking spray.

Punch down the dough and divide into 8 equal portions. Shape into rolls and dip into the orange mixture, covering the entire piece of dough.

Place the rolls in the prepared pan. Loosely cover with plastic wrap and let rise for another 30 minutes.

Preheat the oven to 350°F (180°C, or gas mark 4).

Remove the plastic wrap. Bake for 25 minutes, or until the rolls are golden brown and sound hollow when the bottom is tapped. Let cool on a wire rack.

Yield: 8 rolls

Matcha Spelt Rolls with Bittersweet Chocolate Filling and Almond Icing

We were told these fanciful rolls are a huge hit at a teahouse in New Zealand, where they are being sold. How's that for an awesome endorsement?

For the rolls:

- ¾ cup (180 ml) plain soy or other nondairy milk, heated to 100°F (38°C)
- 2 teaspoons active dry yeast
- ¼ cup (48 g) Sucanat
- 2½ cups (300 g) light spelt flour
- ¾ teaspoon fine sea salt
- 4 teaspoons matcha green tea powder
- 2 tablespoons (28 g) nondairy butter, softened
- 1 teaspoon pure almond extract
- ½ teaspoon canola oil, to coat bowl
- ⅓ cup (58 g) chopped nondairy bittersweet chocolate

For the icing:

- ¼ teaspoon pure almond extract
- ½ cup (60 g) powdered sugar
- 1 to 2 teaspoons plain soy or other nondairy milk, more if needed

To make the rolls: In a medium-size bowl, combine the milk, yeast, and Sucanat. Let stand for about 10 minutes; it should foam and bubble up. If it doesn't, start all over again because your yeast might not be fresh.

In a large-size bowl, combine the flour, salt, and matcha powder.

Stir the butter and extract into the yeast mixture.

Stir the wet ingredients into the dry.

Transfer to a lightly floured surface and knead for 8 to 10 minutes, until the dough is smooth and pliable, adding more flour, a little at a time, if the dough is too wet. Shape into a ball.

Lightly coat a large-size bowl with oil and turn the dough around to coat. Cover tightly with plastic wrap, and let rise until doubled, 60 to 90 minutes.

Line a baking sheet with parchment paper or a silicone baking mat, such as Silpat.

Punch down the dough. Divide into 6 equal portions.

Divide the chopped chocolate into 6 equal portions, placing each in the center of each piece of dough. Fold the dough over the chocolate. Shape into rolls. Place on the prepared baking sheet, loosely covering with plastic wrap. Let rise for 40 minutes.

Preheat the oven to 375°F (190°C, or gas mark 5).

Remove the plastic wrap. Bake for 16 to 18 minutes, or until the rolls are golden brown and sound hollow when the bottom is tapped. Let cool on a wire rack before adding the icing.

To make the icing: Combine the almond extract and powdered sugar in a small-size bowl, and then slowly add the milk; the icing needs to be thin enough to drizzle, but still thick enough to just stick to the back of a spoon. Stir vigorously to remove lumps.

Drizzle on top of each roll.

Yield: 6 rolls

Chapter 16

Cookies and Biscuits

Although it is getting increasingly easier to find amazing and tasty vegan cookies at health food or specialty stores, there is something quite nostalgic and charming about making a batch of your own, especially if your favorite thing is to bite into a gooey, straight-out-of-the-oven treat. The only tricky part will be to pick which kind to prepare first!

Quick reminder: if you aren't fond of baking with whole-grain flours, it is possible to substitute unbleached all-purpose flour for whole wheat pastry, regular, or white whole wheat flour. On the other hand, if you are already accustomed to baking with whole-grain flours but do not have access to whole wheat pastry flour, our recipes were tested with white whole wheat and regular whole wheat flour with great results.

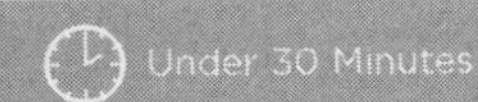
Under 30 Minutes

Chocolate Almond Bake or No-Bake Cookies

The unbaked dough in these cookies is so tasty that you might decide using the oven is an unnecessary step: the fact that they contain no eggs makes it an acceptable thing to do. Simply nix the baking powder if you know you're going to eat the dough in its unbaked form, in which case it would serve no purpose.

1 cup (140 g) whole roasted almonds
1 cup (78 g) quick-cooking oats
½ cup (96 g) raw sugar
¼ teaspoon fine sea salt
1 tablespoon (8 g) arrowroot powder
½ teaspoon baking powder, if baking
3 ounces (85 g) nondairy semisweet chocolate, coarsely chopped, melted, and cooled
¼ cup (60 ml) soy or other nondairy milk, plus more if needed

If you are going to bake the cookies, preheat the oven to 350°F (180°C, or gas mark 4). Line a baking sheet with parchment paper or a silicone baking mat, such as Silpat.

Blend the almonds, oats, sugar, salt, arrowroot powder, and baking powder (if baking) in a food processor until finely ground.

Add the melted chocolate and milk. Process until thoroughly mixed. Add extra milk if the dough doesn't stick together when pinched.

Divide the dough into 12 equal portions, using about 2 tablespoons (38 g) of dough.

Flatten the cookies onto the baking sheet as much as you want them to be, because they don't spread while baking.

Bake for 10 minutes, or until the cookies are set.

Let cool for a few minutes before transferring them to a wire rack to cool completely.

If you are not going to bake them, just shape them however you want, and store in the fridge.

Yield: 12 cookies

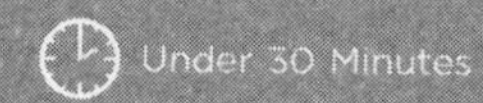

Trail Mix Cookies

Adding healthy ingredients such as nuts, seeds, and dried fruit makes eating cookies sound like just a touch less of an indulgence.

You can substitute any or all of the add-ins to suit your preference. Remember to see chapter 2 of this book for great granola recipes.

¼ cup (56 g) nondairy butter
½ cup (96 g) raw sugar
1 teaspoon pure vanilla extract
2 tablespoons (30 ml) soy or other nondairy milk
1 cup (120 g) whole wheat pastry flour
½ teaspoon baking powder
½ teaspoon baking soda
¼ teaspoon fine sea salt
½ cup (60 g) granola of choice
¼ cup (32 g) roasted sunflower seeds
¼ cup (40 g) dried tart cherries
¼ cup (44 g) nondairy semisweet chocolate chips

Preheat the oven to 350°F (180°C, or gas mark 4). Line a baking sheet with parchment paper or a silicone baking mat, such as Silpat.

In a large-size bowl and using an electric mixer, cream together the butter and sugar until light and fluffy.

Mix in the vanilla and milk. Add the flour, baking powder, baking soda, salt, granola, sunflower seeds, cherries, and chocolate chips, and stir until combined.

Divide the dough into 12 equal portions, using about 2 tablespoons (40 g) of dough.

Place on the prepared baking sheet.

Flatten with your hands, leaving 1 inch (2.5 cm) between the cookies.

Bake for 11 minutes, or until the edges are golden brown.

Let cool for a few minutes before transferring them to a wire rack to cool completely.

Yield: 12 cookies

TB & J Shortbread

Offering a pleasing variation on the more traditional peanut butter and jelly combination, tahini also has the advantage of being rich in calcium as well as flavor. Note that you might have to use more or less milk for the dough, depending on the consistency of your tahini. You want to be able to pinch the dough and have it stick together, without being overly moist either.

Nonstick cooking spray
⅓ cup (85 g) tahini
3 tablespoons (42 g) nondairy butter
½ cup (96 g) raw sugar
½ cup (80 g) brown rice flour
1 cup (120 g) light spelt flour
1 teaspoon pure lemon or other extract (optional)
2½ tablespoons (38 ml) soy or other nondairy milk
½ cup (160 g) jam of choice

Preheat the oven to 350°F (180°C, or gas mark 4). Coat an 8-inch (20-cm) square baking pan with nonstick cooking spray.

In a large-size bowl and using an electric mixer, cream together the tahini, butter, and sugar.

Stir in the flours and extract, if using. Combine until a crumbly meal is obtained.

Set aside ½ cup (about 75 g) of the resulting crumbs.

Stir in the milk until combined: you want the dough to stick together well when pinched. It will still look crumbly, but not dry like it did before the addition of milk.

Sprinkle the dough evenly in the prepared pan; press it down firmly all over the bottom of the pan.

Cover with jam, spreading it all over with a spatula. Sprinkle the reserved crumbs on top, pressing them slightly on top of the jam.

Bake for 40 minutes, until the edges are golden brown and the crumbs are starting to brown up, too.

Let cool on a wire rack, still in the pan, before slicing and serving.

Yield: 12 servings

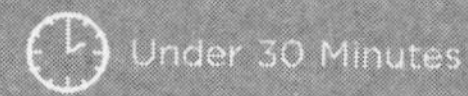

Chewy Ginger Cookies

No one will guess that these perfectly chewy cookies were prepared with fiber-rich whole wheat flour! Good for cravings, and rather healthy, too. Well, as healthy as cookies can be, of course.

¼ cup (56 g) nondairy butter
½ cup (96 g) Sucanat
3 tablespoons (66 g) blackstrap or regular molasses
2 tablespoons (30 ml) almond or other nondairy milk
¼ teaspoon fine sea salt
2 teaspoons ground ginger
1 teaspoon ground cinnamon
1 cup (120 g) whole wheat pastry flour
2 teaspoons cornstarch
½ teaspoon baking soda

Preheat the oven to 350°F (180°C, or gas mark 4). Line a baking sheet with parchment paper or a silicone baking mat, such as Silpat.

In a large microwave-safe bowl, combine the butter, Sucanat, molasses, milk, salt, ginger, and cinnamon. Melt in the microwave for about 1 minute until the Sucanat starts to dissolve, stirring well at the end.

Sift the flour, cornstarch, and baking soda on top of the wet ingredients. Stir the dry ingredients into the wet.

Divide what will be a sticky dough into 12 equal portions, using about 2 tablespoons (31 g) of dough. Place on the prepared baking sheet.

Shape and slightly flatten the dough, using the fleshy part of your hand (close to the thumb): it won't stick as much as if you were to use your fingers.

Bake the cookies for 8 minutes, or until set. Slide the parchment paper off the baking sheet onto the counter, and let the cookies cool.

Yield: 12 cookies

Peanut Brittle Cookies

Peanut aficionados, beware: these cookies have been said to be reminiscent of peanut brittle. You be the judge!

1 cup (112 g) dry-roasted peanuts
2 tablespoons (28 g) nondairy butter
2 tablespoons (30 ml) water
⅔ cup plus ¼ cup (176 g) Sucanat, divided
¼ teaspoon fine sea salt
½ cup (128 g) creamy or crunchy natural peanut butter
¼ cup (60 ml) whiskey
2 tablespoons (30 ml) plain soy or other nondairy milk
2 teaspoons pure vanilla extract
1 cup (120 g) light spelt flour
½ cup (39 g) quick-cooking oats, finely ground
1 teaspoon baking powder

Line 2 baking sheets with parchment paper or silicone baking mats, such as Silpat.

Place the peanuts, butter, water, and ¼ cup (48 g) of the Sucanat in a small-size saucepan.

Heat over medium-high heat, bring to a low boil, and cook for about 4 minutes, stirring constantly, lowering the heat to medium, until the peanuts get some color to them and the liquid is mostly gone. Remove from the heat. Let cool for a few minutes.

Transfer the preparation to a large-size bowl. If it has hardened, break it apart a little bit.

Add the remaining ⅔ cup (128 g) Sucanat, salt, peanut butter, whiskey, milk, and vanilla, and stir until emulsified.

Stir in the flour, ground oats, and baking powder.

Divide the dough into 16 equal portions, using about 2 tablespoons (42 g) of dough.

Place on the prepared baking sheets. Flatten the cookies as much as you want them to be, because they don't spread while baking.

Store in the refrigerator for 1 hour.

Preheat the oven to 350°F (180°C, or gas mark 4).

Bake the cookies for 15 minutes, or until the edges are golden brown.

Let cool for a few minutes before transferring them to a wire rack to cool completely.

Yield: 16 cookies

Brownie Bite Cookies

These big cookies were a huge hit with our testers. Don't let the fact that the recipe looks like a lot of work deter you from giving them a try; they're worth it and not so hard to prepare. The brownie batter makes for a thin layer, which works out well for cutting into chunks for the cookies. Be sure to prepare the brownies in advance so that they have enough time to cool down before being cut into chunks.

For the brownies:

- Nonstick cooking spray
- ⅓ cup (75 g) nondairy butter
- ½ cup plus 2 tablespoons (120 g) Sucanat
- 1 teaspoon pure vanilla extract
- 2 tablespoons (30 g) vanilla soy or other nondairy yogurt
- ¾ cup (90 g) light spelt or (94 g) all-purpose flour
- ¼ cup (20 g) unsweetened cocoa powder
- ¼ teaspoon baking powder
- ⅛ teaspoon baking soda
- ¼ teaspoon fine sea salt

For the cookies:

- 1 cup plus 2 tablespoons (216 g) raw sugar
- ¾ cup (180 ml) walnut, peanut, or canola oil
- 2 tablespoons (30 ml) pure vanilla extract
- ½ teaspoon fine sea salt
- ¼ cup plus 2 tablespoons (90 ml) plain soy or other nondairy milk
- 3 cups (360 g) whole wheat pastry flour
- 1½ teaspoons baking powder

To make the brownies: Preheat the oven to 350°F (180°C, or gas mark 4). Lightly coat an 8-inch (20-cm) square baking pan with nonstick cooking spray.

In a large-size bowl and using an electric mixer, cream the butter and Sucanat until light and fluffy. Stir in the vanilla and yogurt.

Sift the flour, cocoa, baking powder, baking soda, and salt on top of the wet ingredients. Stir the dry ingredients into the wet.

Pour the batter into the prepared pan and level with a spatula.

Bake for 10 minutes, or until the sides of the brownies start to pull away from the pan.

Let cool in the pan, on top of a wire rack, and chill before slicing. Cut into medium to large chunks. Set aside.

To make the cookies: Preheat the oven to 350°F (180°C, or gas mark 4). Line a baking sheet with parchment paper or a silicone baking mat, such as Silpat.

In a large-size bowl, whisk together the sugar, oil, vanilla, salt, and milk until combined.

Sift the flour and baking powder on top of the wet ingredients. Stir the dry ingredients into the wet.

Fold in the reserved brownie chunks, or use your hands to gently incorporate them.

Divide the dough into 12 equal portions, using about ¼ cup (98 g) of packed dough.

Flatten onto the prepared baking sheet: the cookies won't spread much while baking, but leave 1 inch (2.5 cm) in between anyway.

Bake for 16 minutes, or until the edges are golden brown.

Let cool for a few minutes before transferring them to a wire rack to cool completely.

Yield: 12 cookies

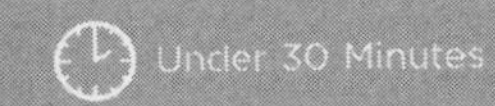

Under 30 Minutes

Tahini Orange Cookies

The summery and refreshing flavor of orange pairs beautifully with the richness of tahini in these buttery cookies. Consider using agave nectar instead of maple syrup, but be sure to preheat the oven to 325°F (170°C, or gas mark 3) in this case. Replacing orange zest with lemon zest is also a nice alternative. Be sure to remove the cookies from the oven after 10 minutes so that they remain chewy and don't get dry.

1 cup (256 g) tahini
2 teaspoons pure vanilla extract
½ cup (120 ml) pure maple syrup or (168 g) agave nectar
¼ cup (48 g) raw sugar
Zest of 1 large-size (organic, preferably) orange or lemon (about 2 heaping teaspoons)
½ cup (40 g) ground oats
½ cup (80 g) brown rice flour
½ teaspoon baking soda
½ teaspoon baking powder
¼ teaspoon fine sea salt
½ cup (88 g) nondairy semisweet chocolate chips

Preheat the oven to 350°F (180°C, or gas mark 4), or 325°F (170°C, or gas mark 3) if using agave nectar. Line 2 baking sheets with parchment paper or silicone baking mats, such as Silpat.

In a large-size bowl, whisk together the tahini, vanilla, syrup, sugar, and zest.

In a medium-size bowl, whisk together the ground oats, flour, baking soda, baking powder, salt, and chocolate chips.

Stir the dry ingredients into the wet.

Divide the dough into 20 equal portions, using about 2 tablespoons (34 g) of dough.

Place on the prepared baking sheets. Flatten a little, because the cookies won't spread much while baking; leave 1 inch (2.5 cm) of space between them.

Bake for 10 minutes, or until the edges are golden brown. Leave the cookies on the sheet for just a couple of minutes until they are firm enough to be transferred to a wire rack to cool completely.

Yield: 20 cookies

Lemon Lavender Cookies

If you are of the mind that lavender belongs solely in soaps, these zesty and buttery cookies should do a good job of proving you wrong.

½ cup (112 g) nondairy butter
¾ cup (144 g) raw sugar
2 teaspoons pure lemon extract
1 teaspoon pure vanilla extract
1½ cups (188 g) all-purpose flour
½ teaspoon baking soda
½ teaspoon baking powder
2 teaspoons cornstarch
¼ teaspoon fine sea salt
2 scant tablespoons (2 g) culinary dried lavender
2 scant tablespoons (30 ml) coconut milk or other nondairy milk

Preheat the oven to 350°F (180°C, or gas mark 4). Line 2 baking sheets with parchment paper or silicone baking mats, such as Silpat.

In a large-size bowl and using an electric mixer, cream together the butter and sugar. Stir in the extracts.

In a medium-size bowl, sift together the flour, baking soda, baking powder, cornstarch, and salt. Stir in the lavender.

Stir the dry ingredients into the wet. Add the milk, as needed: the dough must be neither too dry nor too wet.

Divide the dough into 20 equal portions, using about 1 heaping tablespoon (24 g) of dough. Place on the prepared baking sheets. Flatten a little, because the cookies don't spread a lot while baking.

Bake for 14 minutes, or until the edges are golden brown. If you want chewier cookies, aim for 12 minutes instead.

Wait 2 minutes before transferring them to a wire rack to cool completely.

Yield: 20 cookies

Crisp and Chewy Pumpkin Cookies

If you have been craving a recipe that doesn't yield soft pumpkin cookies, look no further: the name of these cookies says it all.

1 cup (120 g) whole wheat pastry flour
1 cup (80 g) ground oats
1 teaspoon ground cinnamon
2 tablespoons (16 g) arrowroot powder
¼ teaspoon fine sea salt
1 teaspoon baking powder
½ cup (96 g) vegetable shortening
1½ cups (288 g) raw sugar
½ cup (122 g) pumpkin purée
2 teaspoons pure vanilla extract
⅔ to 1 cup (117 to 175 g) nondairy semisweet chocolate chips, to taste

Line a baking sheet with parchment paper or a silicone baking mat, such as Silpat.

In a medium-size bowl, whisk together the flour, oats, cinnamon, arrowroot powder, salt, and baking powder.

In a large-size bowl and using an electric mixer, cream together the shortening and sugar. Stir in the pumpkin and vanilla until combined.

Stir the dry ingredients into the wet. Stir in the chocolate chips.

Divide the dough into 12 equal portions, using about ¼ cup (74 g) of dough. Place on the prepared baking sheet. Flatten the cookies as much as you want them, because they do not spread much while baking.

Place in the fridge for a couple of hours: the longer, the better, because it allows the flavors to blend and the texture to improve.

Preheat the oven to 350°F (180°C, or gas mark 4).

Bake the cookies for 17 minutes, or until the edges are golden brown. Be careful not to bake them too long, or they will dry out.

Wait a couple of minutes before transferring them to a wire rack to cool completely.

Yield: 12 cookies

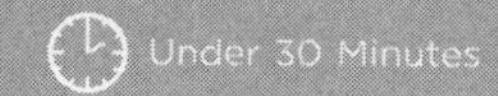

Butterscotch Pecan Cookies

These cookies are unbelievably chewy and caramel-like, and will remind you why making eggless cookie dough is reason enough for anyone to choose an animal-friendly way of life. Just make sure there is enough left to actually bake a few cookies. These are especially great straight from the fridge.

¼ cup plus 1 tablespoon (70 g) nondairy butter
¾ cup (144 g) Sucanat
2 tablespoons (30 ml) almond or other nondairy milk
1 teaspoon pure vanilla extract
¼ teaspoon fine sea salt
1 cup (120 g) whole wheat pastry flour
2 teaspoons cornstarch
½ teaspoon baking powder
¼ cup plus 1 tablespoon (34 g) chopped pecans
½ cup (88 g) nondairy semisweet chocolate chips (optional)

Preheat the oven to 350°F (180°C, or gas mark 4). Line a baking sheet with parchment paper or a silicone baking mat, such as Silpat.

In a large-size microwave-safe bowl, combine the butter, Sucanat, and milk. Melt in the microwave for about 1 minute until the Sucanat starts to dissolve, stirring occasionally. Stir in the vanilla.

Sift the salt, flour, cornstarch, and baking powder on top of the wet ingredients.

Stir the dry ingredients into the wet. Stir in the pecans and chocolate chips, if using.

Divide the dough into 12 equal portions, using about 1 heaping tablespoon of dough for each portion. Place onto the prepared baking sheet. Flatten down just a little with the palm of your hand, and leave 1 inch (2.5 cm) of space between the cookies, because they will spread some while baking.

Bake for 10 minutes, or until the cookies are set. Let cool on the baking sheet.

Yield: 12 cookies

Under 30 Minutes

Open Sesame Cookies

These cookies are wonderfully chewy, with a bit of an attitude thanks to the addition of sesame in both seed and paste form. You can replace the cranberries with any other dried fruit, nut, or chocolate chip you might prefer. These cookies taste even better the next day.

1 cup (120 g) whole wheat pastry flour
1 cup (78 g) quick-cooking oats
1 cup (220 g) firmly packed light brown sugar
½ teaspoon baking soda
¼ teaspoon fine sea salt
¼ cup (32 g) black sesame seeds
¼ cup (32 g) brown sesame seeds
½ cup (61 g) dried cranberries or (80 g) raisins
¼ cup (64 g) tahini
2 tablespoons (30 ml) canola oil
¼ cup (60 ml) almond or other nondairy milk
1 teaspoon pure vanilla extract

Preheat the oven to 375°F (190°C, or gas mark 5). Line 2 baking sheets with parchment paper or silicone baking mats, such as Silpat.

In a medium-size bowl, whisk together the flour, oats, brown sugar, baking soda, salt, sesame seeds, and cranberries.

In a small-size bowl, whisk together the tahini, oil, milk, and vanilla.

Stir the wet ingredients into the dry. If the dough is too dry, add a few extra drops of milk.

Divide the dough into 12 equal portions, using about 2 tablespoons (42 g) of dough.

Place on the prepared baking sheets. Flatten a little, leaving about 1 inch (2.5 cm) of space between the cookies, because they will spread some while baking.

Bake for 9 minutes, or until set. Wait 10 minutes before transferring them to a wire rack to cool completely.

Yield: 16 cookies

Cool Lemon Cookies

Sweet and tart and cool, these delicious little cookies are so yummy, you won't mind the sugary mess on your fingers!

For the cookies:

- ½ cup (60 g) powdered sugar
- ½ cup (100 g) granulated sugar
- ⅓ cup (64 g) vegetable shortening
- ¾ cup (170 g) nondairy yogurt
- 1 teaspoon pure vanilla extract
- 1 teaspoon pure lemon extract
- ¼ teaspoon salt
- 2½ cups (313 g) all-purpose flour
- 1½ teaspoons baking powder
- 1 teaspoon baking soda

For the coating:

- 1 cup (120 g) powdered sugar
- 1 envelope (¼ ounce, or 7 g) unsweetened lemonade drink mix powder, such as Kool-Aid

To make the cookies: Preheat the oven to 325°F (170°C, or gas mark 3). Line 2 baking sheets with parchment paper or silicone baking mats, such as Silpat.

In a large-size bowl and using an electric mixer, beat together the powdered sugar, granulated sugar, shortening, yogurt, vanilla and lemon extracts, and salt until creamy.

Slowly beat in the flour, baking powder, and baking soda. Beat until smooth.

Spoon drop 15 cookies, using about 1 ounce (28 g) per cookie, evenly spaced, onto each of the prepared baking sheets.

Bake for 18 to 20 minutes, or until lightly browned.

To make the coating: While the cookies are baking, place the powdered sugar and drink mix into a resealable plastic bag and shake to combine.

Remove the cookies from the oven and let cool for about 5 minutes.

Add the cookies, 4 or 5 at a time, to the bag and shake to coat.

Yield: 30 cookies

Booze It Up Cookies

Be strong, and have the willpower to share these cookies with friends and coworkers, or you might find yourself greedily devouring the entire batch of chewy, buttery goodness by your own lonesome.

¼ cup plus 3 tablespoons (105 ml) canola oil
¾ cup (144 g) raw sugar
1½ cups (384 g) creamy or crunchy natural peanut butter
1 tablespoon (15 ml) pure vanilla extract
¾ cup (180 ml) coffee-flavored liqueur, such as store-bought or homemade (page 495) Kahlúa, or whiskey
¾ cup (120 g) brown rice flour
¾ cup (90 g) light spelt flour
¾ teaspoon baking powder
¼ teaspoon fine sea salt
¼ cup (44 g) nondairy semisweet chocolate chips

Preheat the oven to 350°F (180°C, or gas mark 4). Line 2 baking sheets with parchment paper or silicone baking mats, such as Silpat.

In a large-size bowl, whisk together the oil, sugar, peanut butter, vanilla, and coffee-flavored liqueur until emulsified.

Sift the flours, baking powder, and salt on top of the wet ingredients. Add the chocolate chips, and stir until well combined.

Divide the dough into 20 equal portions, using about 2 tablespoons (50 g) of dough. Flatten the cookies onto the baking sheet as much as you want them to be, because they don't spread while baking. Decorate with a crosshatch pattern if desired, using a fork.

Bake for 16 minutes, or until the edges are golden brown. Wait 15 minutes before transferring them to a wire rack to cool completely.

Yield: 20 cookies

Maple and Brown Sugar Oatmeal Cookies

We liken these to breakfast cookies. They are not too sweet. They are nice and soft. They taste great alongside a big cup o' jo.

2 cups (156 g) quick-cooking oats
2 cups (250 g) all-purpose flour
½ teaspoon ground cinnamon
¼ teaspoon baking soda
¼ teaspoon baking powder
¼ teaspoon salt
½ cup (112 g) nondairy butter
½ cup (110 g) firmly packed brown sugar
1 teaspoon pure vanilla extract
1 cup (235 ml) soy or other nondairy milk
¼ cup (60 ml) pure maple syrup

Preheat the oven to 350°F (180°C, or gas mark 4). Line 2 baking sheets with parchment paper or silicone baking mats, such as Silpat.

In a mixing bowl, mix together the oats, flour, cinnamon, baking soda, baking powder, and salt.

In a separate bowl, using an electric mixer, beat together the butter and brown sugar until fluffy.

Add the vanilla. Continue to beat for another minute.

Add the milk and syrup and beat until creamy.

Add the wet ingredients to the dry and stir to combine.

Spoon drop about 2 tablespoons (40 g) of the cookie dough onto the prepared baking sheets about 2 inches (5 cm) apart. Bake 12 to a sheet.

Bake for 12 minutes, or until the edges are beginning to brown.

Remove from the oven and let cool for 5 minutes before transferring to a rack to cool completely.

Yield: 24 cookies

VARIATIONS

Not sweet enough for you? Fold in 1 cup (175 g) nondairy semisweet chocolate chips to the batter after you mix the wet ingredients into the dry.

Not healthy enough for you? Substitute whole wheat pastry flour for the all-purpose flour, and fold in 1 cup (160 g) raisins to the batter after you mix the wet ingredients into the dry.

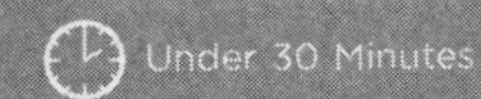

Under 30 Minutes

Ranger Cookies

Not a fan of wimpy cookies that contain nothing but chocolate chips or raisins? Rejoice, for this recipe packs so many ingredients into its dough that your mouth won't know what to do with itself as soon as you have a delicious bite.

1 cup (120 g) light spelt flour
½ teaspoon baking powder
½ teaspoon baking soda
¼ teaspoon fine sea salt
½ cup (112 g) nondairy butter
¼ cup plus 2 tablespoons (72 g) Sucanat
¼ cup plus 2 tablespoons (72 g) raw sugar
2 teaspoons pure vanilla extract
½ cup (39 g) quick-cooking oats
½ cup (47 g) shredded coconut
¼ cup (38 g) granulated or chopped peanuts
½ cup (88 g) nondairy semisweet chocolate chips
⅔ cup (25 g) any cereal flakes

Preheat the oven to 350°F (180°C, or gas mark 4). Line a baking sheet with parchment paper or a silicone baking mat, such as Silpat.

In a medium-size bowl, sift together the flour, baking powder, baking soda, and salt.

In a large-size bowl and using an electric mixer, cream together the butter, Sucanat, sugar, and vanilla until fluffy.

Stir the dry ingredients into the wet. Stir in the oats, coconut, peanuts, and chocolate chips. Delicately stir in the cereal flakes, trying not to crush them too much.

Divide the dough into 12 equal portions, using about 2 tablespoons (52 g) of dough.

Flatten onto the prepared baking sheet. The cookies don't spread much while baking, but leave about 1 inch (2.5 cm) of space between them. The dough may be a bit stiff, but just work it with your hands.

Bake for 10 minutes, or until the edges are golden brown. Wait 4 minutes before transferring them to a wire rack to cool completely.

Yield: 12 cookies

Under 30 Minutes

Spice Cookies

With all the typical flavor you expect to enjoy during the holidays, these spicy cookies are so good you might find yourself dreaming of a year-round white Christmas.

½ cup plus 2 tablespoons (140 g) nondairy butter
⅔ cup (128 g) raw sugar, plus extra for sprinkling on top (optional)
1 tablespoon (22 g) blackstrap or regular molasses
2 teaspoons cornstarch
1½ cups (180 g) whole wheat pastry flour
½ teaspoon baking soda
½ teaspoon baking powder
¼ teaspoon fine sea salt
2 teaspoons ground cinnamon
1 teaspoon ground ginger
1 teaspoon allspice
½ teaspoon ground cloves
½ teaspoon ground cardamom
½ teaspoon ground nutmeg
¼ cup (34 g) crystallized ginger, chopped (optional)

Preheat the oven to 350°F (180°C, or gas mark 4). Line 2 baking sheets with parchment paper or silicone baking mats, such as Silpat.

In a large-size bowl and using an electric mixer, cream together the butter and sugar. Stir in the molasses.

In a medium-size bowl, sift together the cornstarch, flour, baking soda, baking powder, salt, cinnamon, ground ginger, allspice, cloves, cardamom, and nutmeg.

Stir the dry ingredients into the wet. Stir in the crystallized ginger, if using.

Divide the dough into 14 equal portions, using about 2 tablespoons (37 g) of dough.

Place on the prepared baking sheets. Flatten them just a little, because they don't spread much while baking. Sprinkle the extra raw sugar on top, if using.

Bake for 12 minutes, or until set. For chewier cookies, bake only 10 minutes.

Let cool for a few minutes before transferring them to a wire rack to cool completely.

Yield: 14 cookies

Hazelnut Spread Cookies

With so many nondairy chocolate hazelnut spreads available on the market, you shouldn't let yourself believe that the days of digging directly into the jar with a spoon or a knife are but a long-gone memory. Celebrate nostalgia by biting into one of these delicious cookies!

½ cup (112 g) nondairy butter
¼ cup (55 g) firmly packed light brown sugar
¼ cup (50 g) granulated sugar
1 teaspoon pure vanilla extract
¼ cup (74 g) nondairy chocolate hazelnut spread, such as Chocoreale
1 cup (125 g) all-purpose flour
2 teaspoons cornstarch
½ teaspoon baking soda
¼ teaspoon fine sea salt
¼ cup (28 g) hazelnut meal
⅓ cup (58 g) nondairy semisweet chocolate chips

Preheat the oven to 350°F (180°C, or gas mark 4). Line a baking sheet with parchment paper or a silicone baking mat, such as Silpat.

In a large-size bowl and using an electric mixer, cream together the butter, sugars, vanilla, and hazelnut spread.

In a medium-size bowl, sift together the flour, cornstarch, baking soda, and salt. Stir in the hazelnut meal.

Stir the dry ingredients into the wet. Stir in the chocolate chips.

Divide the dough into 12 equal portions, using about 2 heaping tablespoons (42 g) of dough. Place on the prepared baking sheet. Flatten just a little, because the cookies won't spread out much while baking.

Bake for 13 minutes, or until set. For chewier cookies, bake only 10 minutes. Wait 2 minutes before transferring them to a wire rack to cool completely.

Yield: 12 cookies

Pecan Shortbread Cookies

This classic cookie is sure to please. Although pecans are traditional, feel free to substitute any of your favorite nuts here.

1¾ cups (219 g) all-purpose flour
½ teaspoon baking soda
½ teaspoon cream of tartar
¼ teaspoon salt
½ cup (96 g) vegetable shortening
½ cup (100 g) granulated sugar
½ cup (60 g) powdered sugar
¼ cup (60 g) nondairy yogurt
1 teaspoon pure vanilla extract
½ cup (55 g) chopped pecans

Preheat the oven to 350°F (180°C, or gas mark 4). Line 3 baking sheets with parchment paper or silicone baking mats, such as Silpat.

In a medium-size bowl, mix together the flour, baking soda, cream of tartar, and salt. Set aside.

In a large-size bowl and using an electric mixer, cream together the shortening and sugars, then add the yogurt and vanilla.

Slowly beat in the flour mixture. When the dough becomes too thick, use a spoon instead. Fold in the pecans.

Refrigerate the dough for about an hour.

Roll the dough into small balls about 1½ inches (3.8 cm) in diameter, place on the baking sheets, and press slightly to flatten into a disk shape.

Bake for 12 to 15 minutes, or until slightly golden.

Let cool for 5 minutes before transferring to a wire rack to cool completely.

Yield: About 36 cookies

Cherry Almond Cookies

These chewy and spicy cookies are made even more awesome with the addition of tart dried cherries. You will inevitably find yourself reaching for "just one more!"

½ cup (80 g) dried cherries
¼ cup (60 ml) Kirsch
¼ cup (56 g) nondairy butter
¼ cup (60 g) soy or other nondairy yogurt
½ cup (100 g) granulated sugar
½ cup (110 g) firmly packed light brown sugar
1 teaspoon pure almond extract
1 teaspoon pure vanilla extract
½ cup (48 g) almond meal
1 cup (78 g) quick-cooking oats
½ cup (68 g) all-purpose flour
¼ cup (30 g) whole wheat pastry flour
1 teaspoon ground cinnamon
½ teaspoon baking powder
¼ teaspoon fine sea salt

About 1 hour before preparing the cookies, place the cherries in a small-size bowl and combine with the Kirsch. Stir halfway through the soaking time. Drain well, and set aside.

Preheat the oven to 350°F (180°C, or gas mark 4). Line a baking sheet with parchment paper or a silicone baking mat, such as Silpat.

In a large-size bowl and using an electric mixer, cream together the butter, yogurt, and sugars. Stir in the extracts and almond meal.

Place the oats in a medium-size bowl, and sift the flours, cinnamon, baking powder, and salt on top. Stir to combine.

Stir the dry ingredients into the wet. Stir in the cherries.

Divide the dough into 12 equal portions, using about 3 tablespoons (57 g) of dough. Place on the baking sheet, about 1 inch (2.5 cm) apart. Flatten a little, because the cookies don't spread a lot while baking.

Bake for 17 minutes, or until the edges are golden brown.

Let cool for a few minutes before transferring them to a wire rack to cool completely.

Yield: 12 cookies

White Chocolate Lime Cookies

White chocolate and lime make for an interesting and flavorful combination in these buttery, crispy, and irresistible cookies.

½ cup (112 g) nondairy butter
¾ cup (144 g) raw sugar
Zest of 1 lime (about 2 teaspoons)
2 teaspoons fresh lime juice
1 teaspoon pure vanilla extract
1½ cups (188 g) all-purpose flour
½ teaspoon baking soda
½ teaspoon baking powder
¼ teaspoon fine sea salt
1 to 2 tablespoon(s) (15 to 30 ml) coconut milk or other nondairy milk
¼ cup (50 g) nondairy white chocolate chips

Preheat the oven to 350°F (180°C, or gas mark 4). Line 2 baking sheets with parchment paper or silicone baking mats, such as Silpat.

In a large-size bowl and using an electric mixer, cream together the butter and sugar. Stir in the zest, juice, and vanilla.

In a medium-size bowl, sift together the flour, baking soda, baking powder, and salt.

Stir the dry ingredients into the wet. Add the milk, as needed: the dough must be neither too dry nor too wet. Stir in the chips.

Divide the dough into 20 equal portions, using about 1 heaping tablespoon (26 g) of dough. Place on the prepared baking sheets. Flatten a little, because the cookies don't spread a lot while baking.

Bake for 14 minutes, or until the edges are golden brown. If you want chewier cookies, aim for 12 minutes instead.

Wait 2 minutes before transferring them to a wire rack to cool completely.

Yield: 20 cookies

Rum Spice Cookies

You may not carry a parrot on your shoulder, wear a patch on your eye, or roll your "arrs," but you are bound to love the rummy ways of these spicy, deliciously chewy cookies.

½ cup (80 g) raisins
2 tablespoons (30 ml) rum
¼ cup (56 g) nondairy butter
¼ cup (61 g) unsweetened applesauce or pumpkin purée
¼ cup (48 g) raw sugar
¼ cup plus 2 tablespoons (72 g) Sucanat
1 teaspoon rum extract
¼ cup plus 2 heaping tablespoons (56 g) whole hazelnuts, ground
1 cup (78 g) quick-cooking oats
½ cup (60 g) whole wheat flour
¼ cup (40 g) brown rice flour (or more whole wheat flour)
2 teaspoons cornstarch
½ teaspoon ground cinnamon
¼ teaspoon ground nutmeg
¼ teaspoon ground ginger
½ teaspoon baking powder
¼ teaspoon fine sea salt

About 1 hour before preparing the cookie dough, place the raisins in a small-size bowl and combine with the rum. Stir halfway through the soaking time. Set aside.

Preheat the oven to 350°F (180°C, or gas mark 4). Line a baking sheet with parchment paper or a silicone baking mat, such as Silpat.

In a large-size bowl and using an electric mixer, cream together the butter, applesauce, sugar, and Sucanat. Stir in the rum extract and ground hazelnuts.

Place the oats in a medium-size bowl, and sift the flours, cornstarch, cinnamon, nutmeg, ginger, baking powder, and salt on top. Stir to combine.

Stir the dry ingredients into the wet. Stir in the raisins and rum.

Divide the dough into 12 equal portions, using about 2 tablespoons (47 g) of dough. Place on the prepared baking sheet, about 1 inch (2.5 cm) apart from each other. Flatten the dough a bit, because the cookies don't spread a lot while baking.

Bake for 16 minutes, or until the edges are golden brown.

Let cool a few minutes before transferring them to a wire rack to cool completely.

Yield: 12 cookies

Orange Cappuccino Cookies

Crispy at the edges and chewy in the middle, these cookies belong with a nice cup of tea, or even a bona fide cup of cappuccino, if you need even more caffeinated goodness.

1½ cups (180 g) whole wheat pastry flour
½ teaspoon baking powder
½ teaspoon fine sea salt
½ cup (96 g) raw sugar
¼ cup (60 ml) pure maple syrup
¼ cup plus 2 tablespoons (90 ml) canola oil
1 teaspoon pure orange extract
2 teaspoons instant espresso powder
3 tablespoons (45 ml) plain soy or other nondairy milk
⅔ cup (120 g) nondairy bittersweet chocolate chunks

Preheat the oven to 350°F (180°C, or gas mark 4). Line a baking sheet with parchment paper or a silicone baking mat, such as Silpat.

In a medium-size bowl, sift together the flour, baking powder, and salt. Whisk in the sugar.

In a large-size bowl, combine the syrup, oil, extract, espresso powder, and milk, whisking until the espresso powder is dissolved. Stir in the chocolate chunks.

Stir the dry ingredients into the wet.

Divide the dough into 12 equal portions, using about 2 tablespoons (50 g) of dough.

Place on the prepared baking sheet. Flatten the cookies almost as much as you want them, because they don't spread much while baking.

Bake for 14 minutes, or until the edges are golden brown.

Let cool for a few minutes before transferring them to a wire rack to cool completely.

Yield: 12 cookies

Cardamom Sugar Cookies

Delicately flavored with cardamom, these sparkly cookies are a festive addition to a gift basket, but they certainly make a tasty treat anytime.

For the cookies:

3¾ cups (470 g) all-purpose flour, plus more if needed
1 teaspoon baking soda
½ teaspoon salt
2 cups (400 g) granulated sugar
1 cup (224 g) nondairy butter
1 teaspoon ground cardamom
Equivalent of 2 eggs (flax or tofu eggs work well here, or use Ener-G)
1 tablespoon (15 ml) pure vanilla extract
Nondairy milk, if needed

For the spice mixture:

¼ cup (50 g) granulated sugar or sparkling sugar
¼ teaspoon ground cardamom
⅛ teaspoon salt

To make the cookies: Whisk together the flour, baking soda, and salt in a medium-size bowl.

In a separate bowl and using an electric mixer, beat together the sugar, butter, and cardamom at medium speed for 3 to 4 minutes, or until light and fluffy.

Beat in the egg replacers and vanilla.

At low speed, beat in the flour mixture, just until blended.

Add extra flour if your dough is too wet, or a little bit of nondairy milk if it's too dry, to get the dough to come together.

Place the dough on a lightly floured surface and knead just until smooth. Wrap in plastic wrap and refrigerate until firm enough to roll, overnight or up to 2 days.

To make the spice mixture: Combine the sugar, cardamom, and salt.

Preheat the oven to 350°F (180°C, or gas mark 4). Line 2 or 3 baking sheets with parchment paper or silicone mats, such as Silpat.

Remove the dough from the refrigerator and let stand at room temperature until able to roll but still firm. On a lightly floured surface, roll out the dough to about ⅛ inch (3 mm) thick.

Use cookie cutters to cut out desired shapes. Place on the prepared baking sheets.

Liberally sprinkle the spice mixture on top of the cookies.

Bake for 8 to 10 minutes, or until the edges are golden brown.

Let cool for 5 minutes on the baking sheet before transferring to a wire rack to cool completely.

Yield: About 36 cookies, depending on the size of your cutouts

Coconut Drop Cookies

If you've never baked with coconut flour, you are missing out. This silky, gluten-free flour adds softness, natural sweetness, and chewiness to cookies and other baked goods.

3 cups (360 g) shredded coconut, sweetened or unsweetened
2 cups (224 g) coconut flour
1 cup (125 g) all-purpose flour
1 teaspoon baking powder
1 teaspoon baking soda
¼ teaspoon salt
1 cup (120 g) powdered sugar
1 cup (235 ml) soy or other nondairy milk
½ cup (168 g) agave nectar
¼ cup (60 ml) canola oil
¾ cup (170 g) nondairy yogurt
1 tablespoon (15 ml) pure vanilla extract

Preheat the oven to 350°F (180°C, or gas mark 4). Line 2 baking sheets with parchment paper or silicone baking mats, such as Silpat.

In a mixing bowl, mix together the coconut, flours, baking powder, baking soda, and salt.

In a separate bowl, whisk together the powdered sugar, milk, agave, oil, yogurt, and vanilla.

Add the wet ingredients to the dry and mix until a thick batter forms. Drop about 3 tablespoons (45 g) of mixture per cookie onto the baking sheets.

Bake for 20 to 25 minutes, or until the tops begin to turn golden brown.

Let cool for 10 minutes before transferring to a wire rack to cool completely.

Yield: 24 cookies

Lemon Sand Tarts

Cut these lemony roll-out cookies into fun shapes and decorate for gift giving! You can make the dough ahead of time and refrigerate it, or freeze it until you are ready to make a fresh batch of cookies.

For the cookies:

- 1 cup (224 g) nondairy butter
- 1 cup (200 g) granulated sugar
- ¼ cup (80 g) plain, vanilla, or lemon-flavored soy or other nondairy yogurt
- 2 teaspoons pure vanilla extract
- 1 teaspoon pure lemon extract
- 3 cups (375 g) all-purpose flour
- 2 teaspoons baking powder
- ½ teaspoon salt

For the icing:

- 3 cups (360 g) powdered sugar
- 3 tablespoons (45 ml) soy or other nondairy milk
- 1 teaspoon pure vanilla extract
- 1 teaspoon pure lemon extract
- Food coloring (optional)

To make the cookies: In a large bowl and using an electric mixer, cream together the butter and sugar until fluffy.

Add the yogurt, vanilla, and lemon extract.

Sift in the flour, baking powder, and salt. Mix until well combined.

Divide into 4 equal pieces, wrap in plastic wrap, and refrigerate for at least 1 hour.

Preheat the oven to 350°F (180°C, or gas mark 4). Line 3 baking sheets with parchment paper or silicone baking mats, such as Silpat.

Roll out the dough on a floured surface and cut into desired shapes. Transfer to the prepared baking sheets.

Bake for 10 to 12 minutes, or until the edges are golden brown. Remove from the oven and let cool for 5 minutes before transferring to wire racks to cool completely. Meanwhile, make the icing.

To make the icing: Whisk or beat together the powdered sugar, milk, vanilla, lemon extract, and food coloring, if using, until smooth.

Apply to the cooled cookies, and let harden completely before packaging.

Yield: About 36 cookies, depending on the size of your cutouts

Peanut Butter and Jelly Thumbprints

Which two ingredients could be better paired? This simple-to-make little cookie yields big results.

2 cups (250 g) all-purpose flour
½ teaspoon baking soda
½ teaspoon baking powder
2 cups (512 g) creamy or crunchy natural peanut butter
1¾ cups (420 g) your favorite jam or jelly, divided

Preheat the oven to 350°F (180°C, or gas mark 4). Line 2 or 3 baking sheets with parchment paper or silicone baking mats, such as Silpat.

In a mixing bowl, sift together the flour, baking soda, and baking powder.

Add the peanut butter and 1 cup (240 g) of the jam. Every type of peanut butter yields a different moisture content. If your peanut butter is very wet, you may need a little extra flour. If it is very dry, you'll need less. This recipe was made with creamy, no-stir peanut butter.

Mix well. Make sure all the ingredients are well incorporated.

Using 2 tablespoons (30 g) of dough, roll into balls and then flatten slightly into a disk shape. Place on the prepared baking sheets.

Bake for 8 minutes.

Remove from the oven and make a depression in each cookie, using your thumb or the back side of a tablespoon size measuring spoon, which has a nice round, deep well.

Fill the depressions with 1 teaspoon of the remaining ¾ cup (180 g) jam. Bake for an additional 8 minutes.

Let cool for about 10 minutes before transferring to a wire rack to cool completely.

Yield: 30 cookies

Sablés Marbrés

These delicious shortbreadlike cookies are not only tasty, but they're also pleasing to the eye—the combination of vanilla and chocolate dough forms a beautiful pattern you won't get to admire for too long, as you'll find it impossible to resist getting your nibble on.

¾ cup (168 g) nondairy butter
¾ cup (90 g) powdered sugar
½ teaspoon fine sea salt
1 tablespoon (8 g) arrowroot powder
1½ teaspoons pure vanilla extract
1½ cups plus 3 tablespoons (203 g) whole wheat pastry flour
¾ teaspoon baking soda
3 tablespoons (15 g) unsweetened cocoa powder
1½ teaspoons plain soy or other nondairy milk

Preheat the oven to 350°F (180°C, or gas mark 4). Line 2 baking sheets with parchment paper or silicone baking mats, such as Silpat.

In a large bowl and using an electric mixer, cream together the butter and sugar until light and fluffy, 2 to 3 minutes.

Stir in the salt, arrowroot powder, vanilla, flour, and baking soda until well combined.

Gather the cookie dough and shape it into a ball. Divide in half, and set one half aside.

With an electric mixer, beat the cocoa powder and milk into half of the dough, until well combined. Add a little extra milk if the dough is too dry.

Using your hands, flatten both the vanilla and the chocolate doughs separately until they are the exact same shape and size, a small rectangle about ¾ inch (2 cm) thick.

Cut in half and place one on top of the other, patting down gently to glue them together. Make sure that you put a slice of vanilla dough on top of the chocolate, then top with another vanilla, and finally chocolate. Pat down gently to form a rectangular roll. Wrap the dough in plastic, and chill in the fridge for 1 hour.

Cut into 15 equal slices and place on the prepared baking sheets, leaving about 1 inch (2.5 cm) in between each cookie, because they spread just a little bit while baking.

Bake for 15 minutes, or until just slightly golden on the edges and almost firm on top; the cookies will firm up more once they are out of the oven.

Let cool for a few minutes before transferring them to a wire rack to cool completely.

Yield: 15 cookies

Peanut Butter Cookies

Who doesn't like straight-up, sweet peanut buttery cookies? Adding a handful of nondairy chocolate chips would, of course, be anything but wrong.

5 tablespoons (60 g) Sucanat
5 tablespoons (60 g) raw sugar
3 tablespoons (45 ml) plain almond or other nondairy milk
2 tablespoons (30 ml) canola oil
3 tablespoons (45 ml) whiskey
1 teaspoon pure vanilla extract
½ teaspoon ground cinnamon
½ cup plus 2 tablespoons (160 g) creamy or crunchy natural peanut butter
¾ cup plus 2 tablespoons (105 g) whole wheat pastry flour
¼ teaspoon fine sea salt
½ teaspoon baking powder

Preheat the oven to 350°F (180°C, or gas mark 4). Line 2 baking sheets with parchment paper or silicone baking mats, such as Silpat.

In a large-size bowl, combine the Sucanat, sugar, milk, oil, whiskey, vanilla, cinnamon, and peanut butter until emulsified.

Sift the flour, salt, and baking powder on top of the wet ingredients, and stir until combined.

Divide the dough into 16 equal portions, using about 1½ tablespoons (30 g) of dough. Place on the prepared baking sheets, reshaping them a little, then use a fork to flatten them and apply the traditional crosshatch pattern on top of each cookie, if desired. These cookies don't spread much while baking.

Bake for 14 minutes, or until the cookies are set and the edges are golden brown.

Let cool for a few minutes before transferring to a wire rack to cool completely.

Yield: 16 cookies

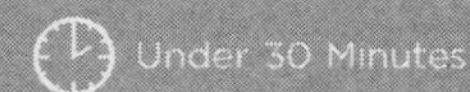

Chocolate Hazelnut Cookies

If you are craving buttery cookies that contain crunchy hazelnuts and irresistibly sweet chocolate chips, this is your lucky day. Hazelnut and chocolate extracts can be hard to find, so consider doubling the amount of vanilla to replace them. The cookies will be just as fantastic.

⅓ cup (75 g) nondairy butter
½ cup (96 g) Sucanat
1 teaspoon pure vanilla extract
1 teaspoon pure hazelnut extract
1 teaspoon pure chocolate extract
1 cup (120 g) whole wheat pastry flour
¼ teaspoon fine sea salt
¼ teaspoon baking powder
3 tablespoons (26 g) hazelnuts, halved
¼ cup (44 g) nondairy semisweet chocolate chips
2 teaspoons plain soy or other nondairy milk

Preheat the oven to 350°F (180°C, or gas mark 4). Line a baking sheet with parchment paper or a silicone baking mat, such as Silpat.

In a large bowl and using an electric mixer, cream together the butter and sugar until light and fluffy, 2 minutes. Stir in the extracts.

Add the flour, salt, and baking powder, and beat until combined, scraping the sides once during the process.

Still using the electric mixer, add the nuts and chocolate chips. Add the milk until the dough is moist enough to stick together when pinched.

Divide the dough into 12 equal portions, using about 1½ tablespoons (32 g) of dough. Place on the prepared baking sheet, about 1 inch (2.5 cm) apart. Flatten them a little; they don't spread much while baking.

Bake for 10 minutes, or until the edges are golden brown. Let cool for a few minutes before transferring them to a wire rack to cool completely.

Yield: 12 cookies

Cherry Oatmeal Chocolate Chip Cookies

These are like a cross between a macaroon and a chocolate chip cookie, with bits of tart cherries thrown in for good measure!

1 cup (125 g) all-purpose flour
1 cup (112 g) coconut flour
1 cup (78 g) quick-cooking oats
1 teaspoon baking soda
1 teaspoon baking powder
1 cup (224 g) nondairy butter, softened
¾ cup (150 g) granulated sugar
¾ cup (165 g) firmly packed brown sugar
¼ cup (84 g) agave nectar
¾ cup (170 g) vanilla soy yogurt
1 teaspoon pure vanilla extract
½ teaspoon salt
1 cup (145 g) dried cherries (any dried fruit would work well here)
1 cup (175 g) nondairy semisweet chocolate chips
½ cup (60 g) sweetened flaked coconut

Preheat the oven to 350°F (180°C, or gas mark 4). Line 2 baking sheets with parchment paper or silicone baking mats, such as Silpat.

In a large bowl, mix together the flours, oats, baking soda, and baking powder.

In a separate bowl, mix together the butter, sugars, agave, yogurt, vanilla, and salt.

Add the wet ingredients to the dry, being careful not to overmix.

Fold in the cherries, chocolate chips, and coconut.

Form into balls using about ⅓ cup (60 g) dough per ball, flatten slightly, and place on the prepared baking sheets about 2 inches (5 cm) apart.

Bake for 12 to 15 minutes, or until lightly browned.

Let cool completely before removing from the baking sheet.

Yield: 24 cookies

Orange Double Chocolate Cookies

Gooey chocolate and sweet citrusy orange goodness. Make sure you have a nice tall glass of ice-cold soymilk to enjoy with these.

1¼ cups (105 g) chocolate graham cracker crumbs, store-bought or homemade (page 414 or 415)
1 cup (125 g) all-purpose flour
¼ cup (20 g) unsweetened cocoa powder
2 teaspoons baking powder
½ cup (96 g) vegetable shortening
1 teaspoon pure vanilla extract
1 teaspoon pure orange extract
2 cups (470 ml) Sweetened Condensed Soymilk (page 399)
1 cup (176 g) nondairy semisweet chocolate chips
Zest from 1 orange

Preheat the oven to 375°F (190°C, or gas mark 5). Line 2 or 3 baking sheets with parchment paper or silicone baking mats, such as Silpat.

In a mixing bowl, combine the graham cracker crumbs, flour, cocoa powder, and baking powder.

In a separate bowl, using an electric mixer, beat together the shortening and extracts, then slowly add the condensed milk.

Add the wet ingredients to the dry, and stir to combine.

Fold in the chocolate chips and orange zest.

Spoon drop about 2 tablespoons (40 g) of cookie dough onto the prepared baking sheets about 3 inches (7.5 cm) apart, because the cookies will spread a lot while baking.

Bake for 12 to 15 minutes.

Let cool for about 5 minutes before transferring to a wire rack to cool completely.

Yield: About 30 cookies

Chapter 17

Pies, Tarts, Crumbles, Crisps, and Crusts

We are of the mind that there is absolutely nothing a good pie won't cure. Add deliciously tender fruit and sinful chocolate or peanut butter delights on top of your pick of a wide selection of tantalizing crusts, and you're on your way to making your world a lot better, one little pie at a time. Just be sure to share with your friends and family so that they can benefit from some probably much-needed extra sweetness, too.

Pie-napple Pie in Macadamia Crust

The slight saltiness of the crust combined with the sweetness of the pineapple filling makes for an absolutely delightful pie with a tropical flair.

For the filling:

2 tablespoons (16 g) arrowroot powder
2 tablespoons (30 ml) unsweetened pineapple juice
1 tablespoon (14 g) nondairy butter
½ cup (96 g) raw sugar
1½ cups (272 g) unsweetened pineapple chunks

Nonstick cooking spray

For the crust:

½ cup (62 g) macadamia nuts
2 cups (240 g) light spelt flour
½ teaspoon fine sea salt
2 tablespoons (30 ml) canola oil
¼ cup plus 2 tablespoons (90 ml) plain soy or other nondairy milk

To make the filling: In a small-size bowl, prepare a slurry by combining the arrowroot powder and juice until the arrowroot is dissolved.

Place the slurry, butter, sugar, and pineapple in a medium-size saucepan. Cook over medium-high heat, stirring often, until the mixture bubbles and thickens and the liquid is almost gone; the syrup will look slightly gelatinous. Let cool before placing on top of the crust.

Preheat the oven to 375°F (190°C, or gas mark 5). Lightly coat an 8-inch (20-cm) round pie plate with nonstick cooking spray.

To make the crust: Grind the nuts in food processor until they begin to look like butter, once they start releasing their oil. This could take a few minutes, depending on the efficiency of the food processor.

Add the flour and salt, and pulse several times until combined.

Add the oil, and pulse several times until combined.

Add the milk, 1 tablespoon (15 ml) at a time, until a dough forms. The dough must hold together when pinched, so if it's too dry, add a little extra milk.

Shape the dough into a disk. Divide into 2 portions, with one portion just slightly larger than the other.

Roll out the dough to a little less than ¼ inch (6 mm) thick.

Place the large piece of dough in the prepared pie plate.

Once the filling is cool enough to proceed, place it in the bottom crust, 1 inch (2.5 cm) from the edge.

Cover with the other piece of dough, using your fingers to seal the edges.

Cut a few decorative holes on the top piece of the crust, for ventilation purposes.

Bake for 35 minutes, or until the crust is golden brown.

Let cool on a wire rack, still in the pan, before cutting and serving, to let the filling set.

Enjoy warm, at room temperature, or chilled.

Yield: One 8-inch (20-cm) pie

Almond Pie with Chocolate Crust

A chewy, simple, yet tasty almond filling tops a delicious chocolate crust. If you have a sweet, sweet tooth, increase the amount of Sucanat to 1 cup (192 g).

For the crust:

- 1¼ cups (150 g) light spelt flour
- 2 ounces (57 g) unsweetened baking or nondairy bittersweet chocolate, finely chopped
- ¼ cup (48 g) raw sugar
- ¼ teaspoon baking powder
- ¼ teaspoon fine sea salt
- ¼ cup (60 ml) canola oil
- 3 tablespoons (45 ml) soy or other nondairy milk

Nonstick cooking spray

For the filling:

- 2 cups (276 g) dry-roasted unsalted whole almonds, ground
- ⅔ cup (128 g) Sucanat
- ¼ teaspoon fine sea salt
- ¼ cup (60 ml) plain almond or other nondairy milk
- 2 tablespoons (30 ml) rum or Kirsch
- 1 teaspoon pure vanilla extract
- 2 teaspoons ground cinnamon or 1 teaspoon pure almond extract

To make the crust: In a food processor, blend the flour, chocolate, sugar, baking powder, and salt until well combined.

Add the oil, 1 tablespoon (15 ml) at a time, and pulse in between each addition. Add the milk, also 1 tablespoon (15 ml) at a time, until a dough forms.

Shape the dough into a disk. Chill for 1 hour before rolling out into an approximately 12-inch (30-cm) round, between 2 pieces of parchment paper or silicone baking mats, such as Silpat.

Preheat the oven to 375°F (190°C, or gas mark 5). Lightly grease an 8-inch (20-cm) round cake pan with spray.

Transfer to the prepared pan. If the dough tears a little, just patch it up. The edges of the crust should be about ½ inch (1.3 cm) high, so push them down if need be, and crimp them for a nice look. Set aside.

To make the filling: In a large-size bowl, combine the ground almonds, Sucanat, and salt. Stir in the milk, rum, vanilla, and cinnamon until well combined.

Pour into the crust and level the filling.

Bake for 20 to 22 minutes, until the filling is set.

Let cool on a wire rack. Serve at room temperature or chilled.

Yield: One 8-inch (20-cm) pie

Peanut Butter Mousse Pie with Candied Nuts and Chocolate Ganache

A very sinful pie, indeed. You will get to choose between two versions for the topping. Both are easy to make and delicious, but the second one is simply ready even faster, if you're a wee bit lazy. If you use agave nectar in the filling, be sure to set a lower oven temperature (325°F [170°C, or gas mark 3]), because agave browns up more quickly.

Nonstick cooking spray

For the crust:

- 1 recipe Chocolate Graham Cracker Crumbs (page 415)
- 2 tablespoons (30 ml) canola oil or (28 g) nondairy butter, softened
- 2 tablespoons (28 g) firmly packed light brown sugar
- Pinch fine sea salt

For the mousse:

- 12 ounces (340 g) firm or extra-firm regular tofu, drained and patted dry
- ½ cup (120 g) nondairy sour cream or soy yogurt
- 1 cup (256 g) creamy no-stir sweetened peanut butter
- 1½ teaspoons pure vanilla extract
- ⅓ cup (80 ml) pure maple syrup or (112 g) agave nectar
- ¼ teaspoon baking powder
- ¼ teaspoon fine sea salt

Preheat the oven to 350°F (180°C, or gas mark 4), or 325°F (170°C, or gas mark 3) if using agave. Lightly grease a 9-inch (23-cm) round baking pan with spray.

To make the crust: Combine the graham cracker crumbs, oil, sugar, and salt in a food processor. Pulse until combined.

Press firmly into the bottom of the prepared pan.

To make the mousse: Combine all the mousse ingredients in a food processor and blend until perfectly smooth, scraping the sides occasionally.

Pour the mousse into the crust. Level with a spatula.

To make the standard topping: Combine all the topping ingredients in a small-size saucepan, and cook over medium heat until the liquid reduces, about 3 minutes, stirring constantly. Remove from the heat. The nuts will darken slightly, but be careful not to let them burn. Let cool.

To make the quicker topping: In a small-size bowl, combine the peanuts and cinnamon, then stir in the agave.

Sprinkle either topping evenly across the filling.

Bake for 20 minutes, or 25 minutes if using agave as a sweetener.

Place the pie, still in the pan, on a wire rack to cool, and freeze once completely cooled for an easier time slicing.

For the standard topping:

¾ cup (114 g) granulated or finely chopped peanuts
1½ teaspoons water
1 tablespoon (14 g) nondairy butter
2 tablespoons (28 g) firmly packed light brown sugar or (30 ml) pure maple syrup
Pinch fine sea salt

For the quick topping:

½ cup (76 g) granulated or finely chopped peanuts
¼ teaspoon ground cinnamon
1 tablespoon (21 g) agave nectar

For the Chocolate Ganache:

¼ cup (60 ml) plain soy or other nondairy milk
½ cup (88 g) nondairy semisweet chocolate chips
1 tablespoon (15 ml) pure maple syrup or (21 g) agave nectar

To make the ganache: Scorch the milk in a small-size saucepan over medium-high heat. Remove from the heat. Add the chocolate chips, and stir until melted. Stir in the maple syrup. You can either decorate with the ganache when taking the pie out of the freezer or upon serving. Drizzle on top of the whole pie or on each individual slice.

Thaw the pie for about 1 hour in the fridge before serving.

Yield: One 9-inch (23-cm) pie

Under 30 Minutes

Avocado Pie

Who knew the creamy flesh of the avocado could be so wonderful in a sweet treat?

Flesh from 4 ripe avocados (about 3 cups [690 g])
1 pound (455 g) nondairy cream cheese
2 cups (240 g) powdered sugar
¼ cup (60 ml) lime juice
1 teaspoon pure vanilla extract
¼ teaspoon salt
1 pie crust, store-bought or homemade, such as Vanilla Cookie Pie Crust (page 417)

Place the avocado flesh, cream cheese, powdered sugar, lime juice, vanilla, and salt in a mixing bowl. Using an electric mixer, beat until smooth.

Pour into the pie crust and refrigerate until ready to serve.

Yield: One 8- or 9-inch (20- or 23-cm) pie

Chocolate Chip Cookie Pie

It's almost like having your milk and cookies in one bite! This pie tastes wonderful when served chilled.

For the cookie crust:

2½ cups (313 g) all-purpose flour
1 teaspoon baking soda
1 teaspoon salt
1 cup (112 g) nondairy butter, softened
1 cup (200 g) granulated sugar
¼ cup (55 g) firmly packed brown sugar
1 tablespoon (22 g) molasses
2 teaspoons pure vanilla extract
1½ cups (264 g) nondairy semisweet chocolate chips

For the vanilla cream filling:

8 ounces (227 g) nondairy cream cheese
1 cup (120 g) powdered sugar
½ cup (56 g) cashews, finely ground into a powder
1 tablespoon (15 ml) pure vanilla extract

Preheat the oven to 375°F (180°C, or gas mark 4). Have ready a lightly greased 9-inch (23-cm) pie dish.

To make the crust: In a mixing bowl, combine the flour, baking soda, and salt. Set aside.

In a large bowl and using an electric mixer, cream together the butter and sugars.

Add the mollases and vanilla and continue to beat.

Slowly add the flour mixture to combine.

Fold in the chocolate chips.

Press the mixture into the prepared pie dish all along the bottom and up the sides to create a thick cookie crust.

Bake for 20 to 25 minutes, or until golden brown.

Remove from the oven and let cool before adding the filling.

While the crust is baking, make the filling: Using an electric mixer, beat together the cream cheese, powdered sugar, cashews, and vanilla.

Spread evenly into the completely cooled crust and refrigerate to chill before serving.

One 9-inch (23-cm) pie

Lemon Ice Box Pie

So simple and so tart! Serve this on a hot summer afternoon for a refreshing break from tradition.

For the sweetened condensed soymilk:

- **3 cups (705 ml) soymilk**
- **1 cup (200 g) granulated sugar**

- **12 ounces (340 g) frozen lemonade concentrate, thawed**
- **12 ounces (340 g) nondairy sour cream**
- **1 cup (120 g) powdered sugar**
- **1 pie crust, store-bought or homemade, such as Vanilla Cookie Pie Crust (page 417)**

To make the condensed milk: Bring the milk and sugar to a simmer over low heat and simmer until reduced to 1 cup (235 ml). Strain any lumps or solids before using.

Using an electric mixer, beat together the condensed milk, lemonade, sour cream, and powdered sugar until creamy.

Carefully pour into the pie crust and place in the freezer for several hours before serving.

Yield: One 8- or 9-inch (20 or 23-cm) pie

Piled High Strawberry Pie

This simple pie really shows off fresh strawberries! Serve garnished with nondairy whipped topping.

For the strawberry glaze:

½ cup (120 ml) water
1 cup (250 g) mashed strawberry pulp
1 cup (200 g) granulated sugar
3 tablespoons (24 g) cornstarch
A few drops red food coloring (optional)

3 pounds (1365 g) fresh strawberries, washed and hulled
1 graham cracker pie crust, store-bought or homemade (page 396)

To make the glaze: In a saucepan, mix together the water, strawberry pulp, sugar, and cornstarch.

Bring to a boil over medium heat. Boil for about 2 minutes, or until thick and translucent. Stir in the food coloring, if using, for a bright red glaze. Set aside to cool.

If you have really large strawberries, cut them in half; otherwise, leave them whole.

Once the glaze has cooled, toss with the strawberries. Pile the strawberries into the pie crust and chill in the refrigerator for a few hours before serving.

Yield: One 8- or 9-inch (20- or 23-cm) pie

Under 30 Minutes Gluten Free Soy Free

Raw Lemon Cheesecake

Trying to cut back on sweets, but still have a sweet tooth? Try this raw cheesecake, which is made creamy with sweet cashew nuts and tangy with fresh lemon juice. If you like things a bit sweeter, you can up the amount of agave nectar.

1 Raw Nut Pie Crust (page 416)
3 cups (336 g) raw cashews
¾ cup (180 ml) full-fat coconut milk
¼ cup (60 ml) fresh lemon juice
¼ cup (84 g) agave nectar
1 vanilla bean, scraped, or 1 teaspoon pure vanilla extract
2 tablespoons (12 g) lemon zest, divided
Fresh raspberries, blueberries, or strawberries, for garnish (optional)

Have ready an 8-inch (20-cm) or 9-inch (23-cm) pie dish. Press the crust into the pie dish.

Combine the cashews, coconut milk, lemon juice, agave, scraped innards of the vanilla bean, and 1 tablespoon (6 g) of the lemon zest in a blender. Purée until silky smooth. If your blender is giving you a hard time and not getting things smooth enough, and you have an immersion blender, try using it. Often it can get things smoother than a countertop blender can.

Pour into the crust and sprinkle with the remaining 1 tablespoon (6 g) zest. Place in the refrigerator for several hours before serving. Keep refrigerated until ready to serve. Serve garnished with fresh raspberries, blueberries, or strawberries, if desired.

Yield: One 8- or 9-inch (20- or 23-cm) cheesecake

Chocolate Cheesecake Pie

This one is not too sinful as far as cheesecakes go. Be sure to give this perfect cheesecake pie enough time to chill for best results!

Nonstick cooking spray

For the crust:

1 recipe Cinnamon Graham Cracker Crumbs (page 414)
2 tablespoons (30 ml) canola oil

For the filling:

1 cup (175 g) nondairy semisweet chocolate chips
2 tablespoons (28 g) nondairy butter
8 ounces (227 g) nondairy cream cheese
9 ounces (255 g) soft tofu, drained
2 tablespoons (10 g) unsweetened cocoa powder
2 tablespoons (30 ml) pure maple syrup
½ cup (96 g) raw sugar
¼ teaspoon fine sea salt
2 teaspoons pure vanilla extract

Preheat the oven to 325°F (170°C, or gas mark 3). Lightly coat a 9-inch (23-cm) pie pan with spray.

To make the crust: Combine the graham cracker crumbs with the oil, using a fork, or pulse in a food processor until combined. Spread the mixture into the prepared pan. Using a spatula or the back of a large spoon, press the mixture firmly on the bottom and sides of the pan.

To make the filling: Melt the chocolate and butter together in a double boiler or in a microwave. Let cool.

In a food processor or blender, blend together the cooled chocolate mixture, cream cheese, tofu, cocoa powder, maple syrup, sugar, salt, and vanilla. Scrape the sides occasionally, and blend until perfectly smooth.

Pour the filling into the prepared crust, spreading it evenly with a spatula.

Bake for 30 minutes. Turn off the oven, and leave the cheesecake in the oven to cool for up to 1 hour.

Refrigerate overnight before slicing and serving.

Yield: One 9-inch (23-cm) cheesecake

Pumpkin Cheesecake Pie

This cheesecake version of pumpkin pie will wow the whole gang next Thanksgiving. Serve with a healthy dollop of nondairy whipped topping for an extra special treat!

For the filling:

1 pound (455 g) nondairy cream cheese
1 can (15 ounces, or 420 g) pure solid-pack pumpkin purée
½ cup (110 g) firmly packed brown sugar
½ cup (100 g) granulated sugar
3 tablespoons (24 g) arrowroot powder
1 teaspoon ground cinnamon
½ teaspoon ground ginger
¼ teaspoon ground nutmeg
¼ teaspoon ground cloves

1 graham cracker pie crust, store-bought or homemade (page 396)

Preheat the oven to 350°F (180°C, or gas mark 4).

To make the filling: In a large bowl and using an electric mixer, beat all the filling ingredients together until smooth.

Pour into the pie crust.

Place a pan of water (about 1 inch [2.5 cm] deep) on the bottom shelf of the oven, to prevent the top of the pie from cracking.

Place the pie on a baking sheet, and place on the top rack of the oven.

Bake for 45 minutes. Remove and let cool, then place in the refrigerator until ready to serve, and to set even more.

Yield: One 8- or 9-inch (20- or 23-cm) cheesecake

Strawberry Rhubarb Frozen Cheesecake Pie

This pink treat will wow the ladies at your next luncheon. Serve with Pink Pomegranate Mimosas (page 496) for a truly girlie afternoon. The strawberry rhubarb mixture used to make this pie also makes an amazing topping for ice cream!

12 ounces (340 g) sliced fresh strawberries
8 ounces (227 g) chopped fresh rhubarb
1 cup (235 ml) water
1 cup (200 g) granulated sugar
¼ cup (60 ml) lemon juice
¼ cup (32 g) cornstarch mixed with ¼ cup (60 ml) water to make a slurry
1 pound (455 g) nondairy cream cheese
2 cups (240 g) powdered sugar
1 Vanilla Cookie Pie Crust (page 417)

To a pot, add the strawberries, rhubarb, water, sugar, and lemon juice.

Bring to a boil, and reduce to a simmer. Simmer, uncovered, for 15 minutes.

Add the cornstarch slurry and stir to thicken.

Remove from the heat and let cool.

Stop here and you have a delcious ice cream topping.

Reserve 1 cup (240 g) of the glaze for topping before serving.

Using an electric mixture, beat in the cream cheese until smooth.

Beat in the powdered sugar, adding 1 cup (120 g) at a time, until smooth.

Pour into the pie crust and freeze for a few hours before serving.

Top with the reserved strawberry rhubarb glaze.

Yield: One 8- or 9-inch (20- or 23-cm) cheesecake

Puddington Pear Galette

The crust in this galette is thick, almost cookielike, giving this dessert a bit of a rustic touch. Be sure to use ripe pears for best results. Leaving the skin on the fruit is up to you, but you will get extra fiber and nutrients by using everything but the core and stem. There will be plenty of time to prepare the custard while the galette is in the oven for the first 20 minutes.

For the galette:

- Nonstick cooking spray
- 1⅔ cups (200 g) whole wheat pastry flour
- ¼ cup (48 g) raw sugar
- ¼ teaspoon fine sea salt
- ¼ teaspoon baking powder
- ¼ cup (60 ml) canola oil
- ¼ cup (60 ml) plain soy or other nondairy milk, plus more if needed
- 2 ripe pears, cored, quartered, and each quarter cut into 4 thin slices lengthwise
- 1 tablespoon (12 g) raw sugar

For the pudding:

- ½ cup (120 ml) vanilla soy or other nondairy milk
- 1 tablespoon (8 g) cornstarch
- 3 tablespoons (36 g) raw sugar
- ¼ teaspoon fine sea salt
- 2 teaspoons pure vanilla extract
- 1 tablespoon (14 g) nondairy butter

To make the galette: Preheat the oven to 350°F (180°C, or gas mark 4). Lightly coat a 9-inch (23-cm) round pie plate with nonstick cooking spray.

In a large bowl, whisk together the flour, sugar, salt, and baking powder.

Add the oil and milk, stirring with a fork or your fingers until it forms a crumbly dough. If your dough is too dry, add 1 tablespoon (15 ml) milk at a time until it is more manageable.

Drop crumbs of dough evenly into the pie plate, and press firmly onto the bottom to form a crust.

Decorate with overlapping pear slices, leaving ½ inch (1.3 cm) around the edges. Sprinkle with the raw sugar.

Bake for 20 minutes.

To make the pudding: In a small-size saucepan, whisk together the milk, cornstarch, sugar, and salt. Cook for approximately 5 minutes over medium heat, or until the mixture reaches a puddinglike consistency, whisking constantly.

Stir in the extract and butter. Set aside.

After the first 20 minutes of baking are done, pour the pudding on top of the pears, avoiding getting too close to the edges. Bake for another 20 minutes, or until the edges are golden brown and the pears are fork-tender.

Place on a wire rack. Let cool before serving.

Yield: One 9-inch (23-cm) galette

Roasted Caramel Nut Tartlets

If you are a fan of nuts, you will absolutely adore this lovely autumnal dessert.

1 cup (139 g) hazelnuts
1 cup (99 g) pecan halves
1 cup (140 g) whole cashews
1 cup (120 g) walnut halves
2 cups (470 ml) Caramel Sauce (page 492)
6 mini tart shells, or 1 pie crust, store-bought or homemade, such as Vanilla Cookie Pie Crust (page 417)
1 cup (175 g) nondairy semisweet chocolate chips

Preheat the oven to 450°F (230°C, or gas mark 8). Have ready a rimmed baking sheet lined with parchment paper or aluminum foil.

Spread the nuts in a single layer on the baking sheet.

Bake for 5 to 7 minutes. Watch carefully so as not to burn the nuts.

Remove from the oven and let cool enough to handle.

Mix the nuts with the caramel sauce. If necessary, heat the caramel sauce in the microwave until soft enough to easily toss with the nuts to coat.

Place an equal amount of caramel nut mixture in each tart shell.

Melt the chocolate chips in the microwave in a small microwave-safe bowl, stirring occasionally to avoid scorching. Alternatively, use a double boiler.

Drizzle an equal amount of the melted chocolate on top of each tartlet using sweeping motions to get a striping effect.

Yield: 6 tartlets

Simply Fruit Tartlets

Certainly you've seen a version of this beautiful tart behind the glass at a bakery, with it's shiny glazed fruit glistening atop a custard-filled tart shell. The beauty of this tart is really its simplicity. The components are quite easy to toss together. The thing that takes the most time is the cutting and arranging of the fruit! That said, the recipe given here is for the glaze and recommendations for the fruits that work best (hint: brightly colored fresh fruits that are sliceable or small). Design and assemby . . . well, that's up to you and your creative imagination!

For the glaze:

½ cup (100 g) granulated sugar
1 cup (235 ml) apple or other clear fruit juice, divided
2 tablespoons (16 g) cornstarch
2 tablespoons (30 ml) corn syrup

1 recipe Coconut Vanilla Pudding (page 479) or Lemon Vanilla Pudding (page 479)
6 mini tart shells, or 1 pie crust, store-bought or homemade, such as Vanilla Cookie Pie Crust (page 420)
Blueberries, kiwifruit, strawberries, blackberries, raspberries, grapes, peaches, and/or pineapple

To make the glaze: In a sauce pot, combine the sugar and ½ cup (120 ml) of the juice and bring to a boil. Boil for 3 minutes to ensure the sugar is completely dissolved.

Meanwhile, in a small-size bowl, dissolve the cornstarch in the remaining ½ cup (120 ml) juice.

Add the cornstarch and juice mixture to the boiling juice and sugar mixture.

Stir in the corn syrup and return to a boil.

As soon as it is boiling, remove from the heat and let cool to room temperature.

Pour the pudding into the tart shells and let set.

While the pudding is setting, cut and prepare the fruit.

Create your masterpiece using the pudding tart as your blank canvas. Use the circular shape as your guide to create a kaleidescope design with your fruits. Use as little or as much fruit as you'd like.

Once your tart is perfected, carefully drizzle the glaze all over the fruit topping to prevent browning and drying out.

Keep refrigerated until ready to serve.

Yield: 6 tartlets

Caraque Pastries

Caraques are scrumptious mini-shortbread crusts filled with chocolate ganache and topped with icing and a piece of chocolate candy. They are quite popular in Switzerland. If you happen to have six 4-inch (10-cm) mini pie pans, the caraques will be perfect shaped like little pies, too. Simply coat the mini pie pans with nonstick cooking spray, and bake the shortbread dough in them.

For the chocolate candy:

- **2 tablespoons (22 g) nondairy semisweet chocolate chips**

For the shortbread:

- **¼ cup (56 g) nondairy butter**
- **¼ cup (30 g) powdered sugar**
- **2 tablespoons (30 ml) soy or other nondairy milk**
- **1 teaspoon pure vanilla extract**
- **¼ cup (32 g) cornstarch**
- **1 cup (120 g) light spelt flour**
- **1 teaspoon baking powder**
- **¼ teaspoon fine sea salt**

- **1 recipe Chocolate Ganache (page 74), slightly cooled**

For the icing:

- **1 cup (120 g) powdered sugar**
- **½ teaspoon pure vanilla extract (optional)**
- **2 to 4 teaspoons plain soy or other nondairy milk**

To make the chocolate candy: Melt the chocolate chips in the microwave in a small microwave-safe bowl, stirring occasionally to avoid scorching.

Drop half teaspoonfuls onto a piece of foil to create 6 circular candies.

Place in the fridge to set for at least 1 hour.

To make the shortbread: In a large bowl and using an electric mixer, cream together the butter, sugar, milk, and vanilla.

In a separate bowl, sift together the cornstarch, flour, baking powder, and salt.

Add in two batches to the butter mixture. Stir until combined, adding a touch of extra milk if the dough is too dry.

Shape into a disk and wrap in plastic. Refrigerate for 30 minutes.

Preheat the oven to 350°F (180°C, or gas mark 4). Line a baking sheet with parchment paper or a silicone baking mat, such as Silpat.

Roll out the dough to a little less than ¼ inch (6 mm) thick. Cut with an approximately 3½-inch (9-cm) cookie cutter, and repeat until you run out of dough. You should get 6 cookies.

Place on the prepared baking sheet, and bake for 14 minutes, or until the bottom is golden brown.

Let cool on a wire rack before applying the ganache.

Apply equal, generous amounts of ganache to each cookie, up to about ¼ inch (6 mm) from the cookie's edges. Place in the fridge for at least 1 hour to set.

To make the icing: In a medium-size bowl, sift the sugar after measuring it. Combine with the vanilla, if using, and a little milk at a time, stirring vigorously with a large spoon until no lumps are left. The icing must stick to the back of a spoon, but still be easily spread on top of the ganache.

Spread equal amounts of icing on top of each cookie, covering the ganache entirely.

Place 1 chocolate candy on top of the icing, in the center of each pastry.

Serve chilled.

Yield: 6 caraques

Peanut Butter and Jam Pastries

This little twist on the good old PB and J of your childhood is not only just as fun to eat as a popular store-bought breakfast pastry, but it's also healthier.

1 cup (120 g) light spelt flour
2 tablespoons (24 g) raw sugar
¼ teaspoon fine sea salt, if using unsalted peanut butter
5 tablespoons (80 g) creamy natural peanut butter, divided
¼ cup (60 ml) plain almond or other nondairy milk, plus extra to brush on top
¼ cup (80 g) all-fruit raspberry spread or other favorite jam, combined with ¼ teaspoon cornstarch

Preheat the oven to 375°F (190°C, or gas mark 5). Line a baking sheet with parchment paper or a silicone baking mat, such as Silpat.

Combine the flour, sugar, salt, if using, and 3 tablespoons (48 g) of the peanut butter in a food processor and pulse a few times. Add the milk, 1 tablespoon (15 ml) at a time, only until a dough forms. If it looks too dry, add a little extra milk.

Divide the dough into 4 equal portions. Roll into circles about ⅛ inch (3 mm) thick. Place 2 circles on the prepared baking sheet.

Divide the remaining 2 tablespoons (32 g) peanut butter and the jam into 2 equal portions and spread across the center of the bottom crusts, being careful to leave enough space at the edges so that the filling cannot escape while baking. Place the remaining 2 crusts on top, and seal the sides with the tines of a fork. Prick the top crust with a fork for ventilation purposes, and brush with a little milk.

Bake for 26 minutes, or until golden brown at the edges and underneath. Let cool on a wire rack.

Yield: 2 large pastries

Variation

Make it even better by applying icing on top. You'll need ¼ cup (30 g) powdered sugar, 1 to 1½ teaspoons plain almond or other nondairy milk, and ¼ teaspoon pure vanilla extract. Combine the sugar, a little milk at a time, and the vanilla in a medium-size bowl, stirring vigorously with a large spoon until no lumps are left. The icing must be thin enough to drizzle, but just thick enough to stick to the back of a spoon, so add the milk accordingly. Drizzle on top of the pastries.

Oatmeal Cookie–Topped Apple Crumble

Maybe you thought that the delicious, hearty dessert that apple crisp already is couldn't be made even more perfect? Not that we're trying to prove you wrong, but see how this recipe takes deliciousness to a whole new level by using cookie dough crumbled on top of perfectly tender baked apple pieces.

For the apples:

2 Granny Smith apples, or other green apples, unpeeled, cored, and cubed
1 Golden Delicious apple, or other yellow apple, unpeeled, cored, and cubed
1 Red Delicious apple, or other red apple, unpeeled, cored, and cubed
1 tablespoon (8 g) whole wheat pastry flour or other flour
1 tablespoon (15 ml) pure maple syrup
3 tablespoons (45 ml) apple juice

For the topping:

½ cup (60 g) whole wheat pastry flour
½ cup (39 g) quick-cooking oats
½ teaspoon ground cinnamon
¼ teaspoon baking soda
¼ teaspoon fine sea salt
2 tablespoons (32 g) creamy natural peanut butter
2 tablespoons (30 ml) canola oil
2 tablespoons (30 ml) plain soy or other nondairy milk
⅓ cup (64 g) Sucanat or (73 g) firmly packed light brown sugar
1 teaspoon pure vanilla extract
¼ cup (40 g) raisins (optional)

Preheat the oven to 350°F (180°C, or gas mark 4). Have an 8-inch (20-cm) baking dish handy.

To make the apples: Combine the apples, flour, syrup, and juice in the baking dish and stir to coat.

Cover with foil, and bake for 30 minutes.

To make the topping: Whisk together the flour, oats, cinnamon, baking soda, and salt in a medium-size bowl.

In a small-size bowl, whisk together the peanut butter, oil, milk, sugar, and vanilla until emulsified.

Stir the wet ingredients into the dry. Stir in the raisins, if using.

Remove the foil; crumble the cookie dough evenly on top of the apples.

Bake for another 10 to 15 minutes, until the apples are tender and the cookie topping is golden brown and cooked through.

Serve warm or at room temperature, or even cold the next morning.

Yield: 6 servings

Blackberry Crumble with Almond Cream

This fruity dish tastes amazing served warm or cold. Be sure to prepare the almond cream ahead of time so that it has time to thicken up in the fridge before being enjoyed.

For the almond cream:

- ½ cup (120 g) nondairy sour cream, store-bought or homemade (page 302)
- ¼ teaspoon pure almond extract
- 1 tablespoon (15 ml) pure maple syrup

For the crumble:

- Nonstick cooking spray
- ½ cup plus 1 tablespoon (68 g) whole wheat pastry flour, divided
- ¼ cup (20 g) quick-cooking oats
- ¼ cup plus 3 tablespoons (84 g) Sucanat, divided
- 2 tablespoons (14 g) chopped pecans
- ½ teaspoon ground cinnamon
- ¼ teaspoon fine sea salt
- ¼ cup (56 g) nondairy butter
- 3 cups (453 g) frozen blackberries
- 1 teaspoon lemon zest
- 1½ tablespoons (23 ml) fresh lemon juice

To make the almond cream: Combine the sour cream, extract, and syrup in a small-size bowl. Whisk until combined. Place in the fridge for 1 to 2 hours to thicken.

To make the crumble: Preheat the oven to 375°F (190°C, or gas mark 5). Lightly coat an 8-inch (20-cm) square baking dish with nonstick cooking spray.

In a medium-size bowl, combine ½ cup (60 g) of the flour, oats, ¼ cup (48 g) of the Sucanat, pecans, cinnamon, and salt.

Cut the butter into small pieces on top of the flour mixture. Combine with a fork or your fingers until a coarse crumble forms.

Place the blackberries in a large-size bowl. Coat with the remaining 1 tablespoon (8 g) flour. Add the zest, remaining 3 tablespoons (36 g) Sucanat, and lemon juice and stir to combine.

Place the fruit mixture into the prepared baking dish. Sprinkle the crumble evenly on top.

Bake for 30 minutes, or until the topping is golden brown.

Enjoy warm or cold. Serve with a dollop of almond cream.

Place on a wire rack and let cool completely before storing in the fridge.

Yield: 4 servings

Mango Blueberry Crisp

This crisp is super simple to throw together. The use of blueberries and mangoes adds not only a twist to a traditional favorite but lots of antioxidants, too! Serve warm or cold, with a nice big scoop of Plain Ol' Vanilla Ice Cream (page 485).

1 pound (455 g) blueberries
1 pound (455 g) mango chunks
½ cup (39 g) quick-cooking oats
½ cup (110 g) firmly packed brown sugar
¼ cup (31 g) all-purpose flour
¼ cup (56 g) nondairy butter
¼ teaspoon ground cinnamon

Preheat the oven to 350°F (180°C, or gas mark 4). Have ready an 8-inch (20-cm) square baking dish.

Toss together the blueberries and mangoes and place in the baking dish.

In a mixing bowl, mix together the oats, brown sugar, flour, butter, and cinnamon. Use your fingertips to work the butter into the mixture until it becomes coarse and crumbly.

Sprinkle the crumb mixture all over the fruit and bake for 30 minutes, or until the fruit is bubbly.

Yield: 6 servings

Old-Fashioned Peach Cobbler

Serve this traditional Southern dessert warm, with a scoop of homemade Plain Ol' Vanilla Ice Cream (page 485). Of course, this tastes best when fresh peaches are in season, but if not, frozen peaches will do just fine.

For the peach filling:

- 2 pounds (908 g) pitted, peeled, and sliced peaches
- ¼ cup (55 g) firmly packed brown sugar
- ¼ teaspoon ground cinnamon
- ¼ teaspoon ground allspice
- ¼ teaspoon ground cloves

For the crust:

- ¾ cup (180 ml) plain soymilk (use soy here, or your milk might not curdle)
- 1 tablespoon (15 ml) lemon juice
- 1 teaspoon pure vanilla extract
- 1 cup (125 g) all-purpose flour
- ¼ cup (50 g) granulated sugar
- ½ teaspoon ground cinnamon
- ½ teaspoon baking soda
- ½ teaspoon baking powder
- ¼ teaspoon salt

For the topping:

- 3 tablespoons (42 g) nondairy butter, chilled and cut into small chunks
- ¼ cup (55 g) firmly packed brown sugar

Preheat the oven to 425°F (220°C, or gas mark 7).

To make the filling: Toss the peach slices with the brown sugar, cinnamon, allspice, and cloves.

Place in an 8-inch (20-cm) or 9-inch (23-cm) square glass baking dish and bake for 10 minutes.

While the peaches are baking, prepare the batter for the crust and the topping.

To make the crust: In a small-size bowl, combine the milk and lemon juice; it will curdle and become like buttermilk.

Add the vanilla to the buttermilk mixture.

In a large-size bowl, mix together the flour, sugar, cinnamon, baking soda, baking powder, and salt.

Fold the wet ingredients into the dry, being careful not to overmix. Set aside.

To make the topping: In a small-size bowl, use your fingertips to work the butter into the brown sugar until it is coarse and crumbly.

Remove the peaches from the oven. Spoon the crust batter over the peaches. Sprinkle the topping all over the batter.

Return to the oven and bake for 25 to 30 minutes, or until the fruit is bubbly and the crust is crisp.

Yield: 6 servings

Cinnamon Graham Cracker Crumbs

If it's as difficult for you, as it has been for us, to find a premade graham cracker crust that does not contain animal-based or hydrogenated ingredients, you'll be thrilled to know that this recipe is not only easy to make but also the perfect vessel for cheesecakes and other delicious pies.

For directions to use the crust, see Chocolate Cheesecake Pie (page 402) or Pumpkin Cheesecake Pie (page 403).

½ cup (112 g) nondairy butter
2 tablespoons (42 g) agave nectar
¼ cup (55 g) firmly packed light brown sugar
1 cup (120 g) white whole wheat flour
¼ cup (30 g) whole wheat pastry flour, plus extra for dusting
1 teaspoon ground cinnamon
½ teaspoon fine sea salt

Preheat the oven to 325°F (170°C, or gas mark 3). Line a baking sheet with parchment paper or a silicone baking mat, such as Silpat.

In a large bowl and using an electric mixer, cream together the butter, agave, and sugar until light and fluffy, about 4 minutes.

Sift the flours, cinnamon, and salt on top of the butter mixture, and combine.

Place the resulting dough on the prepared baking sheet, patting it down into a disk.

Dust with a little extra flour; roll out to about ¼ inch (6 mm) thick.

Bake for 20 to 25 minutes, but start checking a bit sooner to make sure it doesn't get overdone. Let cool for at least 1 hour on the baking sheet.

Break into shards, and then blend into a fine powder in a food processor.

Follow the guidelines in the recipe you need the crumbs for.

Yield: Enough to make one 8- or 9-inch (20- or 23-cm) crust

Chocolate Graham Cracker Crumbs

We include this recipe just because it's impossible not to have a chocolate version of pretty much anything! It's a healthy and tasty recipe that will take already fabulous desserts to the next level. For directions to use the crust, see Peanut Butter Mousse Pie (page 396).

½ cup (112 g) nondairy butter
2 tablespoons (42 g) agave nectar
¼ cup (55 g) firmly packed light brown sugar
1 cup plus 2 tablespoons (145 g) white whole wheat flour, plus extra for dusting
¼ cup (20 g) unsweetened cocoa powder
½ teaspoon fine sea salt

Preheat the oven to 325°F (170°C, or gas mark 3). Line a baking sheet with parchment paper or a silicone baking mat, such as Silpat.

In a large bowl and using an electric mixer, cream together the butter, agave, and sugar until light and fluffy, about 4 minutes.

Sift the flour, cocoa, and salt on top of the butter mixture, and combine.

Place the dough on the prepared baking sheet, patting it down into a disk.

Dust with a little extra flour; roll out to about ¼ inch (6 mm) thick.

Bake for 20 to 25 minutes, but start checking a bit sooner to make sure it doesn't get overdone. Let cool for at least 1 hour on the baking sheet.

Break into shards, and then blend into a fine powder in a food processor.

Follow the guidelines in the recipe you need the crumbs for.

Yield: Enough to make one 8- or 9-inch (20- or 23-cm) crust

Raw Nut Pie Crust

Even if you don't have much patience for homemade pie crusts, this little gem will really fit the bill. With no soy, wheat, or refined sugars, this crust pairs nicely with fresh fruit pies and even richer desserts, such as Raw Lemon Cheesecake (page 401). This recipe yields enough for two crusts. They freeze well, so you can make them ahead of time and just pluck them out of the freezer whenever you need one.

1 cup (120 g) raw walnuts
1 cup (140 g) raw cashews
1 cup (120 g) raw almonds
4½ cups (1065 ml) water, divided
1 cup (142 g) pitted dates
¼ cup (84 g) agave nectar
1 teaspoon ground cinnamon
1 teaspoon pure vanilla extract
Pinch salt

Place each cup of nuts in 1½ cups (355 ml) of the water. Soak the nuts overnight, then drain.

Combine the drained nuts, dates, agave, cinnamon, vanilla, and salt in a food processor and process until a chunky paste is formed.

Press into an 8- or 9-inch (20- or 23-cm) pie pan. Fill with your favorite pie filling.

Yield: Two 8- or 9-inch (20- or 23-cm) crusts

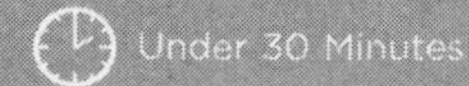

Vanilla Cookie Pie Crust

Use the childhood favorite cookie, vanilla wafers, to make this simple and flavorful pie crust. If possible, try to find cookies that contain no hydrogenated oils.

This crust tastes great with the Piled High Strawberry Pie (page 400) and the Strawberry Rhubarb Frozen Cheesecake Pie (page 404).

10 ounces (284 g) vanilla wafer cookies
¼ teaspoon ground cinnamon
½ cup (112 g) nondairy butter, melted

Turn the cookies into crumbs by either processing in a food processor or placing in a resealable plastic bag and rolling over the cookies to crush them.

Mix the cinnamon into the crumbs.

Pour the crumb mixture into the center of an 8- or 9-inch (20- or 23-cm) pie dish.

Pour the melted butter over the crumbs and work the butter into the crumbs with your fingers.

Press the mixture into the sides and bottom of the dish to form a crust.

Refrigerate for 1 hour to stiffen up.

Preheat the oven to 350°F (180°C, or gas mark 4).

Bake the crust for 10 minutes.

Fill with your favorite pie filling and enjoy.

Yield: One 8- or 9-inch (20- or 23-cm) pie crust

Chapter 18

Cakes and Cupcakes

From decadent Chocolate Cake (page 428) to healthier Pecan Date Cake (page 430), nothing screams celebration like a slice of any dessert, topped with sweet, fluffy frosting, or simply enjoyed with a big scoop of luscious nondairy ice cream.

Nutty Fruitcake

You might just be able to win over even the biggest fruitcake haters with this one, as it contains no fluorescent green or red unidentifiable gelled fruit bits. Rather, it is chock-full of dried fruits and nuts and then topped with candied fruits and nuts. This is a sophisticated fruitcake, if you can believe it! This recipe makes six mini cakes, which makes it perfect for gift giving.

1 cup (120 g) dried cherries
1 cup (160 g) dried apricots, quartered
1 cup (160 g) raisins
1 cup (120 g) dried cranberries
1 cup (120 g) dried pineapple
1 cup (170 g) dried plums, quartered
4 ounces (112 g) pecan halves, broken into smaller pieces
4 ounces (112 g) walnut haves, broken into smaller pieces
1 cup (235 ml) brandy
Nonstick cooking spray
4 cups (500 g) all-purpose flour
2 teaspoons baking powder
2 teaspoons baking soda
½ teaspoon salt
½ teaspoon ground cardamom
½ teaspoon ground cinnamon
¾ cup (170 g) plain or vanilla nondairy yogurt
1¼ cups (180 ml) pineapple juice
1 cup (200 g) granulated sugar
1 tablespoon (15 ml) pure vanilla extract
1 teaspoon pure almond extract
½ cup (120 ml) plain or vanilla soy or other nondairy milk

For the Candied Fruit and Nut Topping:

2 cups (284 g) reserved fruit and nut mixture
2 tablespoons (28 g) nondairy butter
½ cup (100 g) granulated sugar
1 teaspoon pure vanilla extract

In a large-size mixing bowl, toss together the dried fruits and nuts.

Pour the brandy over the mixture, cover, and let sit overnight.

Reserve 2 cups (284 g) of the mixture and set aside to be used later for the topping.

Preheat the oven to 375°F (190°C, or gas mark 5). Lightly coat 6 mini loaf tins with nonstick spray.

In a large-size mixing bowl, whisk together the flour, baking powder, baking soda, salt, cardamom, and cinnamon.

In a separate bowl, whisk together the yogurt, pineapple juice, sugar, vanilla, almond extract, and milk.

Fold the wet ingredients into the dry, being careful not to overmix.

Fold in the fruit and nut mixture.

Divide the mixture equally among the loaf tins.

Bake for 30 minutes, or until a toothpick inserted into the center comes out clean.

While the cakes are baking, make the topping.

To make the topping: In a saucepan, combine the reserved fruit and nut mixture, butter, sugar, and vanilla.

Heat over medium-high heat until the sugar and butter have completely melted, stirring constantly. Take care not to burn.

Remove from the heat and set aside.

Allow the cakes to cool completely before spooning an equal amount of topping over each.

Yield: 6 mini cakes

Cranboozy Cake

Grab a fork and dig into this lovely, fluffy cake! Replace the cranberries with another favorite berry, if you prefer. Be sure to use foil to cover the cake as soon as the batter is firm enough, because agave browns up more quickly than other sweeteners, and by the look of it will have you think the goods are ready when they aren't quite there just yet.

Nonstick cooking spray
2 cups (240 g) whole wheat pastry flour
2 teaspoons arrowroot powder
1 teaspoon baking powder
½ teaspoon baking soda
½ teaspoon fine sea salt
½ cup (120 ml) plain almond or other nondairy milk
2 tablespoons (30 ml) fresh orange juice
2 tablespoons (30 ml) vodka
2 tablespoons (30 ml) triple sec or other orange-flavored liqueur
2 teaspoons pure vanilla extract
¼ cup (60 ml) canola oil
⅔ cup (224 g) agave nectar
1 cup (95 g) fresh or frozen cranberries

Preheat the oven to 325°F (170°C, or gas mark 3). Lightly coat 4 mini Bundt cake pans or the cups of a standard muffin tin with nonstick cooking spray.

In a large-size bowl, whisk together the flour, arrowroot powder, baking powder, baking soda, and salt.

In a medium-size bowl, whisk together the milk, juice, vodka, triple sec, vanilla, oil, and agave.

Fold the wet ingredients into the dry, being careful not to overmix. Fold in the cranberries.

Divide the batter among the prepared pans.

If you use mini Bundt pans: Bake for 20 minutes, then cover with foil. Bake for another 20 minutes, or until a toothpick inserted into the center comes out clean.

If you use a standard muffin tin: Bake for 15 minutes, then cover with foil. Bake for another 5 to 10 minutes, until a toothpick inserted into the center comes out clean.

Let cool on a wire rack for 30 minutes, then remove from the pans.

Let cool completely before enjoying.

Yield: 4 mini Bundt cakes or 12 cupcakes

Orange Almond Cake with Orange Icing

A moist and tender cake with complex flavorings, this scrumptious dessert will make good use of the delicious citrus fruit. Try it with blood oranges, too!

For the cake:

- Nonstick cooking spray
- 2½ tablespoons (18 g) flax meal
- 3 tablespoons (45 ml) water
- 1⅓ cups (160 g) whole wheat pastry flour
- ½ cup (54 g) finely ground toasted almonds
- ½ cup (96 g) raw sugar
- ½ teaspoon ground cardamom
- ½ teaspoon fine sea salt
- 1 teaspoon baking powder
- ¼ teaspoon baking soda
- ¾ cup (180 ml) fresh orange juice
- ¼ cup (60 ml) canola oil
- 1 teaspoon pure orange extract
- ½ teaspoon pure almond extract

For the icing:

- ½ cup (60 g) powdered sugar
- 1 tablespoon (15 ml) fresh orange juice

To make the cake: Preheat the oven to 350°F (180°C, or gas mark 4). Lightly coat an 8-inch (20-cm) square baking pan with spray.

In a medium-size bowl, whisk together the flax meal and water. Set aside.

In a large-size bowl, whisk together the flour, ground almonds, sugar, cardamom, salt, baking powder, and baking soda.

Whisk the juice, oil, and extracts into the flax mixture.

Fold the wet ingredients into the dry, being careful not to overmix.

Pour the batter into the prepared pan.

Bake for 24 minutes, or until a toothpick inserted into the center comes out clean.

Leave in the pan for at least 30 minutes before removing and transferring to a wire rack. Let cool completely before icing.

To make the icing: Combine the sugar and juice (drop by drop) in a medium-size bowl, stirring vigorously with a large spoon until no lumps are left; the icing shouldn't be too thin, so just add the amount of liquid necessary for it to spread easily.

Apply on top of the cake, using an icing spatula.

Yield: 6 servings

Triple Vanilla Cake

A truly vanilla experience. For extra vanilla deliciousness, frost with a double batch of the Cream Cheese Frosting used on the Pumpkin Cupcakes (page 436), adding 1 tablespoon (8 g) of vanilla powder to the mix.

Nonstick cooking spray
3 cups (375 g) all-purpose flour
1 teaspoon baking soda
1 teaspoon baking powder
1 teaspoon vanilla powder
¼ teaspoon salt
¾ cup (170 g) vanilla nondairy yogurt
1 cup (200 g) granulated sugar
¼ cup (60 ml) canola oil
2 tablespoons (30 ml) pure vanilla extract
Scrapings from 1 vanilla bean
2 recipes Cream Cheese Frosting (page 436), optional

Preheat the oven to 350°F (180°C, or gas mark 4). Lightly coat a 9-inch (23-cm) cake pan with nonstick spray.

In a large-size mixing bowl, mix together the flour, baking soda, baking powder, vanilla powder, and salt.

In a separate bowl, mix together the yogurt, sugar, oil, vanilla, and vanilla bean scrapings.

Fold the wet ingredients into the dry, being careful not to overmix.

Pour evenly into the cake pan.

Bake for 25 to 30 minutes, or until a toothpick inserted into the center comes out clean.

Let cool completely before frosting, if desired.

Yield: One 9-inch (23-cm) cake

Yellow Cake

Did you ever wonder what makes yellow cake different from vanilla cake? Butter's the culprit. Not only does it give it that yellow color, but it also adds a touch of buttery richness that makes yellow cake one of the most demanded cakes in town. For a classic combination, frost this cake with Chocolate Agave Frosting (page 447).

Nonstick cooking spray
3 cups (375 g) all-purpose flour
1 teaspoon baking soda
1 teaspoon baking powder
¼ teaspoon salt
½ cup (112 g) nondairy butter, softened
1 cup (200 g) granulated sugar
1 tablespoon (15 ml) pure vanilla extract
¾ cup (170 g) nondairy yogurt
1 recipe Chocolate Agave Frosting (page 447)

Preheat the oven to 350°F (180°C, or gas mark 4). Lightly coat a 9-inch (23-cm) cake pan with nonstick spray.

In a medium-size bowl, combine the flour, baking soda, baking powder, and salt.

In a large-size bowl and using an electric mixer, cream together the butter and sugar.

Add the vanilla and yogurt and beat until creamy.

Slowly add the flour mixture, and beat on low speed to combine.

Pour evenly into the cake pan.

Bake for 25 to 30 minutes, or until a toothpick inserted into the center comes out clean.

Let cool completely before frosting.

Yield: One 9-inch (23-cm) cake

Carrot Cake with Orange Frosting

Get your dose of veggies in cake form! Every bit counts, right? That's our story, and we're sticking to it.

For the cake:

- Nonstick cooking spray
- ⅔ cup (160 ml) plain soy or other nondairy milk
- ¼ cup (60 ml) canola oil
- ⅔ cup (162 g) unsweetened applesauce
- 1 cup (192 g) Sucanat
- 2 teaspoons pure vanilla extract
- 2 teaspoons ground cinnamon
- ¼ teaspoon fine sea salt
- 2 cups (240 g) whole wheat pastry flour
- 2 teaspoons baking powder
- 2 cups (200 g) grated carrots (not packed)

For the frosting:

- ¼ cup (48 g) nondairy vegetable shortening (or more nondairy butter; although less stable than shortening, it works well too, as long as the cake is stored in the fridge)
- ¼ cup (56 g) nondairy butter
- 2 cups (240 g) powdered sugar
- 1 to 3 tablespoon(s) (15 to 45 ml) fresh orange juice
- 2 teaspoons grated orange zest

To make the cake: Preheat the oven to 350°F (180°C, or gas mark 4). Lightly coat two 8-inch (20-cm) round (or square) cake pans with nonstick spray.

In a medium-size bowl, whisk together the milk, oil, applesauce, Sucanat, vanilla, cinnamon, and salt until combined.

In a large-size bowl, combine the flour and baking powder.

Fold the wet ingredients into the dry, being careful not to overmix. Fold in the carrots.

Divide the batter equally between the prepared pans.

Bake for 25 minutes, or until a toothpick inserted into the center comes out clean.

Let cool for a few minutes before transferring the cakes directly onto a wire rack. Let cool completely before frosting.

To make the frosting: In a medium bowl and using an electric mixer, cream together the shortening and butter. Sift the sugar on top, and beat until combined. Add the juice, a little at a time, and beat until the frosting is fluffy, about 2 minutes. Stir in the zest.

Apply a layer of frosting on one cake, then top with the second cake. Spread the rest of the frosting on top of the now layered cake. Store in the fridge.

Yield: One 8-inch (20-cm) double-layer cake

Lemony French Cake with Simple Lemon Icing

This fruity dessert, which is strongly reminiscent of pound cake, tastes even better if you let it sit overnight. Note that the lemon icing makes for a very thin layer, so double it if you have a sweet tooth.

For the cake:

Nonstick cooking spray
1 cup (240 g) plain or vanilla soy or other nondairy yogurt
½ cup (120 ml) canola oil
1 teaspoon pure vanilla extract
2 teaspoons pure lemon extract
1 teaspoon lemon zest
1½ cups (188 g) all-purpose flour
1 cup (120 g) powdered sugar
2 teaspoons baking powder

For the icing:

¾ cup (90 g) powdered sugar
1 to 2 tablespoons (15 to 30 ml) fresh lemon juice

To make the cake: Preheat the oven to 350°F (180°C, or gas mark 4). Lightly coat an 8-inch (20-cm) round cake pan with nonstick cooking spray.

In a large-size bowl, whisk together the yogurt, oil, extracts, and zest.

Sift the flour, sugar, and baking powder on top. Stir to combine, being careful not to overmix.

Pour the batter into the prepared pan.

Bake for 35 to 40 minutes, or until a toothpick inserted into the center comes out clean.

Leave in the pan for 1 hour on a cooling rack before attempting to remove, and let cool completely before icing.

To make the icing: Sift the sugar into a medium-size bowl. Add the juice, a little at a time, and stir until extremely well blended to remove lumps. The icing needs to be thick enough to stick to the back of the spoon, but still be easily spread. Apply on top of the cake with a spatula.

Chill before serving.

Yield: One 8-inch (20-cm) cake

VARIATION

If you want to layer it, simply double the recipe and bake it in two separate pans. Double the Cream Cheese Frosting recipe that is used for the Pumpkin Cupcakes (page 436), replacing the vanilla extract with half the amount of pure lemon extract, or simply add 2 teaspoons lemon zest instead. Apply a layer of frosting on one cake, then top with second cake. Use the rest of the frosting to decorate the top and sides of the now layered cake.

Strawberry Bundt Cake

Rather than a pink artificially colored and flavored excuse for a strawberry cake mix in a box, why not take advantage of what nature intended and bake this dense and luscious cake? Serve simply, dusted with powdered sugar and loaded with a pile of fresh berries.

For the strawberries:

- 12 ounces (340 g) sliced fresh strawberries
- ½ cup (100) granulated sugar
- 1 tablespoon (15 ml) lemon juice

Nonstick cooking spray

For the cake:

- 4 cups (500 g) all-purpose flour
- 2 teaspoons baking soda
- 2 teaspoons baking powder
- ½ teaspoon salt
- ½ teaspoon cardamom
- 1½ cups (355 ml) soymilk (use soy here, or your milk might not curdle)
- 1 tablespoon (15 ml) lemon juice
- 1 tablespoon (15 ml) pure vanilla extract
- ½ cup (112 g) applesauce

To prepare the strawberries: Add the strawberries, sugar, and lemon juice to a saucepan and heat over medium-low heat. Cook, uncovered, for 20 minutes, stirring often.

Remove from the heat and set aside to cool.

Preheat the oven to 350°F (180°C, or gas mark 4). Lightly coat a Bundt pan with cooking spray.

To make the cake: In a large-size mixing bowl, whisk together the flour, baking soda, baking powder, salt, and cardamom.

In a separate bowl, combine the soymilk and lemon juice; it will curdle and become like buttermilk.

Add the buttermilk mixture, vanilla, and applesauce to the strawberry mixture and stir to combine.

Fold the wet ingredients into the dry, being careful not to overmix.

Pour into the Bundt pan and tap gently to remove air bubbles.

Bake for 40 to 45 minutes, or until golden and a toothpick inserted near the center comes out clean.

Let cool completely before inverting onto a serving platter.

Yield: 12 servings

Chocolate Cake (with Sacher Torte Variation)

After spending some time trying to replicate a nonvegan childhood favorite, Celine finally found a way to have her sacher torte and eat it, too. The base recipe is for a plain 8-inch (20-cm) chocolate cake, although there's nothing "plain" about it, but you will find a note at the end of this recipe on how to make Celine's mom's version of the signature Austrian dessert out of it.

Nonstick cooking spray
1 cup (240 g) vanilla soy or other nondairy yogurt
½ cup (120 ml) canola oil
2 teaspoons pure vanilla extract
1 teaspoon pure chocolate extract (optional)
1¼ cups (155 g) all-purpose flour
1 cup (120 g) powdered sugar
¼ cup (20 g) unsweetened cocoa powder
2 teaspoons baking powder
¼ teaspoon fine sea salt

Preheat the oven to 350°F (180°C, or gas mark 4). Lightly coat an 8-inch (20-cm) round cake pan with nonstick cooking spray.

In a large-size bowl, whisk together the yogurt, oil, vanilla, and chocolate extract, if using.

Sift the flour, sugar, cocoa powder, baking powder, and salt on top. Stir to combine, being careful not to overmix.

Pour the batter into the prepared pan.

Bake for 35 to 40 minutes, or until a toothpick inserted into the center comes out clean.

Leave in the pan for 1 hour on a cooling rack before attempting to remove. Chill overnight.

Yield: One 8-inch (20-cm) cake

VARIATION

Double the recipe, and bake in two separate 8-inch (20-cm) round cake pans.

Spread ¼ to ½ cup (80 to 160 g) all-fruit raspberry jam on one of the cakes, then top with the second cake.

Double the Chocolate Ganache (page 74) or use a single recipe of Chocolate Agave Frosting (page 447) to spread on the top and sides. Cool for several hours before serving. (This cake tastes even better if you make it the day before.)

German Chocolate Cake

The funny thing about German chocolate cake is that it's not really German at all. Rather, it is named after Sam German, the developer of a sweet chocolate bar for Baker's Chocolates way back in the day. Reserve this cake for really special occasions, as it is huge! Or, simply halve both the cake and the topping recipes and have a single layer cake.

For the cake:

Nonstick cooking spray
4 cups (500 g) all-purpose flour
1 cup (80 g) unsweetened cocoa powder
1 tablespoon (12 g) baking soda
1 tablespoon (12 g) baking powder
1 teaspoon salt
2 cups (470 ml) soy or other nondairy milk
¾ cup (170 g) nondairy yogurt
½ cup (112 g) applesauce
¼ cup (60 ml) canola oil
1 tablespoon (15 ml) pure vanilla extract

For the filling and topping:

½ cup (112 g) nondairy butter
1 cup (220 g) firmly packed brown sugar
1 cup (235 ml) soy or other nondairy milk
12 ounces (340 g) flaked coconut
6 ounces (170 g) pecans, chopped

To make the cake: Preheat the oven to 350°F (180°C, or gas mark 4). Lightly coat two 9-inch (23-cm) cake pans with cooking spray.

In a large-size mixing bowl, mix together the flour, cocoa, baking soda, baking powder, and salt.

In a medium-size bowl, mix together the milk, yogurt, applesauce, oil, and vanilla.

Fold the wet ingredients into the dry, being careful not to overmix.

Add equal amounts of batter to each of the cake pans.

Bake for 35 to 45 minutes, or until a toothpick inserted into the center comes out clean. Let cool completely.

To make the filling and topping: Add the butter, sugar, and milk to a saucepan. Bring to a boil and boil for 3 minutes to ensure the sugar is fully dissolved.

Remove from the heat and stir in the coconut and pecans.

After the cakes have completely cooled, level one cake by cutting off the dome. Place the leveled cake on a serving plate or cake stand and place a ½-inch-thick (1.3-cm) layer of filling on top. Place the other cake, flat side down, on top of the filling.

From here, you have two choices: you can continue as is, and pile the remaining topping on top of the second layer, purposefully allowing some to drip down over the edges. Or, you can frost the cake using a double batch of Chocolate Agave Frosting (page 447), and then spread with the remaining topping.

Yield: One 9-inch (23-cm) double-layer cake

Pecan Date Cake

If pecans are not your favorite nuts, or dates your favorite dried fruit, feel free to switch them for something closer to your liking, such as walnuts and raisins. Whip up a quick icing, following the instructions in Lemony French Cake with Simple Lemon Icing (page 426), replacing the lemon juice with rum, and adding a few drops of vanilla extract to it. Although this cake is delicious on its own, it is also deserving of the extra attention!

Nonstick cooking spray
1 cup (235 ml) boiling water
1 cup (178 g) chopped dates
1 teaspoon baking soda
2½ tablespoons (35 g) nondairy butter
½ cup (96 g) Sucanat
¼ cup (61 g) unsweetened applesauce
1½ cups (180 g) whole wheat pastry flour
2 teaspoons baking powder
¼ teaspoon fine sea salt
1 teaspoon ground cinnamon
½ cup (55 g) chopped pecans

Preheat the oven to 350°F (180°C, or gas mark 4). Lightly coat a 9-inch (23-cm) round pie plate with spray.

Pour the water over the dates in a medium-size bowl. Stir in the baking soda, and let sit for 10 minutes, or until cooled.

In a large-size bowl and using an electric mixer, cream together the butter and Sucanat.

Stir in the applesauce and the water and dates mixture.

Sift the flour, baking powder, salt, and cinnamon on top of the butter mixture.

Fold the dry ingredients into the wet, being careful not to overmix. Fold in the pecans.

Pour into the prepared pie plate.

Bake for 45 minutes, or until a toothpick inserted into the center comes out clean.

Let cool on a wire rack.

Yield: One 9-inch (23-cm) cake

Blueberry Cocoa Mini Bundt Cakes

There's just something about mini desserts that makes it utterly pointless to try and resist their siren's call. And when these desserts are baked in Bundt pans? That means the stakes are even higher in finding someone strong enough to refuse a bite of the tasty outcome.

Nonstick cooking spray
½ cup (112 g) nondairy butter
1 cup (192 g) raw sugar
1 tablespoon (3 g) instant espresso powder
2 tablespoons (30 ml) warm water
1½ cups (360 g) vanilla soy or other nondairy yogurt
2 teaspoons pure vanilla extract
1 cup (75 g) finely ground hazelnuts
½ cup (40 g) unsweetened cocoa powder
2 cups (240 g) whole wheat pastry flour
½ teaspoon fine sea salt
2 teaspoons baking powder
1 teaspoon baking soda
1 cup (145 g) fresh or frozen blueberries

Preheat the oven to 350°F (180°C, or gas mark 4). Lightly coat 6 mini Bundt pans with spray.

In a large-size bowl and using an electric mixer, cream together the butter and sugar.

In a small-size bowl, dissolve the espresso powder in the warm water.

Add the yogurt, vanilla, ground hazelnuts, and espresso mixture to the butter mixture and stir to combine.

Sift the cocoa, flour, salt, baking powder, and baking soda on top of the butter mixture. Fold the dry ingredients into the wet, being careful not to overmix. Fold in the blueberries.

Divide the batter equally among the prepared mini Bundt pans.

Bake for 35 to 40 minutes, or until a toothpick inserted near the center comes out clean.

Let cool on a wire rack.

Yield: 6 mini Bundt cakes

Gluten-Free Spicy Brownie Cake

Stuck between fudge and cake, these spicy gluten-free brownies will please even those of us who need not keep gluten at bay.

2 teaspoons ground cinnamon
½ teaspoon ground cloves
½ teaspoon ground nutmeg
¼ teaspoon ground white pepper
¼ teaspoon ground cardamom
¼ teaspoon ground ginger
Nonstick cooking spray
4 ounces (112 g) nondairy unsweetened or bittersweet chocolate, coarsely chopped
¼ cup (56 g) nondairy butter
1 cup (227 g) unsweetened applesauce
½ teaspoon fine sea salt
¾ cup (144 g) Sucanat
1 cup (160 g) brown rice flour
1 teaspoon baking powder

Combine the cinnamon, cloves, nutmeg, pepper, cardamom, and ginger in a small-size bowl. Set aside.

Preheat the oven to 350°F (180°C, or gas mark 4). Lightly coat an 8-inch (20-cm) square baking pan with spray.

In the microwave, melt the chocolate and butter a microwave-safe dish for about 1 minute, checking and stirring at least once.

In a large-size bowl, combine the melted chocolate and butter with the spice mixture, applesauce, salt, and Sucanat.

Fold the flour and baking powder into the wet ingredients, being careful not to overmix.

Pour the batter into the prepared pan and level with a spatula.

Bake for 22 minutes, or until the edges of the brownies begin to pull away from the pan and the center appears set.

Let cool in the pan on a wire rack. Chill for several hours in the fridge before slicing.

Enjoy cold. Store in the fridge.

Yield: 6 servings

Pumpkin Chocolate Brownie Cake

Autumnal dessert par excellence, this cloudlike cake deserves a try. We're ready to bet you won't be disappointed.

Nonstick cooking spray
1 teaspoon apple cider vinegar
¼ cup (60 ml) plain soymilk (use soy here, or your milk might not curdle)
½ cup (60 g) whole wheat pastry flour
½ cup (63 g) all-purpose flour
1 teaspoon baking powder
½ teaspoon baking soda
⅓ cup (67 g) granulated sugar
⅓ cup (73 g) firmly packed light brown sugar
2 tablespoons (10 g) unsweetened cocoa powder
1 teaspoon ground cinnamon
½ teaspoon ground ginger
½ teaspoon ground nutmeg
½ teaspoon fine sea salt
½ cup (122 g) pumpkin purée
¼ cup (61 g) unsweetened applesauce
3 tablespoons (45 ml) canola oil
2 teaspoons pure vanilla extract
⅓ cup (58 g) nondairy semisweet chocolate chips

Preheat the oven to 350°F (180°C, or gas mark 4). Lightly coat an 8-inch (20-cm) square baking pan with spray.

Combine the vinegar and soymilk in a medium-size bowl; it will curdle and become like buttermilk.

In a large-size bowl, sift together the flours, baking powder, baking soda, sugars, cocoa, cinnamon, ginger, nutmeg, and salt.

Whisk the pumpkin purée, applesauce, oil, and vanilla into the buttermilk mixture until combined.

Fold the wet ingredients into the dry, being careful not to overmix. Fold in the chocolate chips.

Pour the batter into the prepared pan.

Bake for 23 minutes, or until a toothpick inserted into the center comes out clean.

Let cool in the pan on a wire rack for at least 30 minutes.

Enjoy at room temperature or cold.

Yield: 6 servings

Caramel Chocolate Coconut Cake

Are you ready for a sweet tooth overload? This one has it all: a light chocolate cake topped with ooey-gooey caramel, coconut, chocolate, and pecans! Trust us when we say that you'll only need one piece.

For the cake:

2 cups (250 g) all-purpose flour
½ cup (40 g) cocoa powder
½ teaspoon baking powder
½ teaspoon baking soda
¼ teaspoon salt
¾ cup (170 g) plain or vanilla nondairy yogurt
½ cup (120 ml) soy or other nondairy milk
½ cup (100 g) granulated sugar
1 teaspoon pure vanilla extract

For the additional layers:

2½ cups (300 g) sweetened flaked coconut, divided
¾ cup (175 ml) Caramel Sauce (page 492), divided
½ cup (54 g) chopped pecans
1 cup (175 g) nondairy semisweet chocolate chips

Preheat the oven to 375°F (190°C, or gas mark 5). Have ready an 8-inch (20-cm) square baking dish.

To make the cake: In a large-size mixing bowl, whisk together the flour, cocoa, baking powder, baking soda, and salt.

In a medium-size bowl, mix together the yogurt, milk, sugar, and vanilla.

Pour the wet ingredients into the dry and stir to combine. Spread evenly in the baking dish.

To make the additional layers: Mix together 2 cups (240 g) of the coconut flakes with ½ cup (120 ml) of the caramel sauce. Spread evenly over the cake batter.

Sprinkle the pecan pieces all over the coconut mixture.

Sprinkle the chocolate chips all over the pecans.

Sprinkle the remaining ½ cup (60 g) coconut flakes over the chocolate chips.

Finally, drizzle the remaining ¼ cup (60 ml) caramel sauce over the coconut.

Bake for 30 minutes, until the coconut is golden brown and the chocolate chips are melted.

Let cool before serving.

Yield: 6 servings

Sweet Corn Cake

This traditional Mexican dessert is not like any "cake" you've ever had before. You serve it in scoops! You can wait until the end of dinner, but it is traditionally served right on the plate alongside the rest of the meal.

Nonstick cooking spray
10 ounces (284 g) frozen yellow corn kernels
¼ cup (56 g) nondairy butter
2 tablespoons (24 g) vegetable shortening
½ cup (60 g) masa harina flour (Maseca brand instant masa flour works well here)
3 tablespoons (45 ml) water
3 tablespoons (26 g) yellow cornmeal
¼ cup (50 g) granulated sugar
2 tablespoons (30 ml) soy creamer or nondairy milk
¼ teaspoon baking powder
¼ teaspoon salt

Preheat the oven to 350°F (180°C, or gas mark 4). Lightly coat an 8-inch (20-cm) square baking dish with cooking spray.

Using a blender or food processor, chop the corn kernels into small bits. Set aside.

In a large-size bowl and using an electric mixer, beat together the butter and shortening.

Slowly add the masa flour, then slowly drizzle in the water.

Next, add the cornmeal, sugar, creamer, baking soda, and salt, mixing thoroughly after each addition.

Finally, add the corn and mix together on the lowest speed setting. Your mixture should be thick, sticky, and lumpy from the corn.

Spread the mixture evenly in the prepared dish.

Cover with aluminum foil and bake for 45 to 50 minutes, or until firm but still moist.

Remove from the oven, uncover, and let stand for about 15 minutes before using an ice cream scoop to serve.

Yield: 6 servings

Pumpkin Cupcakes with Cream Cheese Frosting

What would autumn be without pumpkin desserts? Boring, that's what. Have fun decorating these tempting cupcakes, then go play in the leaves and treat yourself to a couple of them upon your return to the coziness of your home.

For the cupcakes:

- 1 teaspoon apple cider vinegar
- ¼ cup (60 ml) plain soymilk (use soy here, or your milk might not curdle)
- ½ cup plus 2 tablespoons (79 g) all-purpose flour
- ½ cup (60 g) whole wheat pastry flour
- 1 teaspoon baking powder
- ½ teaspoon baking soda
- ⅓ cup (67 g) granulated sugar
- ⅓ cup (73 g) firmly packed light brown sugar
- 1 teaspoon ground cinnamon
- ½ teaspoon ground ginger
- ½ teaspoon ground nutmeg
- ¼ teaspoon fine sea salt
- ½ cup (122 g) pumpkin purée
- ¼ cup (61 g) unsweetened applesauce
- 3 tablespoons (45 ml) canola oil
- 2 teaspoons pure vanilla extract

For the Cream Cheese Frosting:

- 2 tablespoons (28 g) nondairy butter
- ½ cup (112 g) nondairy cream cheese
- 1 teaspoon pure vanilla extract
- 2 cups (240 g) powdered sugar, sifted

To make the cupcakes: Preheat the oven to 350°F (180°C, or gas mark 4). Line a standard muffin tin with paper liners.

Combine the vinegar and soymilk in a medium-size bowl; it will curdle and become like buttermilk.

In a large-size bowl, sift together the flours, baking powder, baking soda, sugars, cinnamon, ginger, nutmeg, and salt.

Whisk the pumpkin purée, applesauce, oil, and vanilla into the buttermilk mixture until combined.

Fold the wet ingredients into the dry, being careful not to overmix.

Divide the batter equally among the prepared cupcake liners.

Bake for 18 to 20 minutes, or until a toothpick inserted into the center comes out clean.

Remove from the muffin tin and let cool on a wire rack.

To make the frosting: Cream together the butter, cream cheese, and vanilla with an electric mixer for 2 to 3 minutes, or until fluffy.

Add the powdered sugar ¼ cup (30 g) at a time, beating until fluffy and completely smooth.

Frost the cupcakes once they are completely cool.

Yield: 12 cupcakes

Vanilla Cupcakes

This recipe yields 16 cupcakes if you don't mind a slight muffin top, or 18 if you'd prefer the cupcakes to barely reach the top of the liner, once they're baked. Top them with Chocolate Ganache (page 74) or Chocolate Agave Frosting (page 447), if you please. You're in for a vanill-icious treat!

2 cups (480 g) vanilla soy or other nondairy yogurt
1 cup (235 ml) canola oil
2 tablespoons (30 ml) vanilla extract
3 cups (375 g) all-purpose flour
2 cups (240 g) powdered sugar
4 teaspoons baking powder

Preheat the oven to 350°F (180°C, or gas mark 4). Line 16 or 18 standard muffin cups with paper liners.

In a large-size bowl, combine the yogurt, oil, and vanilla.

Sift the flour, sugar, and baking powder on top.

Fold the dry ingredients into the wet, being careful not to overmix.

Divide the batter equally among the prepared cupcake liners.

Bake for 18 to 20 minutes, or until a toothpick inserted into the center comes out clean.

Remove from the muffin tin and let cool completely before decorating.

Yield: 16 to 18 cupcakes

Cream-Stuffed Cookie Cupcakes

Not quite as unhealthy as some of the other cupcake recipes you might have come across before, these cupcakes still manage to be delicious and satisfying.

Be sure to check the cream-stuffed cookies for ingredients, because they are not always animal-friendly.

3½ ounces (100 g) soft tofu, drained
2 tablespoons (28 g) nondairy butter, softened
¾ cup (180 ml) plain soy or other nondairy milk
½ cup (96 g) raw sugar
1 teaspoon pure vanilla extract
22 cream-stuffed cookies, such as Oreo, blended into fine crumbs, plus 12 whole cookies for decoration
½ cup (60 g) whole wheat pastry flour
2 tablespoons (10 g) unsweetened cocoa powder
¼ teaspoon fine sea salt
2 teaspoons baking powder

Preheat the oven to 350°F (180°C, or gas mark 4). Line a standard muffin tin with 12 paper liners.

Blend the tofu, butter, milk, sugar, and vanilla until perfectly smooth, using an immersion blender or in a regular blender.

In a large-size bowl, whisk together the cookie crumbs, flour, cocoa, salt, and baking powder.

Fold the wet ingredients into the dry, being careful not to overmix.

Divide the batter equally among the prepared cupcake liners. Place a whole cookie flat on top of each cupcake.

Bake for 16 to 18 minutes, or until a toothpick inserted into the center comes out clean.

Let cool on a wire rack before serving.

Yield: 12 cupcakes

VARIATION

Instead of, or in combination with, the cookie decoration, use Chocolate Agave Frosting (page 447), without the orange zest option.

Lemon Lime Cupcakes

Lemon and lime go together like peanut butter and jelly! These fluffy citrusy cuppers are wonderful sprinkled with the lemon sugar mix from the Cool Lemon Cookies (page 371). If you'd like to take them to the next level, top them with a swooping mound of Sour Cream Frosting (page 446) flavored with 1 tablespoon (15 ml) lemon extract, and then sprinkle the tops with lime zest.

2 cups (250 g) all-purpose flour
2 tablespoons (16 g) cornstarch
1 teaspoon baking powder
1 teaspoon baking soda
¼ teaspoon salt
1 cup (235 ml) soymilk (use soy here, or your milk might not curdle)
3 tablespoons (45 ml) lemon juice
3 tablespoons (45 ml) lime juice
1 cup (200 g) granulated sugar
1 tablespoon (15 ml) pure lemon extract
2 teaspoons pure vanilla extract

Preheat the oven to 350°F (180°C, or gas mark 4). Line a standard muffin tin with paper liners.

In a large-size mixing bowl, whisk together the flour, cornstarch, baking powder, baking soda, and salt.

In a medium-size bowl, combine the milk, lemon juice, and lime juice; it will curdle and become like buttermilk.

Add the sugar, lemon extract, and vanilla and stir to combine.

Fold the wet ingredients into the dry, being careful not to overmix.

Divide the batter equally among the prepared cupcake liners.

Bake for 20 to 23 minutes, or until a toothpick inserted into the center comes out clean.

Let cool on a wire rack.

Yield: 12 cupcakes

Chocolate Cherry Cupcakes

These cupcakes do fine on their own without any topping whatsoever. BUT, if you are one of those folks who just can't imagine a naked cupcake, try smothering these in Chocolate Agave Frosting (page 447).

2 cups (250 g) all-purpose flour
½ cup (40 g) unsweetened cocoa powder
1 teaspoon baking soda
1 teaspoon baking powder
¼ teaspoon salt
1 cup (235 ml) soy or other nondairy milk
¾ cup (170 g) nondairy yogurt
1 cup (200 g) granulated sugar
¼ cup (60 ml) canola oil
1 tablespoon (15 ml) pure vanilla extract
1 cup (176 g) nondairy semisweet chocolate chips
1 cup (160 g) dried cherries

Preheat the oven to 350°F (180°C, or gas mark 4). Line 18 standard muffin cups with paper liners.

In a large-size mixing bowl, whisk together the flour, cocoa, baking soda, baking powder, and salt.

In a separate bowl, combine the milk, yogurt, sugar, oil, and vanilla.

Fold the wet ingredients into the dry, being careful not to overmix. Fold in the chocolate chips and cherries.

Divide the batter equally among the prepared cupcake liners.

Bake for 20 to 23 minutes, or until a toothpick inserted into the center comes out clean.

Let cool on a wire rack.

Yield: 18 cupcakes

Smoky Chipotle Chocolate Cupcakes

Chipotle cupcakes? Yep. The smoky heat of chipotle, paired with cinnamon and chocolate, will keep the lucky receivers of these delicious cupcakes wondering, "Why does this taste so good?" Top these with a simple sprinkling of cinnamon and powdered sugar, or go all out and top with Chocolate Ganache (page 74) and a sliver of Mexican chocolate.

1½ cups (188 g) all-purpose flour
½ cup (40 g) unsweetened cocoa powder
1 tablespoon (6 g) ground chipotle powder
1 teaspoon baking soda
1 teaspoon baking powder
1 teaspoon ground cinnamon
¼ teaspoon salt
¾ cup (170 g) nondairy yogurt
¾ cup (150 g) granulated sugar
½ cup (120 ml) soy or other nondairy milk
1 tablespoon (15 ml) pure vanilla extract

Preheat the oven to 350°F (180°C, or gas mark 4). Line a standard muffin tin with paper liners.

In a large-size mixing bowl, whisk together the flour, cocoa, chipotle powder, baking soda, baking powder, cinnamon, and salt.

In a separate bowl, combine the yogurt, sugar, milk, and vanilla.

Fold the wet ingredients into the dry, being careful not to overmix.

Divide the batter equally among the prepared cupcake liners.

Bake for 22 to 25 minutes, or until a toothpick inserted into the center comes out clean.

Let cool on a wire rack.

Yield: 12 cupcakes

Apple Pie Cupcakes

Top this classically flavored cupcake with a dollop of Sour Cream Frosting (page 446) and a drizzle of Caramel Sauce (page 492) for an à la mode effect.

6 ounces (170 g) peeled apple, chopped into small chunks
½ cup (110 g) firmly packed brown sugar
2 tablespoons (28 g) nondairy butter
1 teaspoon ground cinnamon
¼ teaspoon ground cloves
¼ teaspoon ground nutmeg
1 tablespoon (15 ml) lemon juice
1½ cups (188 g) all-purpose flour
1 teaspoon baking soda
1 teaspoon baking powder
¼ teaspoon salt
1 cup (235 ml) soy or other nondairy milk
2 teaspoons pure vanilla extract
½ cup (100 g) granulated sugar
½ cup (55 g) chopped pecans

Add the apples, brown sugar, butter, cinnamon, cloves, nutmeg, and lemon juice to a saucepan and heat over medium-low heat for 10 minutes, stirring often. Remove from the heat and let cool.

Preheat the oven to 350°F (180°C, or gas mark 4). Line a standard muffin tin with paper liners.

In a large-size mixing bowl, whisk together the flour, baking soda, baking powder, and salt.

Add the milk, vanilla, sugar, and pecans to the apple mixture.

Fold the wet ingredients into the dry, being careful not to overmix.

Divide the batter equally among the prepared cupcake liners.

Bake for 20 to 23 minutes, or until a toothpick inserted into the center comes out clean.

Let cool on a wire rack.

Yield: 12 cupcakes

50/50 Bar Cupcakes

Do you remember the days of drive-through dairies? When your mom would buy the box of 50/50 bars that came in a plain brown box? These cupcakes are a throwback to those carefree childhood days.

2 cups (250 g) all-purpose flour
2 tablespoons (16 g) cornstarch
1 teaspoon baking powder
1 teaspoon baking soda
¼ teaspoon salt
1 tablespoon (15 ml) apple cider vinegar
1 cup (235 ml) soymilk (use soy here, or your milk might not curdle)
5 tablespoons (75 ml) orange juice
1 cup (200 g) granulated sugar
1 tablespoon (15 ml) pure orange extract
2 teaspoons pure vanilla extract
1 recipe Cream Cheese Frosting (page 436), adding 1 tablespoon (15 ml) orange extract to the mixture

Preheat the oven to 350°F (180°C, or gas mark 4). Line a standard muffin tin with paper liners.

In a large-size mixing bowl, whisk together the flour, cornstarch, baking powder, baking soda, and salt.

In a separate bowl, combine the vinegar and soymilk; it will curdle and become like buttermilk.

Add the orange juice, sugar, orange extract, and vanilla to the buttermilk and stir to combine.

Fold the wet ingredients into the dry, being careful not to overmix.

Divide the batter equally among the prepared cupcake liners.

Bake for 20 to 23 minutes, or until a toothpick inserted into the center comes out clean.

Let cool on a wire rack completely before frosting.

Yield: 12 cupcakes

Peach Melba Cupcakes

These cupcakes taste even more like a true Melba when frosted with a nice thick layer of Sour Cream Frosting (page 446) prior to drizzling on the topping. The peach and raspberry purée makes them a very unique purplish color, so don't be alarmed when your batter turns gray.

8 ounces (227 g) sliced peaches
4 ounces (112 g) raspberries
1 cup (200 g) granulated sugar
¼ cup (60 ml) water
1 teaspoon pure vanilla extract
¼ cup (60 ml) canola or other vegetable oil
½ teaspoon pure lemon extract
½ cup (120 ml) soy or other nondairy milk
2 cups (250 g) all-purpose flour
2 tablespoons (16 g) cornstarch
1 teaspoon baking soda
1 teaspoon baking powder
¼ teaspoon salt
⅛ teaspoon ground black pepper

Preheat the oven to 350°F (180°C, or gas mark 4). Line a standard muffin tin with paper liners.

In a saucepan, combine the peaches, raspberries, sugar, and water. Heat over medium heat and simmer for 15 minutes, stirring occasionally. Remove from the heat and set aside to cool. Stir in the vanilla.

Purée using an immersion or a countertop blender until mostly smooth, but still a little chunky. Reserve 1 cup (225 g) of purée for topping later.

Add the oil, lemon extract, and milk to the purée and stir to combine.

In a large-size bowl, whisk together the flour, cornstarch, baking soda, baking powder, salt, and pepper.

Fold the wet ingredients into the dry, being careful not to overmix.

Divide the batter equally among the prepared cupcake liners.

Bake for 16 to 18 minutes, or until a toothpick inserted into the center comes out clean.

Let cool for 5 minutes before transferring to a wire rack to cool completely.

Once cooled, spoon an equal portion of the reserved peach and raspberry purée onto each cupcake.

Yield: 12 cupcakes

Angel Food Strawberry Shortcake Cupcakes

Vegan angel food cake? Pretty darn close! Sorry guys, but Ener-G is the only egg replacer that will work in this recipe. Anything else will result in a denser, soggy cupcake that is not nearly as white and fluffy as these.

1 cup (125 g) all-purpose flour, sifted twice
1½ cups (180 g) powdered sugar, sifted, divided
¼ cup plus 2 tablespoons (48 g) Ener-G egg replacer
1½ cups (355 ml) water
1 tablespoon (15 ml) pure vanilla extract
1½ teaspoons cream of tartar
½ teaspoon salt
1 recipe Strawberry Glaze (page 400), divided
1 pound (455 g) fresh strawberries, hulled and quartered
1 recipe Sour Cream Frosting (page 446)

Preheat the oven to 375°F (190°C, or gas mark 5). Line a standard muffin tin with cupcake liners.

In a medium-size mixing bowl, sift together the flour and ¾ cup (90 g) of the powdered sugar.

In a separate large-size mixing bowl, whisk together the egg replacer, water, vanilla, cream of tartar, and salt. Sift in the remaining ¾ cup (90 g) powdered sugar and whisk to combine.

Fold the dry ingredients into the wet, being careful not to overmix.

Divide the batter equally among the prepared cupcake liners.

Bake for 22 to 24 minutes, or until a toothpick inserted into the center comes out clean. These should not brown; if they are beginning to brown, they are overdone.

Let cool for about 5 minutes before transferring to a wire rack to cool completely.

Using your finger, poke a hole in the center of each cupcake and fill with about 1 tablespoon (15 ml) glaze.

Combine the remaining glaze with the strawberries.

Frost the cupcakes with a nice thick layer of frosting.

Top generously with the glazed strawberries just before serving.

Yield: 12 cupcakes

Sour Cream Frosting

This great all-purpose frosting lends itself to the addition of many flavors. Change it up with different flavored extracts to suit your fancy, though the classic vanilla is quite tasty as is. As written, this recipe makes a smooth, spreadable frosting. If you plan on using this to pipe, add more powdered sugar to reach the desired consistency.

¾ cup (170 g) nondairy sour cream, store-bought or homemade (page 302)
½ cup (112 g) nondairy butter
1 tablespoon (15 ml) pure vanilla extract
1 pound (455 g) powdered sugar

In a large bowl and using an electric mixer, beat together the sour cream, butter, and vanilla until creamy.

Beat in the powdered sugar, a little bit at a time, until smooth and silky.

Keep refrigerated until ready to use.

Yield: 2½ cups (700 g)

Gluten Free

Chocolate Agave Frosting

If you are trying to cut down on using refined sugar, this frosting will be great to apply on cakes and cupcakes alike. It's so tasty we've even been known to spread a little (or a lot) of it on a slice of bread, too. This recipe can be doubled, halved, or quartered with great results. If you plan to pipe rather than spread the frosting, double or even triple the recipe.

¼ cup (48 g) vegetable shortening
½ cup (168 g) agave nectar
2 generous teaspoons pure vanilla extract
1 cup (80 g) unsweetened cocoa powder
1 heaping teaspoon orange zest (optional)

Using an electric mixer, cream together the shortening, agave, and vanilla until combined. Sift the cocoa powder on top. Add the zest, if using, and beat together for several minutes at medium-high speed, until fluffy and smooth. Chill for about one hour in the fridge before using.

Yield: About 1 cup (280 g)

Chapter 19

Candies and Bars

Bring back childhood memories by preparing animal-friendly versions of old favorites, such as puffed rice treats or fudgelike brownies and blondies.

If you're in the mood for something new and daring, give a try to bean-based versions of the latter; no one will guess they're actually good for you, while being surprisingly tasty!

Macademia and White Chocolate Crispy Treats

Here's a classic all-white pairing for a new version of the ooey-gooey treat. It's best to melt the white chocolate chips just before stirring them into the agave and nut butter, because the chocolate sets fairly quickly and could become difficult to handle.

1 cup (124 g) macadamia nuts
½ cup (100 g) nondairy white chocolate chips, melted
¼ cup (84 g) agave nectar
1 teaspoon pure vanilla extract
4 cups (64 g) puffed brown rice

Line an 8-inch (20-cm) square baking pan with parchment or waxed paper.

Grind the nuts in a food processor until they begin to look like butter, once they start releasing their oil. This could take a few minutes, depending on the efficiency of the food processor.

In a microwave-safe bowl, melt the chocolate chips in the microwave.

Add the nut butter, agave, and vanilla and stir to combine.

Place the puffed rice in a large-size bowl, pour the nut and chocolate mixture on top, and stir until well combined.

Pour the mixture into the prepared pan and press down firmly, with an extra piece of waxed paper between your hands and the treats to avoid a sticky mess.

Place in the fridge for 1 hour before slicing. Slice into 8 or more treats. Serve cold and store in the fridge.

Yield: 8 treats

S'mores Crispy Treats

If you make your own graham cracker chunks and add them when they're barely out of the oven, they will melt the chocolate, a delicious side effect. The more rice cereal you use, the denser the treats; the less you use, the chewier.

10 ounces (284 g) vegan marshmallow crème, such as Ricemellow
3 ounces (85 g) nondairy semisweet chocolate, chopped
4 to 5 cups (64 to 80 g) puffed brown rice cereal
2 cups (168 g) bite-size chunks vegan graham crackers, store-bought or homemade (page 414 or 415)

Line an 8-inch (20-cm) square baking pan with parchment or waxed paper.

Combine the crème and chocolate in a large-size bowl.

Add the cereal and cracker chunks and stir until well combined.

Pour the mixture into the prepared pan and press down firmly, with an extra piece of waxed paper between your hands and the treats to avoid a sticky mess.

Place in the fridge for 1 hour before slicing. Slice into 8 or more treats. Serve cold and store in the fridge.

Yield: 8 treats

Pecan Turtles

Chewy caramel and pecans, smothered in smooth dark chocolate. Perfection? Just maybe.

1 recipe Cappuccino Caramels (page 455), omitting the espresso powder and cutting into 2-inch (5-cm) squares to yield 16 pieces
8 ounces (227 g) pecans, chopped
2 cups (350 g) nondairy semisweet chocolate chips

On a flat surface lined with parchment or waxed paper, lay out all of the caramels with about 2 inches (5 cm) of space between them.

Add an equal amount of chopped pecans to the top of each caramel.

Using your hands, work the pecans into each caramel, form a ball, and flatten slightly into a disk.

Melt the chocolate chips in the microwave in a small microwave-safe bowl, stirring occasionally to avoid scorching. Alternatively, use a double boiler.

Using a toothpick, dip each caramel into the chocolate to coat, and return to the waxed paper to cool.

Let cool completely to harden.

Yield: 16 turtles

Old-Fashioned Mashed Potato Candy

This is an old family recipe that has been passed down for generations. It's naturally vegan, so no substitutions were necessary. It's also a fun way to use up your leftover mashers, or you can whip up some fresh ones just for the occasion. You can use instant mashed potatoes for these, too.

This batch makes about 200 pieces. So have the kids join in the fun and whip up a batch for the next bake sale, or bag it up in pretty bags for gift giving!

3 cups (227 g) dehydrated potato flakes
2 cups (470 ml) water
1 cup (235 ml) vanilla or plain soy or other nondairy milk
6 pounds (2.7 kg) powdered sugar
2 cups (512 g) creamy no-stir peanut butter

In a large-size mixing bowl, add the potato flakes. In a saucepot, bring the water and milk to a boil. As soon as it begins to boil, remove from the heat and pour over the potato flakes. Stir well, and let cool completely.

Mix in the powdered sugar, 1 cup (120 g) at a time (6 pounds [2.7 kg] equals roughly 18 cups), using an electric mixer.

As the "dough" begins to thicken, you will have to abandon the mixer and knead with your hands. Keep adding sugar until the dough is workable and no longer sticky. Once you achieve a workable dough, divide it into 10 pieces.

On a well-sugared surface, roll out one piece at a time.

Spread on a thin layer of peanut butter, then roll it up.

Slice each rope into 20 equal pieces.

Try wrapping them up individually in squares of waxed paper to give them that old-fashioned homemade look.

Yield: 200 pieces

Gluten Free

Peppermint Bark

What's Christmas without peppermint bark? If you are wondering why on earth you'd put wax in your candy, it's there to make it shine. It also helps the candy harden once cooled. If eating wax isn't appealing, simply leave it out. You'll still get a great candy, albeit not quite as shiny.

1½ pounds (680 g) nondairy semisweet chocolate chips
1 block (4 ounces, or 112 g) baker's wax, such as Parowax
10 ounces (288 g) crushed candy canes (about 24 regular-size canes), divided
1 tablespoon (15 ml) pure peppermint extract

Melt the chocolate chips and wax in a double boiler.

Line 2 baking sheets with parchment or waxed paper.

Mix about three-fourths of the candy canes and the peppermint extract into the chocolate.

Spread half of the mixture on each of the baking sheets.

Sprinkle the remaining one-fourth candy canes on top of the chocolate. Let cool completely in the fridge.

Once completely hardened and cooled, break into pieces to enjoy, or package for gift giving.

Yield: About 2⅓ pounds (1060 g)

VARIATION

Don't limit yourself to peppermint! Eliminate the peppermint extract and candy canes and try using broken pieces of salty pretzels, nuts, or candied fruits—just about anything will work!

Cappuccino Caramels

These caramels are sweet and chewy with a kick of caffeine. They make great gifts, wrapped up individually in waxed paper. That is, if you can bear to part with them!

A candy thermometer is a must here. If the candy does not get hot enough, it won't harden and you will end up with syrup instead of caramels.

1 cup (224 g) nondairy butter
2 cups (400 g) granulated sugar
2 cups (470 ml) soy or other nondairy milk
1 cup (235 ml) light corn syrup
3 tablespoons (21 g) instant espresso powder
1 tablespoon (15 ml) pure vanilla extract

Line an 8-inch (20-cm) square baking pan or dish with parchment paper.

Place the butter, sugar, milk, corn syrup, and espresso powder in a large-size pot, such as a soup pot. Bring to a boil, stirring constantly.

Reduce the heat to medium and continue to cook until the mixture reaches 245°F (118°C) on a candy thermometer.

Remove from the heat and stir in the vanilla.

Carefully pour into the prepared baking pan.

Let cool completely to harden up.

Using a very sharp knife, cut into 1-inch (2.5-cm) squares.

Yield: 64 pieces

No-Bake-Full-of-It-All Candies

Other add-ins than the ones mentioned lend themselves nicely here as well. Dried fruits like cherries or cranberries would give them a nice tart flair. You can also roll your candies in additional coconut flakes or chopped peanuts or dust them with cocoa powder to make them extra fancy. For Valentine's Day, or another special occasion, you could whip up a batch of these in no time, set them in mini cupcake papers, and place them in a pretty box! Ahhh . . . sweets for your sweetie!

2 cups (32 g) crispy rice cereal
1 cup (120 g) powdered sugar
1 cup (256 g) natural peanut butter
1 cup (120 g) coconut flakes
¼ cup (56 g) nondairy butter, softened
½ cup (56 g) dry-roasted peanuts, chopped if desired
14 ounces (385 g) nondairy semisweet chocolate chips, divided

In a large-size mixing bowl, combine the cereal, sugar, peanut butter, coconut flakes, butter, peanuts, and 2 ounces (45 g) of the chocolate chips until you have a massive sticky, gooey mess.

Roll into balls about 1 inch (2.5 cm) in diameter. Place on waxed paper.

Melt the remaining 12 ounces (340 g) chocolate in a microwave or double boiler.

Using a toothpick or skewer, dip each ball into the chocolate and return to the waxed paper to cool and harden.

Yield: 30 truffle-size candies

 Gluten Free

Chocolate Easter Eggs (or Peppermint Patties)

There are so many Easter candies out there it can sometimes leave a vegan feeling a little left out. By making your own, you can control what goes into them, and you can give them as lovely homemade gifts to friends and family. Substitute any flavor extract in the center to make a variety of confections.

½ cup (120 ml) light corn syrup
1 tablespoon (15 ml) pure vanilla extract
3 cups (360 g) powdered sugar, plus more for dusting
A few drops yellow food coloring
12 ounces (340 g) nondairy semisweet chocolate chips

In a bowl, mix together the corn syrup and vanilla. Add the sugar, 1 cup (120 g) at a time. Work in the sugar until you get a dough that is the consistency of Play-Doh.

Divide the dough into thirds. Add yellow food coloring to one-third of the dough. Divide that dough into 12 even pieces and roll into small balls. Dust with extra powdered sugar as you work to prevent them from getting too sticky. Place on a sheet of parchment or waxed paper and set aside.

Divide the remaining two-thirds dough into 12 equal pieces and form into small patties, once again dusting with powdered sugar as you work.

Place 1 "yolk" in the center of each patty and wrap the patty around it. Form into an egg shape, dusting with sugar as you work. Place on parchment or waxed paper and place in the freezer to stiffen up, about 1 hour or so.

While your "eggs" are freezing, melt the chocolate, either in a double boiler or in the microwave.

Using toothpicks, dip each egg into the chocolate and return to the waxed paper to cool and harden. You can place them back in the freezer to speed up the process if you'd like.

Yield: 12 candy "eggs"

VARIATIONS

Peppermint Patties: Instead of dividing into thirds, add 2 tablespoons (30 ml) peppermint extract to the corn syrup and vanilla before adding the sugar. Add a little green food coloring (optional). Divide into 24 equal pieces and form into patties. Follow the recipe from there.

Lemon or Orange Candies: Get creative with the flavors! Add 2 tablespoons (30 ml) lemon or orange (or almond or anise or cinnamon . . .) extract instead of the peppermint. Add a touch of yellow or orange food coloring, or whatever color matches the flavor you use.

Gluten Free

Spicy Pepita Brittle

Yes, there is a lot of sugar in this, but don't be fooled—it's hot and spicy! A candy thermometer is helpful in this recipe. If you don't have one, you can test for doneness by dropping a teaspoonful of the boiling mixture into a bowl of ice water; if it immediately forms into a hard ball, it's ready.

Nonstick cooking spray
2 cups (454 g) hulled pepitas (pumpkin seeds)
2 cups (400 g) granulated sugar
1 cup (235 ml) light corn syrup
1 cup (235 ml) water
½ teaspoon salt
2 tablespoons (28 g) nondairy butter
1 tablespoon (15 ml) pure vanilla extract
1 teaspoon cayenne pepper
1 teaspoon baking soda

Have ready a rimmed baking sheet lined with parchment paper and sprayed liberally with nonstick spray.

In a saucepan over low heat, mix together the pepitas, sugar, corn syrup, water, and salt. Stir until the sugar has melted. Increase the heat to high and bring to a boil. Continue to boil until it reaches 300°F (150°C) on a candy thermometer.

While the mixture is boiling, in a separate bowl, mix together the butter, vanilla, cayenne pepper, and baking soda.

Once the boiling mixture reaches 300°F (150°C), remove from the heat and vigorously stir in the butter mixture. It will foam and fizz.

Quickly pour the mixture onto the prepared baking sheet and spread evenly. Let cool completely before breaking into pieces and enjoying.

Store in an airtight container lined with waxed paper.

Yield: About 40 pieces

Gluten Free

Peanut Butter Chocolate Fudge

Made with coconut milk, this fudge is very creamy and moist! Take extra special care when bringing the mixture to a boil, because if the temperature isn't just right, your fudge will not set, and it would be very sad to have wasted all of those ingredients! In case you have a batch not set, just save it and warm it up for an amazing topping for ice cream.

Nonstick cooking spray
1½ cups (384 g) creamy no-stir peanut butter
1 cup (175 g) nondairy semisweet chocolate chips
1 tablespoon (15 ml) pure vanilla extract
1 cup (235 ml) full-fat coconut milk
3 cups (600 g) granulated sugar

Line an 8- or 9-inch (20- or 23-cm) square baking pan with aluminum foil or parchment paper and lightly coat with nonstick spray.

In a large-size heat-resistant mixing bowl, combine the peanut butter, chocolate chips, and vanilla.

In a saucepan, mix together the coconut milk and sugar. Bring to a FULL boil. (Big rolling bubbles, not little ones.) Boil hard for exactly 1 minute.

Pour the coconut mixture into the peanut butter mixture and stir vigorously until well combined and the chocolate begins to melt. It won't completely melt, and that's okay, because it will marble with the peanut butter as it hardens. You have to work very quickly because the mixture will begin to set almost immediately.

Immediately pour into the prepared pan and let cool and harden completely, about 1 hour.

Cut into small squares and enjoy.

Yield: About 36 pieces

Whiskey Peanut Chocolate Bites

These are not for the children of the household, nor for the faint of heart. Be prepared for the delicious combination of whiskey and chocolate to have you dance the jig. Maybe even literally, depending on how many of these treats you enjoy . . .

Please keep in mind that although the alcohol amount isn't high, these goodies aren't cooked in any way, so the alcohol doesn't get a chance to burn off.

¼ cup plus 2 tablespoons (90 ml) whiskey
1¼ cups (150 g) powdered sugar
1 cup (146 g) dry-roasted unsalted peanuts, coarsely chopped
1¼ cups (219 g) nondairy semisweet chocolate chips, melted and cooled

Line an 8-inch (20-cm) square baking pan with parchment or waxed paper.

Combine the whiskey and sugar in a large-size bowl. Stir in the peanuts and melted chocolate.

Place in the prepared baking pan and level with a spatula or an extra piece of parchment paper.

Place the pan in the fridge for at least 2 hours.

Remove the block of candy from the pan. Peel off the parchment paper. Cut or break the block of candy into the size you want.

Yield: One 8-inch (20-cm) block of candy

No-Bake Chocolate Oat Bites

These chocolate bites are a bit too sweet and indulgent to enjoy for breakfast, but they would make a perfect midmorning or afternoon snack, if you need a boost at work or at school.

Look for peanuts that contain nothing but nuts and salt, because a lot of store-bought peanuts contain animal-derived ingredients. If you cannot find salted peanuts, add ¼ teaspoon fine sea salt to the mix.

10 ounces (283 g) nondairy semisweet chocolate chips
2 tablespoons (28 g) nondairy butter
½ cup (96 g) Sucanat
¼ cup (60 ml) coconut or other nondairy milk
½ cup (73 g) dry-roasted salted peanuts
¼ cup (40 g) raisins
2½ cups (195 g) quick-cooking oats

Line an 8-inch (20-cm) square baking pan with parchment or waxed paper.

In the microwave, melt the chocolate and butter in a microwave-safe bowl for about 1 minute, checking and stirring at least once during the process.

In another microwave-safe bowl, stir the Sucanat into the milk and heat for 30 seconds in the microwave. Combine with the chocolate mixture.

Fold in the peanuts, raisins, and oats.

Pour into the prepared pan and press down firmly, using an extra piece of waxed paper between your hands and the treats to avoid a sticky mess.

Let cool in the freezer for at least 1 hour before slicing. Enjoy cold, and store in the fridge.

Yield: 16 bites

Chocolate Tahini No-Bake Barley Bars

Crispy and intense with a delicious chocolate and extremely subtle tahini flavor, these bars are so quick and easy to put together that there will be no more excuses for a trip to the vending machine in the middle of the afternoon.

¼ cup (84 g) agave nectar
3 tablespoons (48 g) tahini
2 ounces (57 g) nondairy unsweetened or semi-sweet chocolate, chopped
¼ teaspoon ground cinnamon
1½ teaspoons pure vanilla extract
3 cups (288 g) wheat and barley cereal, such as Grape-Nuts

Line an 8-inch (20-cm) square baking dish with parchment or waxed paper.

Combine the agave, tahini, and chocolate in a microwave-safe bowl. Heat in the microwave until melted, stopping and stirring to accelerate the process.

Add the cinnamon, vanilla, and cereal; stir until thoroughly combined.

Pour into the prepared pan and press down firmly, using an extra piece of waxed paper between your hands and the treats to avoid a sticky mess.

Place in the freezer to set. Slice into 6 bars. Store in and enjoy straight from the freezer or fridge.

Yield: 6 bars

Black Bean Brownies

The first time we saw fellow blogger Activist Mommy whip up a batch of black bean brownies, we thought she had lost her mind. Her own version was tasty, but we put a big spin on it and are now addicted to these healthy treats. Give them a try: you will be surprised how tasty they are.

Nonstick cooking spray
½ cup (39 g) quick-cooking oats
½ cup (47 g) shredded coconut
¼ cup (48 g) raw sugar
¼ cup (30 g) carob powder
½ cup (100 g) roasted chestnuts or other nuts
1 can (15 ounces, or 425 g) cooked black beans, drained and rinsed
2 ripe bananas
8 dried dates, pitted
2 tablespoons (30 ml) unsweetened almond or other nondairy milk, plus more if needed
1 teaspoon pure vanilla extract

Preheat the oven to 350°F (180°C, or gas mark 4). Lightly coat an 8-inch (20-cm) square baking pan with spray.

Place the oats, coconut, and sugar in a food processor. Blend until finely ground.

Add the carob powder, chestnuts, beans, bananas, dates, milk, and vanilla. Blend until perfectly smooth, scraping the sides occasionally. Add more milk if the batter is too dry.

Pour into the prepared pan and level the batter with a spatula.

Bake for 27 minutes, or until set and firm to the touch.

Let cool on a wire rack, still in the pan. Chill for at least 4 hours before slicing and serving.

Enjoy cold, and store in the fridge.

Yield: 8 brownies

Gluten Free   Soy Free

Chickpea Blondies

This fudgelike, chewy, and healthy treat has a wonderful texture and flavor. It is perfect for those days when you feel like something sweet, without going overboard in fat and calories. Be bold and give them a try!

Nonstick cooking spray
1 can (15 ounces, or 425 g) cooked garbanzo beans, drained and rinsed
½ cup (96 g) raw sugar
½ cup (160 g) strawberry or other all-fruit spread
¼ cup (64 g) crunchy natural peanut butter or tahini
2 teaspoons pure vanilla extract
¼ cup plus 2 tablespoons (42 g) flax meal
2 tablespoons (20 g) brown rice flour
½ teaspoon baking powder

Preheat the oven to 350°F (180°C, or gas mark 4). Lightly coat an 8-inch (20-cm) square baking pan with spray.

In a food processor, combine all the ingredients and blend until perfectly smooth, scraping the sides occasionally.

Pour into the prepared pan and level the batter with a spatula.

Bake for 26 minutes, or until set and firm to the touch.

Let cool on a wire rack, still in the pan. Chill for a few hours before slicing and serving.

Enjoy cold, and store in the fridge.

Yield: 8 blondies

Peanut Butter Blondies

Prepare yourself to be wowed by this melt-in-the-mouth, somewhat fudgelike, irresistible treat, made even more delicious when served with all-fruit jam or a drizzle of Chocolate Ganache (page 74).

Nonstick cooking spray
½ cup (128 g) creamy natural peanut butter
½ cup (96 g) raw sugar
¼ cup (60 g) vanilla soy or other nondairy yogurt
¼ cup (60 ml) vanilla soy or other nondairy milk
2 tablespoons (30 ml) peanut or canola oil
1 teaspoon pure vanilla extract
½ teaspoon fine sea salt
¾ cup (90 g) light spelt flour
¼ teaspoon baking powder

Preheat the oven to 350°F (180°C, or gas mark 4). Lightly coat an 8-inch (20-cm) square baking pan with spray.

In a large-size bowl and using an electric mixer, cream together the peanut butter, sugar, and yogurt until light and fluffy, about 2 minutes.

Stir in the milk, oil, vanilla, and salt.

Sift the flour and baking powder on top. Stir until just combined.

Pour into the prepared pan and level the batter with a spatula.

Bake for 22 to 25 minutes, or until golden brown and the edges pull away from the pan.

Let cool on a wire rack, still in the pan. Chill for a few hours before slicing and serving.

Enjoy cold, and store in the fridge.

Yield: 8 blondies

Butterscotch (or White) Chocolate Fudge Brownies

It would be a lie to say we never devoured a whole pan of these chocolate-rich, decadent brownies in ten seconds flat. Word of advice: be sure to share with friends, family, or neighbors!

Nonstick cooking spray
1½ cups (263 g) mix of nondairy butterscotch (or white chocolate) and semisweet chocolate chips, melted and cooled
1 cup (255 g) sweet potato purée
2 tablespoons (30 ml) canola oil
2 tablespoons (30 ml) soy creamer or any nondairy milk
1 teaspoon pure vanilla extract
¼ cup (30 g) powdered sugar
½ cup (60 g) light spelt flour
2 tablespoons (10 g) unsweetened cocoa powder
¼ teaspoon fine sea salt
¼ teaspoon baking powder
½ cup (88 g) mix of nondairy butterscotch (or white chocolate) and semisweet chocolate chips

Preheat the oven to 350°F (180°C, or gas mark 4). Lightly coat an 8-inch (20-cm) square baking pan with spray.

In a large-size bowl, combine the melted chips, sweet potato purée, oil, creamer, and vanilla.

In a medium-size bowl, sift together the sugar, flour, cocoa powder, salt, and baking powder.

Fold the dry ingredients into the wet, being careful not to overmix. Fold in the extra chips.

Pour into the prepared pan and level the batter with a spatula.

Bake for 28 minutes, or until the middle is set and the sides pull away from the pan.

Let cool on a wire rack, still in the pan. Chill for a few hours before slicing and serving.

Enjoy cold, and store in the fridge.

Yield: 8 brownies

VARIATION

If finding nondairy butterscotch or white chocolate chips is the equivalent of searching for the Holy Grail, depending on where you live, use more semisweet chocolate chips instead, and double the amount of sugar.

Gluten-Free Fudge Brownies

Gluten freedom doesn't have to mean boredom! If you feel like being especially indulgent, add ½ cup (88 g) nondairy semisweet chocolate chips to the batter of these fudgelike brownies.

Nonstick cooking spray
1 cup (175 g) nondairy semisweet chocolate chips, melted and cooled
½ cup (128 g) sweet potato purée
2 tablespoons (30 ml) canola oil
¼ cup plus 2 tablespoons (90 ml) soy creamer or nondairy milk
1 teaspoon pure vanilla extract
½ cup (60 g) powdered sugar
⅓ cup (53 g) brown rice flour
2 tablespoons (10 g) unsweetened cocoa powder
¼ teaspoon fine sea salt
¼ teaspoon baking powder
1 tablespoon (8 g) instant coconut milk powder (optional, check for ingredients if using)

Preheat the oven to 350°F (180°C, or gas mark 4). Lightly coat an 8-inch (20-cm) square baking pan with spray.

In a large-size bowl, combine the melted chocolate, sweet potato purée, oil, creamer, and vanilla.

In a medium-size bowl, sift together the sugar, flour, cocoa powder, salt, baking powder, and coconut powder, if using.

Fold the dry ingredients into the wet, being careful not to overmix.

Pour into the prepared pan and level the batter with a spatula.

Bake for 26 minutes, or until the middle is set and the sides pull away from the pan.

Let cool on a wire rack, still in the pan. Chill for a few hours before slicing and serving.

Enjoy cold, and store in the fridge.

Yield: 8 brownies

Molasses Cake Bars

These healthy and tasty cakelike bars are perfect for breakfast or as a nutritious boost for a midmorning or midafternoon break.

Nonstick cooking spray
1 tablespoon (15 ml) apple cider vinegar
1 cup (235 ml) plain soymilk (use soy here, or your milk might not curdle)
1 cup (120 g) whole wheat pastry flour
¾ cup (60 g) ground oats
2 teaspoons ground cinnamon
1 teaspoon ground ginger
1 teaspoon baking powder
1 teaspoon baking soda
½ teaspoon fine sea salt
½ cup (176 g) blackstrap or regular molasses
2 tablespoons (30 ml) canola oil
¼ cup plus 2 tablespoons (60 g) raisins
½ cup (55 g) chopped pecans or (59 g) walnuts (optional)

Preheat the oven to 350°F (180°C, or gas mark 4). Lightly coat an 8-inch (20-cm) square baking pan with spray.

Combine the vinegar and milk in a medium-size bowl; it will curdle and become like buttermilk.

Whisk the flour, ground oats, cinnamon, ginger, baking powder, baking soda, and salt in a large-size bowl.

Whisk the molasses and oil into the buttermilk mixture.

Fold the wet ingredients into the dry, being careful not to overmix. Fold in the raisins and nuts, if using.

Pour the batter into the prepared pan.

Bake for 25 minutes, or until a toothpick inserted into the center comes out clean.

Place on a wire rack, still in the pan, for about 15 minutes before transferring directly to the rack, and let cool completely before slicing or storing.

Yield: 6 servings

Monkey Bars

Peanut butter, bananas, caramel, and chocolate come together in what we think must be monkey heaven!

For the Peanut Butter Cookie base:

- Nonstick cooking spray
- 1 cup (125 g) all-purpose flour
- ¼ teaspoon ground cinnamon
- 1 cup (256 g) creamy no-stir peanut butter
- 1 banana, mashed
- ½ cup (100 g) granulated sugar
- ½ cup (120 ml) soy or other nondairy milk
- 1 teaspoon pure vanilla extract

For the Caramel Banana topping:

- 2 firm bananas
- ½ cup (120 ml) Caramel Sauce (page 492)
- ½ cup (88 g) nondairy semisweet chocolate chips

To make the cookie base: Preheat the oven to 350°F (180°C, or gas mark 4). Lightly coat an 8-inch (20-cm) square baking dish with cooking spray.

In a large-size mixing bowl, stir together the flour and cinnamon.

In a medium-size bowl, combine the peanut butter, banana, sugar, milk, and vanilla.

Fold the wet ingredients into the dry, being careful not to overmix. Spread the mixture evenly in the baking dish.

To make the topping: Slice the bananas into thin slices about ⅛ inch (3 mm) thick. Layer the bananas evenly over the cookie dough.

Drizzle the caramel sauce all over the bananas.

Sprinkle the chocolate chips all over the top.

Bake for 30 minutes, or until the caramel is bubbly and the chocolate is melted.

Place on a wire rack, still in the pan, for about 15 minutes before transferring directly to the rack, and let cool completely before slicing or storing.

Yield: 16 squares

Maple Pine Nut Bars

The unusual addition of pine nuts to this rich dessert bar makes a gourmet statement that will have your friends and family thinking you are pure genius!

Nonstick cooking spray
2 cups (250 g) all-purpose flour
1 teaspoon baking soda
1 teaspoon ground cinnamon
½ teaspoon salt
½ teaspoon ground nutmeg
1 cup (220 g) firmly packed brown sugar
¼ cup (60 ml) pure maple syrup
⅔ cup (168 g) nondairy butter, softened
¾ cup (170 g) nondairy yogurt
¼ cup (60 ml) soy or other nondairy milk
1 teaspoon pure vanilla extract
1 cup (142 g) chopped, pitted dates
1 cup (120 g) pine nuts

Preheat the oven to 350°F (180°C, or gas mark 4). Lightly coat a 9 x 13-inch (23 x 33-cm) baking dish with cooking spray.

In a large-size mixing bowl, combine the flour, baking soda, cinnamon, salt, and nutmeg.

In a medium-size bowl, mix together the brown sugar, maple syrup, butter, yogurt, milk, and vanilla.

Fold the wet ingredients into the dry, being careful not to overmix. Fold in the dates and nuts.

Spread evenly in the prepared baking dish.

Bake for 25 to 30 minutes, or until the edges are golden brown.

Place on a wire rack, still in the pan, for about 15 minutes before transferring directly to the rack, and let cool completely before slicing or storing.

Yield: 24 bars

Cinnamon Apple Pie Bars

No need to wait for fall to enjoy the flavor of apple pie! These oatmeal cookie bars taste almost like the real thing. For extra goodness, drizzle the top with some Caramel Sauce (page 492).

For the Oatmeal Cookie base:

- 1 cup (78 g) quick-cooking oats
- 1 cup (125 g) all-purpose flour
- ½ teaspoon baking soda
- ½ teaspoon baking powder
- ¼ teaspoon cinnamon
- ¼ teaspoon salt
- ½ cup (120 ml) soy or other nondairy milk
- ¼ cup (55 g) firmly packed brown sugar
- 2 tablespoons (30 g) nondairy yogurt
- 1 teaspoon pure vanilla extract

For the apple topping:

- 6 ounces (170 g) peeled and cored apples, cut into small chunks
- ¼ cup (56 g) nondairy butter, melted
- 2 tablespoons (25 g) firmly packed brown sugar
- ¼ teaspoon cinnamon

To make the cookie base: Preheat the oven to 350°F (180°C, or gas mark 4). Have ready an 8-inch (20-cm) square baking dish.

In a large bowl, mix together the oats, flour, baking soda, baking powder, cinnamon, and salt.

In a medium bowl, combine the milk, brown sugar, yogurt, and vanilla.

Fold the wet ingredients into the dry, being careful not to overmix. Spread the mixture evenly in the prepared baking dish. Set aside.

To make the topping: In a medium bowl, toss the apple chunks with the melted butter, brown sugar, and cinnamon.

Spread the apple mixture evenly on top of the cookie mixture.

Bake for 30 minutes, or until the apples are tender.

Place on a wire rack, still in the pan, for about 15 minutes before transferring directly to the rack, and let cool completely before slicing or storing.

Yield: 16 squares

Baklava

Baklava is a traditional Greek dessert that is so easy to make and yields such impressive results.

1 package (1 pound, or 455 g) frozen phyllo dough
1¼ cups (280 g) nondairy butter
6 ounces (170 g) pecans
6 ounces (170 g) walnuts
6 ounces (170 g) almonds
1 teaspoon ground cinnamon
1 cup (235 ml) water
1 cup (200 g) granulated sugar
1 cup (336 g) agave nectar
1 tablespoon (15 ml) pure vanilla extract

Thaw the phyllo according to the package instructions.

Preheat the oven to 350°F (180°C, or gas mark 4). Have ready a 9 x 13-inch (23 x 33-cm) glass baking dish.

Rub a bit of the butter all over the bottom and sides of the dish.

Melt the remaining butter in the microwave in a small microwave-safe bowl.

Add all of the nuts to a resealable plastic bag. Using a rolling pin or a kitchen mallet, smash the nuts.

Add the cinnamon to the bag and shake to combine with the nuts.

Unfold the phyllo and cut the entire stack in half, to fit into the bottom of the dish.

Place 2 sheets of phyllo in the bottom of the dish and brush with melted butter. Add 2 more sheets, and brush on more butter. Repeat 2 more times. You should now have 8 layers of phyllo. For structure, the bottom and top will have more layers of phyllo.

Sprinkle a handful of the nut mixture all over the top. Cover with 2 more sheets of phyllo and brush with butter.

Repeat this process until you have 6 to 8 sheets of phyllo left, then repeat as you did on the bottom, with 2 sheets, butter, 2 sheets, butter, with no nuts.

Brush the top layer with butter.

Using a very sharp knife, cut the baklava into 12 equal squares, then cut each square into 2 triangles. Triangles are the traditional shape for baklava.

Bake for 45 to 50 minutes, or until the top is golden brown and flaky.

While the baklava is baking, make the syrup.

In a saucepot, bring the water and sugar to a boil and boil until the sugar is completely dissolved. Reduce to a simmer.

Add the agave and vanilla and simmer for about 20 minutes.

When the baklava is done baking, remove from the oven and immediately drizzle the syrup evenly all over the top.

Let cool completely before serving.

Do not cover, because your baklava will become soggy if you do.

Yield: 24 pieces

Chapter 20

Puddings, Mousses, Ice Creams, and Libations

When you find yourself wanting to reach for something sweet (and sinful) to seal the end of a meal, but don't feel like biting into a treat that might weigh you down and make you fall asleep at your desk or in front of the television, reach for one of the following desserts or drinks that will please everyone (of legal age, for the latter), and in the case of frozen treats, also make for cheaper alternatives to air-conditioning in the dog days of summer.

Butterscotch Pumpkin Pudding

Pumpkin: fall's unavoidable delicious fiber- and vitamin-packed squash is presented here in pudding form. If you're not a fan of cloves—it would appear there are quite a lot of us out there—just leave them out of the recipe.

½ cup (96 g) Sucanat
2 tablespoons (28 g) nondairy butter
¼ teaspoon fine sea salt
1 cup (244 g) pumpkin purée
1¼ cups (295 ml) soy or other nondairy milk
1 tablespoon (15 ml) rum
1 tablespoon (22 g) blackstrap or regular molasses
1 teaspoon ground cinnamon
½ teaspoon ground ginger
Pinch ground cloves (optional)
1 tablespoon (8 g) cornstarch
1 teaspoon pure vanilla extract

In a medium-size saucepan over medium heat, melt the Sucanat, butter, and salt for about 1 minute, until the sugar crystals are dissolved.

Stir in the pumpkin, milk, rum, molasses, cinnamon, ginger, cloves, if using, and cornstarch. Cook until thickened, whisking constantly.

Remove from the heat and stir in the vanilla.

Divide among 4 small-size dessert dishes, and chill for several hours in the fridge before serving.

Yield: 4 servings

Baked Chocolate Almond Pudding

This pudding is so tasty, healthy, and easy to make that you won't believe the main ingredient is tofu! Sift some powdered sugar on top of each, just upon serving, to make these decadent, soufflé-like individual desserts even fancier.

2 tablespoons (28 g) nondairy butter, plus extra for coating dishes
½ cup (69 g) roasted whole almonds
2 tablespoons (20 g) brown rice flour
1 pound (455 g) firm silken tofu, cut into cubes
½ cup (96 g) raw sugar
1 teaspoon pure almond extract
1 teaspoon pure vanilla extract
¼ teaspoon fine sea salt
½ teaspoon baking powder
¼ cup (20 g) unsweetened cocoa powder

Lightly coat 4 oven- and microwave-safe 8-ounce (235-ml) ramekins with nondairy butter.

Preheat the oven to 350°F (180°C, or gas mark 4), placing a baking sheet in the oven while it preheats. Placing the ramekins on it while the soufflés are in the oven ensures a more even baking.

Grind the almonds into a fine powder in a food processor. Add the butter, flour, tofu, sugar, extracts, salt, baking powder, and cocoa. Blend until perfectly smooth, scraping the sides occasionally.

Divide the batter equally among the ramekins.

Bake for 30 minutes, or until set. Serve immediately.

Yield: 4 servings

Chocolate Tapioca Pudding

Chewy tapioca paired with chocolate makes for a great, light ending to a meal.

⅓ cup (50 g) small dry pearl tapioca
¾ cup (180 ml) water
2 cups (470 ml) chocolate-flavored soy or other nondairy milk
¼ cup (44 g) nondairy semisweet chocolate chips
¼ cup (48 g) raw sugar
½ teaspoon pure vanilla extract
¼ teaspoon ground cinnamon (optional)

In a medium-size saucepan, soak the tapioca in the water for 30 minutes.

Stir the milk into the tapioca mixture; bring almost to a boil over medium-high heat. Immediately lower the temperature and simmer, uncovered, for 10 to 15 minutes, stirring often. The tapioca will be translucent when it is done cooking. The darkness of the chocolate milk might make it hard to see, so carefully spoon out some of the tapioca to check if it's done.

Add the chocolate chips, sugar, vanilla, and cinnamon, if using, to the tapioca, stirring until the chips are melted. Remove from the heat.

Divide among 4 small-size dessert dishes. Let cool completely before chilling in the fridge for several hours or overnight. Serve cold.

Yield: 4 servings

Gluten Free

Coconut Vanilla Pudding

This classic dessert is made simple here by the use of arrowroot powder. Garnish with fresh berries or layer berries and pudding in a glass for a delectable parfait.

¼ cup (32 g) arrowroot powder
1¼ cups (295 ml) vanilla soy or other nondairy milk, divided
1 can (14 ounces, or 414 ml) coconut milk
1 cup (192 g) raw sugar
1 tablespoon (15 ml) vanilla extract

In a small bowl, mix the arrowroot into ¼ cup (60 ml) of the milk to create a slurry and set aside.

In a saucepan, combine the coconut milk, the remaining 1 cup (235 ml) milk, and the sugar. Bring to a boil. As soon as it begins to boil, remove from the heat.

Stir in the arrowroot slurry and stir until it thickens.

Add the vanilla and continue to stir.

Immediately pour into dessert cups and refrigerate to cool and continue to thicken.

Yield: 4 servings

Lemon Vanilla Pudding

This pudding tastes absolutely divine when paired with fresh blueberries, raspberries, or strawberries.

3 cups (705 ml) soy or other nondairy milk (do not use coconut)
1 cup (200 g) granulated sugar
½ cup (64 g) cornstarch
½ cup (120 ml) lemon juice
1 tablespoon (15 ml) pure vanilla extract

In a saucepan, combine the milk, sugar, cornstarch, and lemon juice and stir until smooth.

Heat over medium heat, stirring constantly to prevent lumps and scorching, until thickened.

Remove from the heat and stir in the vanilla.

Pour into 6 dessert cups or a bowl and refrigerate until ready to serve.

Yield: 6 servings

Chocolate Peppermint Pudding

Here is a smooth and creamy dessert that can be prepared in no time; waiting for it to chill will be the most strenuous part of the preparation.

½ cup (96 g) Sucanat
2 tablespoons (16 g) cornstarch
2 tablespoons (10 g) unsweetened cocoa powder
¼ teaspoon fine sea salt
2 cups (470 ml) chocolate or vanilla soy or other nondairy milk
3 ounces (85 g) nondairy bittersweet chocolate, chopped
2 tablespoons (28 g) nondairy butter
¼ teaspoon pure peppermint extract (optional)

In a medium-size saucepan, combine the Sucanat, cornstarch, cocoa, and salt. Slowly whisk in the milk. Cook over medium-high heat until it starts to thicken, whisking constantly.

Whisk in the chocolate and butter, and cook until melted and thickened. Stir in the extract, if using.

Divide among 4 small-size dessert dishes. Let cool completely before chilling in the fridge for 2 hours or overnight. Serve cold.

Yield: 4 servings

VARIATIONS

If you only like your mint in toothpaste form, replace it with 1 teaspoon pure vanilla extract instead.

If you love fancy desserts, try layering this recipe with Peanut Butter Pudding (page 481). Don't forget to omit the peppermint extract, in this case.

Peanut Butter Pudding

Try layering this dessert with the Chocolate Peppermint Pudding (page 480), omitting the peppermint extract in the latter. Choosing natural peanut butter is key here for its flavor to shine through.

½ cup (96 g) Sucanat
½ teaspoon ground cinnamon
2 tablespoons (16 g) cornstarch
¼ teaspoon fine sea salt
1 tablespoon (8 g) instant coconut milk powder (optional, check for ingredients if using)
2 cups (470 ml) vanilla soy or other nondairy milk
½ cup (128 g) creamy natural peanut butter

In a medium-size saucepan, combine the Sucanat, cinnamon, cornstarch, salt, and coconut powder, if using. Slowly whisk in the milk. Cook over medium-high heat until it just starts to thicken, whisking constantly.

Whisk in the peanut butter, and cook for another couple of minutes, until thickened again.

Divide among 4 small-size dessert dishes. Let cool completely before chilling in the fridge for several hours or overnight. Serve cold.

Yield: 4 servings

Baked Apples with Thyme

This is a little twist on a reliable baked apple recipe, with the addition of thyme. Any other jam and ground nut can be substituted, and the thyme is absolutely optional, although the testers agreed that it was an extremely pleasant addition to this lovely, typically autumnal dessert. If the nondairy butter that sits at the bottom of the dish starts bubbling a little too merrily in your oven, lightly cover the dish with a piece of foil.

3 tablespoons (42 g) nondairy butter, divided
1 tablespoon (15 ml) water
2 baking apples (such as Granny Smith or Golden Delicious), halved and cored
¼ cup (24 g) ground toasted almonds
2 tablespoons (40 g) sour cherry or other jam
1 teaspoon dried thyme (optional)

Preheat the oven to 375°F (190°C, or gas mark 5). Place 1 tablespoon (14 g) of the butter and water in an 8-inch (20-cm) square baking dish.

Place 1½ teaspoons of the remaining butter in each apple cavity, then top with 1 tablespoon (6 g) ground almonds and 1½ teaspoons jam. Sprinkle each halved apple with ¼ teaspoon dried thyme.

Bake for 25 to 30 minutes, or until the apples are tender but not mushy.

Let the apples rest for a few minutes before serving. You can also serve these at room temperature, or even cold.

Yield: 4 servings

Macadamia and White Chocolate Pudding

This luscious and light white dessert will be the perfect ending to a delicious meal.

¾ cup (150 g) nondairy white chocolate chips
¼ cup (84 g) agave nectar
¾ cup (93 g) macadamia nuts
14 ounces (397 g) silken tofu, drained, patted dry, and cut into cubes
2 teaspoons pure vanilla extract
1 teaspoon grated lemon zest

Combine the white chocolate chips and agave in a microwave-safe bowl and melt in the microwave. Stir occasionally, being careful not to scorch.

Grind the nuts in a food processor until they begin to look like butter, once they start releasing their oil. This could take a few minutes, depending on the efficiency of the food processor.

Add the melted chocolate, tofu, vanilla, and zest to the food processor. Process until perfectly smooth, scraping the sides occasionally.

Divide among 4 small-size dessert dishes.

Chill overnight before enjoying, to let the flavors develop.

Yield: 4 servings

 Gluten Free

Rich and Thick Chocolate Mousse

If you are sensitive to any or all nut butters, don't be sad thinking that you won't get to enjoy a deliciously rich dessert that's actually rather good for you: avocados contain healthy fats that make for a perfectly creamy and indulgent dessert, just like nut butters do.

1 pound (455 g) firm silken tofu, cut into cubes
1 ripe avocado, halved, pitted, and peeled
¼ cup (84 g) agave nectar or (60 ml) pure maple syrup
1 teaspoon pure vanilla extract
2 tablespoons (16 g) instant coconut milk powder (optional, check for ingredients if using)
2 cups (350 g) nondairy semisweet chocolate chips or chopped bittersweet chocolate, melted and cooled

Place the tofu in a food processor and blend until smooth. Add the avocado, agave, vanilla, coconut milk powder, if using, and melted chocolate. Blend until perfectly smooth, scraping the sides occasionally.

Divide among 6 small-size dessert dishes. Chill for at least 2 hours or overnight before serving.

Yield: 6 servings

Peanut Butter Mousse

It may seem odd not to use a smoother, softer tofu like the silken kind in a dessert, but have no fear—it really works. You won't look back on dairy-based mousses after trying this protein-packed, lusciously creamy and smooth dessert that we found to be slightly reminiscent of whipped cream.

12 ounces (340 g) firm or extra-firm regular tofu, drained, patted dry, and cut into cubes
½ cup (120 g) nondairy sour cream, store-bought or homemade (page 306)
1 cup (256 g) creamy no-stir sweetened peanut butter
1½ teaspoons pure vanilla extract
½ cup (120 ml) pure maple syrup or (168 g) agave nectar
¼ teaspoon fine sea salt

Place the tofu, sour cream, and peanut butter in a food processor. Blend until smooth, scraping the sides occasionally.

Add the vanilla, maple syrup, and salt. Blend until perfectly smooth, scraping the sides occasionally.

Divide among 8 small-size dessert dishes and chill for several hours or overnight before enjoying.

Yield: 8 servings

Chocolate Raspberry Mousse

This rich mousse is best made with fresh berries, but if frozen is all that is available, you will still get to enjoy a luscious dessert. To make it extra fancy, serve garnished with a chocolate-dipped mint leaf.

12 ounces (340 g) nondairy semisweet chocolate chips
1 pound (455 g) silken tofu, cut into cubes
½ cup (60 g) powdered sugar
1 tablespoon (15 ml) pure vanilla extract
¼ cup (80 g) raspberry jam
4 ounces (112 g) fresh raspberries

Melt the chocolate chips in the microwave in a microwave-safe bowl, stirring occasionally to avoid scorching. Set aside.

To a blender or food processor, add the tofu and blend for about 1 minute.

Add the sugar and vanilla and continue to blend.

Add the jam and continue to blend.

Drizzle in the melted chocolate a little bit at a time until it is all incorporated. Your mixture should be like that of thick sour cream.

Divide among 4 dessert bowls and chill for about 1 hour. Top each bowl with an equal amount of fresh berries upon serving.

Yield: 4 servings

Plain Ol' Vanilla Ice Cream

Vanilla may be the plainest of flavors, but it is also one of the best. This simple vanilla ice cream boasts the richness of true vanilla bean. Its deep vanilla flavor makes it perfect on its own, or as a fine accompaniment to many of the pies, cobblers, crisps, and crumbles in chapter 17.

3 cups (705 ml) vanilla soy creamer or other nondairy creamer or milk
1 cup (200 g) granulated sugar
¼ cup (32 g) cornstarch
Scrapings from 1 vanilla bean
1 tablespoon (15 ml) pure vanilla extract

In a saucepan, mix together the creamer, sugar, cornstarch, and scrapings from the vanilla bean.

Bring to a boil, stirring often. As soon as it begins to boil, remove from the heat and stir in the vanilla extract.

Cover and place in the refrigerator to cool for an hour or so, then follow the instructions on your ice cream maker.

Yield: 4 servings

Making Ice Cream without an Ice Cream Maker

Although we all scream for ice cream, we also know that not everyone has access to an ice cream maker. Here are some simple instructions (although a bit more laborious) to make delicious homemade ice cream without one.

The purpose of an ice cream maker is to aerate the ice cream and prevent it from becoming too crystallized as it freezes. This can be accomplished with an electric mixer, as long as you have a few hours to spend. Don't worry. Most of that time is downtime.

After following the recipe up to the point where it tells you to follow the directions on your ice cream maker, follow these simple steps.

Pour the ice cream mixture into a mixing bowl and chill in the refrigerator for 2 hours, then place it in the freezer for about a half hour.

Remove it from the freezer and beat with a mixer until creamy. Put it back into the freezer for another half hour.

Repeat this process three times before placing it in the freezer for the final freeze, usually overnight, for a nice, firm ice cream.

Gluten Free

Kahlúa Ice Cream

Finally, a sweet frozen delight for grown-ups only! This tastes amazing topped with chocolate syrup. There are two methods here: a no-cook method and a stove-top method. Both yield creamy, delicious results. Remember that alcohol does not freeze, so you can keep this in the freezer for months and it will always remain perfectly scoopable!

2 tablespoons (16 g) Instant Clear Jel (no cook) or arrowroot powder (stove top)
2 cups (470 ml) vanilla soymilk, divided
2 cups (470 ml) soy vanilla creamer
1 cup (235 ml) coffee-flavored liqueur, such as Kahlúa, store-bought or homemade (page 495)
1 cup (200 g) granulated sugar

No-cook method: Dissolve the Instant Clear Jel in 1/4 cup (60 ml) of the milk.

Combine the Clear Jel and milk mixture with the remaining 1 3/4 cups (410 ml) milk, creamer, liqueur, and sugar and follow the directions on your ice cream maker.

Stove-top method: Dissolve the arrowroot in 1/4 cup (60 ml) of the milk.

In a pot, bring the creamer, remaining 1 3/4 cups (410 ml) milk, liqueur, and sugar to a simmer.

Add the arrowroot mixture to the pot and stir until beginning to thicken.

Remove from the heat and follow the instructions on your ice cream maker.

Yield: 6 servings

VARIATION

No ice cream maker? Follow the instructions on page 485 for making ice cream without one.

Soy Free

Peanut Butter Ice Cream

A fellow blogger put us to the test one day by requesting a peanut butter ice cream that would be free of soy. We're happy to report that Amy was very pleased with the result, but wasn't sure whether to give thanks or not, considering the dessert is deliciously addictive and not exactly figure-friendly. We're of the mind that it's perfectly fine to go ahead and indulge every now and then, so add chocolate chips, graham cracker pieces, chocolate syrup, or brownie chunks during the last few minutes of churning, to make it absolutely worth your while. Celine's recipe can also be found in Alisa Fleming's Go Dairy Free *book.*

1 cup (256 g) crunchy or creamy natural peanut butter
2 teaspoons pure vanilla extract
1 cup (235 ml) plain rice milk
1⅓ cups (315 ml) coconut milk
¾ cup (165 g) firmly packed light brown sugar

Place all the ingredients in a food processor. Blend until perfectly smooth, scraping the sides occasionally. Chill overnight.

Transfer to an ice cream maker and follow the manufacturer's instructions.

Place in the freezer for at least 1 hour if you want the dessert to have an even firmer consistency.

Yield: 6 servings

Intensely Chocolate Frozen Dessert

If you prefer chocolate to be dark, sometimes completely unsweetened, but always absolutely intense, this treat should make you happy! If you have a sweet tooth, you will want to be a bit more heavy-handed with the agave.

1 cup (235 ml) plain soy creamer
1 cup (235 ml) soy or other nondairy milk
½ cup (40 g) Dutch-processed or unsweetened cocoa powder
3 tablespoons (48 g) crunchy natural peanut butter
3 tablespoons (24 g) cornstarch
2 teaspoons pure vanilla extract
¼ to ½ cup (84 to 168 g) agave nectar
¼ cup (44 g) nondairy semisweet chocolate chips

Combine the creamer, milk, cocoa, peanut butter, and cornstarch in a medium-size saucepan. Cook over medium-high heat for about 5 minutes, whisking constantly, until the mixture has thickened a bit.

Stir in the vanilla and ¼ cup (84 g) of the agave, and taste to see whether some extra sweetener is needed to suit your preference. Cool completely before placing in the fridge for 2 hours or up to overnight.

Transfer to an ice cream maker and follow the manufacturer's instructions. Add the chocolate chips a few minutes before the end of the process. Place in the freezer for at least 1 hour if you want the dessert to have a firmer consistency.

Yield: 6 servings

VARIATION

No ice cream maker? Follow the instructions on page 485 for making ice cream without one.

Frozen Chocolate Peanut Butter Treat

This favorite treat is so easy to prepare, and it is not entirely bad for you because of the protein in the peanut butter, the calcium in the nondairy yogurt, and . . . well, chocolate tastes good, and that's its biggest redeeming quality. Adjust the amount of agave depending on how big of a sweet tooth you have, and how sweet the nondairy yogurt you use is.

4 cups (960 g) vanilla soy or other nondairy yogurt
12 ounces (340 g) nondairy semisweet chocolate chips, melted and cooled
1 cup (256 g) crunchy or creamy natural peanut butter
2 to 4 tablespoons (42 to 84 g) agave nectar

Place all the ingredients in a food processor. Blend until perfectly smooth and thickened, scraping the sides occasionally.

Place in the freezer overnight and thaw for 10 seconds in the microwave when you are ready to enjoy.

Yield: 12 servings

Frozen Tiramisu

A perfectly decadent dessert, minus (just a little bit of) the guilt.

8 ounces (227 g) nonhydrogenated, nondairy cream cheese, such as Tofutti
8 ounces (227 g) firm silken tofu
⅔ cup (160 ml) soy or other nondairy milk
¾ cup (165 g) firmly packed light brown sugar
¼ cup (60 ml) coffee liqueur, such as Kahlúa, store-bought or homemade (page 495)
1 tablespoon (15 ml) rum
Pinch fine sea salt
¼ cup (20 g) unsweetened cocoa powder

Place the cream cheese, tofu, milk, sugar, liqueur, rum, and salt in a food processor and blend until smooth, scraping the sides occasionally.

Strain using a fine-mesh sieve. Chill overnight.

Transfer to an ice cream maker and follow the manufacturer's instructions.

Layer and alternate the ice cream with the cocoa powder in 4 small-size dessert dishes.

Place in the freezer for at least 1 hour if you want the dessert to have an even firmer consistency.

Yield: 4 servings

Gluten Free

Peppermint Chocolate Frozen Treat

Almost too easy to make, this frozen treat will have you running to the freezer when you're craving something tasty and cold during the dog days of summer.

1 cup (175 g) nondairy semisweet chocolate chips
2 tablespoons (28 g) nondairy butter
2 cups (480 g) vanilla soy or other nondairy yogurt
2 tablespoons (42 g) agave nectar
2 tablespoons (30 ml) coffee liqueur, such as Kahlúa, store-bought or homemade (page 495)
¼ teaspoon pure peppermint extract

In a large-size, microwave-safe bowl, combine the chocolate chips and butter, and melt in the microwave in 45-seconds increments, stirring often, until smooth. Let cool for a few minutes.

Add the yogurt, agave, liqueur, and extract. Using an immersion or a countertop blender, blend all ingredients until perfectly smooth, scraping the sides occasionally.

Divide among 4 small-size dessert dishes. Place in the freezer overnight and thaw for 10 seconds in the microwave when you are ready to enjoy.

Yield: 4 servings

VARIATION

For the true peppermint aficionados out there, increase the extract to ½ teaspoon. For a subtler flavor, leave as is. And if you're not a fan of peppermint, replace it with 1 teaspoon pure vanilla extract.

Lemon Raspberry Gelato

No crazy equipment is needed here. The untraditional addition of fruit pectin makes this frozen treat soft and scoopable straight out of the freezer. Feel free to cut back on the sugar if you so choose.

2 cups (470 ml) vanilla soymilk
½ cup (120 ml) fresh lemon juice
Zest of 1 lemon
1 cup (200 g) evaporated cane juice or granulated sugar
2 tablespoons (28 g) nondairy butter
1¾ ounces (49 g) fruit pectin
6 ounces (170 g) fresh or frozen raspberries

Combine the milk, lemon juice, zest, cane juice, and butter in a pot.

Bring to a boil, then reduce to a simmer. Stir often to prevent overflow. Simmer for 10 minutes.

Slowly sprinkle in the pectin and whisk vigorously to dissolve completely. Continue to simmer for about 2 more minutes. Remove from the heat.

Stir in the berries and pour into an airtight container.

Freeze overnight.

Yield: 4 servings

 Under 30 Minutes  Gluten Free

Red Wine Hot Fudge Sauce

This is a seriously serious chocolate sauce. Serve it over ice cream, drizzle it over cheesecake, or dip into it with strawberries. However you enjoy it, know that this is one special hot fudge.

2 cups (350 g) nondairy semisweet chocolate chips
1 cup (235 ml) Cabernet Sauvignon or your favorite red wine
1 cup (200 g) granulated sugar
2 tablespoons (28 g) nondairy butter
¼ cup (32 g) cornstarch mixed with ¼ cup (60 ml) soymilk to make a slurry
1 tablespoon (15 ml) pure vanilla extract
2 teaspoons pure almond extract

Add the chocolate chips, wine, sugar, and butter to a saucepan and heat over medium heat.

Bring to a boil and continue boiling for 3 minutes, stirring constantly.

Add the cornstarch slurry and stir until thickened.

Remove from the heat and continue to stir.

Add the vanilla and almond extracts and keep stirring until shiny and smooth. Let cool. Store in mason jars in the refrigerator until ready to use.

Warm in the microwave or run the jar under hot water for a warm fudge sauce.

Yield: 3 cups (705 ml)

Caramel Sauce

This amber-colored sweet syrup tastes delicious poured over Plain Ol' Vanilla Ice Cream (page 489) and is a necessary ingredient in the Caramel Chocolate Coconut Cake (page 434). Before you begin, be sure to have all of your ingredients measured and within arm's reach, as things can happen quickly here, and we wouldn't want you to burn your caramel.

1 cup (235 ml) light corn syrup
2 cups (400 g) granulated sugar
½ cup (112 g) nondairy butter, cut into cubes
1 cup (235 ml) soy or other nondairy milk
2 tablespoons (16 g) cornstarch
2 teaspoons pure vanilla extract

In a saucepan, melt the corn syrup and sugar over medium heat, stirring often. It will begin to bubble and turn golden amber in color.

Add the butter cubes and stir until melted.

In a small-size bowl, combine the milk and cornstarch to make a slurry.

Add the milk and cornstarch mixture to the sugar mixture, stirring constantly. The mixture will bubble and froth as you add the milk.

Remove from the heat and stir until completely smooth and silky.

Stir in the vanilla and let cool to thicken.

Pour into mason jars and store in the refrigerator until ready to use.

Yield: 2½ cups (588 ml)

Balsamic-Glazed Roasted Strawberries

This is a sophisticated dessert indeed! Serve alongside a simple slice of Triple Vanilla Cake (page 423) for a truly elegant presentation.

1 cup (200 g) granulated sugar
½ cup (120 ml) balsamic vinegar
1 pound (455 g) whole fresh strawberries

In a saucepan, bring the sugar and vinegar to a boil over medium heat. Boil for 3 minutes to ensure the sugar is fully dissolved.

Remove from the heat and let cool for about 15 minutes.

Preheat the oven to 350°F (180°C, or gas mark 4). Line the bottom of an 8-inch (20-cm) square baking dish with a single layer of strawberries.

Pour the balsamic syrup evenly over the strawberries.

Bake, uncovered, for 15 minutes.

Let cool before serving.

Yield: 6 servings

Mexicannolis

Looking for the perfect dessert to serve on Mexican Food Night? Roll these on for size. Light and crispy and sweet, these are the perfect way to end a Mexican meal.

For the filling:

½ cup (112 g) nondairy butter
8 ounces (227 g) nondairy cream cheese
1 teaspoon ground cinnamon
½ teaspoon ground cardamom
1 teaspoon pure vanilla extract
5 cups (600 g) powdered sugar

For the cannoli shells:

Canola oil, for frying
1 cup (200 g) granulated sugar
¼ teaspoon ground cinnamon
8 flour tortillas

To make the filling: Add the butter and cream cheese to the bowl of your stand mixer. Beat until creamy and fluffy.

Add the cinnamon, cardamom, and vanilla and continue to beat.

Add the powdered sugar, 1 cup (120 g) at a time. Beat until fluffy, cover, and store in the refreigerator until ready to use.

To make the cannoli shells: Pour the oil into a frying pan or skillet to a depth of ½ inch (1.3 cm) and heat over high heat to 350° to 375°F (180° to 190°C), or when a drop of water sizzles immediately upon contact.

While the oil is heating, mix together the sugar and cinnamon in a large-size shallow dish. Set aside.

Line 2 plates with paper towels.

Roll up a tortilla so that the opening on either end is about 1 inch (2.5 cm) in diameter. Hold the tortilla's shape with tongs and place in the oil to fry for about 7 to 10 seconds, then carefully roll to fry evenly on all sides.

Transfer to the paper towel-lined plate to quickly drain the excess oil, and then immediately place in the sugar and cinnamon mixture to coat.

Transfer to the second plate to cool completely.

Repeat with the remaining tortillas.

Using a piping bag and your largest star piping tip, or a resealable plastic bag with the corner snipped off, pipe the filling into each end of the cannoli shell so that a tiny bit pops out of the opening.

Yield: 8 cannolis

VARIATION

Looking for an even lighter, quicker dessert? Skip the filling entirely and cut each tortilla into 6 triangles. Fry the triangles in oil, about 3 at a time, for 7 to 10 seconds on each side. Transfer to a paper towel-lined plate to drain the excess oil and then immediately dip into the sugar and cinnamon mixture to coat. Transfer to a second plate to cool completely. Repeat with the remaining triangles.

Horchata

The commercial availability of rice milk makes having a nice cool glass of sweet horchata only a few minutes away!

4 cups (940 ml) rice milk
1 cup (235 ml) Simple Syrup (page 498)
1 teaspoon pure vanilla extract
¼ teaspoon ground cinnamon

Stir together all the ingredients in a large-size pitcher. Serve over ice.

Yield: 4 servings

 Low Fat  Gluten Free  Soy Free

Gramma Nan's Homemade Kahlúa

This recipe came from Joni's Gramma Nan. It takes at least thirty days for it to fully develop, but it's worth the wait. If you plan ahead of time, these make wonderful gifts, especially if you adorn the bottles with fancy labels. You'll need two empty quart-size bottles and caps or corks to make this drink.

4 cups (800 g) granulated sugar
2 ounces (56 g) instant coffee crystals
2 cups (470 ml) boiling water
2 cups (470 ml) vodka
1 vanilla bean, cut in half

Combine the sugar and coffee crystals in a large-size pot. Add the boiling water and stir until completely dissolved. Cool thoroughly.

Add the vodka and pour into the bottles.

Add a ½ vanilla bean to each bottle.

Cap, date, and use after standing for at least 30 days.

Yield: 2 quarts (1880 ml)

 Low Fat  Gluten Free  Soy Free

Sparkling Pink Grapefruit Sangria

Want to impress your guests at your next dinner party? Wow them with this sparkling punch!

1 bottle (750 ml) your favorite red wine
1 cup (235 ml) pink grapefruit juice
1 cup (235 ml) pineapple juice
8 ounces (225 g) sliced peaches
8 ounces (225 g) blueberries
8 ounces (225 g) strawberries, halved
3 cups (705 ml) sparkling Italian soda

Combine the wine, grapefruit juice, pineapple juice, peaches, blueberries, and strawberries in a punchbowl or a large-size pitcher and refrigerate overnight.

Right before serving, add the sparkling soda and stir to combine.

Yield: 2 quarts (1880 ml)

 Under 30 Minutes  Low Fat  Gluten Free  Soy Free

Pink Pomegranate Mimosas

Pomegranate juice has long been known to contain many health benefits. Cholesterol-reducing antioxidants are just one of the reasons to enjoy this fruit juice often.

The recipe here is for one serving. You can easily make a whole pitcher to serve many at a time.

Garnish with a few pomegranate arils and an orange wedge for a fancy presentation.

½ cup (120 ml) pink champagne
¼ cup (60 ml) pomegranate juice
¼ cup (60 ml) orange juice

Stir together and serve.

Yield: 1 serving

 Under 30 Minutes  Gluten Free  Soy Free

Mango Coladas

Don't imbibe? That's okay. This tropical treat tastes great sans the alcohol. To make it extra fancy, serve it up in a sugar-rimmed margarita glass garnished with a little umbrella holding a cherry and a chunk of fresh pineapple.

2 bananas
8 ounces (227 g) frozen mango chunks
¾ cup (177 ml) pineapple juice
1 can (14 ounces, or 414 ml) coconut milk
1 cup (235 ml) coconut rum or light rum

Place all the ingredients in a blender and blend until smooth.

Yield: 4 servings

 Under 30 Minutes  Low Fat  Gluten Free  Soy Free

Joni's Jubilee

This sweet and dangerous libation made itself known when Joni was camping with friends at the Colorado River one very hot summer. Joni, who was not known as much of a drinker, was trying to find a concoction that was tasty and refreshing in scorching hot weather. Needless to say, this has become her signature drink, and many fond and not-so-fond memories have come of it!

½ cup (120 ml) grapefruit soda
½ cup (120 ml) orange juice
½ cup (120 ml) coconut rum
Ice

Mix the soda, juice, and rum and pour over ice.

Yield: 1 powerful drink

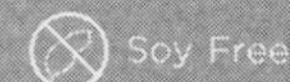

Summer Sweet Tea

Use the warmth of the summer sun to make this deliciously refreshing sweet tea!

For the Simple Syrup:
4 cups (940 ml) water
2 cups (400 g) granulated sugar

For the tea:
12 cups (2820 ml) water
12 whole leaves fresh mint
1 lemon, sliced into 8 slices, peel intact
1 orange, sliced into 8 slices, peel intact
8 plain green or black tea bags
Ice

To make the Simple Syrup: Bring the water to a boil. Add the sugar and stir until completely dissolved.

To make the tea: Add the water, syrup, mint, lemon slices, and orange slices to a large-size mason jar or a pitcher with a lid and stir.

Add the tea bags and seal the container.

Place in a warm, sunny location for about 4 hours.

Remove the tea bags.

Serve over ice.

Yield: 1 gallon (3.8 l)

Berry Bonanza

This berry delight can be used many ways. Sans the alcohol, it makes a fine breakfast treat or summer afternoon refreshment. Add the vodka and you've got yourself a stunning spring or summer cocktail, especially when served in a sugar-rimmed glass garnished with a wedge of lime and a fresh mint leaf.

1 cup (155 g) frozen blueberries
1 cup (300 g) frozen strawberries
1 cup (250 g) frozen raspberries
2 cups (470 ml) orange juice
1 cup (235 ml) vodka

Add all the ingredients to a blender and blend until smooth.

Yield: 4 servings

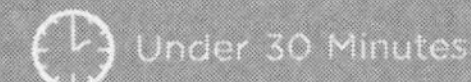

Sunrise—or Sunset—Smoothie

You choose. This amazing smoothie tastes great either way. For an extra boost in the morning, try adding some soy protein powder. To dress it up for the evening, why not add a shot of tequila?

1 ripe banana
2 cups (600 g) frozen strawberries
1 cup (235 ml) orange juice (Sunset), or 1 cup (235 ml) apple juice (Sunrise)

Add all the ingredients to a blender and purée until smooth.

Yield: 1 serving

Resources

Following is a list of various online shops, sites, and other places we truly enjoy.

Our Sites

www.havecakewilltravel.com (Celine's site)
www.justthefood.com (Joni's site)
www.flickr.com/groups/500veganrecipes
(Join the fun! Here you can see pictures of our recipes taken not only by us, but also by you!)

Recipes

This page would never end if we were to list all the sites we visit religiously, but you will find links to a lot of fantastic blogs if you get a chance to visit the ones listed here.

www.blog.fatfreevegan.com
www.dietdessertndogs.com
www.everydaydish.tv
www.seitanismymotor.wordpress.com
www.tofufortwo.net
www.veganappetite.com
www.veganmenu.blogspot.com
www.veganyumyum.com
www.veggiemealplans.com

General Information for Vegans

Whether you're new to veganism or a seasoned veteran, there's always something new to learn!

www.godairyfree.org
www.theppk.com (With forums, for added support.)
www.vegweb.com (A good starting point fpr people new to veganism.)
www.vegan.com
www.veganrepresent.com
www.barnivore.com (Is your beer/wine/liquor vegan?)
www.vegetarisme.fr (Veganism in France)
www.ivu.org (Veganism internationally)
www.foodnotbombs.net

Cruelty-Free Shopping

It is important to speak with our wallets. Please support vegan companies and companies that offer vegan products. Here are some sites that we visit often:

www.cosmosveganshoppe.com (If you're craving nondairy white chocolate chips and many other awesome strictly vegan items, look here.)
www.herbivoreclothing.com (Great-looking printed tees, wallets, and books.)

www.veganessentials.com

www.foodfightgrocery.com

www.shophumanitaire.com (Vegan shoes, handbags, accessories, and more.)

www.bobsredmill.com (Grains, flours, TVP, gluten-free baking mixes, and more.)

www.bulkfoods.com (Nutritional yeast, nuts, dried fruit, and vital wheat gluten galore.)

www.veganbasics.com (German-based online store; check to see if they ship to your country.)

www.vega-trend.de (German-based online store; check to see if they ship to your country.)

www.vegan-wonderland.de (German-based online store; check to see if they ship to your country.)

www.goodnessdirect.co.uk (UK-based online store; check to see if they ship to your country.)

www.seasonedpioneers.co.uk (UK-based online store, for spices; check to see if they ship to your country.)

www.aroma-zone.com/aroma/accueil_fra.asp (Vegan cosmetics in France.)

www.rootsofcompassion.org (German resource for vegan clothing items, food, and books.)

Cookbooks

We read cookbooks like romance novels. You might already be a cookbook addict like we are, or you will find yourself quickly becoming one. Here are a few of our favorite titles:

Cozy Inside, Joni Marie Newman
Yellow Rose Recipes, Joanna Vaught
Eat, Drink & Be Vegan, Dreena Burton
The Joy of Vegan Baking, Colleen Patrick-Goudreau
The Vegan Table, Colleen Patrick-Goudreau
Simple Treats, Ellen Abraham
Vegan with a Vengeance, Isa Chandra Moskowitz
Veganomicon, Isa Chandra Moskowitz and Terry Hope Romero
Vegan Cupcakes Take Over the World, Isa Chandra Moskowitz and Terry Hope Romero
Vegan Planet, Robin Robertson
Get It Ripe, Jae Steele
My Sweet Vegan, Hannah Kaminsky
The Ultimate Uncheese Cookbook, Jo Stepaniak
The Native Foods Restaurant Cookbook, Tanya Petrovna
The Vegan Scoop, Wheeler del Torro

Informative Books

Animal Ingredients A to Z, The E. G. Smith Collective
Becoming Vegan, Brenda Davis and Vesanto Melina
Go Dairy Free, Alisa Marie Fleming (with recipes)
The Vegan Sourcebook, Jo Stepaniak and Carol J. Adams (with recipes)

Acknowledgments

Many thanks to Amanda Waddell and Will Kiester at Fair Winds Press, for turning a dream into reality, while also offering their support and expertise any time we needed it.

Thank you, Karen Levy, for your patience and for the awesome editing job, and to Sylvia McArdle for the beautiful design of this book.

Celine and Joni would like to thank the testers who graciously offered their invaluable feedback and support: Karyn Casper, Jamie Coble, Lisa Coulson, Melissa Elliott, Kristi Garboushian, Amy Gedgaudas, Kat Hindmarsh, Ashley MacDonald, S.D. Mocquet-McDonald, Monique and Michel Narbel, Constanze Reichardt, Luciana Rushing, Amanda Somerville, Liz Wyman, Bahar Zaker, and Kat Zemmel.

Special thanks to Lauren Ulm, for her unwavering support from day one.

Celine would like to thank her husband for licking his plate clean and being an ever-enthusiastic taste-tester.

Thank you, Mamou et Papou, for never scoffing first at vegetarianism and then at veganism, for being inspired to embrace the lifestyle too, and for testing almost every single recipe to make sure the metric measurements worked well.

Thank you to Willow and Buffy, for showing support in your own way by never failing to hope some of the food would magically drop right in front of your kitty noses.

Last but definitely not least, many thanks to Joni, my awesome partner in crime, for making this cookbook-writing experience as enjoyable as they come.

Joni would like to thank her sisters Kristen, Bethany, and June. Ladies, your constant support, encouragement, and love, from nearby and afar, have been invaluable in helping me take the chance to follow my dreams.

Special thanks also to my husband, Dan, for sticking by my side in our tiny home, as my crazy kitchen antics take over the entire house, all while sharing a bed with all three of the mutts and the cat, because I simply won't make them sleep on the floor.

Celine, I am grateful for this experience, for having you in my life, for your ever-watchful eye, and for your patience with my last-minute frenzies.

About the Authors

Celine Steen is the founder of the blog *Have Cake, Will Travel*. After more than a decade of vegetarian eating, she finally made the switch to a vegan lifestyle in 2004. She was born and raised in Switzerland and currently resides in California with her husband, Chaz. You can contact her at celine@havecakewilltravel.com.

Joni Marie Newman is the author of *Cozy Inside: Delicious and Comforting Cruelty-Free Recipes* and founder of the blog *Just the Food*. After dabbling in vegetarianism since high school, she finally decided to get real and do it right, making the switch to veganism in 2004. She was born and raised in Southern California and currently resides in Trabuco Canyon with her husband, Dan. You can contact her at joni@justthefood.com.

Index

D

E

M

N

O

P